THE
WAR
ON
HERESY

R. I. MOORE

THE
WAR
ON
HERESY

THE BELKNAP PRESS OF HARVARD UNIVERSITY PRESS

Cambridge, Massachusetts / 2012

Copyright © R. I. Moore, 2012
All rights reserved
Printed in the United States of America

First published in the United Kingdom in 2012 by
Profile Books LTD
3A Exmouth House
Pine Street
London EC1R 0JH

Library of Congress Cataloging-in-Publication Data

Moore, R. I. (Robert Ian), 1941–
The war on heresy / R. I. Moore.
— 1st Harvard University Press ed.
p.   cm.
Includes bibliographical references (p.   ) and index.
ISBN 978-0-674-06582-6 (cloth : alk. paper)
1. Heresy—History.   2. Christian heresies—History—
Middle Ages, 600–1500.   I. Title.
BT1319.M67 2012
273′.6—dc23   2012001269

For Elizabeth

CONTENTS

LIST OF MAPS

LIST OF ILLUSTRATIONS

While every effort has been made to contact copyright-holders of illustrations, the author and publishers would be grateful for information about any illustrations where they have been unable to trace them, and would be glad to make amendments in further editions.

PREFACE

Old men often reflect on the errors of their youth and are seldom given the opportunity to correct or (alas) to repeat them. If, as I hope, this book does more of the former than the latter, it is almost entirely thanks to the students, colleagues (known and unknown) and friends who have read, written and argued about heresy in general and my heresies in particular for more than forty years. During that time, as the Afterword explains, the scholarly basis of our knowledge of medieval heresy has been transformed to such an extent that the whole story now needs to be retold, and its significance rethought, from the beginning.

The growth of heresy and accusations of heresy in Europe between 1000 and 1250 is the backdrop for some of the most spectacular and portentous events in medieval European history – the Albigensian Crusade, which subjected what is now the southern part of France to the French monarchy, persecution and mass burnings, the foundation of the papal inquisition. It is a story not only interesting for modern Europeans but also central to our history. It prompts serious questions that we still need to ask ourselves about how we got here and where we are going. I have therefore concentrated on the positive tasks of telling what happened and why, and making clear my reasons for thinking so. Conversely, I have tried as far as possible to avoid the distraction (both for myself and the reader) of pointing out when and why I differ from my predecessors and colleagues, as I do repeatedly and often fundamentally. Such explanation is, of course, essential for scholars and scholarly purposes. It may be found, with a full academic apparatus, bibliography and references, at www.rimoore.net.

I have incurred specific and often heavy debts for answering questions, pointing to and even providing materials, and commenting on ideas and portions of draft to Stuart Airlie, Christine Caldwell Ames, Scott Ashley, Alan Bernstein, Jean-Louis Biget, Peter Biller, Christopher Brooke, Caterina Bruschi, Niall Campbell, Kate Cooper, John Gillingham, Bernard Hamilton, Edmund King, Robert Lerner, Anne E. Lester, Conrad Leyser, David Luscombe, Gerald Moore, Olivia Moore, Richard Moore, Claire Taylor, Bruce Venarde, John O. Ward and Anders Winroth. Hilbert Chiu and Monique Zerner have allowed me, with the greatest generosity, to make use of their unpublished and fundamental work. Maureen Miller has read several chapters, corrected many errors and taken pains to educate my eyes and ameliorate my ignorance of Italy. She has also been immensely helpful in identifying and securing illustrations. René Weis has read the whole book with a far better sense than mine of the readership I hope to reach. Mark Pegg has lived with it for almost as long as I have. It owes more than I can count to his learning and unstinting support at every point and in every way – above all, in time and in comradeship. To draw once again on the expertise and unfailing encouragement of John Davey has been a constant pleasure, as has been every aspect of being published by Profile.

It need hardly be said that none of these is in any degree responsible for my errors and opinions. Neither is A. E. Redgate, who has devoted countless painful hours to making my prose accessible. The dedication acknowledges much else besides.

R. I. Moore
February 2012

Europe

300 miles
400 kilometres

♦ Landmark burnings

SCOTLAND

North
Sea

DENMARK

Atlantic Ocean

ENGLAND

Oxford
1165

London

Bremen

Hamburg

Elbe

Magdeburg

Cologne
1163

Goslar

Liège

GERMAN

Cambrai
1076

Rouen

Soissons
1114

Mainz

Worms
1231-33

Prague

Paris
1210

Reims

Mont-Aimé
1239

Rhine

Nuremberg

Oléans
1022

Seine

Regensburg

Danube

Tours

Vézelay
1167

Poitiers

Dijon

Zurich

Augsburg

Loire

Cluny

EMPIRE

Lyons

Compostela

Duero

Ebro

Garonne

LEON

Toulouse

Saragossa

Rhône

Milan
1028

Po

Verona
1233

Venice

Agen
1246

Minerve
1210

Avignon

Marseille

Tajo

Toledo

ARAGON

Narbonne

Florence

Lisbon

Guadiana

Montségur
1244

Rome
1231

CASTILE

Barcelona

Seville

Valencia

Grenada

Naples

Mediterranean Sea

Palermo

FATIMID CALIPHATE

DEATH AND A MAIDEN

It is always disturbing when intelligent people seriously talk nonsense ... The hardest things to understand about much of the past are its errors and delusions.

J. M. Roberts

In the year 1163 some heretics of the sect of the Cathars came to Cologne from Flanders and stayed secretly in a barn near the city. But when they did not go to church on Sunday they were found out by their neighbours. They were brought before the church court and thoroughly examined about their sect. When they would not be corrected by sound arguments and stubbornly maintained their position, they were summarily expelled from the church and handed over to the lay court. On 5 August four men and a girl were taken outside the city and burned. The girl would have been saved by the sympathy of the people if she had been frightened by the fate of her companions and accepted better advice, but she tore herself from the grasp of those who were holding her, threw herself into the flames and was killed.[1]

Dreadful though this story is, it does not quite fit the image of the medieval world as an 'age of faith', in which the burning of heretics provided regular entertainment for multitudes of the applauding pious.

The onlookers at Cologne were shocked because in 1163 this was by no means a commonplace event. No heretic had been executed in western Europe for almost 600 years after the end of the Roman empire until, in 1022, about sixteen people were burned alive at Orléans by order of King Robert II of France. In 1028 the nobles of Milan insisted over the protest of the archbishop on burning 'many'– but we have no idea how many – whose bodies 'were reduced to wretched ashes'.[2] In the following 140 years heretics, real or alleged, were burned on five other occasions we know of, but the numbers involved were much smaller.

The burning at Cologne in 1163 was a turning point. From this time forward burnings became much more frequent. Because their victims were not only the preachers or leaders of alleged heretical sects but their ordinary followers, they sometimes involved much larger numbers of people. This was the war against heresy that did so much to fix the primitive, blood-stained image of medieval Europe and foreshadowed burnings in far larger numbers at the beginning of the modern epoch, in the sixteenth and seventeenth centuries. Along the way it restructured the relationship between church and people, reshaped the kingdom of France into the hexagon we know today and helped to mould Europe's universities and its legal and governmental systems. Like other world-changing wars, it originated in profound long-term changes in social relations, the climate of ideas and the distribution of power as well as in ordinary, and extraordinary, human idealism, opportunism, vanity and greed.

———

The burning of 1163 was widely reported in the Rhineland region and beyond. The report of the *Chronica regia Coloniensis* quoted above illustrates a great deal about how both the perception of heresy and the treatment of those accused of it were changing in Europe in the middle of the twelfth century, as well as about the problems of recovering its history. To begin with, although this is the version of the story that historians almost always quote or have in mind when they tell it, it is not the earliest or most authoritative, for it was written some sixty years after the events it describes. The nearly contemporary *Annals of Aachen*, a short distance to the west of Cologne, and the *Annals of Erfurt*, some way to the east, both compiled in the 1160s, say only that 'Some heretics were burned at Cologne. A woman among them threw herself into the fire without being pushed.' The identical wording of these two notices suggests that they reproduce a written report circulated immediately after the trial and burnings. Dietrich, a monk of the nearby abbey of Deutz who died in 1164, gives a fuller account:

> On August 2, 1163, six men and two women were arrested in Cologne as Catafrigians, or Cathars, with their leaders Arnold, Marsilius and Dietrich, who were condemned and excommunicated by the clergy and handed over to the judges and people of the city because they refused to accept the catholic faith and renounce their impious sect. When they were burned near the Jewish cemetery, on the hill called 'Jew Hill', they showed themselves so obstinate in their belief that, inspired by the devil, some of them threw themselves into the fire.[3]

Even among these three strictly contemporary sources there is an apparent discrepancy on the vital question (we might think) of the number of people – one woman or two? – who were burned. But it was through later versions that the episode came to be well known. They included not only the *Chronica regia Coloniensis* and other thirteenth-century chronicles but also a widely circulated collection of stories for the instruction and edification of Cistercian novices (the Cistercians being the order of monks most closely associated with the identification and pursuit of heresy), Caesarius of Heisterbach's *Dialogue of Miracles*, composed like the *Chronica regia Coloniensis* in the early 1220s.

As might be expected, the story was polished in the retelling, the better to illustrate the lessons it was intended to teach. A lone girl makes a more pitiable figure than two women and by the 1220s would have reminded many listeners of another famous story, of another burning, in the late 1170s, which we owe to another Cistercian chronicler, Ralph of Coggeshall. It tells how Gervase of Tilbury, an English clerk in the service of the archbishop of Reims, was attracted by a young girl whom he saw working alone in a vineyard. When she declined his amorous advances, pleading that the loss of her virginity would bring her to certain damnation, 'Master Gervase realised at once that she belonged to the blasphemous sect of the *Publicani,* who were being searched out and destroyed all over France.'[4] The girl was arrested and taken to the archbishop's palace for questioning. It transpired that she had an instructress in the city, who, she was confident, would be able to answer the arguments that were being advanced against her beliefs. Found and brought before the court,

> the woman was bombarded by the archbishop and his clerks with questions and citations of the holy scriptures to convince her of the greatness of her errors, but she perverted all the authorities which they brought forward with such subtle interpretations that it was obvious to everybody that the spirit of all error spoke through her mouth.

The two women, refusing to recant their errors, were condemned to the stake, but the elder escaped:

> When the fire had been lit in the city, and they should have been dragged by the archbishop's servants to the punishment that had been allotted to them, the wicked mistress of error called out, 'Madmen! Unjust judges! Do you think that you can burn me on your fire? I neither respect your judgement nor fear the fire which you have prepared.' So saying she took a ball of thread from her breast, and threw it through the great window, keeping one end of the thread in her hand, and calling loudly in everyone's hearing, 'Catch!' At this she was raised from the ground in front of everyone, and flew through the window after the ball of thread. We believe that she was taken away by the same evil spirits who once lifted Simon Magus* into the air, and none of the onlookers could ever discover what became of the old witch, or whither she was taken.
>
> The girl, who had not yet achieved such madness in the sect, remained behind. No reason, no promise of wealth, could persuade her to give up her obstinacy, and she was burned. Many admired the way in which she let forth no sighs, no wailing, and bore the torment

---

*A magician encountered by the apostles, described in Acts 8: 9–24. The greatest heresy of this period, that of selling the gifts of the Holy Spirit, was named after him (see below, Chapter 5).

of the flames firmly and eagerly, like the martyrs of Christ who (for such a different reason!) were once slain by the pagans for the sake of the Christian religion.

It is easy to see how much more fancifully the story from Reims has been elaborated in successive tellings than the one from Cologne, but the message is the same. To the young monks and courtiers who made up the primary audience the steadfast and courageous young women represented mortal temptation as well as corrupted innocence. Their fates gave a dreadful warning of the seductive power of the heresies believed to be rampant at this time. The introduction at Reims of the older woman, who 'replied so easily, and had such a clear memory of the incidents and texts advanced against her, both from the Old and New Testaments, that she must have had great knowledge of the whole Bible, and had plenty of practice in this kind of debate', showed not only that the heretics were in the service of the devil but also that they were well organised, and capable of fighting the faith with its own weapons.

The miraculous escape brings out some of the dilemmas of interpretation that narrative sources always present. Both of these stories (as we shall see more fully in later chapters) originated in real events; Ralph of Coggeshall's is corroborated by the remark of the biblical commentator Peter the Chanter, about 1191, that laywomen in Flanders had been unjustly suspected and condemned as Cathars solely because they resisted clerical attempts on their chastity.[5] Both stories were polished over much the same period of half a century or so, for much the same audience, to point the moral and fit the episodes into a changing picture of the world, and of the danger that heresy presented. But what is the relation between the old story and the new, between what really happened and what the sources tell us? It is easy to accept the burnings and dismiss the ball of thread, but is the reported presence among the heretics of an educated woman in a position of leadership a genuine reflection of the composition and appeal of some heretical sects at this time or simply a monastic nightmare, designed to show how heretics pervert the divine order in every possible way? Did the groups uncovered in Cologne and Reims belong to the same sect, sharing the same heretical beliefs, even though they are given different names by their respective chroniclers? If so, does the greater degree of organisation portrayed at Reims suggest a histori-cal development that took place within the sect between 1163 and 1180 or only the hindsight and commitment of authors writing after western Europe had been enthralled, and appalled, by a full-blown war against heresy – the Albigensian Crusade, proclaimed in 1208 by Pope Innocent III to root out heresy from the lands of the count of Toulouse – and the barrage of stories about heretics, true and false, that accompanied it?

———

The burning of six men and two women at Cologne may seem a rather small affair by comparison with that bloody and savage war of conquest, and with the manhunts, torture and burnings that marked the century from the establishment of the papal inquisition at Toulouse in 1233 through the persecution of sects, real and imaginary (among whom the 'Cathars'* and Waldensians are only the most notorious), to the trial of the Templars in France (1307–14) and the hunting down of the Spiritual Franciscans in Italy (1317–27), which provided the setting for Umberto Eco's *The Name of the Rose*. The conflicts that gave rise to those horrors also established institutions and mentalities that pervaded the culture and shaped the growth of Europe, including both the tendency to recur-rent and frequent persecution of more or less arbitrarily defined minori-ties and the development of defences against it. Denunciation, arbitrary arrest and imprisonment without charge, judicial torture and burning alive, became ordinary features of European life until the eighteenth century and beyond: a 'witch' was burned at Beaumont-en-Cambrésis, in northern France, in 1835.[6] Those threatened included people accused or suspected not only of heresy but also of being Jews or Muslims, of being homosexual, of being lepers, of being witches and so on, and on. The stereotypes and ideologies that fuelled and rationalised these procedures were devised by intellectuals and public servants bent (often from the loftiest, most idealistic motives) on extending the power and

---

* The indiscriminate use of the term 'Cathars' (*Cathari*) by medieval writers, and even more by modern ones, is a problem addressed throughout this book. It is seldom clear in medieval sources that it refers to an identifiable set either of beliefs or of people (see further pp. 167–170, 332–6 below). I have placed it in quotation marks where it seems particularly necessary to emphasise this uncertainty.

effectiveness of governing institutions, secular and ecclesiastical, but they were quickly disseminated, to drive and justify persecution, violence and discrimination in many forms, and at all levels of society.

In 1163 these horrors lay in the future. Although the burning of heretics is now commonly thought of as an ordinary, even routine, expedient in medieval society, it did not become so until late in the twelfth century. The earliest cases, beginning at Orléans in 1022, do not reveal a settled method of dealing either with heresy accusations or with people found or alleged to be heretics. A burning at Bonn in 1143 was the first since the one at Milan in 1028 in which it is clear that what became the standard procedure was followed – that is, the heretics were condemned by a church court and then handed to the secular power for punishment. Before that, a hanging at Goslar in 1052, at the order of the German emperor, was the only other occasion on which we can be sure that heretics were put to death through a formal legal process. At Cambrai in 1077, Soissons in 1114, Liège in 1135 and/or 1145, and Cologne in 1147 contemporary sources assert with varying degrees of plausibility that alleged heretics were burned by 'the people' after being found guilty by ecclesiastical tribunals, but against the wishes of the clergy concerned. Two famous heretic preachers were killed without any formal procedure: in 1115, when Tanchelm of Antwerp was murdered by a priest; and in c. 1139, when Peter of Bruys was thrown by the citizens of St Gilles-du-Gard in Provence on to a bonfire of crosses that had been made by his own followers. Another, Eon (or Eudo) *de Stella*, died in prison after being found heretical but mad at the Council of Reims, presided over by Pope Eugenius III, in 1148, and an unknown number of his principal followers were burned.

In all of those cases the victims were leaders, accused of spreading heresy, not just of accepting or believing in it. Two years after the burning at Cologne, however, in the winter of 1165–6, Henry II of England had 'rather more than thirty people, both men and women', branded, stripped to the waist and flogged from the city of Oxford into the intolerable cold, forbidding his subjects to give them any help or succour. 'Nobody showed the slightest mercy towards them,' remarks the chronicler with satisfaction, 'and they died in misery.' Except for their leader, these were simple, uneducated people, 'Germans by race and language', who had come to England allegedly to spread their faith – they were said to have converted one old woman, who disappeared as soon as they were arrested – but more probably as refugees.[7] Compared with the 140 people burned at Minerve in 1210, the 60 at Verona in 1233, the 180 at Mont-Aimé in 1239 and the 200 at Montségur in 1244, this was a modest affair. Nevertheless, these wandering Germans should be remembered as the first victims of the mass repression of heresy in European history.

———

The systematic, violent and large-scale repression brought to western Europe by the war on heresy of which these events in the 1160s were the opening shots had no earlier parallel. There was indeed nothing new, or even specifically Christian, about the idea that religious dissent should not be tolerated. In ancient China, as in ancient Rome, it was held to be the emperor's duty to uphold the proper observance of religious rites and respect for the gods. During the bitter struggles between warring Christian sects from which the catholic church emerged victorious in the fourth and fifth centuries AD punishments such as the destruction of places of worship, fines and confiscation of property and the deprivation of the legal right to testify or to dispose of property by will were occasionally imposed on heretics, notably the Donatists of North Africa and the Manichees, as they were on Jews and others. In his definitive codification of Roman law (AD 534) the Emperor Justinian I equated heresy with treason, a principle that was revived by Pope Innocent III in 1199.

Many died in the often long and savage conflicts that revolved around these disputes, but the exaction of capital punishment seems to have been relatively rare; indeed, at least up to the reign of Diocletian (284–305), Christians bent on martyrdom were sometimes frustrated by the reluctance of magistrates to accommodate them. Similarly, although the eastern (Byzantine) part of the Roman empire, which survived until 1453, always demanded strict religious orthodoxy of its subjects and religious dispute was commonplace, intense and often central to both political and social conflict, the persecution of heresy was intermittent throughout its history, and the execution of heretics rare. The very different relationship between religious and political structures and authority in the Islamic world makes direct comparison less straightforward, but again it may be said that though the right, and indeed duty, to persecute heretics was generally maintained and acknowledged, it was seldom widely or systematically exercised for sustained periods.

The key questions to be discussed in this book, then, are why the persecution of people described by some of their contemporaries as heretics became widespread and frequent in western Europe after the middle of the twelfth century, and why from that time it was conducted against a much greater variety of people and on a much larger scale than ever before. That is to ask why 'heresy' appeared to become more threatening, or at least more evident, and what danger it presented, or appeared to present, to twelfth- and thirteenth-century Europeans. Even if religious dissent was becoming more widely supported or theologically more radical just then, it would still be necessary to account for the suddenness, scale and savagery of the response. And hence to ask what part was played in persecution by the clergy, by secular rulers and authorities, by the population at large? How much reliance can we place on accounts of 'heretics' and their doings produced almost exclusively by their enemies, and how can we hope to understand these events on the basis of such accounts? Was the confrontation between 'heretics' and their persecutors purely a clash between religious fundamentalists, fanatics or idealists (depending on your point of view), or did it in some way arise from or embody broader political, social or cultural issues?

The problem posed by the victims is still more difficult. The strenuous efforts both at Cologne and at Reims to persuade the condemned women to abandon their beliefs were no mere formalities. Heresy was defined by Robert Grosseteste in the thirteenth century as 'an opinion chosen by human perception, contrary to holy scripture, publicly avowed and obstinately defended'. It was in stubbornly refusing to abjure such beliefs, even after their error had been repeatedly and exhaustively demonstrated, and every incentive to repentance and reconciliation with the church offered, that the essence of heresy lay. It was the bounden duty of every cleric who confronted alleged or suspected heretics to do everything he possibly could to persuade them to recant and save their souls. With some notorious exceptions, that duty was taken seriously. The burning represented a failure, not a triumph, for those who authorised it. It follows that on most occasions the victims, like the women at Cologne and Reims, chose their fate knowingly and deliberately. That is one reason why they made so profound and disturbing an impact on the onlookers. Few things could be more unnerving than the spectacle of young, gifted, attractive people insisting on, even glorying in, a terrible death for an utterly incomprehensible cause, 'like the martyrs of Christ who (for such a different reason!) were once slain by the pagans for the sake of the Christian religion'. In the course of this book it will be necessary to clear away a luxuriant overgrowth of falsehood and legend that has gathered around these heretics – especially, but not only, the so-called 'Cathars' – during the thousand years since the burning at Orléans. To deny the myths is not to deny the victims themselves, or their dreadful fate. On the contrary, the only reparation that we can now offer to their memory is to try to reach a better understanding of what it was they died for.

Part One

CRY HAVOC

1

THE AVENGING FLAMES

Clovis, who believed in the Trinity, crushed the heretics with
divine help and enlarged his dominion to include all Gaul;
but Alaric, who refused to accept the Trinity, was therefore
deprived of his kingship, his subjects and the life hereafter.
Gregory of Tours, *History of the Franks*, III

On 28 December (Holy Innocents' Day) 1022, by order of the French
king Robert II, often called 'the Pious', a number of prominent clerics
and others, of both sexes, were burned at Orléans. 'Thirteen of them
were in the end delivered over to the fire,' says Ralph the Bald,

but when the flames began to burn them savagely they cried out as
loudly as they could from the middle of the fire that they had been
terrribly deceived by the trickery of the devil, that the views they had
recently held of God and Lord of All were bad, and that as punishment for their blasphemy against Him they would endure much
torment in this world and more in that to come. Many of those standing near by heard this, and moved by pity and humanity, approached,
seeking to pluck them from the furnace even when half roasted. But
they could do nothing, for the avenging flames consumed them, and
reduced them straight away to dust.[1]

These were the first people to be put to death as heretics since the end of the western Roman empire six hundred years ago. They could hardly have been more different from the modest young women who would later choose the stake at Cologne and Reims or the illiterate and destitute migrants driven into the Oxfordshire countryside in the winter of 1165. Their leaders were canons of Orléans cathedral, and therefore – although we know nothing about the particular connections or previous careers of these individuals – men of the highest standing and influence. Cathedral clergy were normally drawn from the leading families of the region, though canonries could also be used to recruit and support men whose particular talents and abilities might be of use to the ruler – who, for example, needed someone to write his letters – or the bishop. The leaders among those convicted in 1022 were royal favourites; one of them had been the queen's confessor. Their trial and condemnation, rumours of which reverberated through northern France for at least two generations afterwards, averted a scandal capable of threatening the monarchy itself.

The earliest surviving report of the affair at Orléans is in a letter evidently written soon after the trial by John, a monk of the Catalan monastery of Ripoll, to Oliba, its abbot. Oliba had sent John to the great monastery of Fleury (St Benoît-sur-Loire), near Orléans, to secure for Ripoll a fragment of the relics of St Benedict, for which Fleury was famous. 'If you have heard a rumour of heresy in the city of Orléans', John wrote,

> it is quite true. King Robert has had about fourteen of the most repu-
> table clerks and noble laymen of the city burned alive. These people,
> odious to God and hateful on earth and in heaven, absolutely denied
> the grace of holy baptism, and the consecration of the body and blood
> of the Lord. They would also deny forgiveness to those who had com-
> mitted mortal sins. Moreover, they rejected the bonds of marriage.
> They abstained from foods that the Lord has created, meat and animal
> fats, as impure. Enquire carefully in your abbey and in your diocese
> [Oliba was also bishop of Vich] in case there are some who under the
> cover of false religion have secretly fallen into these errors – may it
> never happen![2]

John was well placed to confirm the rumour and to describe the heresy, for his host was the king's half-brother Abbot Goslin of Fleury, also archbishop of Bourges, who had been present at the trial. John's summary of the heretics' beliefs accords well with the account of the trial that another monk, André of Fleury, provides in his biography of Goslin. This was not written until after Goslin's death twenty years later, but André had probably attended the trial himself, as one of the senior monks from Fleury he mentions who had accompanied Goslin. He describes the heretics as 'certain clerks, raised from childhood in holy religion and educated as deeply in sacred as in profane letters ... Some were priests, some deacons, some sub-deacons. The chief among them were Stephen and Lisois.'[3] Like John, André reports that the heretics denied the efficacy of baptism, the sanctity of marriage and the possibility of redemption from mortal sins, and adds that they did not believe in the church as an institution or the rank of bishops or their capacity to ordain priests. More shockingly still, 'They boasted that their own mothers resembled in every respect the Mother of God, who was like no other woman and has had no successor.' On the other hand, André does not mention the denial of the eucharist or the abstention from meat and animal fats, on which John had commented.

———

As John anticipated, the burnings at Orléans created a considerable sensation, and they appear, as he recommended to Oliba, to have been followed by something of a witch-hunt. Before turning to the more lurid descriptions of the affair that circulated in its aftermath, we should pause to consider what we are told by these two, the closest to the event and to the main actors. Both were struck first by the denial of baptism, to which André attributed a wider significance than John had noted:

they pretended to believe in the Three-in-One, and that the Son of God had become flesh; but it was a lie, for they denied that the baptised could receive the Holy Spirit in baptism, or in any other way secure redemption after commiting a mortal sin.

Here is a cast of mind that would become the hallmark of the inquisitor at work. In André's view the accused had made statements about their beliefs that were logically incompatible: they could not both believe in the Holy Trinity and the incarnation of Christ, as they claimed, and disbelieve in the sacrament of baptism and the forgiveness of sins. André, in other words, chose to prefer his own understanding of what the statements of the clerks implied to what they had actually said. Whether he was logically, or theologically, correct is, of course, irrelevant to the historical question of whether the accused were deliberately lying, as André supposed, for even highly educated people may be capable of believing at once several things logically inconsistent with each other. As it happens, André, as Archbishop Goslin's biographer, had an interest in maintaining that Stephen and Lisois had lied about their beliefs all along: it excused the king's patronage and exonerated Goslin himself from any suspicion of complicity in the heresy to which, as we shall see, he may have been exposed.

Real or apparent, the contradiction does point to the source of Stephen's and Lisois's beliefs. During the century and a half before their time a way of thinking had become fashionable (though not predominant) in Francia which explains what they said, or what André thought they said. This was neoplatonism, whose influence on some of the most popular works from antiquity such as the *Confessions* of Augustine and Boethius's *Consolation of Philosophy*, had been reinforced by the work of the most learned scholar of the ninth century, John Scotus Eriugena. His translation (from Greek into Latin) of the works of an unidentified but probably fifth-century writer now known as the pseudo-Dionysus, and his commentaries on them, circulated widely in tenth- and early eleventh-century monasteries and schools.[4]

There were dangers inherent in this way of thought. Combining the teachings of the church with the methods and conclusions of Classical Greek philosophy had always been a source of inspiration, but also of difficulty, for Christians. Plato's insistence, especially as expounded by Plotinus of Alexandria (AD 205–270) and his followers, on the unity of creation, on the flowing of all things from the Word (*Logos*), in which they began, on the permanence and purity of idea and spirit as opposed to the transience and corruptibility of material things, had great religious potential. Plotinus's vision of the soul striving to free itself from the prison of the flesh to reunite with the divine essence from which it had been parted offered a powerful appeal to Christian mystics, and to those who sought the religious life. But these ideas also presented serious obstacles to some of the fundamentals of catholic teaching – most obviously that God was Three as well as One, had assumed human flesh through the virgin birth, had lived on earth and been crucified as a man with a human body. So neoplatonism, in many manifestations and formulations, has been a recurrent influence in Christian history, especially at times of religious revival and renewal. But it has also been a fertile source both of heresy and of accusations of heresy, because even when those inspired by it have succeeded in resolving the difficulties to which it gives rise in stating Christian doctrine, the resulting complexities have often left them highly vulnerable to misunderstanding or misrepresentation.

Whether Stephen and Lisois had indeed strayed into heresy or were misunderstood or misrepresented there is now no means of knowing. Either way, the very brief and, of course, hostile summaries given by John and André show quite clearly that we are in the presence of neoplatonist language, and therefore in one way or another of neoplatonist belief. Thus, neoplatonists might deny that the Holy Spirit was contained in the water of baptism, or conveyed by the hands of the priest in blessing, or of the bishop in ordination, without (in their own view) necessarily denying the sacraments themselves – especially at a time when the nature and indeed the number of the sacraments was still by no means clearly defined. Others might easily fail to grasp the distinction, with or without malice. The difficulty is evident in André's tortuous explanation that Stephen and Lisois did not believe in the church because 'that which is contained cannot be defined by the container'. The meaning seems to be that the power and workings of the Holy Spirit could not be restricted by the confines of a human institution, or perhaps within the material fabric of a church building. Neoplatonist distrust of matter, and so of the flesh, certainly encouraged abstinence both from sex and from meat, and therefore tended to the disparagement of marriage, though not necessarily to denial of its validity. On the other hand, the heretics' assertion that Mary was no different from their own mothers might as easily reflect an affirmation of Christ's humanity as a denial of it.

The story of what had happened at Orléans spread rapidly and was embroidered in the process. That is quite evident in the accounts of two more monks whose writings provide our most extensive, and most controversial, information about early eleventh-century heresy accusations, Adémar of Chabannes, of the abbey of St Cybard at Angoulême, and Ralph the Bald (Glaber), of St Germanus, Auxerre. Adémar, writing about 1025, gives a brief account of the trial and executions at Orléans, giving the number burned as ten, and saying that their leader was Lisois, 'a man whom the king had once loved for his apparent holiness'. He adds that

> a canon of Orléans, a cantor named Theodatus, had died in this heresy, according to trustworthy witnesses, three years before, though he had seemed to be correct in religion. After this was proved his body was taken from the cemetery by order of Bishop Odalric, and thrown into waste ground.[5]

This is a more explicit indication than we had from either John of Ripoll or André of Fleury that there were tensions behind the burnings that went back some way beyond the exposure of Stephen and Lisois. Theodatus has been plausibly identified as a former master of the cathedral school at Orléans whose neoplatonist interpretations of the doctrines of the Trinity, baptism and the eucharist had been attacked some years earlier by Bishop Fulbert of Chartres, the teacher of Bishop Odalric. Odalric's disputed claim to the bishopric was one of the political conflicts behind the trial of 1022, about which André of Fleury remained discreetly silent.

Adémar has nothing to say about what Stephen and Lisois taught or believed. He explains instead that

> they had been led astray by a peasant who claimed that he could give them great strength and who carried about with him dust from dead children which quickly made anyone who came into contact with it into a Manichee. They worshipped the devil who appeared to them on

one occasion in the guise of an Ethiopian and on another as an angel of light, and brought down money for them every day. In obedience to him they secretly rejected Christ, and in private committed sins and crimes which it would be sinful even to mention, while in public they pretended to be true Christians.

Here Adémar betrays his own agenda. Historically, 'Manichees' were the followers of Mani (d. AD 231), a prophet and visionary whose faith had flourished mightily in the Roman and Persian empires 600 years or so before Adémar's time and been fiercely persecuted. Among their followers had been at one time Augustine of Hippo (354–430), subsequently perhaps the most famous (after St Paul) of all converts to Christianity. Augustine was the most influential, in the Latin tradition, of the fathers of the church whose writings laid down the authoritative account of Christian doctrine and practice upon which medieval – and indeed modern – catholicism would be founded. His vivid descriptions of the Manichees, of their belief in two gods – one good, who presided over the realm of the spirit, and one evil, who ruled the material universe – and of their refusal to perpetuate the domain of the latter by eating meat or procreating, made this the most feared of all ancient heresies. Adémar of Chabannes was convinced that it had reappeared in his own lifetime, and that it was being spread among 'the people' – that is, the poor and the unfree – by 'emissaries of Antichrist'. Whether his fears were justified is a question for a later chapter, but the peasant preacher with his magic dust is as manifestly fictitious as he is an improbable prophet of the sophisticated neoplatonism of the canons of Orléans, about which Adémar says nothing. The magic dust itself, and the dead children from whom it was made, are also revivals from the ancient past, echoing stories directed by Roman pagans against the early Christians, and later by Christians against their own heretics.[6]

Ralph the Bald also attributed the appearance of the heresy to contamination from the lower reaches of society, this time 'a woman from Italy', who converted 'not just the uneducated and peasants but even many who passed amongst the most learned of the clergy'. His account of the content of the heresy is somewhat confused: he likens it to the Epicureans – not Christian heretics at all, but a school of ancient philosophy

— 'in that they did not believe that carnality was a sin meriting avenging punishment'. Nevertheless, he took it seriously enough to devote
several pages to his own rebuttal of it, and in doing so reflects, though
apparently without understanding, the neoplatonist influence that lay
behind it. Ralph's description of the circumstances in which the heresy
had spread and been discovered, and of the people involved, however,
adds significantly to what we learned from John and André. He identifies as its leaders Lisois, whom we have already met, 'the [royal] favourite
among the clerks in the cathedral', and Heribert, master of the school at
another church in the city, St Pierre-le-Puellier. Enthusiastic to spread
their teaching to other cities, they made contact with a priest in Rouen,
who reported the approach to Duke Richard of Normandy. Richard in
turn informed King Robert, who summoned a meeting at Orléans of
'many bishops and abbots and some religious laymen' to look into it.

> When inquiry was made among the clergy of the city to see what each
> felt and believed about the truths which the catholic faith by apostolic
> precept unchangingly observes and preaches, Lisois and Heribert did
> not deny their divergent beliefs but revealed all that they had previ-
> ously kept hidden. Then many others professed themselves adherents
> of this sect, and declared that nothing could ever separate them from
> their fellows.

Refusing to retract, 'on the king's orders and with the consent of the
whole people' thirteen of them were consigned to the flames.

Ralph the Bald was a highly inventive writer with an agenda of his own.
But he was also very well informed, and had a wide circle of acquaintance
in the high political and clerical circles in which the burning at Orléans
and its aftermath reverberated. In some of its essentials he supports, or
is corroborated by, the fullest but most questionable surviving account,
that of yet another monk, Paul, of the abbey of St Père at Chartres.
Paul's story is a sort of extended footnote to a compilation of documents
that he put together to replace the abbey's records, destroyed in a fire

in 1078.[7] It is best known for its more elaborate version of the prurient rumours that Adémar of Chabannes had circulated half a century earlier:

> They met on certain nights in the house which I have mentioned, each holding a light in his hand, and called a roll of the names of demons, like a litany, until suddenly they saw the devil appear among them in the guise of some wild beast. Then, as soon as they saw that sight, the lights were put out and each of them grabbed whatever woman came to hand, and seized her to be put to ill use. Without regard to sin, whether it were a mother, or a sister, or a nun, they regarded that intercourse as a holy and religious work. On the eighth day they lit a great fire among them, and the child who was born of this foul union was put to the test of the flames after the manner of the ancient pagans, and burned. The ashes were collected and kept with as much reverence as the Christian religion accords to the body of Christ, to be given as a last sacrament to the sick when they are about to depart this life. There was such power of diabolic evil in this ash that anyone who had succumbed to the heresy and tasted only a small quantity of it was afterwards scarcely ever able to direct his mind away from heresy and back to the truth.

Paul's account of how the heresy came to be discovered and unveiled is almost equally melodramatic. It begins with Heribert, a clerk in the household of Harfast, brother-in-law of Duke Richard of Normandy, who went to Orléans (which at this time 'shone more brightly than other cities with the light of wisdom and the torch of holiness') to study, met Stephen and Lisois, and was converted to their heresy. When he got home, he announced the good news to Harfast, who, horrified, went straight to the duke, asking him to warn King Robert and offer to help root out the heresy. The king responded by ordering Harfast himself to Orléans. On the way he stopped at Chartres to consult Bishop Fulbert, the most celebrated teacher of the day. Fulbert was away, but Harfast was briefed instead by Everard, a senior canon of the cathedral, who 'advised him to seek the help of the Almighty every morning, to go to church, devote himself to prayer and fortify himself with the holy communion of the body and blood of Christ'. 'Thus protected by the sign of the cross,' Everard continued, 'he should proceed to listen to the wickedness of the heretics, contradicting nothing that he should hear them say, and pretending that he wished to become their disciple, while he quietly stored everything away in his heart.'

While Harfast won the confidence of the heretics in this way, preparations were made for the dénouement. King Robert, Queen Constance and a number of bishops came to Orléans, and when Harfast gave the word, 'the whole wicked gang' – Harfast among them – 'was arrested by royal officials at the house where they met, and brought before the king and queen and an assembly of clerks and bishops at the church of Ste Croix'. Harfast now identified himself and described the teachings that he had heard from Stephen and Lisois, who 'had prepared for themselves a dwelling with the devil in hell, and replied that he had remembered accurately, and they did hold and believe those things'. Then

from the first until the ninth hour of that day everyone put forward various arguments to make them renounce their errors, and they resisted with the obstinacy of iron. Then they were all commanded to put on the holy vestments of their order, and immediately stripped of them again with full ceremony by the bishops. At the King's command, Queen Constance stood before the doors of the church, to prevent the common people from killing them inside the church, and they were expelled from the bosom of the church. As they were being driven out, the Queen struck out the eye of Stephen, who had once been her confessor, with the staff which she carried in her hand. They were taken outside the walls of the city, a large fire was lit in a certain cottage, and they were all burned, with the evil dust of which I have spoken above, except for one clerk and a nun, who had repented by the will of God.

Paul told his tale more than a half a century after the event. Some of it is impossible and much of it improbable. On the other hand, its hero, Harfast, had retired to St Père as a monk, probably in 1026, when he gave land to the abbey. Everard, whom Harfast had consulted on his way to Orléans, also became a monk at St Père. Both were probably long dead when Paul did his work – Harfast was grown up by 990, when he witnessed a charter of Duke Richard I of Normandy, and

Everard was already a senior canon of Chartres in 1022 – but we may accept that their recollection of the events of 1022 was preserved, if also elaborated, in the monastery. Its importance is that the story it gives us, like Ralph the Bald's, is not that of the French royal court, as seen from Fleury by John of Ripoll and André. The most obvious difference is that Paul's version, like Ralph's, involves a much wider cast of characters than André's, suggesting that the initiative in uncovering the heresy (if that is what it was) came not from King Robert II or from within his court but from the circle of Duke Richard of Normandy, with the assistance of senior clergy of Chartres, the chief city of Count Odo of Blois. This contrast is sharpened by the silence of King Robert's official biographer, Helgaud – yet another monk of Fleury – who makes no mention of the trial of 1022. Helgaud, writing immediately after Robert's death in 1031, was anxious to present him as a God-fearing and actively Christian king: for example, he describes Robert as curing sufferers from scrofula, thus inaugurating the tradition of touching for 'the King's evil', which lasted in France and later in England until the eighteenth century. That image would certainly have been enhanced if Robert could have been credibly represented as energetically rooting out heresy.

———

We should not argue from silence, but neither should we ignore the questions that silence can prompt. The essential clue to explaining the silences of the writers with close links to the royal court is the behaviour of Queen Constance. Stephen had been her confessor, Paul of St Père says, and she struck out his eye with her staff as he was driven from the church at the end of the trial. Constance was King Robert's third wife, the daughter of Count William of Arles and, more importantly, a first cousin of Count Fulk Nerra ('the Black') of Anjou. Robert had married her in 1006, after repudiating his second wife, Bertha, widow of Count Odo of Blois. That is to say, he had married the cousin of one of his greatest enemies after discarding the mother of the other, Odo II of Blois. These three great lords – Robert, Fulk and Odo – were the main protagonists in a contest for power in the vast and wealthy region between the Loire and the Meuse that had been gathering since the

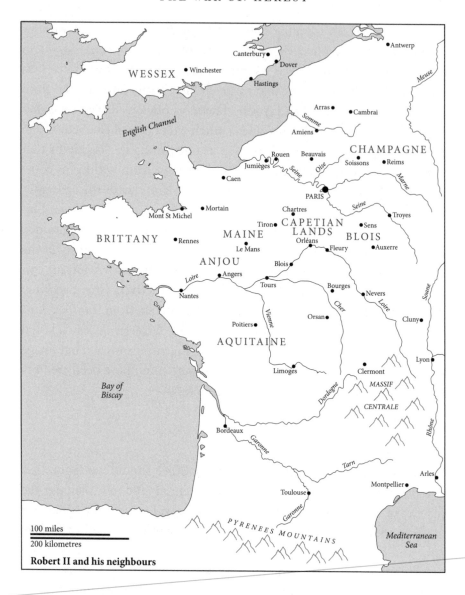

Antwerp

Canterbury
Dover
WESSEX   • Winchester
Hastings

Meuse

Arras •
• Cambrai
Somme
Amiens •

English Channel

Rouen   Beauvais   CHAMPAGNE
Jumièges •   Soissons • • Reims
• Caen   *Seine*   *Oise*   *Marne*

PARIS

Mortain   Chartres   *Seine*
Mont St Michel   Tiron •   Troyes
CAPETIAN
BRITTANY   • Rennes   MAINE   LANDS   • Sens
Le Mans   Orléans   BLOIS
• Auxerre
ANJOU   Fleury
Blois •   *Loire*
• Angers
Loire   Tours   Bourges
Nantes   • Nevers   *Saône*
Vienne   Orsan •   *Cher*   Cluny •
Poitiers •   • Lyon

AQUITAINE

Limoges •   Clermont •   Lyon •
Dordogne   MASSIF   *Rhône*
Bay of   CENTRALE
Biscay

Bordeaux •   *Garonne*
Tarn   Arles •
Montpellier •
Toulouse •
100 miles   *Garonne*
200 kilometres   PYRENEES MOUNTAINS   Mediterranean
Sea
Robert II and his neighbours

middle of the ninth century and which would not be settled until the
great victory of King Philip II of France (Philip Augustus) at Bouvines
in 1241. The prestige of the monarchy had been greatly reduced when
the last king descended in the male line from Charlemagne* died in 987.

---

* Charles, king of the Franks 768–814, crowned Holy Roman Emperor in 800 and widely
regarded, for the territorial extent of his empire and the durability of the institutions and
culture associated with it, as the 'founder of Europe'.

The election as his successor of Robert's father, Hugh Capet, turned out to have inaugurated a dynasty that lasted until 1789, but at the time it was a sign less of strength than of weakness, or at least of the extent to which he seemed unlikely to threaten his neighbours. Among those neighbours the closest, strongest and therefore most dangerous were the counts of Blois and Anjou, both energetically extending their lordships, and in Robert's reign fiercely pitted against each other for domination of the Touraine. This, like Odo's annexation of the county of Champagne in 1019, was a major threat to the Capetian interest. To the north the counts of Rouen, descendants of Viking pirates soon to style themselves dukes of Normandy (as they are called here), were consolidating their command over an unruly territory and establishing their claim to an acknowledged position among the great princes of the realm.

For king and counts alike this meant securing the allegiance or alliance of as many as possible of the lords of those territories, who were in turn engaged at their own levels in the same struggle for control over lands and revenues. In the shifting patterns of alliance and counter-alliance which they struck in the unending pursuit of tactical advantage the exchange of sisters and daughters in marriage was a crucial stratagem, while the establishment of the lasting dynasties to which they all aspired required the fathering of sons by acknowledged, legitimate wives. The two necessities did not always sit easily together. Robert had repudiated Bertha some time between 1001 and 1006 and replaced her with Constance. We do not know whether this was because Bertha bore him no children or through hostility to her son Odo of Blois, but after Constance had promptly produced the two sons he urgently needed he repudiated her in turn, tried to get the pope to order him to take Bertha back and then changed his mind yet again, in favour of Constance. In the continuing struggle for ascendancy at court between the interests represented by the two women that these vacillations reflected (irrespective of Robert's personal feelings, whatever they may have been), the accusation of heresy against Stephen and Lisois was a manoeuvre by the supporters of the Blois faction, still hoping for the restoration of Bertha, against those of Constance and her Angevin connections.

It was a move very dangerous to the king. He was able to counter it only by dissociating himself from his former favourites at a hastily summoned trial. As Paul of St Père described it, 'The king and Queen Constance had come to Orléans, as Harfast had asked, with a number of bishops, and at his suggestion the whole wicked gang was arrested by royal officials at the house where they met, and brought before the king and queen and an assembly of clerks and bishops at the church of Ste Croix.' This was more like a kangaroo court than the formal assembly of leading men of the realm which would ordinarily come together to consider its affairs at one of the three great feasts of the year, or be summoned in an emergency. Nor was it a properly constituted council or synod of the church: the only senior clerics on record as present were Archbishop Léger of Sens, Abbot Goslin of Fleury, Bishop Franco of Paris, Bishop Odalric of Orléans and Bishop Guarin of Beauvais. Léger was a long-standing supporter of the king and, as such, regularly criticised by Fulbert of Chartres for his role in ecclesiastical appointments; Goslin was the king's half-brother, whose promotion to the archbishopric of Bourges had been strenuously resisted by Fulbert and the Blois faction; Franco was the king's chancellor; Odalric was a nephew of Odo of Blois whose long and bitter struggle for the bishopric of Orléans against King Robert's candidate, Thierry, seems to have been brought to a successful conclusion by this affair; Guarin was a friend of Fulbert of Chartres and another supporter of the Blois interest.

Léger might have been expected to preside in what was, after all, his own archiepiscopal province, but it was Guarin of Beauvais who conducted the interrogation, at whose conclusion Constance felt obliged to disown her confessor in so brutal and dramatic a fashion. In a final humiliation for the royal party Goslin himself, at the end of the proceedings, publicly recited a confession of faith. Whether it was required or volunteered, the implication can only be that he, and his office, had been directly threatened by association with the condemned heretics. The aftermath of the trial also included, by order of Odalric, the disinterment of Theodatus, the canon who had died some three years earlier and was now said to have been one of the heretics – and, no doubt, a supporter of Thierry for the bishopric. Several other churchmen felt it necessary to dissociate themselves in one way or another from the heretics and the ideas that had been associated with them.

In 1022 the allegation of heresy among the canons of Orléans was not in itself sufficiently remarkable or shocking to account for the violence of the outcome. Although the threat of heresy was extremely dangerous in principle, it did not in practice inspire widespread or urgent anxiety. Accusations were not uncommon, and not usually particularly serious. They were part of the currency of debate, and especially of disputes over property and office such as those in the diocese of Orléans which lay behind the trial in 1022. They generally went no further. The label was used and intended for rhetorical effect, neither alleging nor implying specific errors of doctrine. Abbo of Fleury (Goslin's predecessor as abbot) often likened his opponents (including the bishop of Orléans) to ancient heretics, especially when he was accusing them of usurping revenues which he thought rightfully belonged to his church. Fulbert of Chartres called a layman, Count Raginard of Sens, a heretic for the same reason. Sometimes it was used simply as a term of general abuse, as when (in the 1040s) Archbishop Adalbert of Hamburg-Bremen became unpopular for despoiling his diocese to fund his political ambitions and 'everyone hissed him and his followers as though they were heretics'.

The repercussions of the Orléans affair are attributable to the high social standing of the accused, the roots of the accusation in the royal court and the prominence of the king himself in the proceedings. The combination is typical of another kind of accusation, less common than of heresy but in practice much more serious – that of sorcery. In 1028, for example, Count William of Angoulême died after a lingering and mysterious wasting illness. Before he died, his eldest son, Alduin, accused a woman of having caused the illness by witchcraft and had her tortured to extract a confession. She resisted, but three of her friends, tortured in their turn, did not. Acting on the information thus secured, Alduin's men dug up from various places of concealment figures of the count that the women confessed to having buried. Count William from his sickbed ordered the women pardoned, but Alduin, engaged in a bitter succession dispute with his younger brother, had them burned as soon as his father was dead. Alduin succeeded his father, but his sons did not succeed him. A fine modern analysis confirms the obvious suspicion that the witchcraft (which later rumours attributed to Alduin's wife) was fabricated to cover up Alduin's own part in his father's death.[8] Such episodes cropped up intermittently throughout the middle ages, especially when ambitious newcomers sought to discredit and displace courtiers of traditional status and influence, or the old hands to disparage the upstarts. In 834, for example, Lothar, rebellious son of the emperor Louis the Pious, had Gerberga, sister of Count Bernard of Septimania, tortured and thrown into the River Saône in a barrel, to be drowned as a witch. It was a time, like the aftermath of the Capetian succession in 987, when factional rivalry was particularly intense and political legitimacy vulnerable to challenge.

The resemblance of the Orléans affair to a sorcery trial is one more confirmation that the tensions and motives that lay behind it were essentially political. But there was a crucial difference. To accuse a ruler's servants or intimates of sorcery did not implicate the ruler himself. On the contrary, by suggesting that he had been deceived or himself attacked by the sorcerer's magic, it cast him as an innocent victim, allowing him to accept without losing face what was in fact a political reverse. This was the function of the sorcery-like elements, the secrecy and the orgies, with which Paul of St Père, so long after the event, embellished his account of the activities of Stephen and Lisois.

To save King Robert's face had been no part of the original plot. The whole history of the Frankish monarchy since the baptism of its founder, Clovis, 500 years before this time, had been interwoven with its claim to protect the faith against its enemies, and specifically against heresy. The greatest of those monarchs, Charlemagne, whose successor Robert II precariously claimed to be, had renewed the Christian empire when Pope Hadrian I crowned him in St Peter's on Christmas Day 800. Since heresy, by definition, was openly propagated, to accuse royal favourites of heresy was indirectly to accuse the king himself of spectacular weakness or incompetence at best, and at worst of the basest perfidy in the most fundamental responsibility of his office, and in a role on which his legitimacy depended. In 1022 the monarchy was highly vulnerable to attacks both on its legitimacy and on its competence. The weakness of his own situation and the ambition of his neighbours made Robert's court a snakepit of overt and covert contention between the

representatives of competing interests, in which only the ruthless aban-
donment of their accused favourites allowed the royal couple to survive,
if not unscathed, at least without formal censure or open reverse.

————

For the next hundred years and more accusations of heresy played a
prominent part in the political rivalries of northern France.[9] None of
those we know of ended in flames, as they had at Orléans, but we should
not underestimate how easily they might have done so. This was the
age of the 'wandering scholars', when activity in the schools and the
exchange of masters and students between them were increasing rapidly.
Disagreements among the masters were continued in rivalries between
their pupils, conspicuously including those of Gerbert of Aurillac and
Fulbert of Chartres. And behind the masters, usually well concealed
from modern eyes, stood the political patrons for whom they acted,
or were treated, in some degree as representatives and surrogates. The
most celebrated case in the eleventh century was that of Berengar of
Tours, who was repeatedly accused of denying that the bread and wine
of the eucharist 'really' became the body and blood of Christ. A formidable debater, Berengar was condemned by a series of councils over
three decades, the last at the Lateran in Rome in 1079, presided over by
Pope Gregory VII himself. Berengar, a pupil of Fulbert of Chartres and
apparently a hereditary canon of Tours, enjoyed the patronage of the
counts of Anjou, whose court he joined around 1040 after establishing
his reputation as a teacher. His principal critics at every stage were associates or subjects of Duke William of Normandy. It was William who
convened the first of the series of councils to attack Berengar's teachings
during that decade, at Brionne in 1050. Berengar's final, ablest and most
relentless opponent was Lanfranc of Bec, William's closest ecclesiastical
adviser and eventually archbishop of Canterbury.

Peter Abelard's debating skills were even more celebrated and feared
than Berengar's, his enemies even more numerous and influential. His
fortunes throughout his career were intimately connected with those of
the shadowy but formidable figure of Stephen de Garlande, archdeacon of Paris and Chancellor of King Louis VI of France. The first of

Abelard's several famous confrontations with other masters took place a little before 1100, while he was still a student. It was with William of Champeaux, a bitter enemy of Garlande and thenceforth of Abelard, and later a friend and counsellor of Bernard of Clairvaux, the most famous preacher and miracle worker of the day. It may even be that Abelard had been brought to Paris from the Loire valley in order to confront and humiliate William. At any rate, for the rest of his life Abelard rode high when Garlande prospered. In the early 1120s, when Garlande lost royal favour, Abelard was driven into exile in Champagne and then in Brittany; he came back to Paris when Garlande returned to power in 1132. Abelard's fame now waxed greater than ever, until the final eclipse of Garlande after the death of Louis VI in 1137 opened the way for his enemies to prepare his nemesis at Bernard's hands, at the Council of Sens in 1141.

In Abelard's case, as in Berengar's, it is impossible to weigh precisely the significance of the political connections and rivalries of his patrons in the total context of his life and career – but insignificant they were not. One thing demonstrated by both is that right up to the middle of the twelfth century the accusation of heresy retained the public force and political menace that had been unleashed at Orléans in 1022. In the long contest for supremacy between the kings of France, the counts of Anjou and of Blois-Champagne and the dukes of Normandy, a successful accusation of heresy against a well-known supporter or protégé would be a serious reverse – as indeed it remained, though in greatly changed circumstances, thereafter. Heresy was a public matter. It touched the powerful and their relations with one another, whether they were clerics or laymen, with an intimacy that they could not ignore. When all authority was precarious, nobody who claimed it could allow the legitimacy of his claim to be impugned or be seen to have faltered in discharging its obligations.

This was made abundantly clear by the dénouement of the Orléans trial. 'At the king's command Queen Constance stood before the doors of the church, to prevent the common people from killing them inside the church, and they were expelled from the bosom of the church', says Paul of St Père. By this account 'the common people' had no part in the accusation, the trial or the sentence but nevertheless contributed to the drama of the occasion, adding to the pressures under which the leading actors performed. 'As they were being driven out,' Paul continues, 'the queen struck out the eye of Stephen, who had once been her confessor, with the staff which she carried in her hand.' A similar effect is suggested by Abelard's account of how before his first trial for heresy, at Soissons in 1121,

> my two rivals spread such evil rumours about me amongst the clerks and people that I and the few pupils who had accompanied me narrowly escaped being stoned by the people on the first day we arrived, for having preached and written (so they had been told) that there were three Gods.[10]

A few years earlier another famous heretic of whose actual teaching almost nothing is known, Roscelin of Compiègne, complained to Bishop Ivo of Chartres that, while visiting that city, he had been set upon by 'certain violent people' by whom, after being robbed and stripped, he was stoned. Far from sympathising, Ivo – who, as bishop, was responsible for law and order in the city – said it served him right for repeating heretical opinions that he had renounced at an earlier council at Soissons, in 1092. Roscelin fled to England, and at Canterbury again recanted his heresies – but only, according to Archbishop Anselm, because he was afraid, once more, of being killed by 'the people'.[11] It is not clear in any of these cases who 'the people' were, or what was their role and the role of their religious beliefs in public affairs, including the business of heresy. The establishing of answers to those questions during the next two centuries is an important part of our story.

2

THE GIFT OF THE
HOLY SPIRIT

*Human souls are of necessity more free when they continue in
the contemplation of the mind of God and less free when they
descend to bodies, and less free still when they are imprisoned
in earthly flesh and blood.*

Boethius, *The Consolation of Philosophy*

When Harfast thought that Stephen and Lisois were playing for time
with evasive answers, 'trying to cloud over their views with a shield of
verbiage', according to Paul of St Père's account of their interrogation at
Orléans, he interrupted their interrogation with these words:

> You taught me that nothing in baptism merits forgiveness of sin; that
> Christ was not born of the Virgin, did not suffer for men, was not
> truly buried, and did not rise from the dead; that the bread and wine
> which through the operation of the Holy Spirit seem to become a
> sacrament on the altar cannot be turned into the body and blood of
> Christ in the hands of priests.[1]

This, for Harfast, was the core of the heresy that he had been taught.
The accused did not deny it, but 'replied that he had remembered accurately, and they did hold and believe those things'. Their acquiescence

suggests that what Harfast had taken for evasion had been rather the attempt, not unfamiliar when intellectuals are explaining positions that seem to run counter to the conventional wisdom, to show that the matter was not so simple as their adversaries were making out. Nevertheless, such a statement was profoundly shocking to an audience which took it for granted that salvation in the next world, and order, justice and social harmony in this one, depended on universal and unquestioning acceptance of the revealed truths of the Christian religion, as they were understood and expounded by its duly appointed and ordained authorities. Among the miscellaneous and bizarre beliefs and practices attributed to the canons of Orléans, Harfast's summary listed their central teachings, as understood by their accusers. Agreement on these points between John of Ripoll, André of Fleury and Paul of St Père is clear, and so similarly expressed by the last two as to suggest a common origin, such as a written record of the interrogation.

Such teachings, or the appearance of them, would be quite consistent with the suspicion of neoplatonist influence that was prompted by John of Ripoll's and André of Fleury's descriptions of the heresy. The doctrines of the incarnation of Christ and the presence of his body and blood in the eucharistic sacrifice had frequently caused trouble in the hands of Christian platonists and would often do so again. It easily led them into either heresy itself or explanations so subtle and complex as to expose them to the accusation of it. The suggestions that the heretics avoided meat and marriage and scorned the institutions and buildings of the church are equally consistent with neoplatonist distrust of the flesh and of all material things.

The mystical language in which Paul of St Père describes the attempted conversion of Harfast is also distinctly neoplatonist in flavour. 'We regard you', the canons had said to him,

as a tree in a wood, which is transplanted to a garden, and watered regularly, until it takes root in the earth. Then, stripped of thorns and other excess matter, and pruned down to the ground with a hoe, so that a better branch can be inserted into it, which will later bear sweet fruit. In the same way you will be carried out of this evil world into our holy company. You will soak in the waters of wisdom until you have taken shape, and armed with the sword of the Lord, are able to avoid the thorns of vice. Foolish teachings will be shut out from your heart and you will be able with a pure mind, to receive our teaching, which is handed down from the Holy Spirit.

Similarly,

until now you have lain with the ignorant in the Charybdis of false belief. Now you have been raised to the summit of all truth. With unimpeded mind you may begin to open your eyes to the light of the true faith. We will open the door of salvation to you. Through the laying of our hands upon you, you will be cleansed of every spot of sin. You will be replenished with the gift of the Holy Spirit, which will teach you unreservedly the underlying meaning of the scriptures, and true righteousness. You will want for nothing, for God, in whom are all the treasures of wealth and wisdom, will never fail to be your companion in all things.

The assertions of the accused that 'neither prayers to the saints and martyrs nor good works could secure the forgiveness of sins' and the rejection of episcopal authority on the ground that 'a bishop is nothing, and cannot ordain priests according to the customary rules, because he has not the gift of the Holy Spirit' are, in this context, entirely consistent with the powerful conviction of personal revelation and salvation that Stephen and Lisois evidently entertained. They were neither the first nor the last Christian enthusiasts to do so. The suggestion not only of neoplatonism but also of spiritual elitism is confirmed by the impatience with which they brushed aside the questions and arguments put to them by Guarin of Beauvais:

You may tell all this to those who are learned in earthly things, who believe the fabrications which men have written on the skins of animals. We believe in the law written within us by the Holy Spirit, and hold everything else, except what we have learned from God, the maker of all things, empty, unnecessary and remote from divinity. Therefore bring an end to your speeches and do with us what you will.

Now we see our king reigning in heaven. He will raise us to his right hand in triumph and give us eternal joy.

One monk and one nun accepted the opportunity to recant, but Stephen and Lisois believed what they said. The political rivalries in which they had found themselves embroiled meant nothing to them. For their faith in their revelation they and some dozen followers who went with them to the flames were ready to embrace a dreadful death.

———

The faith of Stephen and Lisois naturally raises the question whether they belonged to a religious movement wider than their own aristocratic circle in Orléans. There is nothing to suggest that they preached to 'the people' or sought converts among them. By this time there were some among the religious in every part of Europe, including the neighbourhood of Orléans, who had come to feel that the vast and increasing distance in wealth and status between the small and highly privileged elite and the mass of the labouring and generally unfree population was contrary to the spirit and teaching of the gospels. But the expression of such sentiments, by word or deed, was regarded with the deepest distrust, as at best eccentric and at worst dangerous, behaviour that marked those who indulged it as inspired, either by God or the devil.

On the other hand, the circle of the higher clergy and nobility of the Orléanais was not the only one to which Stephen and Lisois belonged. Those who had been educated in the schools that every cathedral church was obliged to maintain had been shaped by a common culture and formation, in which the Latin writers of the Classical age figured as prominently as the scriptures, and not always with less moral authority. A master's reputation for learning and eloquence might add greatly to the prestige both of his church and of his patron. His bearing and demeanour, based especially on Cicero's prescriptions for the qualities and conduct befitting those with public responsibilities, provided a model and example for the young noblemen in his care.* That is what

---

* Marcus Tullius Cicero (106–43 BC), Roman lawyer and orator, generally considered the greatest of Latin prose writers; on these matters his letters and his treatise *De officiis* were particularly influential.

André of Fleury meant when he described Stephen and Lisois as 'raised from childhood in holy religion and educated as deeply in sacred as in profane letters.'[2] Within this tradition the links between particularly influential or charismatic masters and their former students were often strong, intimate and assiduously maintained, as the surviving letter collections of Gerbert of Aurillac (Pope Sylvester II) and Fulbert of Chartres bear witness. The tradition itself was mistrusted by many, especially in monastic circles. St Odo, the first abbot of Cluny (near Mâcon, in Burgundy), which led the greatest monastic movement of the age, once dreamed of an extraordinarily beautiful vase filled with writhing serpents, which he took to be a divinely inspired representation of the poetry of Virgil. Another dreamer, according to Ralph the Bald (himself a Cluniac monk), was Vilgardus of Ravenna, 'deeply learned in the art of grammar', to whom demons appeared in the form of Virgil, Horace and Juvenal. Seduced by their promise of a share in their fame, 'he began arrogantly to preach against the holy faith, saying that the sayings of the poets should be believed in everything', and was condemned as a heretic, some time before 971, by Bishop Peter of Ravenna.[3] This may reflect nothing more than a rhetorical swipe at the pretensions of the schoolmasters and bears no resemblance to what we are told about Stephen and Lisois, but it illustrates the cultural climate of their time.

A closer resemblance to the teachings of Stephen and Lisois, and to their social milieu, is revealed in another story from Italy, which records another large-scale burning, that of Gerard of Monforte d'Alba and his disciples, at Milan in 1028. We have only one account of it, composed long after the event, around 1100, by Landolf Senior.[4] It appears to be based on a formal record of the interrogation of Gerard by Archbishop Aribert II of Milan, and Landolf Senior was a capable and well-informed writer. He was also, however, passionately partisan in the events that tore Milan apart in the 1050s, '60s and '70s, when a party of religious reformers, the Patarenes, tried to wrench the city from the control of the archbishop and the established ruling families. Landolf, an opponent of the Patarenes and himself a married clerk, included the story of Monforte in his chronicle to illustrate how dangerous to the church even apparently admirable religious enthusiasm might be. We cannot exclude the possibility that he elaborated it, not to deceive but to clarify the danger as he understood it.

Archbishop Aribert was staying at Turin when he 'heard that a new heresy had recently been established in the castle above the place called Monforte and immediately ordered one of the heretics from the castle to be brought to him, so that he could have a trustworthy account of it'. Gerard came forward as spokesman, 'prepared to answer every question with alacrity'. He presented as the foundation of the group's way of life the fact that

> We value virginity above everything. We have wives, and while those who are virgins preserve their virginity, those who are already corrupt are given permission by our elders to retain their chastity perpetually. We do not sleep with our wives, we love them as we would mothers and sisters.

'We never eat meat', he went on. 'We keep up continuous fasts and unceasing prayer; our elders pray in turn by day and by night, so that no hour lacks its prayer. We hold all our possessions in common with all men.' He added that 'We believe in the Father, Son and Holy Ghost. We believe that we are bound and loosed by those who have the power of binding and loosing. We accept the Old and New Testaments and the holy canons, and read them daily.'

If this were all, we should have no difficulty in identifying this as one of the communities of pious lay people, appearing all over Europe at this time, who retired from the world to live in what they believed to be the manner of the early Christian 'desert fathers'. So it may have been, but Aribert pressed for explanation. It became clear that while Gerard, an educated man, doubtless based his views on the New Testament and the contemporary lives and writings of the desert fathers, he interpreted them in a strongly platonist fashion, and with some implications disturbing to the archbishop. His definition of the Trinity was strikingly expressed, potentially though not necessarily heterodox: 'I mean by the Father eternal God, who created all things and in whom all things come to rest. I mean by the Son, the soul of man beloved by God. I mean by the Holy Spirit the understanding of divine wisdom, by which all things are separately ruled.'

Archbishop Aribert continued:

'What have you to say, my friend, of our Lord Jesus Christ, born of the Virgin Mary by the word of the Father?'

'Jesus Christ of whom you speak is a soul sensually born of the Virgin Mary; born that is to say, of the holy scriptures. The Holy Spirit is the spiritual understanding of the holy scriptures.'

'Why do you marry if it is not to have children? How are men to be born?'

'If all men married without corruption the human race would increase without coition, as the bees do.'*

For Aribert the crucial issue was ecclesiastical authority:

'Where do we find absolution from our sins? From the pope, or from a bishop, or from any priest?'

'We do not have the Roman pontiff, but another one, who daily visits our brothers, scattered across the world. When God gives him to us spiritually we are given complete absolution from our sins.'

Finally, Aribert 'asked Gerard whether he believed in the catholic faith held by the Roman Church, in baptism and in the Son of God born in flesh of the Virgin Mary, and that his true flesh and true blood are sanctified by the word of God through the catholic priest, even if he is a sinner?' Gerard replied, 'There is no pope but our pope, though his head is not tonsured, and he is not ordained.'

Gerard's allegorical imagery was very like that used to Harfast by Stephen and Lisois in Orléans. His Latin vocabulary for theological and spiritual issues is not just generally platonist but specifically that used and taught in the cathedral schools of northern Europe, where many

---

* This was a reminder of the accepted view that sex was necessary only because of original sin: bees often appear in both Classical and Christian literature as models of industrious and self-denying virtue.

Italian bishops and senior churchmen had been trained.[5] In describing his beliefs he said nothing absolutely heretical, but he gave grounds for the suspicion of heresy. In respect of constituted ecclesiastical authority he was at least evasive. Archbishop Aribert, like many subsequent commentators, was particularly struck by Gerard's revelation that 'None of our number ends his life except in torment, the better to avoid eternal torment ... We rejoice to die through torment inflicted on us by evil men; if any of us is dying naturally his neighbour among us kills him in some way before he gives up the ghost.' His words, if accurately reported and intended literally – neither to be depended on – remain unexplained and unparalleled, except, at a very great distance, by another dubious and uncorroborated assertion that two and a half centuries later some of the so-called 'Cathar' heretics of southern France hastened their deaths by avoiding food.

Gerard's final comment, on the pope, was the last straw. 'When it was thus clear what their faith was and the truth was apparent,' Landolf continues,

Aribert sent a large body of soldiers to Monforte, and took all of them that he could find into custody. Among them the countess of the castle was taken, as a believer in this heresy. He took them to Milan and laboured to convert them to the catholic faith, for he was greatly concerned that the people of Italy might become contaminated by their heresy. For whatever part of the world these wretches had come from they behaved as though they were good priests, and daily spread false teachings wrenched from the scriptures among the peasants who came to the town to see them. When the leading layman of the town heard of this a huge funeral pyre was set alight, and a holy cross erected near by. Against Aribert's wishes the heretics were brought out, and this decree ordained, that if they wanted to embrace the cross, abjure their wickedness, and confess the faith which the whole world holds, they would be saved. If not, they must enter the flames, and be burned alive. So it was done: some of them went to the holy cross, confessed the catholic faith, and were saved. Many others leapt into the flames, holding their hands in front of their faces, and dying wretchedly were reduced to wretched ashes.

Aribert's protest was not necessarily hypocritical, or merely formal. The church disapproved of bloodshed, and least one other eleventh-century bishop considered violence an inappropriate response to heresy, as we shall see. The affair at Orléans had ended in flames for political, not religious, reasons. We know much less about the background and circumstances of this case, but there is enough to suggest that purely religious considerations were not the only ones at work. The community came to Aribert's attention because he was carrying out a visitation in the diocese of one of his subordinate bishops, in a part of his large province that, as an energetic and ambitious bishop and lord, he was anxious to bring more firmly under his grip. The source of the reports that reached him about the heresy is unspecified, but the castle and its countess represented a centre of local power, and therefore of possible competition. The *majores* (great men) of Milan who according to Landolf insisted on the executions were the *capitanei*, the heads of the noble families that dominated the region and controlled its lands. As the traditional elite of the wealthiest and most rapidly growing urban community in western Europe they were under challenge, actually or potentially, from several quarters, including the merchants and moneylenders who led the city's commercial growth, the weavers, journeymen, craftsmen and casual workers who precariously underpinned it, and, most conspicuously, their own knights (*valvassores*), who bitterly resented the fact that they were not permitted to transmit their landholdings to their sons. These were germs of tensions and rivalries that a few years later led to open insurrection against Aribert's rule, and which in the longer run made Milan the scene of bitter and effectively continuous civil conflict in the thirty years following his death.

The victims of Orléans and Monforte died for their faith, but it was not really because of their faith that they were put to death. Their ill fortune was to have provided convenient targets for the enemies of those who could be represented as protecting them – in the first case, King Robert and Queen Constance of France; in the second, perhaps the countess of Monforte, or Archbishop Aribert himself, or one or another of the Milanese factions. There was no direct connection between the two condemned groups, but through their education and religious outlook their leaders had a great deal in common. The neoplatonism that was widely influential in the schools in which they were formed had led them beyond philosophical speculation to religious revelation. Guided by their personal illumination rather than the formal rituals of the church, they were convinced that this was the only path to salvation. That conviction fostered both disdain for the ecclesiastical hierarchy and ultimately the authority of the church, and the commitment to their own vision and the ties it forged between its devotees that brought them to the flames. Neither group was secretive about its teachings. They were quite ready and indeed eager to explain them when asked.

This debate echoed widely in the church of the early eleventh century. The handful accused of heresy were far from being alone in finding the ordinary precepts and routines of the church inadequate to their spiritual ambitions. The influential William of Volpiano (friend and mentor of the chronicler Ralph the Bald) renounced the world and the flesh to seek his inspiration directly from the holy spirit by meditation upon the divine, perceived by what Bishop Ratherius of Verona had called the *interioris oculus*, the inner eye. Confidence in that inner guidance might have practical consequences. Authoritative figures such as Abbo, Goslin's predecessor as abbot of Fleury, or Gerbert of Aurillac, could appeal to their private conviction of righteousness against those who accused them of attacking the church when they argued for its reform. There was, in other words, a latent but widely experienced tension between the urge to individual spiritual progress and the authority of the church.

Not everybody who encountered neoplatonist ideas was influenced by them, nor was everybody who was influenced by them influenced in the same way. Texts, or the ideas they describe, do not necessarily lead to given conclusions, still less to given actions, except as they are understood by particular readers. In the twentieth century Marxism was endorsed as a coherent intellectual system only by a minority of the many whose outlook and thinking were influenced by it in various degrees. Those who did endorse it took it to justify a wide range of political stances, from libertarian pacifism through democratic socialism to authoritarian communism. Similarly, in the eleventh century platonism, or neoplatonism, was a widely pervasive and variously received way of thinking, which might encourage those influenced by it in certain identifiable directions but led of necessity to none. No single, authoritative version existed, or could have been universally accepted if it had.

For this reason historians have found helpful the idea of a 'textual community' – that is, a group of people who base their outlook and way of life on a particular text or set of texts which they understand in the same way, generally that of a particular leader or interpreter.[6] Both leader and followers may indeed be quite unconscious of this 'crucial mediating role. Who has not heard the indignant, and perfectly sincere, denial, 'this isn't just what I say; it is what the scriptures say'? In the eleventh century, as in others, episcopal authority and anticlericalism, catholic devotion, discord and terror, heresy and schism, persecution and martyrdom, arose from the same passionate devotion to differing and equally sincere interpretations of the same scriptures. The choice between interpretations, however, and not only that of the vast illiterate majority, was most often based not on scrutiny of the texts themselves, or even the arguments about them, but on the reputed probity and virtue, the personal force, of the individuals who advanced the arguments and expounded the texts. For the followers of Stephen and Lisois and of Gerard of Monforte charismatic leadership had carried the spiritual understanding of the scriptures beyond mere intellectual influence to the point of religious rebirth, with tragic consequences.

———

The potentially subversive impact of neoplatonist teachings was certainly both recognised and mistrusted. Shortly after Christmas 1024 Bishop Gerard of Cambrai held a synod at Arras to deal with people who had been reported to him as heretics. It was a magnificent occasion, on which, after questioning the prisoners briefly about their beliefs, the bishop embarked on a sermon that, no doubt considerably embellished, runs to some 20,000 words of Latin (two to three chapters of this book) in its surviving form. When he finished, the accused 'could only reply that they believed that the sum of Christian salvation could consist in nothing but what the bishop had set out'. They signed a confession of faith which Gerard dictated, and returned to their families with his blessing.[7]

This is a story, rare in these pages, that ended happily. The accused in question were not cathedral canons or residents of a castle but humble people. Gerard's long sermon, far from being addressed to what they had told him about their beliefs (which will be considered in the next chapter), ignored most of what they had said and rebutted a great deal that they had not said. In other words, following a common literary convention, he had used the examination as the occasion for saying, or writing, what he had already intended to say in any case.

Gerard came from the aristocracy of the region around Liège, subject politically to the German emperor Henry II but ecclesiastically to the archbishopric of Reims, where he attended the cathedral school and belonged to the chapter before becoming a chaplain to the emperor. In 1012 Henry had appointed him to the bishopric of Cambrai, which carried with it the office of count, exercising royal powers to do justice, levy taxes and call men to arms. His position was therefore a highly political one, demanding the defence of his authority and prerogative against the competing pretensions of French king and German emperor as well as an assortment of powerful local rivals.

The sermon that Gerard preached at Arras amounted to a systematic demolition of the neoplatonist understanding of the scriptures that had been maintained at Orléans by Stephen and Lisois, and of its implications for the teaching, practices and authority of the church. 'You believe that nothing of a material nature should be found in the church', the bishop says. Nothing so rarified had even been hinted at by the people actually before him, but it had been the starting-point for the views of Stephen and Lisois three years earlier, and would be again by the other Gerard, at Monforte three years later. This was the position against which Bishop Gerard defended the use of water in baptism and of chrism in the communion service, of incense and bells on the altar, of church buildings themselves and of the church as a material structure. He insisted on the necessity of marriage for the laity and of celibacy for the priesthood, to which was reserved sole authority to teach and to perform the sacraments, ruling the church as the mind rules the body. Beyond the rebuttal of individual heretical propositions, Gerard of Cambrai's central concern was to drive it home that mere spiritual illumination was not enough. Salvation could be attained only by divine grace, pursued through specific and concrete acts of devotion, submission and contrition, with the aid of relics of the saints, of miracles, reverence for the cross, prayers for the dead, the rituals and sacraments of the church. He sought to show the faithful an accessible faith, a path to salvation that could be followed in simple, practical steps by all who sought it sincerely.

———

In this way Bishop Gerard of Cambrai identified the danger that enthusiasm held for the church universal: that it threatened to create a spiritual elite, to whose members alone was reserved the knowledge of God, perceptible only by the inner eye of the spirit. Such elitism had been exemplified by the contempt of the clerks of Orléans for 'what men have written on the skins of animals' – that is, for the church's, as opposed to their own, reading of the scriptures. On his way to Orléans, Harfast had been disappointed to find that Bishop Fulbert of Chartres, whose advice he sought, was away from the city. But Fulbert had given his answer some thirty years previously, when he (or possibly one of his pupils) wrote about the proper relation of inspiration to faith. Knowledge of the divine, he said, could not be secured by unaided human wisdom. The will of God must be discovered by turning outwards, to the disciplined study of the scriptures, of the law of the church and the writings of its fathers. Reliance on the unguided impulses of the inturned spirit had given birth to all the great heresies of the patristic age. Nobody might dismiss the services and requirements of the church as elaborations and superfluities, for the *via legis divine* (path of the divine law) was a single road, the same for all Christians. There was not one law for the perfect and another for the imperfect.

There is nothing to suggest that Stephen and Lisois tried to disseminate their beliefs by evangelism among the population at large, and it was only after their capture that Gerard of Monforte and his companions 'daily spread false teachings wrenched from the scriptures among the peasants who came to the town to see them'. Nevertheless, it is an obvious question whether ideas capable of exciting such passionate faith, or fanaticism, among the social elite of early eleventh-century Europe may not also have spread among other sections of the population.

3

THE APOSTOLIC LIFE

And the multitude of believers had but one heart and one soul. Neither did any one say that aught of the things which he possessed was his own: but all things were common unto them.

Acts of the Apostles 4: 32

The people whom Bishop Gerard of Cambrai questioned at Arras had tried to escape after being reported to him as heretics but were caught and brought before him. A preliminary interrogation seemed to confirm the rumours, so he had them detained for three days while a full hearing was prepared.

On the third day, a Sunday, the bishop in full regalia, accompanied by his archdeacons bearing crosses and copies of the Gospels, processed to the church of Notre Dame, with a great crowd of clerks and of the populace, to hold a synod. The appointed psalm, 'Let God arise and let his enemies be scattered', was sung. Then, when the bishop was seated in his court with the abbots, religious and archdeacons placed around him according to their ranks, the men were taken from their place of confinement and brought before him. After addressing a few words about them to the people, the bishop asked, 'What is your doctrine, your discipline and your way of life, and from whom have you learned it?'[1]

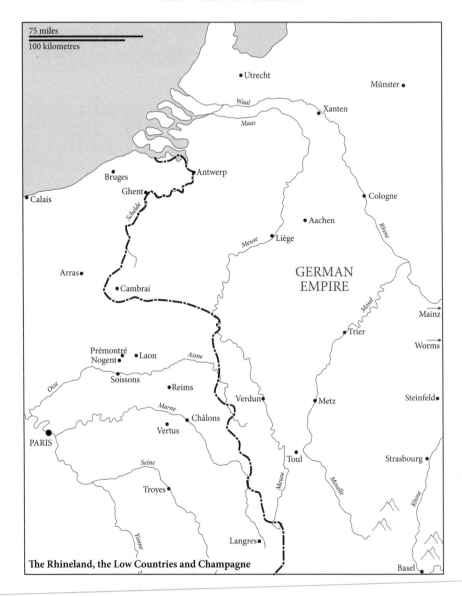

75 miles

100 kilometres

• Utrecht

Münster •

Waal

Xanten •

Maas

• Antwerp

Bruges

Ghent•

Schelde

Calais •

Cologne •

• Aachen

Meuse • Liège

Rhine

Arras •

GERMAN
EMPIRE

• Cambrai

Mosel

Mainz →

• Trier

Worms →

Prémontré •
Nogent •

• Laon

Aisne

Soissons

• Reims

Verdun •

• Metz

Steinfeld •

Marne

• Châlons

Vertus

PARIS

Seine

Toul •

Strasbourg •

Troyes •

Meuse

Moselle

Rhine

Yonne

Langres •

The Rhineland, the Low Countries and Champagne

Basel •

The prisoners said that they were followers of an Italian named Gundolfo, from whom 'they had learned the precepts of the Gospels and
the apostles, and would accept no other scripture but this, to which
they would adhere in word and deed'. Gerard proceeded to question
them about baptism, the eucharist, the sanctity of marriage, the authority of the church, the value of confession and the cult of martyrs, all of
which he had heard that they denied. When he asked them how they

46

could defend their views against passages of scripture that he cited, they replied:

> Nobody who is prepared to examine with care the teaching and rule which we have learned from our master will think that they contravene either the precepts of the Gospels or those of the apostles. This is its tenor: to abandon the world, to restrain the appetites of the flesh, to provide our food by the labour of our own hands, to do no injury to anyone, to extend charity to everyone of our own faith. If these rules are followed baptism is unnecessary; without them it will not lead to salvation.

They justified their denial of baptism as a sacrament on three grounds:

> first, that the evil life of the minister cannot be a vehicle for the salvation of him who is baptized; second that the vices which are renounced at the font may be resumed later in life; third, that the child who neither wills it nor concurs with it, knows nothing of faith and is ignorant of his need for salvation, does not beg for rebirth in any sense, and can make no confession of faith: clearly he has neither free will nor faith, and makes no confession of it.

This is all that we have directly from the accused. The sermon that followed, whether or not it was actually delivered to the synod, was addressed in the form we now have to a much wider and quite different audience. When Gerard had finished,

> those who a little while before had thought themselves invincible by words, incapable of being swayed by any manner of argument, stood stupefied by the weight of his discourse, and the evident power of God, as though they had never learned any better argument. Speechless, they could only reply that they believed that the sum of Christian salvation could consist in nothing but what the bishop had set out.

They were called upon to renounce their former beliefs and to subscribe to a confession of faith solemnly pronounced by bishop and clergy before the whole assembly.

As on most such occasions, the confession was formulaic, not tailored to the people who were required to subscribe to it. It repudiated a number of errors of which they had not been accused but did not mention the suggestion that the efficacy of the sacraments depended on the merits of the priest, a most serious heresy that their statement had clearly implied. The confession was recited in Latin, which the accused did not understand, and in the vernacular. Thereupon 'they confessed with a solemn oath that they abjured what had been condemned, and believed what is believed by the faithful', put their crosses to the document 'and returned to their families with the blessing of the bishop'. The public translation, and if necessary attestation, of Latin documents translated into the local vernacular was a familiar procedure. This was how the decrees and exhortations of the Carolingian rulers had been conveyed to their subjects at least since the ninth century.

The report of the assembly at Arras is unusual in quoting directly (or purporting to do so) the words not of clerics or lay dignitaries but of ordinary working men and women. But it is also suspect. It is known only in a single copy, made around 1200 at Cîteaux, the principal house of the monastic order that was leading the war against heresy at that time, and energetically collecting evidence of the danger that heresy represented. It is also uncorroborated. The diocese of Cambrai is one of the best-documented in northern Europe for this period, but the synod of Arras is mentioned by no other surviving source.

On the other hand, as we saw in the last chapter, the lengthy sermon that Bishop Gerard composed for this occasion was well designed to counter the kind of heresies associated with learned neoplatonism that had appeared at Orléans two years earlier. Close examination of its language and reasoning confirms that they belong to the early eleventh century and suggests that they should not be placed later. For example, there is no echo of the arguments that raged around the teaching of Berengar of Tours in northern Francia in the second half of the century. It is possible that Gerard simply invented the story of these heretics as the occasion for a treatise that he intended to publish in any case – it would have been a perfectly acceptable rhetorical device – but if so, he might easily have made the heresy it described resemble more closely the one that he really meant to attack. On balance, therefore, it seems likely that he used a real episode to which (as we shall see) he attached no great importance in itself, as an opportunity to contribute to theological-political debate at a level far beyond the horizons of the simple people he had actually confronted, and that the description of the questioning of the heretics and the public ceremonial attending it which precedes the sermon is a contemporary account of real events.

———

We must take their words on the way of life prescribed by the scriptures and on baptism as a statement of the core beliefs of the people questioned by Gerard. If they acknowledged or commented on any of the other heresies that he had mentioned or heard rumours of, he did not think it worth recording. As such a statement, for all its brevity, it is revealing. It confirms, to begin with, that whatever their beliefs may have been, these people constituted a sect, implicitly distinguishing as objects of their charity 'others of our own faith' from the generality of the population, or of Christians at large. They had derived this faith from a leader or teacher, for, not themselves literate, they were confident of the basis of their beliefs in the text of the New Testament, so Gundolfo was probably more than a convenient fiction. The message that they had heard from him was of stark insistence on the responsibility of each individual for his or her own fate. Salvation would be secured through steady adherence to a simple code of abstemious and charitable behaviour modelled on that of Christ and the apostles, and not by the intercession of a fallible church and its sinful priests. That they 'would accept no other scripture but this' suggests a rejection of any teaching but Gundolfo's, rather than the outright denial of the authority of the Old Testament that would sometimes be expressed in later centuries.

Rejection of infant baptism, here specified as a tenet of reported heretics for the first time in our period, would become one of the most regular elements in heresy accusations. Infant baptism had been unusual among early Christians, who often postponed the ceremony until late in life to minimise the risk of repeating the sins which it required them to abjure – a caution echoed in the second objection of the Arras sectaries.

Charlemagne, however, had proclaimed baptism as defining the Christian community, and from his time on it was expected to take place early in life. Insistence on infant baptism, and therefore the possibility of resistence to it, must have become more general with the reform of the church, however, and in particular with the widespread growth of the parish system in the eleventh and twelfth centuries.

While this was the only heresy avowed by the sectaries of Arras, their defence of it had drawn them, perhaps unwittingly, into two others. In saying that baptism was unnecessary if their rules of conduct were observed and would not lead to salvation if they were not, they denied the necessity of grace, and of membership of the church. Their anxiety that baptism might be invalidated by the sins of those who administered it denied the catholic teaching that salvation lay by God's grace in the sacrament itself, and not in the vehicle through whom it flowed. Theologically these were, respectively, the Pelagian and Donatist heresies, which had been identified by Augustine as two of the gravest threats to the early church and resoundingly condemned.

The claim that the efficacy of the sacraments, including ordination, was nullified by the sins of the clergy – Donatism, though by this time seldom called by that name – was about to become once again the most widespread and persistent threat to the authority of the church and would remain so throughout the period considered in this book. Gerard of Cambrai was therefore perfectly correct in identifying what he heard here as, in principle, a repudiation of the authority and universality of the institutional church in favour of the esoteric spiritual elitism against which his treatise was directed. But by the same token, in choosing not to categorise and condemn their error by describing the people before him as Pelagian or Donatist heretics – as, of course, he was perfectly capable of doing if he had thought it appropriate – he showed that he did not regard them as conscious or dangerous agents of that threat. This they confirmed in their ready acceptance of his authority, and he in his lenient treatment of them.

———

Such information as we are given about the people who were examined by Bishop Gerard lends itself almost too readily to explanation. In 1025 Arras was at the very beginning of its medieval prosperity as a centre of the international cloth trade, launched by the invention of a new kind of standing loom, on which broader and better bolts of cloth could be woven than on the traditional hand loom. Consequently Arras merchants were already seeking markets as far afield as Novgorod (near modern St Petersburg), and consolidating the connection between Flanders and Lombardy, one of the great axes of the trade of medieval Europe. That brought prosperity, employment and growth – but also privilege, exploitation and bitter social division. The new looms required not only capital but also workshops, in which men and women were employed by the owners of the looms, instead of working on their own account, in their own homes. Social division rapidly achieved political expression. It is at this time that we find the first indications of the presence of legally privileged families among the townspeople of Arras, the ancestors of the proud and wealthy burghers of the high middle ages.

There we have a context not only for the Italian Gundolfo but also, more importantly, for the determined individualism that led these people – practitioners, perhaps, of the weavers' trade whose association with heresy would become proverbial – to insist on the child's innocence of the sins of others and on the adult's responsibility for his own, unbuffered by the mediation of priest or godparents, and on providing their food by the labour of their own hands, repudiating the exploitation inherent in the new system of manufacture. It is an attractive and plausible conjecture, consistent with such facts as we have, and adding very little to them by way of additional hypothesis. But it is no more than that. Gundolfo, though given a name, may have been merely the stereotypical carrier of wickedness from Italy whom we have already met. The insistence on 'providing our food by the labour of our own hands' may have been merely a striking expression of the communal ideal described by St Paul. Our sectaries may have been masons drawn to Arras by the church under construction there, or peasants (also becoming subject to much harsher exploitation at this time), or even possessors of the privilege renounced by many others in the pursuit of the apostolic life. Their illiteracy is a probable, though by no means certain, pointer to humble standing, but apart from the suggestion of the highly suspect introductory letter that they were tortured or threatened with torture, which would indicate servile status, there is no positive evidence of their social position.

———

Other reports of heresy at work among the people of eleventh-century northern France tell us less about either its nature or its appeal than about the apprehensions of the reporters. Ralph the Bald provides a characteristically lively account of Leutard of Vertus, near Châlons-sur-Marne, a farm hand who dreamed as he slept in the fields that his body was invaded by a swarm of bees.[2] On their orders he separated from his wife, smashed the crucifix in the local church and took to preaching. He won a considerable popular following but was exposed as ignorant and a heretic by his bishop and, humiliated, committed suicide by throwing himself into a well. Whether Leutard was indeed a heretic remains a mystery, for although Ralph describes behaviour that might have been prompted by heretical beliefs – most obviously, breaking the crucifix – his only specific assertion about what Leutard preached is 'that it was completely unnecessary and mere folly to pay tithes'. That was not a heresy. This is an example of the rhetorical application of the label of heretic to anyone who was accused of attacking ecclesiastical property. That Leutard 'aspired to be a great teacher', justified separating from his wife by 'pretended reference to evangelical precept', that he 'declared that though the prophets [of the Old Testament] had said many good things, they were not to be believed in everything', and, when questioned by his bishop, began to wish 'that he had not learned to take texts from Holy Scripture for his own purposes' suggests that he had embraced the apostolic life, inspired by his own or more probably somebody else's unauthorised reading of the New Testament.

Leutard's bishop was either Gebuin I (d. 998) or Gebuin II (d. 1014) of Châlons-sur-Marne. If Gerard of Cambrai's introductory letter to the account of the synod at Arras is authentic, it was addressed to Gebuin II's successor, Bishop Roger I. It accuses Roger of having captured and examined, but failed to convict and punish, heretics whose missionaries had carried the heresy into the diocese of Cambrai. They who falsely claimed to follow the teaching of the apostles and the Gospels, said that the ceremony of baptism and the sacrament of the body and blood of Christ were nothing, and should be avoided, unless taken for the sake of deception; that penance does not help us towards salvation; that married people cannot aspire to heaven, and other things which are set out in this pamphlet.

Between 1043 and 1048 Bishop Roger's own successor in Châlons-sur-Marne, Roger II, asked the advice of Wazo of Liège on how to deal with some peasants 'who following the perverse teaching of the Manichees were holding secret meetings' and 'make anyone they can join their sect, abhor marriage, shun the eating of meat, and believe it profane to kill animals, presuming to assimilate to their heresy the words of the Lord in the commandment which prohibits killing'.[3] This last phrase, together with the assertion 'that if uncouth and ignorant men become members of this sect they immediately become more eloquent than the most learned Catholics', points clearly to a textual community, or incipient sect, whose leaders the bishop regarded as uneducated. They may have been successful in their evangelism, for he was 'more worried about their daily corruption of others than about their own damnation'.

Wazo's biographer Anselm of Liège also mentions the hanging at Goslar, in 1052, on the orders of the Emperor Henry III, of heretics who he thought belonged to the same sect. 'I have most diligently tried to find out what passed at this discussion,' he says, 'and can discover no justification for the sentence except that the heretics refused to obey the order of the bishop to kill a chicken.' Anselm's interest, and the fact that the heretics had been arrested and brought to the imperial court by Duke Godfrey of Upper Lorraine, may suggest that they also had come from this or a neighbouring region. But speculation is empty on so limited a basis. Another possibility is suggested by the fact that the flourishing silver mines near Goslar were attracting many itinerant craftsmen at this time, while the involvement of Duke Godfrey, out of imperial favour but soon to recover it, is a reminder that political motives for heresy accusations can never be excluded.

It is not surprising that the diocese of Châlons-sur-Marne should occasionally have experienced religiously informed dissidence at this period. Relatively long- and densely settled and farmed, the plain of Champagne was both turbulent and prosperous. It exhibited, sometimes in extreme form, many of the forces that were gathering to transform European society. Merchants were already connecting its fairs and markets, famous a century later, to places as far afield as Lombardy, Catalonia and Russia. A political vacuum left by the Carolingians, one of whose heartland territories this had been, was filled not by a great principality like those of Aquitaine or Anjou but by episcopal lordships, among which Châlons was one of the greatest, and a multitude of small castellanies. The consequent social tensions were acute. The tithes against which Leutard rebelled enriched secular lords as well as churchmen; the distinction was largely a formal one in these terms as in others. The transformation of the cloth industry by the invention of the broad loom that we suspected in Arras began here. If, as so often in later history, the elevation of personal sanctity through austerity in matters of sex and diet, repudiation of privilege and of personal wealth was a response to brutally accelerating social differentiation and the exploitation and ostentation that went with it, its persistence in this region is not difficult to account for.

―――――

Their denial of infant baptism apart, the statement of the people arraigned before Bishop Gerard at Arras was not only unexceptional but typical of what are often considered the most inspiring religious sentiments of the age. The hangings at Goslar are mentioned in several sources, but only in passing. All the other reports of episodes discussed in this chapter are uncorroborated, and all, in varying degrees, conform to other agendas. They differ too much, even if they could be relied on, to support any suggestion of connection, still less continuity, between the groups they describe. The only point on which they agree is that those accused or suspected of heresy claimed, explicitly or implicitly, to follow the apostolic life.

The precepts of the gospels and the apostles have always moved Christians to seek better lives, but they assumed a particular appeal and universal resonance in the eleventh century. The apostolic life (*vita apostolica*) was marked, as it was then understood, not only by simplic-ity and devotion but also, above all, by its collective character, sustained by the renunciation of personal property, which conferred a unique moral authority. From this time onwards its popular appeal would be repeatedly attested in descriptions of preachers conspicuous for personal austerity. Robert of Arbrissel (d. 1116), 'wearing a pig-hairshirt, shaving his beard without water, scarcely knowing but one blanket, refraining altogether from wine, and from fine or rich food, abusing natural frailty by rarely getting half a night's sleep', 'preached to the poor, called to the poor and gathered the poor around him' in great numbers, and often to the consternation of his ecclesiastical superiors.[4] This would be the greatest force behind the storms that overtook the church in the second half of the eleventh century, to transform it, and Europe with it, beyond recognition.

4

MONKS, MIRACLES
AND MANICHEES

*Alice laughed. 'There's no use trying,' she said, 'one can't
believe impossible things.' 'I daresay you haven't had much
practice,' said the Queen. 'When I was your age I always did
it for half an hour a day. Why, sometimes I've believed as
many as six impossible things before breakfast.'*
Lewis Carroll, *Through the Looking Glass*

Preachers of heresy in early eleventh-century Aquitaine, although allegedly more numerous, are less substantial figures than their northern
counterparts. In a famous passage of his *History*, Adémar of Chabannes,
writing in 1025–6, says that in 1018

> Manicheans appeared in Aquitaine, leading the common people
> astray. They denied baptism, the cross, the church and the redeemer
> of the world, marriage and the eating of meat, and all sound doctrine.
> They did not eat meat, as though they were monks, and pretended to
> be celibate [that is, they claimed to lead the apostolic life], but among
> themselves they enjoyed every indulgence. They were messengers of
> Antichrist, and caused many to wander from the faith.[1]

Adémar also interrupted his description of the Orléans trial of 1022 to report that 'Manichaeans were found and put to death in Toulouse in that year, and messengers of antichrist appeared in various parts of the West, concealing themselves in hideouts and corrupting men and women whenever they could.' In 1028, he tells us, 'Duke William summoned a council of bishops and abbots to Charroux, to wipe out the heresies which the Manichaeans had been spreading among the people.' He returned to the 'Manichaeans' or, as he often called them, simply 'the heretics', in a number of sermons that he wrote around 1031, associating them particularly with the denial of baptism, the eucharist and the sanctity of marriage, and hostility to the veneration of the cross. His comment that many of them, when tortured, preferred execution to conversion implies continuing persecution, but there is nothing to connect it with particular occasions or events.

This information comes from a writer of immense energy and talent, but very questionable judgement. Adémar's life – including his dream-life – and writings were dominated by an intense belief in the imminence of the apocalypse, and he interpreted events accordingly. He therefore believed that St Paul's prophecy of heretics 'forbidding marriage and the eating of meat' would be fulfilled in his time. To this was added, as he grew older, an obsessive determination to prove that Martial, patron saint of the great monastery at Limoges, with which Adémar had close family and personal connections, was one of the apostles. He apparently had a major breakdown following a public humiliation in that endeavour, when in 1029 he was challenged to debate Martial's claim by a monk from Italy named Benedict of Chiusa and worsted before a jeering crowd. His remaining years were consumed by unsuccessful and increasingly bizarre attempts to rescue the project, his reputation and perhaps his sanity from a very public disgrace.

The difficulty of weighing Adémar's statements about the 'Manichaeans' is compounded by the fact that his are the only explicit reports we have that heresy was being preached to the people of Aquitaine in these years. The absence of any other reference to the Council at Charroux in 1028, an important public event, is especially noticeable because another council reported by Adémar in lengthy and circumstantial detail, at Bourges in 1031, was either wholly or partly invented by him as the occasion when his campaign for the apostolicity of St Martial was upheld by the church – which it certainly was not.

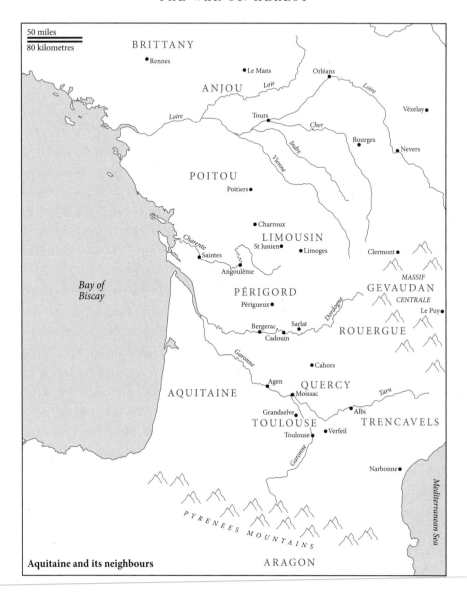

50 miles
80 kilometres

BRITTANY
• Rennes

ANJOU

• Le Mans
Orléans
Loir
Loire
Vézelay •

Loire
Tours
Cher
Bourges •
Nevers •

Indre
Vienne

POITOU
Poitiers •

• Charroux
LIMOUSIN
St Junien •
• Limoges
Clermont •

Charente
• Saintes
Angoulême •

MASSIF
GEVAUDAN
CENTRALE
Le Puy •

Bay of
Biscay

PÉRIGORD
Périgueux •

Dordogne

Bergerac •
Sarlat •
• Cadouin

ROUERGUE

Garonne

• Cahors

Agen •
Moissac •
QUERCY
Tarn

AQUITAINE

Grandselve •
TOULOUSE
Toulouse •
• Verfeil
• Albi
TRENCAVELS

Garonne

Narbonne •

Mediterranean Sea

Aquitaine and its neighbours
ARAGON

P Y R E N E E S   M O U N T A I N S

There is only one other text from the first quarter of the eleventh century that speaks of heresy in this region. It purports to be a letter written by a monk named Heribert, warning that heresy was being disseminated in the Périgord by 'pseudo-apostles' who refused meat and wine, prayed a hundred times a day and denied the real presence in the Mass. They would not accept alms, held their funds – 'seemingly honestly possessed' – in common and attacked liturgical chant as 'a vanity invented to please men'. At face value this may seem to corroborate Adémar's assertions, but it is more likely to be a satirical attack on the practices of the monastery of Cluny, lately introduced to the region at Sarlat, which was greatly elaborating its liturgy at this time, and whose critics accused it of excessive elaboration of the liturgy, too much interest in the acquisition of property and too little in the mortification of the flesh. Either reading, however, confirms that traditional monasticism in the region was under attack from advocates of the apostolic life.[2]

It is hard to know what to make of Adémar's 'Manichaeans'. Much significance has been attached to them, largely because of the association of the 'Cathar' heresy and the Albigensian Crusade, 200 years later, with the southern part of modern France. His possibly significant but again uncorroborated report of burnings at Toulouse in 1022 offers no detail but seems to refer to an elite conflict comparable to the affair at Orléans. Otherwise, however, Adémar locates his heretics not in the so-called 'Cathar country' but somewhat to the north, in the area between Poitiers and Limoges. They clearly occupied a large and growing place in his mind, with a vividness and immediacy that to modern readers suggest first-hand experience, but then so does his vision of a weeping Christ nailed to the cross, which he saw in the night sky in 1010, symbolising the seizure of Jerusalem by the antichrist – and corroborated by Ralph the Bald, who reports a similar vision from, of all places, Orléans. Adémar does not record a single direct encounter with the 'Manichees', or any particular occasion or incident in which they were involved, or name or describe a single heretic. He was sure that their influence lurked behind many of the evils that, for him, abounded in his time, but he would not, or could not, explain exactly how.

————

If heresy was indeed being preached in Aquitaine, as Adémar so fervently believed, the absence of specific information about the preachers points to wider issues than his personal credibility. In all the cases from the dioceses of Cambrai and Châlons-sur-Marne discussed in the previous chapter our knowledge arises from a confrontation between the bishop and the supposed heretics. All the reports indicate, albeit imperfectly, the nature of the charges and procedures involved. It was in that region that the efforts of the Carolingian rulers to improve the administration of the church and delivery of its services had been most active. The northern bishops, for all the turbulence of their times, still enjoyed the lordship, secular and spiritual, of substantial territories, tenaciously though it was necessary to defend them, and still expected to wield the full authority of their office. In doing so, they still looked to royal authority for support not only in the empire, where it was firmly exercised, but also, despite its difficulties, in the French kingdom as well. Their brethren south of the Loire were differently situated. The Carolingian reforms had much less purchase here, and the Capetian monarchy, which had succeeded (or supplanted) the Carolingian in 987, was barely recognised. In most places it was the monasteries, not cathedral or local churches, that acted as the focal points of popular piety. In principle, of course, the bishops had the same pastoral powers and responsibilities as their northern counterparts, but in practice, as far as their flocks were concerned, there was very little to show for them.

It is not surprising, then, that when change began in the south it was brought from the north. When Count Geoffrey Greymantle of Anjou died, around 975, his younger brother Guy succeeded him as both bishop and count of Le Puy. His sister Adelaide was already the wife of Stephen, count of the neighbouring Gevaudan and Forez. Guy found himself immediately confronted by the problems of keeping the peace, and of dealing with 'the goods of the church which had been forcibly siezed by the thieves of this region'.[3] To that end he summoned a meeting of prominent warriors and farmers (*milites ac rustici*) to Laprade, near Le Puy, and asked them to swear an oath to keep the peace, refrain from pillaging the goods of the poor and the churches and return what they had stolen already. They declined. Guy, however, had taken the precaution of getting his nephews to bring their militias to a nearby rendezvous. During the night they surrounded the meeting place, and in the morning the assembled dignitaries swore the oath and provided hostages to guarantee that they would observe it; various lands and castles were returned to Notre Dame at Le Puy and other churches.

In principle this was a restoration of royal power. As count, Guy, whose election as bishop had at least the approval of King Lothar, was the king's deputy. His prime responsibility was to maintain and enforce the king's peace. The 'thieves' (*raptores*) were the local noble families, who had themselves used delegated royal powers to take over church lands. One means of doing this was by making some of their sons canons of the cathedral, so that they could divide its property among themselves. The meeting at Laprade, comprising not only nobles but also free cultivators, was in form a traditional assembly, at which the royal will was proclaimed and endorsed by the people.

As so often in times of change, what was intended to restore the old ways turned out to foreshadow new and potentially revolutionary ones. The paragraph of the chronicle of Le Puy following the one that describes Guy's dramatic victory over the *raptores* reveals that the restoration of church lands had not been unconditional. Henceforth the canons of Le Puy led the common life – that is, they accepted the rule of celibacy and held their property in common. Bishop Guy divided the newly enhanced revenues of his cathedral so that one third was devoted to the support of the canons and another third to his own expenses.

Arrangements of this kind would be the basis and the hallmark of the reform of the church for the next two centuries. Their immediate effect was to assure the families that the land they returned to the church would not be divided among married canons to become a potential basis for rival dynasties. It would remain available in future generations for the support of their descendants' younger sons. In the long run, as the details were worked out and established case by case, innumerable such agreements divided the land of western Europe into two distinct and watertight categories, transmitted on one side through blood and the sword, on the other by ordination and appointment to office. To be qualified to hold land in either capacity was ipso facto to be disqualified from doing so in the other. So fundamental was this distinction to the new European society being shaped in the eleventh and twelfth centuries that its dismantling by reformation and bloody revolution between the sixteenth and nineteenth centuries is now considered an essential precondition of modernity.

Such an outcome, of course, was neither intended nor foreseen by Bishop Guy and those with whom he negotiated. They were dealing with the practical question, always urgent and acute in changing times, of how to maintain social order when the means of acquiring wealth and power had outrun the traditional mechanisms of control. The meeting at Laprade was the forerunner of what, south of the Loire, became the Peace of God – a movement whose very name proclaimed it a substitute for the lost peace of the king, more effective in hindsight than it probably had ever been in reality. The principles of the Peace of God were developed at a series of meetings beginning at Charroux in 989 and including a second at Le Puy, convened by Bishop Guy himself, in 994. The goods of the church and the poor would be protected by the threat of excommunication from the depredations of the armed warriors who controlled the countryside; the church itself would be reformed. Specifically, the Council of Poitiers (1000 or 1014), summoned by the duke of Aquitaine in conjunction with the bishops of the region, ordained that payments would not be demanded or accepted ('unless freely given') for the administration of the sacraments, and that priests or deacons who were found to have women in their houses (that is, to be married) would be degraded from holy orders. The force of that decree is illustrated by Adémar's report that 'Duke William, always intent on doing the will of God, restored regular discipline at Charroux, throwing out the most powerful Abbot Peter, who had obtained the position through the heresy of simony [that is, by paying for it] and administered it in a secular fashion [that is, not enforcing the common life].'[4] In 1016 the duke enforced the reform at St Hilaire in Poitiers, prohibiting its canons from selling goods or property belonging to the church, 'which is henceforth to be held in common in the manner of the apostles'. Resistance, he made clear, would be attributed to 'the pullulation of wicked deeds sprung from the Arian heresy, not only among the people but even in Holy Church' – and, the implied threat is obvious, those who resisted would be treated as heretics.[5]

The peace councils appear in the sketchy record of their conclusions as an alliance between the princes and the bishops to assert authority over disorderly warriors and ill-disciplined clergy. According to the monastic chroniclers, they were accompanied by intense popular excitement. They were great public occasions, attended, says Letaldus of Micy, describing the first of them, at Charroux in 989, by 'a great crowd of many people from Poitou, the Limousin, and neighbouring regions'. 'Many bodies of saints were also brought there', he continues. 'The cause of religion was strengthened by their presence, and the impudence of evil people was beaten back. That council – convoked, as it was thought, by divine will – was adorned through the presence of these saints by frequent miracles.'[6] Great crowds flocked to see the relics as they were borne through the countryside, eager for the miracles that showed divine power at work.

The pious enthusiasm of the monastic writers to record the power of the relics in their care, and the vigour of their language in denouncing the 'evildoers who had sprung up like weeds, and ravaged the vineyard of the lord', doubtless exaggerates the impression conveyed by their descriptions of the Peace of God, of something like a spontaneous popular uprising against the warriors who terrified the countryside. Nevertheless, these accounts help to illuminate key tensions and anxieties. The central political fact of the century ahead would be that the increasingly highly trained mounted warriors, the knights (*milites*) against whom the rhetoric of the Peace of God was directed, constituted collectively a new monopoly of violence. Power, in its most brutal and direct form, lay with those who maintained or could afford to hire them. Its nature was very clearly displayed when – just before or just after 1000 – certain *conventicula* (meetings or gatherings) of Norman peasants protested to Duke Richard II about tolls or services that had been imposed on them contrary, as they thought, to former custom. Richard's representative, his cousin Count Ralph of Caen, dealt with them by cutting off the hands and feet of the negotiators, leaving them to crawl back to their fellows as his answer. What could a box of old bones avail against such savage intransigence?

———

'Several things occurred when the relics of the holy father Junianus were brought forth from their monastic enclosure', says Letaldus.

Not far from the monastery [of Nouaillé, near Poitiers] those who carried the bundle containing the saint stopped and put down their holy burden. After the most holy relics departed, the faithful in their devotion erected a cross in order to memorialize and record the fact that the relics of the holy father had rested there. From that time to this, whosoever suffers from a fever and goes there is returned to their former health through the invocation of the name of Christ and the intercession of this same father Junianus. At the place where the relics had rested in the little village called Ruffec faithful Christians erected a sort of fence from twigs, so that the place where the holy body had lain might remain safe from the approach of men and animals. Many days later a wild bull came by and wantonly struck that same fence with his horns and side, when suddenly he retreated from the fence, fell down and died. In that same place a little pool was created by placing a gutter tile to allow run-off water to be stored. Because of the reverence for the holy relics, this pool served as an invitation for many people to wash. Among these there was a woman who suffered from leprosy. When she washed herself with that water, she was returned to her former health.

Here Letaldus shows us religious belief in action. He was naturally anxious to emphasise the devotion inspired by the relics of his patron saint wherever they went. But he describes something more than a passive response to a spectacle orchestrated by the monks. It was not they but the communities themselves who created shrines at the places where the relics had rested, places now charged with the power of the sacred, which showed itself at Ruffec punishing the impious bull as well as by curing the afflicted. These things did not just happen. People decided that they had happened. This is the magic of small communities, later dismissed by the literate as superstition. Through it distress is alleviated, quarrels resolved, norms of behaviour established and enforced. It was memorably evoked in a famous description, by the great anthropologist Edward Evans-Pritchard, of how – and why – the Azande, in the Sudan, might see witchcraft in everyday events:

If blight seizes the groundnut crop it is witchcraft; if the bush is vainly scoured for game it is witchcraft; if women laboriously bale water out of a pool and are rewarded by but a few small fish it is witchcraft; if termites do not rise when their swarming is due and a cold useless night is spent waiting for their flight it is witchcraft; if a wife is sulky and unresponsive to her husband it is witchcraft; if a prince is cold and distant with his subject it is witchcraft; if in fact any failure or misfortune falls upon anyone at any time and in relation to any of the manifold activities of his life it may be due to witchcraft.[7]

The emphasis here is on 'may'. Everybody knows that a roof *may* collapse at any moment if the post that holds it up has been eaten away by termites. But if, in fact, it collapses just at the particular moment when I am passing under it, the possibility is there to be considered that it was bewitched by someone who wishes to harm me, maybe because I have injured or offended them. My neighbours will decide, after due consideration, whether to dismiss the matter as mere coincidence or to investigate it further, leading perhaps to a settlement of the quarrel.

If, substituting good for evil, we bear in mind that 'if in fact any success or good fortune falls upon anyone at any time and in relation to any of the manifold activities of her life it *may* be due to a miracle', the miracle stories that abound in early medieval narratives work in just the same way. Wild animals damage fences often enough, and wild animals die. The connection that makes it a miracle (as Letaldus implies) represents a conclusion of the community of Ruffec – which became more a community in reaching the conclusion, and provided itself with a shrine around which many of its future actions and concerns would be arranged. Similarly, when it was concluded that a man who was put to the ordeal by water had floated, and so been rejected by the water and must be a heretic after all (as at Soissons in 1114: see below, p. 94), when fits of madness abated and the sight of the blind was restored by the touch of a holy man whose sanctity was thereby affirmed (see below, p. 121), and an oppressive official was seized by a stroke after refusing the injunction of another saint to make reparations to his victim (see below, p. 83), the communities involved had pronounced their verdict as to where right lay, and in whom holy power was vested.

The apparent simplicity of our sources, almost all of them monastic, is deceptive. Their authors, like Letaldus, needed to record the triumphs of their relics not just for prestige but because this was often the only protection they had in a violent world. When the monks of Ste Foy at Conques paraded a statue of their patron saint through the fields to define the boundaries of her property; when the canons of St Martin at Tours laid the reliquaries of their saints on the floor of the church in front of the altar, and 'humiliated' them by covering them with thorns to protest against the invasion of their cloister by Count Fulk Nerra and his armed retainers,[8] they advertised the misdeeds of their enemies to the world and summoned the carefully orchestrated forces of public opinion, of shame and dishonour, to their aid. Sometimes it worked, and when it did, they made sure to record it in terms that would provide the maximum reinforcement in the next emergency.

Whatever allowance we make for the interests and prejudices of the sources, we cannot dismiss these manifestations of popular sentiment as merely part of the armoury of ecclesiastical rhetoric. That, certainly, they were, but any comparison with the work of modern students of peasant communities – such as the one offered above through the observations of Evans-Pritchard – quickly shows that, as well as being skilful propagandists, our monks were shrewd social anthropologists. Their accounts of the behaviour and motivations of 'the common people' may be manipulated, but they are not fabricated. The skills of traditional religious leadership lay precisely in persuading the *vulgus* – the people – where authority lay, and getting their endorsement and support in return. It was not a negligible quantity. Even the fiercest and greediest of warriors liked to appear in a favourable light, to display the qualities of justice and magnanimity that characterised good lordship as well as the ferocity and singleness of purpose that were necessary to sustain any lordship at all. Even in a world of immense and increasing disparity between 'the powerful' and 'the poor' – to use the revealing conventional antithesis of the time – the fear of revolt was real and present, though seldom acknowledged. One of the most successful and ruthless descendants of Duke Richard II was King Henry I of England. While in Normandy in 1130 he had a nightmare, vividly illustrated in a famous manuscript now in Corpus Christi College, Oxford, in which peasants armed with scythes and pitchforks appeared before him to protest against the weight of his taxes, and his ship was tossed by a terrible storm, which abated only when he promised remission.[9]

Those accused of spreading heresy in the early eleventh century had one thing, and only one thing, in common: they claimed to live the apostolic life. In that they were far from being alone. Everywhere the same impulse led to the foundation of many new monasteries and the reform of many old ones. The sense that the church was failing in its mission to the world was widely felt, and frequently expressed by reference to the teachings of the New Testament. Its critics commonly appealed to the ideal of the apostolic life, and often themselves aspired to live according to its precepts as they understood them, surrendering their property, living communally and renouncing the pleasures of the flesh. The New Testament, more widely disseminated with rising levels both of active and of passive literacy, and often studied under the influence of neoplatonist distaste for the flesh and distrust of the material, was by far the most influential source of such ideas.

This conception of the apostolic life passed in various forms from the tiny literate minority into the working population, with the assistance of growing trade and improving communications both locally and over long distances. Its attractiveness was enhanced by grievances arising from widening disparities of wealth and power, as when Leutard of Vertus preached against tithes. 'Spiritual' and 'material' considerations were not antithetical or mutually exclusive causes of religious dissent. One of the opinions most frequently expressed by those accused of heresy, for example, at a time of ambitious and splendid church-building – notably in Aquitaine – was that the church had no need of material structures. Who is to say whether such sentiments arose from a sense that the grandeur, the expense, the increased social distance between clergy and people, associated with those great buildings contradicted the simple values of the gospels, or because those who were injured or offended by these developments found endorsement of their grievance in the New Testament? Much more voluminous and authoritative sources than we possess would not provide the window into people's souls to make that distinction visible – or tell the chicken from the egg.

The only rational appraisal that the sources support is that in the first half of the eleventh century heresy among the common people did not present any coherent or concerted challenge either to the authority of the church or to the structure of society. At the distance of a thousand years that judgement is bound to be qualified by the scantiness of those sources and the difficulty of interpreting them. But it is considerably reinforced by the judgement of contemporaries. Only Adémar of Chabannes believed that the 'messengers of Antichrist' formed a concerted heretical movement, brought to Aquitaine by outsiders and spreading beyond it through the peasant from the Périgord who, according to him, converted the scholars of Orléans. His view has been (and still is) widely accepted, and has the advantage of all conspiracy theories that it cannot be disproved. Nobody we know of agreed with him at the time. Even Ralph the Bald, who collected all the stories of heresy he could find, sometimes in sensational terms, because he thought they were signs of the approaching apocalypse, did not suggest any direct connection between the various episodes he recounted.

The bishops who actually dealt with the recorded cases saw them differently. They knew, to begin with, that heretical ideas are not at all the same thing as heresy. All manner of religious ideas, Christian and non-Christian, were current in early medieval Europe, as in all peasant societies. Among them, inevitably, were many that had been condemned as heretical in the writings of the fathers of the church and by its formal councils. Anyone might pick up such ideas, in any number of ways. But those who did so would become heretics only, as Gerard of Cambrai demonstrated at Arras, if they refused to abandon them in the face of episcopal correction. Behind that formal requirement lies no mere academic sophistry or legalistic quibble but profound differences of temperament, experience and outlook on the world between those who might become pertinacious heretics and those who would remain, instinctively, good catholics.

Wazo of Liège understood this very clearly. When Bishop Roger II of Châlons-sur-Marne consulted him about 'peasants who followed the perverse teaching of the Manichees', Wazo replied, 'The heresy of the people you write about is clear. It was discussed of old by the fathers of the church, and rebutted by their brilliant arguments' – of which he provides a brief summary, concluding, 'The Christian religion abhors this view and finds these heretics guilty of the Arian sacrilege.' At first sight this is puzzling. Wazo was one of the best-read men of his time. He knew perfectly well that the heresies described by Roger – avoiding marriage, refusing to eat meat or to kill animals – were indeed to be expected from Manichees, whereas Roger had made no mention of the Holy Trinity, or of the nature of Christ, to which the heresy of Arius related. But Arius was the prince of heretics, associated above all with the terrible schism that had torn the church apart for generations after his condemnation at the Council of Nicaea in 325. Hence his name stood for division in the church, and the accusation of reviving his heresy was routinely invoked against those who rebelled against episcopal authority, as it had been by Duke William of Aquitaine against the canons of St Hilaire. By introducing it here, Wazo deliberately moved the issue from wild theological speculation to the firm ground of ecclesiastical discipline, courteously but clearly reminding Roger where the essence of his duty lay. He must assert his episcopal authority to maintain the unity and discipline of his flock, without being distracted by the possibly bizarre but certainly unimportant particulars of what these 'ignorant and uneducated' people might believe.

Wazo concluded by setting his face firmly against calling in the secular authorities to persecute these supposed heretics.

> We must always remember that we who are called bishops do not receive the sword of the secular power in ordination, and are anointed to bring life, not death. Of course, you must take action against these heretics. You must deprive them, as you well know, of the catholic communion, and proclaim publicly to everybody the advice of the prophet, 'Go out of the midst of them: touch no unclean thing' of their sect, because 'he that toucheth pitch shall be defiled with it' (Isaiah 52:11; Eccles. 21:31).

Wazo's advice to Roger, in short, was not to panic but to use the ordinary powers of his office in the ordinary way – as, he might have added, Roger's predecessor Gebuin had done in the case of Leutard, and as Gerard of Cambrai had done at Arras. So, indeed, had Frankish bishops been doing through the six centuries since the heroic days when the founders of their sees, gathering the relics of their patron saints around them, staked their claims against all comers to a monopoly of holy power, and of the right to interpret the commands of the scriptures. The tremendous scene at Arras, when the bishop in full regalia, surrounded by his clergy, confronted and corrected his lost sheep, was not especially remarkable. If Gerard had not, as authors do, been on the look-out for something to make the book he was about to write 'relevant', and if the Cistercians had not almost two centuries later been collecting material on heresy to support a war on the 'Cathars', we would never have heard of the trial at Arras, precisely because those involved were *not* pertinacious heretics. This was one of innumerable mundane and usually unrecorded occasions when, with more or less pomp and ceremony, as appropriate, people were told, and accepted, what their catholic faith required of them. That is what bishops did. Historical discussion of the reports from the early eleventh century considered in these first four chapters has been dominated by the views of two intelligent but very excitable monks, Adémar of Chabannes and Ralph the Bald. Gerard of Cambrai and Wazo of Liège were no less intelligent, no less learned and no less determined to secure the church against its enemies – but, as capable pastors and experienced men of the world, they were rather better equipped to assess who those enemies were, and how seriously they needed to be taken.

5

THE SIMONIAC HERESY

For throughout the region up to Romuald's time the custom of simony was so widespread that hardly anyone knew this heresy to be a sin.

Peter Damiani, *Life of Romuald*, Chapter xxxv

At the beginning of the twelfth century the Cistercian order represented all that was most admired in the monastic movement. One of the great historians of the period, Orderic Vitalis of the Norman abbey of St Evroul, describes how it began. In the 1080s, in one of the most famous acts of 'reform', Robert, abbot of the traditional ('Black Monk'*) monastery of Molesmes, in Burgundy, 'examined the Rule of St Benedict very carefully and studied the writings of other holy fathers'. The Rule, believed to have been laid down by Benedict in the sixth century for the monks of Monte Cassino, and founded on their vows of poverty, chastity and obedience to the abbot and the Rule itself, had become the basis of monastic life everywhere in Latin Christendom. Robert, however, concluded that 'we have many customs which are not laid

---

* The Cistercians were known as 'White Monks' because they did not dye their woollen habits, holding it, on the principle set out by Robert in this passage, to be a superfluous addition to the provisions of the Rule of St Benedict. For the same reason they wore no undergarments. Conversely, those who adhered to the traditional interpretation which Robert criticised were, and are, often called Black Monks.

Monastery
Battle

Como
Milan
Brescia
Verona
Aquilea
Turin
Po
Pavia
Cremona
Padua
Venice
Piacenza
Po
Monforte
Parma
Genoa
Bologna
Ravenna
Lucca
Camaldoli
Pisa
Florence
Vallombrosa
Fonte Avellana
Perugia
Tiber
Sutri
ROME
Sora
Civitate
Monte Cassino
Capua
Benevento
Bari
Naples
Salerno
Brindisi
Palermo
Messina
Reggio di Calabria
SICILY

Ligurian Sea

CORSICA

Adriatic Sea

SARDINIA

Tyrrhenian Sea

Ionian Sea

M E D I T E R R A N E A N   S E A

100 miles
160 kilometres

The Italy of the Patarenes

down there, and we have carelessly overlooked a number of its precepts.'

We do not work with our hands, he told his assembled brethren, as we read that the holy fathers did. We receive abundant food and clothing from the tithes and oblations of churches, and by casuistry or force take for ourselves the tithes which belong to the priests. In this way we are gorged with the blood of men and are participators in sin.[1]

When his fellow monks, declining to accept his interpretation, refused to give up what Robert regarded as unsanctioned practices, he left Molesmes with the few who agreed with him to form the community that became the new foundation of Cîteaux.

Robert's description of tithes reflected both a long-standing religious attitude to property and a realistic view of how it was acquired. Monastic writers were eager to praise those who refrained from abusing power in the pursuit of wealth. Bezo, a minor lord from Cucciago, near Milan, for example, and his wife, Beza, detested greed (*rapacitas*) so heartily that they would not allow their retainers to ride down other people's standing corn. Destroying peasants' crops was a notorious means of driving them into poverty, and so into servitude. Another was stealing their livestock, a practice strenuously denounced by the peace councils. When the hermit Romuald of Ravenna (d. 1027) cursed the bailiff of a 'proud and greedy count' who refused to return the cow he had stolen from an old woman, causing him to choke to death on its meat, Romuald was resisting, or avenging, an attempt to usurp the old woman's land. This was a miracle much in demand from early eleventh-century saints. Its subversive potential is clearly intimated in a posthumous miracle of Romuald's, when another old woman whose cow was being driven off rushed to his tomb, with an offering of two hens, to implore his help. 'Wonderful news. Hardly had the bailiff left the woman's house than he was struck by an arrow. He let the cow go on the spot, and on reaching home died instantly.'[2] We need not be told where the arrow came from to see that the prestige of the saint is here endorsing what the bailiff, or his lord, would have described as an act of rebellion. The contrast with Ralph of Caen's treatment of the Norman peasants who complained of the same kind of oppression is obvious.[3]

———

These connections between the gathering currents of religious reform and accelerating social change emerge especially plainly in the lives of the hermit preachers of early eleventh-century Italy, men such as Romuald, John Gualberti and Dominic of Sora. Among them the mightiest voice was that of the biographer of Romuald quoted above. He was

the youngest of several sons of a nobleman of Ravenna. 'How shame-
ful', one of his brothers had greeted Peter's birth, in 1007. 'There are so
many of us that this house will hardly hold us – so many heirs for so
small an inheritance.'[4] That brother spoke for his generation. The concentration of property in the hands of a single heir, often the eldest son,
was a widely and ruthlessly pursued family strategy, and the reason for
many savage and desperate feuds. The traditional alternative of dividing
it between all the children (partible inheritance) might also be produc-
tive of bitterness and division, as this story shows, if the property was not
large enough to sustain the consequent fragmentation.

Fortunately for Peter, orphaned when he was two years old, he had
another, kinder brother, Damian, who rescued him from a desperately
cruel childhood and whose name he took as he would have a father's. For
fifteen years he was educated, and then became a teacher, in the schools
of northern Italy. In 1035 he abandoned the schools and the world to
devote himself to the monastic life at Fonte Avellano, at a remote spot
in the Apennines, near Gubbio, becoming prior a few years later. Fonte
Avellano was a monastery of the new style, in which the monks, imitating the desert fathers of old, sought salvation through the most extreme
humiliation of the flesh. They lived almost as hermits, some near the
church, two to a cell, others alone on the mountainside, their continuing ascent into greater solitude and harsher conditions symbolising their
progress in the spiritual life. They devoted themselves to prayer, reading
and chanting, coming together only for worship on Sundays and great
feast days. They went barefoot in all seasons and restricted their diet to
water, bread and salt, supplemented on three days of the week by a few
herbs or vegetables.

For Damiani only such a pattern of life contained the possibility
of union with God and of defeating the two great forces of sin by
which, in his eyes, the world was ruled: sex and power. In two remarkable books he described how they dominated the church. The *Book
of Gomorrah* assailed the sexual laxity of clerks and monks in terms so
frank and vivid that until late in the twentieth century it was considered
impossible to edit or translate it in full, even for scholarly purposes. The

Book of Graft* discussed the evils that arose from payment for ordination, for office in the church and for the sacraments. In these works, as in all Damiani's voluminous writings, sexual indulgence and the improper conferring of the sacraments, especially that of ordination, were excoriated as vices which disabled the church and surrendered the world to the devil.

It is easy to dismiss the horror of sexual desire – and especially same-sexual desire – so obsessively expressed by Damiani and many of his contemporaries as 'medieval' superstition. But eleventh-century Europe was no different from almost every other known society in understanding its customs regarding who could do what with whom, and on what conditions, as fundamental to its organisation and social structure. The turmoil of its social relations, at every level, was naturally expressed and indirectly discussed in its impassioned debates about sex and the agonising efforts necessary to control it. Count Gerald of Aurillac, the saintly layman whose *Life* had been written by Odo of Cluny around 920, was saved by a miracle when a serf's daughter by whose clear skin he was 'tortured, allured and consumed as though by a blind fire' became hideous in his eyes, just when he had arranged with her parents to have her placed at his disposal. To preserve himself from further temptation he ordered her father to give her away in marriage, gave her her liberty and presented her with a smallholding.[5] Dominic Loricatus, whose biography Damiani wrote, discharged his guilt for the payment his socially ambitious father had made to have him ordained priest while still a child, by wearing instead of a hair shirt next his skin the coat of chain mail (*lorica*) from which he took his name and becoming a virtuoso in the art of flagellation, said to inflict on himself 300,000 lashes in a six-day period.

The relentless competition for control over land and those who worked it, common everywhere in Europe, was intensified in Lombardy and Tuscany by the rising profits of increasing local and long-distance commerce and the revenues from markets and tolls associated with it. Both in the countryside and in the cities, which by the end of the

---

*The meaning of Peter's title, *Liber gratissimus*, is not clear: I take something more than a liberty in attributing to him a pun on *gratia*, which meant a favour or gift, in every sense from that of divine grace to an outright bribe.

tenth century were growing rapidly, the terrifying force of change was embodied in the man of power and wealth who was constrained by no law in the pursuit of his own advantage – or, it goes without saying, of sexual gratification. It was in contrast to such a man that Bezo and Beza of Cucciago, 'although they could freely threaten their neighbours in every way, and could be constrained by none of them if they didn't want to be', voluntarily submitted themselves to 'every decent custom'; in contrast to him that John Gualberti, in embracing the religious life, renounced 'landed honours and false riches'. These are references to the power of the seignurial ban, the pretext of delegated – but long since usurped – royal authority to exact services and seize animals and goods that provided the theoretical justification of these practices. Gualberti, who as the son of a noble had been born to such power, demonstrated his renunciation in saintly fashion when, seeing a fine herd of cattle grazing in an Apennine meadow, he called on Paul, his patron saint, to give him one of them for the poor.

> At his words one immediately fell dead, and he ordered its body to be cut up and distributed among the poor. When it was eaten, he took another by praying in the same way, and a third, and a fourth.[6]

At this point the unfortunate herdsmen tried to save their flock by driving it off to another part of the mountain, to be told sharply that they might evade Gualberti that way, but not St Paul. To make himself clear Gualberti took another beast, followed by a sixth, a seventh, an eighth and a ninth. The herdsmen plucked up their courage and told the saint that he would do better to go back to his monastery than deprive poor men of their animals. He took the point, promised to do them no more harm and kept his word, thenceforth confining his charity to the distribution of such animals as came to him by way of gift.

What makes this an example of Gualberti's holiness is not his power to take the cattle but his magnanimity in forgoing it. These stories show how immediately the universal touchstones of holiness – chastity, the renunciation of property, extreme bodily asceticism, devotion to prayer and spiritual exercises – appealed to people who were troubled by rapidly increasing disparities of wealth and power. The miracles of these

Italian holy men, demanded and acknowledged by popular acclamation, cast them in the roles of ideal lordship, settling disputes, feeding the hungry, protecting the weak and punishing the wicked and the oppressor. The holy men themselves tended to come from families that expected or aspired to exercise lordly powers, but were not so grand as to do so securely, or to be immune from the turns of fortune and the whims of the great. They knew both the temptations of avarice and the anxieties of the poor. Gualberti and others like him abjured the ambitions of lordship in its worldly form but now exercised its prerogatives in a nobler cause, in the service of a greater and more potent lord, and often in quite explicit opposition to the customs and behaviour of their brothers who had remained in the world. This did not mean that their ideas and values were embraced only by the poor. The eleventh century was not the last time in European history when the most passionate and radical critics of privilege and its abuses included some of those who had been born to it.

———

One such was Bezo's and Beza's son Ariald, educated as a clerk, who on 10 May 1057 launched a public attack on the clergy of Milan, gathered for the solemn translation of the relics of one of the city's many saints. Not only did they live in concubinage, as everybody knew, he said, but they were so deeply involved in the heresy of simony that none of them, from the highest to the lowest, had been admitted to any degree of holy orders or held any office in the church unless he had bought it as he might have bought a cow. He urged the people to stay away from their churches, which were as filthy as stables, and to refuse their sacraments, which were no better than dog turds. He started a riot, and many of the clergy were seized by the crowd and forced, under threat of death, to swear oaths of celibacy.[7]

Ariald's sermon began a period of nineteen years during which, if the Patarenes (as his followers were derisively called by their enemies, after the lowliest workers in the cloth trade) did not rule Milan themselves, they made it ungovernable by the archbishop and the nobles. The city had been restless since the bloody suppression of a rising against

Archbishop Aribert II (whom we met at Monforte in Chapter 2) some years before his death in 1045. Aribert's successor, Guido da Velate, was objectionable to traditionalists as neither nobly born nor a member of the higher clergy of the city, and despised by reformers as 'an illiterate man, living in concubinage, a simoniac without any shame'.[8] Ariald had begun to preach reform in the villages around before moving into the city itself. His closest associates were Landolf Cotta, a notary from one of the ruling families, and Landolf's brother Erlembald. Some said they had been put up to it by a priest from another aristocratic family, Anselm of Baggio, of whom Archbishop Guido rid himself by commending him to the imperial court, where he made a good enough impression to be appointed bishop of Lucca; in 1062 he became Pope Alexander II. Among Ariald's lay supporters were Benedetto Rozzo, who had founded the church that the Patarenes took over as a base for their worship and operations, and Nazarius, both members of an influential group of citizens who had the hereditary privilege of striking coin, and so had been well placed to take advantage of the rapid growth of Milan's markets and the dizzy rise in land prices over the previous half-century or so. For Ariald's biographer, Andrew of Strumi, the movement divided not so much classes as families: 'One household was entirely faithful, the next entirely faithless; in a third the mother believed with one son while the father disbelieved with another. The whole city was thrown into disorder by this confusion and strife.'[9]

Ariald formed around him a community of priests who had renounced the service of the archbishop, and of laymen and women. Abjuring all possessions, they lived chastely under a common rule – so their community became known as the Canonica – in a cloister that they built beside the church that Nazarius had given them. From this base Aribert organised what amounted to an alternative clergy for the city, preaching and conducting services for people who flocked from the nearby towns and villages. Every day, surrounded by his followers, he left the Canonica to visit Milan's many shrines, praying and chanting at each, and in the process creating and consolidating a close identification between his movement and the community of the city, openly and successfully challenging the authority of the archbishop and clergy, whose legitimacy he continually disparaged.

Ariald is readily recognisable as a product of the currents of reform that flowed in early eleventh-century Europe. He was a zealous and educated devotee of the apostolic life – his sermons used the neoplatonist language that had been heard at Orléans and Monforte – who had found the condition and practices of the church at odds with what his reading had led him to believe it should be. To his followers he was a saint. He became a martyr in 1067, when he was murdered by the servants of a niece of Guido da Velate. His horribly mutilated body was dumped in Lake Como, to be recovered by his followers and borne in solemn procession back to the city for burial. From the beginning it was as heretics, not merely as sinners, that he had denounced the Milanese clergy. 'They deserve to be overthrown', he said, in the sermon that launched the rising, 'because every kind of pollution, including the simoniac heresy, is rife among the priests and deacons and the rest of the clergy; they are all Nicolaitists and simoniacs.'

The clergy of Milan accepted neither this valuation nor Ariald's authority to pronounce it. To them he was a heretic in his turn, and the founder of a heretical sect. Their see had been founded in the fourth century by St Ambrose, one of the greatest of the chuch fathers, and they firmly maintained that Ambrose had established the customs attacked by the Patarenes, including their right to marry and to observe distinctive liturgical observances, such as a three-day feast before Pentecost. In insisting on the authority of their patron saint, the Milanese clergy were not simply rationalising privilege. The bishoprics of Italy and Gaul had been established under the Roman empire, and their bishops spoke directly as the successors of their founding saints and martyrs. Their authority as such was not understood to be diminished by the acknowledged primacy of the bishop of Rome. In the eleventh century the burgeoning cults of their patron saints fostered and symbolised the vigour and independence of the emerging cities, among which Milan itself was the richest and most powerful. This became increasingly a source of tension after 1046, when popes began to convene councils that claimed general authority and to send representatives (legates) acting in their name to enforce their decrees and intervene in local disputes. The Milanese clergy responded that the Ambrosian church was not subject to Roman laws, or to the authority of the Roman bishop. They were not, historically speaking, strictly correct, but their view was deeply rooted and widely shared in their time.

———

The conditions that identified Milan so closely with the sin of simony had been formally established in 987. In that year the archbishop distributed the extensive and wealthy lands of his church as fiefs among a number of the leading families of the region, whose heads became known as the *capitanei* ('captains'). Thenceforth the offices of the church and the benefices that went with them, from canonries of the cathedral downwards, were disposed of to the families and followers of these lords. What seems to have made the practice especially unacceptable was not only the sense that was growing everywhere in Europe that the church, its ministers and its services ought to be disentangled from the sordid and undignified structures of secular power but also the fact that here in Lombardy, most of all in Milan, money was now flowing in ever greater quantity and ever more visible streams as a great commercial revival got under way. The return that was made for appointment to a position in the church, or for a baptism or a funeral, was increasingly likely to be a bag of coins rather than a share of the annual vintage or a gift of livestock or produce, such as the two hens the widow brought to Romuald when she sought his help against the rapacious count. The offices of the church of Milan, it began to be said, were available for purchase on a fixed tariff. The cost would be recovered from the profits of the ecclesiastical duties attached to them, including the administration of the sacraments.

The sin named after Simon Magus had not always been as easy to recognise as to condemn. His offence had been that, seeking to buy from the apostles their power to confer the Holy Spirit, he 'offered them money, saying "Give me also this power, that on whomsoever I lay hands he may receive the Holy Spirit." But Peter said unto him, "Thy money perish with thee, because thou hast thought that the gift of God may be purchased with money"' (Acts of the Apostles 8: 18–20).

In the early middle ages money was not much used from day to day. Goods and services were generally exchanged in kind, and the services of the church, like any others, were expected to be reciprocated. Additionally, Christians had had from the earliest times a religious duty to devote a tenth of all their revenues and produce to the support of the church and the poor. In the eighth century the Carolingian kings made this a civic obligation, which meant that everybody had to pay, and therefore to be attached to a particular church, and that collection was enforced, in principle, by royal authority. Churches and monasteries were supported by endowments of land from which, like any other landlord, they took the profits both from direct cultivation by slaves or serfs and from the rents and services of tenants. Since the bishopric was usually among the largest landholders of its region and the holdings of other churches and monasteries were often substantial, these were very considerable and dependable sources of income, and therefore also of power. Control over them became ever more desirable and rivalry among the followers correspondingly intense in the tenth century, as the ability of the kings to reward, and therefore to restrain, their followers declined. All land came to be treated for practical purposes as family land, whose revenues could be divided, distributed and redistributed to support the retinues and secure the alliances necessary for survival in a fiercely competitive world.

Rulers were not indifferent to the dangers that these facts held for religion and learning. In 909 the duke of Aquitaine founded at Cluny, in Burgundy, a monastery whose security as a haven of prayer for the redemption of his soul and those of all its friends and patrons was to be assured by the paradoxical device of granting it immunity from the powers of ducal officers – who would have used those powers to annexe its land and income for their own use. Later in the century the pope was persuaded to grant it the same exemption from the authority of the bishop of Mâcon. The formula was repeated all over Europe. Many new monasteries were founded in imitation of Cluny, and many old ones placed under the authority of its abbot, who became the head of a chain of monasteries – what would later become known as an order – that spread through Burgundy and the Auvergne, then into northern Italy and beyond. Similar developments were associated with Gorze in the Rhineland, Brogne in Flanders, St Victor in Marseille and Winchester in England.

Reform was not always a peaceful process. When Odo of Cluny was entrusted with the reform of Fleury – which subsequently became itself a centre of reform – there were threats that the monks would kill him rather than submit to his authority. They did not go so far, but when he began 'to persuade them to give up eating meat, to live sparingly and to possess nothing of their own', they gave away the property of the monastery to their relations rather than return it to the common holding, and tried to exhaust their supply of fish so that Odo would be forced to let them eat meat again.[10]

––––––––

In the middle decades of the eleventh century the currents of reform which had flowed occasionally and intermittently came together in a raging torrent that swept the old world away. It was precipitated not only by social tensions of the kind that were so divisive in Milan but also by the scandals of the Roman papacy. In Rome, as in other cities, the bishopric was the object of intense rivalry between the leading families. Its special standing lent them high visibility and occasionally attracted outside intervention, as on the famous occasions in 800, when Charlemagne had come to rescue Pope Leo III from deposition and found himself crowned Holy Roman Emperor, and in 961, when Otto I secured the same reward for a similar service to Pope John XII. The intervention of Henry III came after Benedict IX was expelled from the city to be replaced by Sylvester III, and then restored, to resign shortly afterwards, in May 1045, in favour of a reformer, John Gratian, who assumed the pontificate as Gregory VI. Such sensational events were naturally accompanied by scandalous accusations. Bonizo of Sutri, for example, a committed reformer writing some forty years later, claimed that Benedict, 'after committing many squalid adulteries and murders with his own hands', gave up the papacy because he wanted to marry his cousin the daughter of Gerald de Saxo, who demanded this price for her so that he could place his own man on the papal throne as Sylvester III.[11] However all that may have been, the accession of Gregory VI, Benedict's godfather and a high official of the papal court, was received with rejoicing by Italian reformers, Peter Damiani among them, in whose eyes he had done a fine thing in persuading Benedict to stand down for a second time.

The emperor took a different view. Benedict's resignation had been expensive. To procure it John Gratian, a wealthy man, had paid him off with a very large sum of money. It was generally acknowledged that he had done so to secure the abdication of his universally despised predecessor rather than to buy the office for himself, but the distinction was too fine to save him from the accusation of simony. Henry, anxious to be crowned by an undisputed pope, summoned synods at Sutri and Rome in 1046, which – Benedict IX and Sylvester III having revived their claims – deposed all three. In their place the emperor appointed a German bishop, who was killed within a year by the foul air of the Roman marshes, and then another, who lasted for two months. With a persistence worthy of Gualberti, Henry sent in his kinsman Bishop Bruno of Toul, who was made, in every sense, of sterner stuff. In his five years (1049–54) as Leo IX, he inaugurated a transformation of the papacy that turned out, when the dust eventually settled (if it ever has), to have been a decisive moment in European history.

One of Leo's first acts was to hold a synod in Rome at which simony was outlawed and several bishops found guilty of it deposed. Among them was the bishop of Sutri, who had intended to brazen it out with the help of false witnesses but suffered a fatal stroke as he was on the point of doing so. 'All who heard of it were so terrified', says Leo's biographer, 'that no one thereafter attempted to escape ignominy by taking a false oath in the presence of the pope.'[12] The lesson was driven home at the consecration of the new basilica of St Remigius at Reims a few months later, when Leo placed the relics of the saint on the high altar and demanded that every bishop and abbot present should stand up, one at a time, and swear before them that he had paid no money for his office. The archbishop of Besançon was struck dumb as he was about to embark on the defence of a notorious simoniac, Bishop Hugh of Langres, and recovered his speech only with the aid of Leo's fervent prayers on his behalf.

These were two of a dozen synods in Italy, Germany and France in which Leo, making the solemn progress of a monarch through his dominions, placed the war against simony at the top of the church's agenda. In doing so he also served notice that papal leadership would henceforth be exercised much more vigorously and directly than through the letters and decrees that had sufficed even the most active of his predecessors. Not many of his successors travelled as often and widely as he had done, except when compelled by their political misfortunes, but from now on they were represented increasingly frequently, and often very effectively, by legates whom they appointed to act in their name and with their authority. What immediately ensured that Leo's policies and influence would outlast his brief pontificate, however, was the cadre of committed and talented reformers whom he brought to Rome as cardinals, many of them from his native Rhineland and several of them future popes. Among them were: Humbert, a monk from Moyenmoutier in Leo's former diocese of Toul, who became a formidable polemicist of reform and the hammer of everything that he saw as heresy or the source of heresy, above all the simoniacs and the Greeks; Peter Damiani, wrenched from his mountainside to wage his battle against the flesh on a wider front; and Hildebrand, nephew and devoted admirer of Gregory VI, who had followed his uncle into exile but now returned to become ever more influential, and an ever more uncompromising proponent of papal supremacy.

———

The new men in Rome soon became closely allied with the Milanese Patarenes. In 1057 Ariald and Landulf Cotta were excommunicated by Archbishop Guido da Velate for their assault on his authority and his clergy. They appealed to the pope, who sent as legates to deal with the dispute the bishop of Lucca, their old ally Anselm of Baggio, and Cardinal Hildebrand. In 1059 Anselm was dispatched again, this time with Peter Damiani, who imposed a settlement in line with the argument of his *Book of Graft*. The clergy of Milan were required to give up simony and marriage, and to do penance for their sins, but on those conditions were permitted to retain their offices. It was a compromise that in the short run satisfied nobody, but which in the longer term avoided an error that might easily have been fatal to the authority of the Roman church. If the Patarenes had had their way the argument of Cardinal

Humbert's thunderous *Books against the Simoniacs* (1058) would have been applied, and the orders of the Milanese clergy declared invalid on the ground that, as simoniacs, they were heretics and had been ordained by heretics. This would have raised inescapably the question whether anybody remained in the Latin church who had been validly ordained. Damiani had acted on the crucial distinction that Augustine of Hippo had made in his writings against the Donatist church of north Africa. The ordination conferred by a bishop known to be a heretic could not be accepted as valid. But sacraments, including ordination, received in good faith even from a sinful minister were valid in God's eyes. As Augustine had put it, 'Let it be God's merit in giving and my faith in receiving: for me two things in this are certain, God's goodness and my own faith. But if you [the priest] intervene how can I know anything for certain?'[13] The priest was the conduit of God's grace. That a conduit should be correctly connected to its source is essential; its inner cleanliness, though much to be desired, is not. Failure to insist on this principle would have created insuperable difficulties for the church. As many heretics would point out in the centuries to come, an authority transmitted from the time of the apostles must inevitably have passed through a succession of mortal sinners.

Despite this settlement, the Patarenes did not abandon their struggle against 'the captains and the lesser vassels, the sellers of churches and their kindred and the kinsmen of their concubines'. Nor did they lose their supporters in Rome in consequence. Indeed, when Anselm of Baggio became Pope Alexander II, in 1061, he appointed Erlembald as his personal representative in Milan, presenting him with a 'banner of St Peter' to proclaim the office. With that impetus, and it was said with funds provided by Hildebrand, the Patarene movement spread to other cities in Lombardy and Tuscany. At Brescia, when the bishop, a reformer, read out the papal decree against simony, 'he was beaten by the clergy and almost killed', but there, as in Cremona and Piacenza, married and simoniac priests were driven out of the churches, and their services boycotted.[14] In Florence a similar campaign, led by John Gualberti and his monks of Vallombrosa, triumphed when an enormous crowd watched a monk named Peter, from that day known as Petrus Igneus, walk unscathed through the flames to prove their charges of simony and concubinage against the bishop and his clergy. As it turned out, these were early battles in a war that would rage through Italy for decades to come.

6

ROUTING OUT THESE DETESTABLE PLAGUES

Go your ways: behold, I send you forth as a lamb among wolves. Carry neither purse nor scrip, nor shoes: and salute no man by the way.

Luke 10: 3–4

In 1073 Cardinal Hildebrand succeeded to the papacy as Gregory VII. His pontificate entrenched the confrontation between the papacy and the (German) empire, and thence between church and state, which for the next two hundred years largely shaped the political and governmental agendas of Latin Europe and its emerging national monarchies. Gregory himself is remembered as the pope who humiliated the emperor Henry IV, forcing him in 1076 to save his throne by grovelling in the snow at Canossa – and, his triumph short-lived, for his dying words, nine years later: 'I have loved righteousness and hated iniquity and therefore I die in exile.'[1]

At the Roman synod in Lent 1075 Gregory ordered that people should no longer accept the services of uncelibate or simoniac clerks, including in the latter category those who allowed themselves to be invested with the symbols of their office by lay rulers. The synod was followed up by a stream of violently worded letters demanding support for bishops who were enforcing the decrees, and resistance to those who were not. 'As most dear sons,' Gregory wrote to the people of Lodi, 'we urge that, in treading underfoot and utterly routing out these detestable plagues, namely the simoniac heresy and the fornication of ministers at the sacred altar, you must take urgent steps together' – in this case, to support one of his allies, Bishop Opizo. But if the bishop failed to give a lead in the right direction 'the faithful' must take matters into their own hands. 'We have heard', Gregory wrote to 'all the clergy and laity of Germany', that

> certain of the bishops who dwell in your parts condone, or fail to take notice of, the keeping of women by priests, deacons, and sub-deacons. We challenge you in no way to obey these bishops or to follow their precepts, even as they themselves do not obey the commands of the apostolic see or heed the authority of the early fathers of the church.[2]

The identification and proclamation of the *simoniaca haeresis* as the root of the church's entanglement with the world made every call to reform a potential accusation of heresy, and every defence a counter-accusation against the reformers. The demand for a boycott, in the Patarene style, made clerical authority itself, and even by implication the validity of clerical orders, a matter for the judgement of 'the faithful'. That term (*fideles*) usually refers to men of noble and knightly rank, but to the Patarenes and many like them it also meant those who shared their reformist convictions. Inevitably, the practical basis for judgement was reputation and the ability to command it, for better or worse. The question on which a priest's authority depended was to be not whether he had, as a matter of fact and public record, been ordained by the bishop but whether he had paid for his job or the bishop had paid for his, or whether the woman who cooked his meals and cleaned his house also shared his bed. These, by their nature, were seldom matters capable of objective verification, or of effective rebuttal in the eyes of an unsympathetic community. The judgement they invited, like that of the public confrontation or of trial by ordeal, or the acknowledgement of miracles, was that of public opinion. It involved more than clerical discipline, more even than ecclesiastical authority. It was capable of embracing any faction, any dispute, in any community.

In the half-century or so after Gregory's election the programme and tactics of the Patarenes were extended by papal decree from Italy to the whole of Europe. It was a time of acute political instability, of conquests and crusades, of conspiracies, rebellions and revolts, as well as of the confrontation of empire and papacy. But the demand for religious reform and resistance to it did more to foment popular unrest and social turmoil at the local level than the great events that preoccupied the nobility and wrote the conventional historical headlines. The issues at stake bore immediately on the lives of ordinary people and communities. As the Flemish chronicler Sigebert of Gembloux, whose sympathies were with the emperor, asked:

> Whatever their sex, rank or fortune, whatever their religious connections, who can ignore this dreadful turmoil? What else are women everywhere talking about at their spinning-wheels, and craftsmen in their workshops, but the confusion of all human laws, the overthrow of Christian standards, sudden unrest among the people, crazed assaults on ecclesiastical decorum, servants plotting against their masters and masters mistrusting their servants, betrayals among comrades, treacherous plots against the powers ordained by God, friendships broken and faith neglected, malicious and perverse doctrine contrary to the Christian religion brought in by official licence – and worst of all, all these monstrosities allowed by the permission, supported by the consent, endorsed by the authority, of those who are called the leaders of Christendom.[3]

The ferment set off by the Patarene papacy continued to seethe and occasionally to explode in northern Europe, at times in the form of demands for religious reform, at others of accusations and counter-accusations of heresy. It led to burnings at Soissons in 1114, in the diocese of Liège in 1135 and perhaps again in 1145, and in the diocese of Cologne, at Bonn in 1143 and in Cologne itself in or a little before 1147. It would seem natural to suspect a common source of these incidents, and of the discovery of heresy at Ivoy, in the diocese of Trier, around 1115 and perhaps in the diocese of Toul in the early 1130s, in some new teaching or sect. But the surviving accounts of all these episodes are too fragmentary, and for several of them date from too long after the events, to corroborate the presence of anything like a concerted or coherent heretical movement. Even this list of places and dates is tentative. We can, however, see how some people at least were thinking, or worrying, about heresy, though not much about the heretics themselves, such as they were. We can also see these events as a sort of seismograph of social tension, registering conflicts of loyalty and value in the communities in which they occurred.

———

Sigebert of Gembloux had some justification for saying that the disturbances of which he complained so bitterly were 'supported by the consent, endorsed by the authority, of those who are called the leaders of Christendom' – that is, that they were being at least condoned by the papacy and perhaps deliberately fomented by its emissaries. Gregory VII, when he was cardinal–deacon under Pope Alexander II (himself one of the first Patarenes), had fostered the Patarene movement and supported its spread from Milan to other Lombard cities. As pope, Gregory licensed Wederic of Ghent (of whom nothing else is known except that he was of noble birth) to preach against simoniac and uncelibate clergy in Sigebert's own region, Flanders, overriding the authority of the local bishops in doing so. He also approved, at least in retrospect, the preaching of Ramihrd of Esquerchin, whose burning at Cambrai in 1077 was the first recorded since the one at Milan in 1028, and of many in Flanders and the Rhineland in the years to come.

This affair began when, in September 1076, Bishop Gerard II of Cambrai heard that Ramihrd was preaching in the villages of his diocese, and had won a large following.

> He immediately inquired into the man's life and teaching, decided that he ought to answer the charges, and ordered him to be brought to his seat at Cambrai, where they could be discussed in full. On the appointed day Ramihrd was brought before a group of abbots and learned clergy and questioned about the Catholic faith.[4]

The case arose, that is, in just the same way as the one at Arras in 1025, and

Bishop Gerard followed the same procedure as his predecessor had done on that occasion. The outcome, however, was very different. Ramihrd's answers were satisfactory on every point of doctrine, but when Gerard ordered him to confirm his sincerity by taking communion he refused, 'saying that he would not accept it from any of the abbots or priests present, or even from the bishop himself, because they were up to their necks in simony and other avarice'. That Ramihrd was obeying a papal injunction availed him nothing. He was denounced as a heresiarch, and the meeting was adjourned. Some of Gerard's servants dragged Ramihrd away, shut him into a hut and set it on fire.

Pope Gregory was outraged. 'It has been reported to us', he wrote to Bishop Josfred of Paris, 'that the Cambraiers have delivered a man to the flames because he had ventured to say that simoniacs ought not to celebrate Mass, and that their ministration ought in no way to be accepted.' He demanded immediate investigation and, if the story turned out to be true, excommunication of those responsible. The pope concluded with a sharp reminder to Josfred and his fellow bishops 'through all France' that married priests must not be allowed to celebrate the Mass and were to be boycotted if they persisted in doing so. Shortly afterwards Gerard of Cambrai made the journey to Rome to resign his see, confessing that after being elected by the clergy and people of the diocese he had been invested with the symbols of his office by the emperor Henry IV. Pleading ignorance of the prohibition of this custom in 1075, and of the subsequent excommunication of the emperor, Gerard was restored to his position on condition that he would affirm that ignorance on oath before the papal legate, his archbishop and his fellow diocesan bishops of the province of Reims.

When Bishop Gerard's servants came to take Ramihrd to his death, with or without the complicity of their master, he went 'not reluctantly, but without fear, and, they say, prostrate in prayer'. Afterwards, 'many of those who had been his followers took away some of his bones and ashes for themselves. In some towns there are many members of his sect to this day [c. 1130], and it is thought that those who make their living by weaving belong to it.' We know nothing else of Ramihrd's life and actions and are given no flavour of his preaching beyond the passionate repudiation of the higher clergy of the diocese, in accordance with papal policy, which may be inferred from his response to Bishop Gerard.

That Ramihrd was a layman, as seems likely, need not have prevented him from having, like Wederic, a papal commission to preach reform. At any rate the pope hailed him as a martyr, at the least legitimising his activity in retrospect. Nor does it greatly matter how many of the scores of travelling preachers whose execration of the sins of the clergy drew adoring crowds around them in the following decades acted with the prior approval of their ecclesiastical superiors, though certainly many did. Idealists and enthusiasts had no need of papal mandates to make the connection regularly proclaimed by the reformers, that only those who led the apostolic life were fit to preach. From there it was a short step to claim that living the apostolic life was all the licence a preacher needed. Thus, at Coutances in Normandy, some time around 1100, 'a certain archdeacon who had a wife and children, accompanied by a crowd of priests and clerks of the diocese', demanded of Bernard of Tiron by what right he denounced the shortcomings of their clergy to the people of the town. Bernard replied, 'A preacher of the church ought to be dead to the world. He earns the licence to preach by virtue of his mortification. Therefore the fact that I am a monk and dead to the world, far from depriving me of the right to preach, confers it upon me the more.'[5]

———

The burning at Soissons in 1114 is described by one of the liveliest and most intelligent writers of his time, though also one of the most imaginative, and one increasingly haunted in old age by anxiety about the dangers that threatened the world as he knew it. Guibert, born near Beauvais in the early 1050s or early 1060s, was abbot of the small Black Monk house of Nogent-sous-Coucy, so-called because of its proximity to the mighty stronghold of the lords of Coucy, near Laon. He is best known for his memoir of his own life, written a year or two after this episode, in which he provides, among much else, a riveting description of his boyhood and upbringing in the care of a neurotic and ambitious mother and an incompetent and sadistic tutor, and a vivid and detailed account of the rising of the citizens of Laon in 1112 against their corrupt and tyrannous bishop, the assassination of the bishop, and the bloody suppression of the revolt.

One of Guibert's last stories – written down within months of the event in 1114 – is that of two peasants from the village of Bucy-le-long, near Soissons, brothers named Everard and Clement, who were summoned by Bishop Lisiard to answer charges of organising religious meetings unauthorised by the church, and being reputed among their neighbours to be heretics.[6] Guibert does not say how the charges arose, but he mentions two witnesses who failed to turn up at the trial, 'a certain lady whom Clement had been driving mad during the past year, and a deacon who had heard Clement say the most perverse things'. Everard was surprised to be accused and quoted the words of the Gospel *beati eritis* ('blessed are you': John 13: 17), which, not knowing Latin, he thought meant 'Blessed are the heretics.' Although the brothers did not deny holding meetings, all their answers to Lisiard's questions were impeccably orthodox. Lisiard was not satisfied, however, because, as everybody knew, heretics did not give truthful answers, so he ordered Clement and Everard to be put to the ordeal by water and got Guibert to question them again while the ordeal was prepared. Clement, duly bound, was thrown into a vat of water, where to the jubilation of the assembled multitude he floated like a straw: the water would not accept him. Everard promptly confessed his heresy but refused to abjure it and was bound in chains with his brother and with two others, whom Guibert describes as well-known heretics from the nearby village of Dormans, who had incautiously, or bravely, come to watch. The bishop and Guibert then set out for an ecclesiastical council which was meeting at Beauvais, to ask what should be done with them. 'But in the meantime the faithful people, fearing the weakness of the clergy, ran to the prison, forced it open, and burned the heretics on a large pyre they had lit outside the city.' 'Thus,' Guibert concludes, 'the people of God, fearing the spread of this cancer, took the matter of justice into their own zealous hands.'

To Guibert's questions, as to Bishop Lisiard's, Clement and Everard answered submissively, as obedient but ignorant catholics: 'For God's sake, do not expect us to search so deeply … We believe everything you say.' Guibert did not believe them, but in the absence of the two witnesses he recommended that the ordeal should proceed. His note of the interrogations is preceded by a general description of what he thought he was dealing with, though he was unable to get the accused to confirm it. 'This is not the sort of heresy whose teaching is openly defended by its holders', he begins. 'Rather, it crawls clandestinely like a serpent and reveals itself only through its perpetual slitherings.' It is an interesting comment, since heresy, to be condemned as such, must according to canonical definition be openly avowed, as Guibert certainly knew. Nor is it altogether consistent with the charge against Clement and Everard of holding unauthorised meetings. Perhaps Guibert, as an intelligent and serious churchman, was embarrassed in the face of accusations of corruption or immorality against his clerical colleagues that he knew to be just. No heretic could have surpassed Guibert's own scathing account of the election and conduct of Bishop Gaudry of Laon. In that case he may have felt it necessary to offset the plausibility of Clement's and Everard's charges, apparently supported by simple precepts from the Gospels, by hinting that there was more wickedness behind the activities of Clement and Everard than their public utterances betrayed.

Guibert goes on to say that the heretics rejected the sacraments, including infant baptism and the eucharist ('because they call the mouth of any priest the mouth of hell'), burial in sacred ground, matrimony and procreation. 'Indeed wherever they are scattered throughout the Latin world one might see men living with women, without taking the name of husband and wife.' This amounts to the hostile view of the apostolic movement that we will encounter repeatedly, in which the combination of veneration for personal asceticism and the avoidance of corrupt priests gave the appearance, or fell into the reality, of heresy. That is how Guibert seems to have understood it, for he concludes that 'originally started by well-educated people, this heresy filtered down to the peasants who, claiming to be leading the apostolic life, have read the Acts of the Apostles and little else.' Since he had earlier gone out of his way to remark that Clement and Everard did not know Latin, his assumption here must be that they, or their leaders, had access to a translation of at least this much scripture into the vernacular. We shall see again that such translations did exist, particularly of the Acts of the Apostles, although churchmen increasingly disapproved of them.[7]

The teachings of Clement and Everard were not necessarily the reason for the enthusiasm with which they were condemned to the stake. Trial by ordeal, of which this story of Guibert's is a classic illustration, was in effect a test of reputation in the community. Whether the accused sank or floated – whether or not he was 'received' by the water – was not an objective fact, but a judgement of the onlookers, and not always so unambiguous as it was held to be here.[8] A source other than heresy of the unpopularity of Clement and Everard is not hard to identify, for they had been favourites of Count John of Soissons, one of the most outrageous characters in Guibert's gallery of wicked barons. Count John came of bad stock: his mother had employed a Jew, later burned at the stake for the deed, to poison one of her brothers, and had ordered the tongue of a deacon who had displeased her to be pulled out of his throat, and his eyes to be gouged out. John himself, 'whose sexual abuses spared neither dedicated women nor cloistered nuns', used a Jew as a pimp, in whose squalid house he used to meet a repulsive old hag whom he found attractive. He tried to get rid of his beautiful young wife by trumping up a charge of adultery, ordering one of his followers to impersonate him in bed. The trick failed because 'his wife immediately knew from the feel of the man's body that it was not the count, whose skin was covered in scabs' and raised the alarm. John's most shocking quality was his blasphemous irreligion. He had been heard to deny the divinity and the resurrection of Christ, and when asked by a daring cleric why, in that case, he attended church for the Easter vigil, replied, 'It's all piss and wind, but I enjoy watching the beautiful women who spend this night here.' Even on his death-bed he refused to repent his debaucheries. 'Do you think I'm going to hand out money to some arse-licking priests? No, not a penny. I have learned from many people far cleverer than you that all women should be in common, and that this sin is of no consequence.'[9]

———

The deaths of Clement and Everard of Bucy and their nameless brethren from Dormans tells us that there was at least one established group of committed heretics in this area, for otherwise they would not have refused to recant. It also implies that the known presence of such a group had not in itself triggered a prosecution. Guibert refers to the men from Dormans as *probatissimi heretici* – proven, or certain heretics – and (unless they were bent on martyrdom) some of them had evidently, if mistakenly, felt it safe to join the crowd at the trial of Clement and Everard. We cannot say much about what they were committed to, except that, like the other heresies that occasionally cropped up in this socially turbulent region, it was probably apostolic in inspiration and egalitarian and anticlerical in its appeal.

The way in which Guibert tells the story, on the other hand, shows a great deal about how clerical attitudes to heresy among the people, and the nature of clerical anxiety about it, were changing. His highly coloured descriptions of John of Soissons, and of other castellans of the region, belong to a venerable tradition of monastic invective against those who preyed on church lands, usurped ecclesiastical revenues and exploited the church's peasants – which, of course, is not to say that he was wrong or that these were good people. In the eleventh century such diatribes had often been associated with the label of heresy. Being a patron of heretics had been, and remained, evidence of a ruler's illegitimacy. To this mixture Guibert added a potent new ingredient, in depicting Count John as an associate also of Jews, and as using them to pander to his egregious sexual appetites. Later in the twelfth century the equation of heretics and Jews, and of both with sexual debauchery, would become part of a standard and enduring pattern of Christian anti-Semitism, but now the stereotype was in its infancy, and Guibert one of its pioneers: he was the first to portray what became another of its regular features, a Jew summoning the devil to effect a magical cure in return for a libation of semen.[10]

In fact it was Jews, not heretics, whom Guibert regarded as a major threat to the Christian faith. The Jews of northern France at this time were not the wretched, downtrodden creatures of the later stereotype. Their communities were prosperous, reflecting their essential role as connected to an international trading network and as specialists in the uses of money, indispensable to the opening up of new land to cultivation and the establishment and growth of markets that underlay the economic take-off of western Europe in the twelfth century, and which were transforming the area around Laon and Soissons just at this time. Wherever the Jews went, they had schools, for (as a pupil of Abelard said),

1. (a) Fonte Avellana, near Gubbio, where Peter Damiani lived as a hermit.

(b) The fall of Simon Magus, a popular subject in the early twelfth century depicted here by Gislebertus of Autun, *c.* 1135.

2. (a) The nightmare of Henry I: the sleeping king of England is surrounded by angry peasants.

(b) Pope Innocent II (left), in S. Maria in Trastavere, Rome, which he had rebuilt between 1140–43 to celebrate the end of the schism and the reassertion of papal authority.

3. The story of Alexis inspired many vocations to the apostolic life, perhaps including that of Valdès of Lyons (see p. 221). The first known version in French is in the St Albans Psalter, prepared *c.* 1140 for the influential English hermit Christina of Markyate.

4. An eleventh-century chasuble from St Peter's, Salzburg. To the hermit-preachers vestments like these typified the pride and worldliness of the twelfth-century church.

5. The Golden Chamber of St Ursula, Cologne. Construction of the basilica of St Ursula began in 1135 on the site of the Roman cemetery where the bones of St Ursula and the 11,000 virgins had been found. The Golden Chamber was built to house the relics in 1643, its walls decorated with patterns made from the bones.

6. St Augustine debates with Faustus the Manichee. Until the end of the twelfth century the heretics who appeared in visual images were figures from antiquity, not those reported to be active at the time, and were not caricatured or represented as personally depraved.

7. The enemies of the church: Jews, tyrants, false brethren and heretics. From the 1220s contemporary heretics are frequently represented and clearly recognisable, associated (as here in the first *Bible moralisée*, probably prepared for Louis VIII of France) with Jews and other enemies of the faith and with the devil, who regularly appears as a black cat, the recipient of the obscene kiss.

8. The murder of Peter Martyr in 1252 became a popular subject of religious instruction. In this version, painted around 1400 by Taddeo di Bartolo, a bishop tells two Dominican friars how Peter was attacked and killed, acquiring a martyr's halo in the process.

the Jews, out of the love of God and zeal for the law put as many sons as they have to letters ... A Jew, however poor, if he had ten sons would put them all to letters, not for gain as the Christians do, but for the understanding of God's law, and not only his sons, but his daughters.[11]

The superiority of Jewish culture was recognised, and admired, by many Christians of this generation, but it was also becoming a source of anxiety to others, especially because, in denying the incarnation and the resurrection of Christ, Judaism pointed directly at the areas in which Christian scholars were experiencing the greatest difficulties in working out a logical and compelling account of their own theology, and in some cases the greatest threat to their personal faith. It seems that Guibert of Nogent's was one such case, for he had experienced a considerable humiliation when he wrote a short treatise on the eucharist which turned out to be heretical and had to be hastily and furtively patched over.[12]

————

The history of Clement and Everard of Bucy illustrates how apostolic preaching might, as Guibert put it, 'filter down to the peasants', especially when social differences were increased and the tensions associated with them exacerbated by growing wealth and the harshness both of secular and of ecclesiastical lords – between whom, in this, there was little to choose – in exploiting it. The appeal of the ideal is vividly conveyed by a south German reformer, Bernold of Constance, writing a little before 1100:

An innumerable multitude not only of men but also of women entered a way of life of this kind at this time so that they might live in common under the obedience of clergy or monks and might most faithfully perform the duty of doing service like maidservants. Also in the villages innumerable peasants' daughters strove to renounce marriage and the world and to live under the obedience of some priest. But even the married people never ceased to live devoutly and to obey the religious with the greatest devotion. Such zeal blossomed with particular decorum, however, everywhere in Swabia. In that province many villages dedicated themselves wholly to religion and ceaselessly strove to surpass each other in the holiness of their morals.[13]

A more sceptical observer – a Guibert of Nogent, for instance – might have reflected how well this describes conditions ideal for generating heresy as well as reform. Yet if it was the principal source of heresy accusations at the beginning of the twelfth century, we must ask not why we hear so many of them, but so few. Wherever we look in Europe – and especially in Flanders, the Rhineland and Champagne – conditions were thoroughly conducive to the circulation and acceptance of all manner of religious ideas and enthusiasms. The means available to the bishops of controlling or correcting them, on the other hand, were limited. Apart from the political difficulties in which bishops were so regularly entangled, the parish system in most regions was still at best rudimentary and patchily developed, the quality and training of clergy at best uncertain and erratic. The crucial question, therefore, is not what was the source of the heresies specified in the handful of cases we know of (even supposing them to be accurately reported) or how they were disseminated. It is why, among a myriad of vanished alternatives, these few in particular became the objects of accusations of which a record survives. That must return our attention to the other familiar consequence of reform preaching. The claim that the services of the established clergy were vitiated and its authority negated by the circumstances of their appointment and the manner of their lives implied an attack on local structures of power and patronage. An obvious response to such attacks was to denounce the accusers as heretics.

Certainly, it is not always easy to be sure which was the reformer and which the heretic. Around 1115, for example, two priests and two laymen were accused at Ivoy, in the diocese of Trier, of 'denying that the substance of bread and wine blessed on the altar by priests is truly transformed into the body and blood of Christ, and that the sacrament of baptism helps infants to salvation'.[14] One of the priests, Frederick, defended his view and refused to recant, but in the excitement he managed to escape through the crowd and was condemned in his absence. The other, Dominic William, 'who had two names to obscure the wickedness of his infamy', denied the accusation, was ordered to affirm his denial by reciting a Mass – the form of ordeal appropriate to his status – and completed it without breaking down, even though the archbishop interrupted him at the critical moment with a solemn warning: 'If you have dared to say impiously that the life-giving sacrament of our salvation which you hold in your hand is not the true body and blood of Christ I forbid you, in its presence, to receive it. If your belief is not that, but the Catholic one, take it.'

Dominic William's escape disturbed the chronicler, who was relieved to report that soon afterwards he was taken in adultery 'and met a death worthy of his wickedness' after all. One of the laymen also escaped, and the other swore on the relics not to persist in his heresy. The description of the hearing is somewhat ambivalent. Was it a purely clerical affair, or was it a public assembly? 'Everybody approved' of the suggestion that Dominic William should be put to the ordeal, which he survived, and the insistence of the chronicler on the hostility to the accused of those present adds to the suspicion that the archbishop was seeking to consolidate public support rather than simply exercising his authority. If so, the fact that two of the four accused contrived to escape may point to some sympathy in the community for reformers who advocated avoidance of the services of the local clergy (which for pious Christians would imply seeking an alternative) or even argued that they were invalid.

This suggests that the incident at Ivoy reflected, at least indirectly, the presence of dissenters in the area. Some witnesses 'claimed that they had chanced across a meeting of these heretics and found one of the accused priests taking part in it'. The same uncertainty as to whether an accusation of heresy really arose from attacks on the church from outside rather than dispute within it is left by a letter written by an Augustinian canon named Hugh Metel to Bishop Henry of Toul (1126–65), probably in the early 1130s, claiming that there were heretics in that diocese 'who detest marriage, abominate baptism, laugh at the sacraments of the church and deride the Christian name'.[15]

––––––––

The apostolic ideal, and the demand for reform of the clergy that went with it continued to flourish in the Low Countries. Around 1110 a canon of Utrecht, Ellenhard by name, resigned his position to embrace a life of poverty. He later changed his mind but was accused of heresy, apparently in retaliation for criticism of his brother canons. A year or two later these same canons of Utrecht were the authors of a remarkable letter which implored Archbishop Frederick of Cologne not to release from custody a preacher named Tanchelm (or Tanchelin), who they said had

> raised his voice to the heavens, and dared to excite a heresy against the sacraments of the Church which was long since refuted by its fathers. Swelling with spiritual pride (which is the root of all heresy and apostasy), he maintained that the pope and archbishops, priests and clerks are nothing; hacking at the columns of the Church of God, the very rock of our faith, it was Christ that he presumed to divide. He maintained that the Church consisted only of himself and his followers; the Church which Christ received from his Father, 'Gentiles for his inheritance and the utmost parts of the earth for his possession', was to be a Tanchelmite dominion.[16]

The canons' account of Tanchelm's activities was indeed alarming. He had begun to preach, they said, on the Frisian coast, 'where the population is backward and infirm in the faith', securing his first followers by sleeping with women, both old and young, and then converting their husbands.

> After that he moved out of the shadows and bedrooms and began to preach from the rooftops, giving sermons in the open fields, surrounded by huge crowds. He used to preach as though he were a king summoning his people, as his followers crowded around him, carrying swords and flags like royal insignia. The deluded populace listened to him as though he were an angel of God.

Such was Tanchelm's popularity, the canons asserted, that he distributed his bathwater to be drunk 'as a benediction' and would carry out a blasphemous parody of the wedding service in which he married the Blessed Virgin, represented by a wooden statue whose hand he held while repeating the marriage vows.

Then he would say, 'There, beloved followers. I have married the Blessed Virgin. Let us have the cost of the betrothal and the wedding.' Placing one purse in the left, and one in the right hand of the statue, he would continue, 'Let the men put their offerings in this purse, and the women in the other. I will see now which sex shows the greater generosity towards me and my wife.' Sure enough, the deluded people rushed upon him with gifts and offerings. The women showered him with earrings and necklaces, and by this monstrous sacrilege he made a great deal of money.

According to a later source, Tanchelm

led many of the people of those parts into his errors, and they believed him in everything so firmly that some three thousand armed men used to follow him about, and no prince or magnate would resist him or kill him. He dressed in gilded clothes, and glittered because of the gold twisted into his hair, and the many ornaments which he wore.

But these details – a companion named Mary, the gifts of gold and silver, the three thousand followers – were based on a famous description by the sixth-century historian Gregory of Tours of a preacher who had appeared at Bourges claiming to be Christ.[17]

It seems that the canons of Utrecht failed to persuade Archbishop Frederick to keep Tanchelm in custody, for he was attacked and killed with a stone by a priest, while crossing a river in a rowing boat. He was not simply the deranged demagogue of the canons' letter. He was a man of rank, for in about 1110, before these events, he had visited Rome as a diplomatic envoy of the count of Flanders to secure the transfer of part of the diocese of Utrecht to that of Thérouanne. That might go some way to account for the hostility and anxiety of the canons of Utrecht. The rhetoric of their letter obscures a hostile but unmistakable outline of the reform programme and echoes its language. When Tanchelm claimed that 'the churches of God should be thought of as brothels; that the office of priests at the altar is worthless – they should be called pollutions rather than sacraments', when he 'urged the people not to receive the sacraments of the body and blood of Christ, and not to pay their tithes to the ministers of the church', he spoke with the voice of Ariald of Cucciago, and of Pope Gregory VII. So we may suspect that behind the charade with the wooden statue lay a brilliant, or brutal, satire on clerical marriage. One of Tanchelm's associates was 'a blacksmith named Manasses (who) following the example of his wicked master founded a sort of fraternity commonly called a guild. It was composed of twelve men, representing the twelve apostles, and a woman as Mary.' The canons had their inevitable suggestion as to the nature of Mary's role in this group, but pious congregations with members of both sexes were a universal product and vehicle of reform, and it was a normal expectation that a new religious community should comprise a superior and twelve brethren, because that was the number of the apostles. Another associate was a priest named Everwacher, who had accompanied Tanchelm on the mission to Rome and now 'fell upon the tithes of the brothers of the church of St Peter (of Ghent), and drove the priests themselves from their church and altar by force of arms' – as the Patarenes had done in Milan, and so many of their followers in so many places since.

It was a short distance from boycotting the services of simoniacal or married priests as a matter of discipline to holding as a matter of doctrine that their orders and the sacraments they conferred were invalid, and from witholding tithes from the corrupt to witholding them altogether. Whether his enthusiasm, or his anger, carried Tanchelm or some of his followers over that short but crucial leap we cannot tell. It is what the canons of Utrecht believed, or affected to believe. The most serious part of their letter is devoted to a rebuttal of the proposition that the efficacy of the sacraments proceeded from the merits and holiness of the ministers. This is the Donatist heresy, and they quoted the crucial argument of its great antagonist, St Augustine of Hippo, that it was the faith of the recipient, not the virtue of the priest, that mattered.[18]

It may be that Tanchelm had been aroused to violent hostility to the clergy and their pretensions in reaction to the wordliness and venality of the papal court after seeing its business at first hand. But it is equally possible that, like Wederic and perhaps Ramihrd, he had returned from

Rome with a papal mandate to advance the cause of reform in this part of the imperial territories. In either case, and whatever the justice of their charges against him or his against them, the canons' letter identified correctly the greatest danger that the spread of reform sentiment held for the church. If its legitimacy and the efficacy of its sacraments depended on the freedom of its ministers from sin, there could be no church at all. By the second decade of the twelfth century that spectre haunted the dreams of many besides the canons of Utrecht.

7

SOWERS OF THE WORD

You stay among barbaric and rude men; it seems to you that you can do no good there. There you find simoniacal clergy, bishops and abbots and priests; wicked and thieving princes; adulterers and incestuous people ignorant of God's law.

Robert of Arbrissel, letter to Countess Ermengarde of Brittany[1]

They say that you go into the crowd, having discarded your canonical dress, skin covered by a hairshirt and a worn out cowl full of holes, your legs half naked, your beard long and your hair trimmed at the brow, bare foot, offering a strange spectacle to all who look on, such that you lack only a club to complete the outfit of a lunatic. All this procures for you not so much the moral authority among the 'simple folk', as you are wont to claim, as the suspicion of madness among the wise men.[2]

Thus Marbod (*c.* 1035–1123), bishop of Rennes, schoolmaster and poet, wrote in or about 1098 to the hermit preacher Robert of Arbrissel. His words catch the difficulties and ambiguities raised by successful preaching to popular audiences, and the dangers that it seemed to hold. Robert of Arbrissel was no fly-by-night rabble-rouser. He preached by the authority of Pope Urban II, who had commissioned him to advance the reform of the clergy throughout what is now western and south-western France. A year or two after this letter was written he established a convent for his followers at Fontevraud, a few miles from the confluence of the Loire and the Vienne, on the borders of Touraine, Anjou and Poitou. When he died in 1116, Fontevraud was the head of dozens of priories. It would become one of the richest and most powerful monasteries in Europe and the burial place of King Henry II of England, his wife, Eleanor of Aquitaine, and his son Richard the Lionheart. But its founder has never become a saint of the Roman Catholic Church, despite vigorous efforts by determined and influential advocates in the seventeenth century and again in the nineteenth.

Robert was born at Arbrissel in Brittany, not far from Rennes, around the middle of the eleventh century, the son of a priest and of a priest's daughter – which in that part of the world and at that time carried none of the stigma that such a description would later imply. Priesthood was hereditary in Brittany, as it was and would long remain in many parts of Europe, despite the prohibitions on the ordination of priests' sons which had been reiterated by ecclesiastical councils at least since the 1030s. In a region not yet dominated by lords with castles the priestly family was generally the chief property owner in its community, to which it gave leadership in matters not just of religion but also of practical everyday life, business included.[3]

'At the time when Gregory VII held the papacy in Rome', says Robert's biographer, 'he went as a student to Paris, where he found the teaching in literature proportionate to his longing.'[4] The story that follows describes the classic 'roots' conflict of the provincial student, between the cosmopolitan values and culture that he embraced at university and the local traditions and loyalties of his home and family – but it was a new story in the eleventh century, which is as good a symbol as any of why the eleventh century is when the history of modern Europe begins. In the late 1080s Robert was brought back to Rennes by Bishop Sylvester de la Guerche, a layman who had been simoniacally elected to the see in 1076 and became a reformer. Sylvester made Robert archpriest of the diocese with responsibility for clerical discipline, including 'putting a stop to the sinful fornications of the clergy and laity', and to simony, now held to include all family influence in church appointments. In other

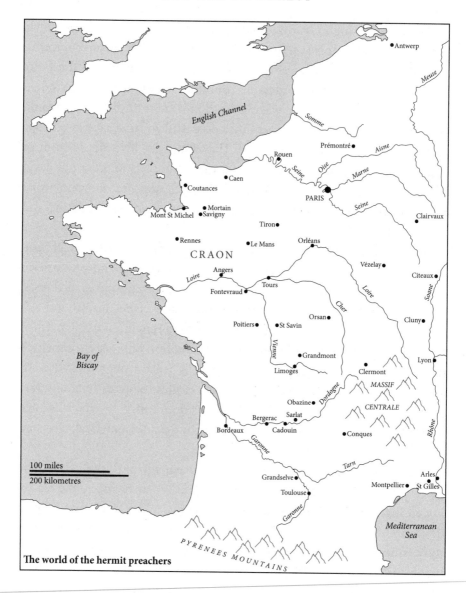

Antwerp

Meuse

English Channel

Somme

Prémontré •

Aisne

Rouen •

Seine

Oise

Marne

• Caen

• Coutances

PARIS

Seine

• Mortain

Mont St Michel • Savigny

Tiron •

Clairvaux •

• Rennes

• Le Mans

Orléans •

CRAON

Vézelay •

Citeaux •

Loire

Angers •

Loire

Saône

Tours •

Fontevraud •

Cher

Cluny •

Orsan •

Poitiers • • St Savin

Vienne

Lyon •

Bay of Biscay

• Grandmont

Limoges •

Clermont •

MASSIF

Obazine •

Dordogne

CENTRALE

Bergerac • Sarlat

Bordeaux • Cadouin

• Conques

Rhône

Garonne

Tarn

Arles •

100 miles

Grandselve •

Montpellier • St Gilles

200 kilometres

Toulouse •

Garonne

Mediterranean Sea

PYRENEES MOUNTAINS

The world of the hermit preachers

words, Robert was given the task of dismantling the social structure that had sustained his family and its world for generations, and in which he himself had grown up. Small wonder that when Sylvester died in 1093, Robert 'remained alone, an orphan among orphans, because his fellow clerics resented his probity, and already their resentment had turned to hatred'. He fled from Rennes, first to Angers as a student again, where he took to wearing an iron tunic next to his skin, and then to become a hermit in the forest of Craon, on the borders of Maine and Brittany. In the 1080s this great wilderness was a nursery for hermit preachers who became scourges of the clergy and then, needing to provide for the followers attracted by their preaching and the austerity of their lives, founders of religious houses.

Among the hermits of Craon were two others with whom Robert became closely associated. In their cases too the personal crises that brought them to the forest involved, though in very different ways, alienation from the social position, and especially the structures of power, in which they had grown up. Bernard, later of Tiron, began a turbulent religious life as a monk at St Cyprian in Poitiers. From there he was sent as prior to St Savin-sur-Gartempe, fled to the forest to avoid being made its abbot, was persuaded to return as abbot of St Cyprian itself and fled again to the forest, in despair, when the claim of Cluny to authority over that house involved him in two highly political and fruitless trips to the papal court. It seems to have been that experience, rather than disillusionment with conventional monastic life itself, that precipitated Bernard's final break. St Cyprian was a wealthy Black Monk house, and some of the decisions that led in the years around 1100 to the building of the wonderfully elegant church at St Savin (now a World Heritage site) and the painting of its superb frescos must have been taken while Bernard was there. Nevertheless, when he came to found his own house at Tiron in Normandy, in 1109, it embraced the plainness and austerity of the new orders modelled on Cîteaux.

To Bernard's biographer Geoffrey Grossus the forest of Craon at this time was 'another Egypt', filled by hermits devoted to the exaltation of the spirit through the humiliation of the flesh, in the manner of the desert fathers.[5] When Bernard entered the forest, he was intercepted by some hermits and questioned closely on his motives and intentions, welcomed to the community and offered his choice of the cells and huts that had been constructed among the roots of fallen trees and in the rocky beds of streams. He confirmed his spiritual fitness by selecting the dampest and most uncomfortable, to the gratification of the man who had contrived it, and everybody celebrated with a banquet of berries and spring water.

The lead in Bernard's examination was taken by Vitalis, a Norman clerk of family and education sufficient for him to have become chaplain to Count Robert of Mortain, who had made Vitalis a canon of his church of St Evroul at Mortain. Robert was a half-brother of Duke William and one of the leading magnates of William's Anglo-Norman empire. Why Vitalis left his household and gave up the canonry is not clear – one story is that it was in revulsion after finding the countess in tears because of her husband's brutality – but in worldly terms it was a dramatic abdication. Many a glittering career in the El Dorado that was opened to talented young Normans by the exploits of William the Conqueror was built on smaller advantages.

———

In February 1096 Pope Urban II visited Angers to consecrate the church of St Nicholas, and Robert of Arbrissel was summoned to preach before him. He made such an impact that 'the pope appointed Robert his deputy as God's word-scatterer and urged him to pursue this mission wherever he went'.[6] It seems that Bernard and Vitalis received similar commissions at about the same time, and in discharging them the three experienced and illustrated all the tensions and turbulence associated with the drive for reform in this generation.

While Bernard and Vitalis worked chiefly in Normandy and Maine, Robert ranged across western France, mainly south of the Loire. His golden eloquence and spectacular austerity drew crowds wherever he went. Most of the score or so of priories that had been established for his followers when he died in 1116 were in Poitou and Berry, but they were to be found as far afield as Hautes-Bruyères, just south of Paris, Espinasse, near Toulouse, and Beaulieu-le-Roannais, on the upper Loire not far from Lyon. He 'preached to the poor and gathered the poor around him', including lepers, who were apparently at this time the victims in many regions of increasing fear and social hostility. One of the four houses that comprised Robert's chief foundation at Fontevraud, dedicated to St Lazarus, was a leper hospital. He asked on his death-bed, in vain, to be buried among its inmates. But his special mission was to women, of every rank and background. Fontevraud and its many priories were governed by the abbess of the mother house because Robert laid it down firmly that this should be so, and that the place of the monks in his order (who observed the rule of regular canons) was solely to serve the spiritual needs of the nuns, to whom they were subordinate in all respects. Fontevraud had two houses for women, dedicated to St Mary the Virgin and St Mary Magdalen, in accordance with the condition of their respective residents.

The depth of Robert's popular appeal was dramatically illustrated by the events surrounding his death, so sensational that the account of them written by Andreas of Fontevraud, probably his chaplain, for Petronilla of Chemillé, whom Robert had made abbess, seems to have been suppressed by her successors and has come fully to light only in the last thirty years.[7] Early in 1116, hard at work in the region of the Berry, Robert felt his last illness at hand, asked his companions to carry him to the priory that had been founded by some of his followers at Orsan, and sent to Petronilla at Fontevraud to let her know that he was dying. When the news got out, 'people came from everywhere, and nearly the whole city of Bourges assembled at Orsan.' A desperate struggle followed for his body, partly orchestrated by Robert himself. Archbishop Léger of Bourges and the local lord, Alardus, whose wife was the prioress of Orsan, were determined to keep the precious relic there. Petronilla arrived in the nick of time. Using every weapon from threatening an appeal to Rome to organising a hunger strike by the nuns, she won the day, and Robert's body, apart from his heart (which was left at Orsan), returned to Fontevraud. A military escort was necessary to prevent it from being stolen on the journey, and at the end 'all the brothers of Fontevraud, and also all the people of the town from the least to the greatest walked alongside the body.' They did so not least to protect it from the men of neighbouring Candes, 'peaceful enemies' who wanted Robert to spend a night in their church and 'insisted on it to the point of striking religious men and women', whose prayers and orisons happily prevailed over the swords and cudgels of their rivals. Such were the tensions and passions that the holy man, dead or alive, had the power to arouse and focus.

We cannot know how closely Robert's popular appeal was related to his attacks on the clergy. He had, as Marbod observed pointedly, discarded his clerical clothing. The animal skins in which he dressed, like most hermits, were a sign of poverty and exclusion. They dissociated him from the division and exploitation of labour represented by agriculture and by weaving – even domestic weaving – thus declaring him outside the established social order. Those who gathered around him and followed him through the countryside were said to be the poorest and most wretched, conspicuously including many described as prostitutes. He made a habit of sleeping among, but not with, his female followers, an ancient ascetic practice known as synacteism. It naturally aroused the darkest suspicions of his critics, but in the eyes of his disciples it would have confirmed his freedom from the taint and corruption of ordinary human passions and jealousies, and from a routine abuse of power. Who these 'prostitutes' were is hard to tell. Such towns as there were had their brothels no doubt, but by comparison with the Rhineland or the Low Countries, let alone Lombardy, this was still a backward region, still relatively untouched by long distance commerce or manufacture. Economic growth was represented rather by the clearing of forests and draining of marshes for cultivation, accompanied by increasingly harsh enserfment of the cultivators. Its victims certainly included women who had been cast off or pushed out, or who had escaped, for many reasons – because they could not work or be found husbands or bear children, for instance. No doubt some of them had been encouraged by Robert, or by their own or their husbands' inclination, to abandon priests or clerks to whom they had been partners, but the slowness of that aspect of the reform and the strength of resistance to it caution against exaggerating their number.

The austerity that inflamed the devotion of Robert's admirers was to Marbod mere eccentricity, or exhibitionism, unbefitting his clerical and social status. His followers, at least disreputable if not hypocritical, were to be seen 'running around different lands, clad in coarse garments. Identifiable by the length of their beards, they go about through the fields in shoes, it is said, but barefoot in villages and towns', where they would be seen. Robert's relations with the women and young girls among them must at best give rise to suspicion. Even if his chastity was not found wanting, the same could not be said of all his followers, for 'some have slipped away, jailbreakers ready to give birth; others have had their babies in these cells.'

According to Marbod, the sermons preached to 'crowds of common and ignorant people … censure not only the vices of those present – as is fitting – but also those of absent churchmen. You enumerate the crimes not only of those in orders but even in high office – which is not fitting – and you slander and abuse … this is not to preach but to undermine.' His complaints were echoed a few years later in a similar letter from another senior churchman, Abbot Geoffrey of Vendôme. On the other hand, Robert's preaching, licensed and approved as it had been by the pope, was supported by prelates no less distinguished than Marbod and Geoffrey, including Bishop Peter of Poitiers, Archbishop Léger of Bourges and Hildebert, bishop of Le Mans and later archbishop of Tours. Nevertheless, like the manner of life that proved his credentials to his admirers, it breached or threatened to breach social boundaries of every kind – not only between virgins and women of the world, or between the adherents of local ecclesiastical hierarchies sustained by custom which had become simony and the new men who carried the banner of reform from Rome, but also between men and women, rich and poor, the respectable and the disreputable. Robert of Arbrissel seemed to threaten not only the clerical order but also the social one.

———

Marbod's and Geoffrey's anxieties were all too vividly realised in the very year of Robert's death, 1116, when a preacher named Henry appeared in the neighbourhood of Le Mans, 'with the haggard face and eyes of a shipwrecked sailor, his hair bound up, unshaven, tall and of athletic gait, walking barefoot even in the depths of winter, a young man always ready to preach, possessed of a fearful voice'.[8] He aroused great excitement in the area. He was said to be a man

> of unusual holiness and learning … whose eloquence could move a
> heart of stone to remorse. It was claimed that all monks, hermits and

canons regular ought to imitate his pious and celibate life, and that God had blessed him with the ancient and authentic spirit of the prophets, and he saw in their faces, and told them about, sins which were unknown to others.

At the beginning of Lent, Henry sent two of his followers into the city to seek the bishop's permission for him to preach there during the penitential season. They 'carried a standard in the way that doctors bear staves, with a cross of wrought iron fixed at the top'. The iron of the cross was a symbol of penitence, contrasting with the precious metal and rich jewellery of those that would have been carried before the bishop or worn by the cathedral canons.

Bishop Hildebert was about leave the city to attend the Easter synod in Rome, but granted Henry permission to preach in his absence. The result was calamitous. Henry

turned the people against the clergy with such fury that they refused to sell them anything or buy anything from them and treated them like gentiles or publicans. Not content with pulling down their houses and throwing away their belongings, they would have stoned and pilloried them if the count and his men had not heard of their wicked and vicious exploits and suppressed them by force instead of by reason, for a monster admits no argument.

When some of the clerks tried to negotiate, 'they were viciously beaten and had their heads rolled in the filth of the gutter; they were scarcely able to escape alive from the attack of these brutal people.'

Unable to challenge Henry in person, the canons wrote a letter accusing him of blasphemy, sedition and heresy, and forbidding him to preach or teach 'anywhere in the diocese of Le Mans, in private or in public', on pain of excommunication. The letter was delivered and read aloud under the protection of the count's steward, and Henry 'nodded his head at each sentence of the letter, and replied in a clear voice, "You are lying".' He remained in control of the city at least until Pentecost (that is, for about three months) and was driven out only when Hildebert returned and succeeded in rallying opinion against him.

This affair was not as straightforward as it looked, or as its only chronicler, Hildebert's official biographer, thought best to present it. Hildebert was a fine poet and a distinguished man of letters and of the world. As archdeacon before his elevation to the bishopric he had fathered at least two sons, one of whom became a canon of the cathedral. But he was also a reformer and a friend of reformers, including Robert of Arbrissel, who had roamed western France for the previous twenty years, dressed much as Henry is described and inciting crowds against married and simoniac clergy as Henry did – and as Robert had been commissioned to do by Pope Urban II. Robert and others like him were sometimes called in by newly appointed reforming bishops to rally opinion against cathedral clergy who were the sons of local noble families determined to go on supporting their wives and families on the income of their canonries. Among Henry's supporters in Le Mans were some of the younger canons, perhaps appointed by Hildebert. It was they who 'prepared a platform from which the demagogue addressed the crowds of people who followed him' and 'sat weeping at his feet' as he thundered against the sins of their senior colleagues. When Henry was expelled from the city, two of these young clerks followed him. They later returned, and Hildebert wrote a letter to say that they were truly repentant and should not be penalised for the excesses of their youthful enthusiasm.

It looks, then, as though Hildebert had allowed – or even invited – Henry to preach while he was away as part of his own campaign to reform his cathedral clergy, and found that he had lit a bigger fire than he intended. Bernard of Clairvaux later said that Henry had left Lausanne under a cloud (he is usually known as Henry of Lausanne, as the first place with which he can be connected) before he appeared at Le Mans, where his approach aroused some excitement, so perhaps he already had a reputation as a fiery preacher. Some of the the fuel for the flames he lit at Le Mans can be identified. That the count of Maine should have protected and by implication supported the canons is to be expected, but he did not suppress the rising with the pitiless savagery regularly deployed by the nobles of this period against any sign of unrest among peasants or townsmen. His restraint suggests that Henry commanded significant support in the city and its suburbs, including that of such notables as it possessed. Le Mans was no Milan or Cologne. It was a small town in a backward region, its trade and manufacture heavily dependent on the expenditure of the church. When the bishop put the city under interdict in 1092,

> the inn-keepers, the jesters, the butchers and bakers, the women who sold trinkets of little value, everybody who in normal times made good profits from the affluence of the people of the province, murmured angrily against the bishop, through whom they were deprived of the profits of their business.

In 1070 the leaders in a demand for a commune here, one of the earliest in Europe (and firmly suppressed by William the Conqueror), had been known by earthy and unpretentious nicknames – 'Witless', 'Fathead,' 'Threeballs,' 'Farter' – more suggestive of labouring or artisanal backgrounds than of the dignified family names that would in time be assumed by sober and prosperous bourgeois. Nevertheless, this was not a simple story of perennial hostility between arrogant clerics and resentful dependants. The churches of Le Mans, including the cathedral, fostered a lively and apparently well-integrated civic life through feasts and celebrations, confraternies, prayer associations and the like. Ironically enough, this may have contributed to the solidarity that the citizens displayed during the crisis in 1116, and perhaps to the intensity of anger against the clergy, if Henry's denunciation of their sins and malfeasances created a sense of betrayal where previously there had been a degree of trust.

———

As to what Henry actually said, we are told nothing, except for an account of two extraordinary, and in the eyes of the chronicler scandalous, episodes:

> He summoned sacrilegious meetings at the churches of St Germain and St Vincent, where he pronounced a new dogma, that women who had not lived chastely must, naked before everybody, burn their clothes and their hair. No one should accept any gold or silver or

goods or wedding presents with his wife, or receive any dowry with her: the naked should marry the naked, the sick marry the sick, and the poor marry the poor, without bothering about whether they married chastely or incestuously. On his advice many of the young men married the prostitutes, for whom he bought clothes to the value of four *solidi*, just enough to cover their nakedness, with money he had collected for the purpose.

We are given this remarkable story because it illustrates and reinforces, in the chronicler's eyes, the invective that throughout his narrative sought to discredit Henry by depicting him as a sexual libertine and a fomenter of anarchy. When he first preached outside the city,

women and young boys – for he used both sexes in his lechery – who associated with him openly flaunted their excesses, and added to them by caressing the soles of his feet and his buttocks and groin with tender fingers. They became so excited by the lasciviousness of the man, and by the grossness of their own sins, that they testified publicly to his extraordinary virility.

When Henry heard that Hildebert was on his way back from Rome, he retired to a castle outside the town. There on Whit Sunday, which everybody should devote to prayer, he 'caroused all day until mid-day' in bed with the wife of the castle's lord. The meetings that he held in the churchyards were themselves scenes of his lechery for, while the repentant prostitutes were stripping and burning their clothes, 'he admired their beauty, and discussed which ones had fairer skin or better figures than the others'. The marriages that had been entered into with his encouragement were miserable failures: the men were reduced to poverty and despair by the debauchery of their new wives and fled the city, leaving the destitute women to return to their former trade.

The chronicler, in short, protests a very great deal. He was still determined, years after the event, to show that Henry's appeal had been fraudulent, and to discredit his memory. Events spoke differently. When Bishop Hildebert entered the city on his return from Rome he was greeted by jeers and anger:

We don't want your blessing. Bless the dirt! Sanctify filth! We have a father, a bishop and defender greater than you in authority, fame and learning. These wicked clerks of yours opposed him, and contradicted his teaching. They have hated it and rejected it as sacrilege because they are afraid that their crimes will be revealed by his prophetic spirit. They wrote letters attacking his heresy and his bodily unchastity. Their sins will be speedily turned against them when they presume so audaciously to forbid his heavenly preaching of the word of God.

Hildebert managed to recover control, with God's help in manifesting His anger by means of a sudden and devastating fire in the suburbs, and Henry was expelled from the city. But although 'Hildebert took every precaution to calm by reason and humility the popular fury which Henry had seditiously stirred up against the clergy, the people had become so devoted to him that even now his memory can scarcely be expunged, or their love for him drawn from their hearts.'

———

Even the hostile chronicler, then, reluctantly admits that Henry had tapped deep and lasting passions and grievances in Le Mans. The meetings in the churchyards point directly to one important source of his appeal. In urging that marriage should be governed (as he implied) by the will of the partners alone, without regard to dowry and 'without worrying about whether they married chastely or incestuously', Henry struck directly at one of the most profound and far-reaching changes that was taking place in European society at this time. The church was increasingly treating marriage as a sacrament, which meant that it should be performed before the altar and not, as was commonly the case, outside in the churchyard, customarily the forum of the community rather than the domain of the priest. This brought marriage, the most fundamental of social institutions, and therefore the conditions under which it could take place, under the control of the church itself rather than the community.

The sacralisation of marriage greatly facilitated the enforcement of another change yet more radical in its consequences. All systems of social organisation are based on rules governing who may or may not sleep with whom, and on what conditions. Changes in those rules are always bitterly contentious and always indicative of profound social or political change. The most important of them determine what constitutes incest – what degrees of kinship are so close as to prohibit marriage. Christians had long agreed that this was the seventh degree, which was calculated by counting back from both partners to their nearest common ancestor, and adding the results. Thus I am related to my sister in the second degree, to my first cousin in the fourth, and so on. In the middle of the eleventh century, however, led in this by none other than Peter Damiani, the church had proclaimed a change in the method of counting. Henceforth it was to be seven steps back from *each* partner to the common ancestor, not from both combined. On that basis I am related to my sister in the first degree, and to my first cousin in the second.

The effect of this change was to multiply the number of people whom one could *not* marry, on average, by a factor of about twenty. It meant that in a world of small communities, where almost everybody was related more or less closely to almost everybody else, almost every feasible marriage was incestuous, and therefore could not take place or, if it had already done so, was invalid. At first sight it seems extraordinary that such a change should have been widely accepted, as apparently it was (though later in the twelfth century the rule began once again to be more flexibly interpreted), especially since there was no mechanism to enforce it except the support of those involved. And that was the point. Almost any marriage would indeed be invalid – unless everybody agreed to keep quiet about it and, in the priest's words, for ever hold their tongues. A marriage could take place, therefore, only with the agreement of everybody who might possibly be concerned. The restriction provided an immensely powerful instrument for parents to control the marriages of their children, and lords of their serfs. This was critical for many noble and knightly families. Prosperity and its transmission down the generations were now being seen more and more to depend on the accumulation and effective management of landed property. This depended, among other things, on preventing its fragmentation through the claims that would otherwise arise on the marriage either of sons or of daughters, all of whom, traditionally, had until now had equal claims.

The theoretical justification of this more stringent definition of incest, and its practical enforcement through the sacralisation of marriage, was the church's main contribution to the reordering and stabilisation of the lay aristocracy in our period. In return its own immense endowments of property were acknowledged and confirmed, on the condition that the beneficiaries would be celibate, so that they could not use the land to establish rival dynasties. This was reinforced by the growing expectation that a woman should enter marriage with a dowry, so that if her family could not or would not provide a sufficient dowry she was ipso facto unmarriageable. For great landholders, and for property owners generally, these changes, though often extremely irksome, were in the long run not only advantageous but essential to the consolidation of their power and prosperity. Henry's success in Le Mans shows very clearly how hardly they might bear on ordinary people – and the danger of effective preaching against them not only for the church but for the privileged laity.

Thirty years later Henry became the target of a famous and influential campaign when Bernard of Clairvaux, the greatest preacher of the age, undertook a mission to cleanse his influence from the lands of the count of Toulouse.[9] Henry's activities in the interim are obscure. After leaving Le Mans in 1116 he went south into Aquitaine,

> to spread the germ of his heresy in remote places ... and he has created so much disturbance that soon Christians will scarcely enter the doors of the churches: they reject the holy mystery, refuse offerings to the priests, first fruits, tithes and visits to the sick, and withdraw their habitual piety.

In 1135 the archbishop of Arles – in whose province, therefore, Henry had been active – brought him before an important church council at Pisa. He was 'convicted, and by agreement labelled a heretic', but, according to Geoffrey of Auxerre, who acted as secretary to Bernard of Clairvaux, Henry (who had once been a Black Monk) 'renounced the heresies which he was preaching, and was handed over to the abbot (that is, Bernard), from whom he had received letters to enable him to become a monk at Clairvaux.'

If Henry ever got to Clairvaux, he did not stay there but contrived to return to his life as an itinerant preacher. In 1145 Bernard, in the company of a papal legate, Cardinal Alberic of Ostia, and a senior bishop, Geoffrey of Chartres, undertook a preaching mission to combat the effects of his activities. The letters in which Bernard announced the mission to Count Alphonse Jordan of Toulouse and in which Geoffrey of Auxerre described it to the monks of Clairvaux contain the rest of what we know of Henry's life and activity. Bernard called him an educated man (which is confirmed by the author of the treatise *Against Henry*; see note 10 below) and alleged that he earned money by preaching and was forced by his dissolute habits to live an itinerant life: 'Enquire if you like why he left Lausanne, Le Mans, Poitiers and Bordeaux. There is no way at all of return open to him in any of these places, because of the foul traces [in the shape of angry husbands] he has left behind him.' A lurid picture follows of the devastation that Henry's preaching had left in his trail:

Churches without people, people without priests, priests without the deference due to them, and Christians without Christ. The churches are regarded as synagogues, the holiness of God's sanctuary is denied, the sacraments are not considered sacred, and holy days are deprived of their solemnities. Men are dying in their sins, and souls are everywhere being hurled before the awesome tribunal unreconciled by repentance, unfortified by communion. The grace of baptism is denied, and Christian children are kept away from the life given by Christ.

———

Leaving aside the rhetorical exaggeration to be expected in a public document such as this letter, intended to justify the intrusion into the count's lands not only in his eyes but in those of his subjects and neighbours, Bernard was mistaken in attributing whatever shortcomings he found or heard of solely to the influence of Henry or others like him.

The church as he understood it was far less developed in large parts of this vast and varied territory between the Rhône and the Loire than the lowland regions, both north and south of the Alps, with which Bernard was more familiar. Much of the Mediterranean and Atlantic coasts and their hinterlands, including the Charente and the plain of Poitou, had maintained a degree of urban living and social organisation since Roman times. But the mountainous and relatively undeveloped lands between the Alps, the Massif Central and the Pyrenees had been little touched by the work of Charlemagne and his successors in the ninth century, which had not only given schools to the cathedrals of the north but made them in varying degrees hubs of parochial organisation and services. The monastic movement of the tenth and eleventh centuries also provided such services in many places and contributed much to the Christianisation of the countryside, but it too had a much less general impact south of the Loire. On these foundations, inadequate and even corrupt though they may have come to seem, the reformers of our period were building in Italy and in northern France, the Low Countries and Germany.

Christianity south of the Loire was often, for this reason, very different from that of other parts of Europe, at any rate as it is shown in the written texts of the period, which come to us overwhelmingly from those other regions. Communities, as we saw in relation to the eleventh-century Peace of God, attached great importance to religious ritual, language and gesture in the regulation of social life and the resolution of conflict and difficulty, and occasionally in rallying and uniting people against injustice or repression. Local saints and their festivals, commemorations and customs were cherished with corresponding fervour. Doctrine, on the other hand, cannot have been at all clearly or precisely disseminated or understood among lay people, and was doubtless subject to a good deal of local variation in its expression. It is most unlikely that its refinements had much to do with the reception afforded to the preachers who began to appear in the twelfth century – much later than in many parts of Europe – practising spectacular fleshly austerities, preaching the gospels and calling the people to repentance. This was the stamping-ground of Robert of Arbrissel and of at least one other of his companions from the forest of Craon, Gerard of Salles. In the Limousin, Stephen of Muret and, on the borders of the Périgord, the Corrèze and the Auvergne, Stephen of

Obazine are remembered as saints, hermits and holy men, the founders of great churches and religious orders, but in the first place as practitioners of spectacular personal austerity and as charismatic preachers.

———

Bernard left Poitiers at the end of April 1145 to pursue Henry, or his influence, through Bergerac, Périgueux, Sarlat and Cahors to Toulouse and Albi, a distance on modern roads of at least 700 kilometres. As he went, people of all sorts and conditions clamoured to have their problems solved and their conflicts settled, and acclaimed his successes as miracles, enthusiastically described by Geoffrey. In Bergerac he cured a nobleman who had been seriously ill, and another man, destitute because he was too weak to work, began to recover 'after he had followed us for a few days and eaten bread blessed by the abbot'; in Cahors he restored the sight of one of the bishop's servants, who had been blinded when he was struck on the head in a fight. Wherever he went, Bernard was followed by the restoration of temporary loss of sight or of speech, and the loosening of withered or crippled fingers, conditions that may have originated in shock, hysteria or social isolation.

Bernard caught up with Henry in Toulouse, which he reached at the beginning of June. Henry had won many followers there, including prominent citizens. Bernard's reception was cool at first, but he gradually won support, assisted by a flow of miracles in different parts of the city, and among various groups of people, until he judged his moment and secured from the citizens a promise that 'nobody would give the heretics any support thereafter unless they came forward for public debate'.

Henry, who had taken refuge in a nearby village, ducked the challenge and fled with his closest followers.

> Their supporters renounced them, and we believed that the city was wholly free of the infection of heresy. Some of the knights promised to drive them out and not to support them in future. To make sure that this would not be infringed by anybody who might be bribed by the heretics, judgement was pronounced that the heretics, their supporters and anybody who gave them any help would not be eligible to give

evidence, or seek redress in the courts, and nobody would have any dealings with them either socially or commercially.

This is the first time we hear of civic sanctions against those adjudged heretical. Such measures would later become standard.

Bernard's greatest triumph was in Albi, which he reached at the end of the month, after chasing Henry through the villages where he had won support among the lordlings, impoverished masters of small and fragmented holdings, who 'hated clerks and enjoyed Henry's jokes'. Hitherto Bernard had not been uniformly successful. It was long remembered at Clairvaux that at Verfeil, 'that seat of Satan', the nobles walked out of the church during his sermon and, when he followed them into the public square, still preaching, retired into their houses and banged on their doors to drown him out, so that those who had stayed to listen could not hear him. Bernard laid a curse on Verfeil as he left, and yet the clamour had not been the most rational of responses to his preaching, or one that suggests that support for Henry was unanimous.

The papal legate reached Albi first. 'Its people, who we had heard were more contaminated with heresy than any others on our route … came out to meet him on donkeys, beating drums, and when the signal was given to call the people together for mass scarcely thirty came.' When Bernard arrived two days later, preceded by the news of his miracles, he was greeted with enthusiasm but declined to accept the devotion of people of whom he had heard such ill reports. The following day, 1 August, he preached to a packed congregation and, beginning with the eucharist, carefully rebutted Henry's teachings one by one. Whether it was his theology or his charisma, when Bernard asked them which opinions they would choose,

the whole people began to execrate and decry the wickedness of the heretic, and joyfully to receive the word of God and the Catholic faith. 'Repent', said the abbot. 'Each of you is contaminated. Return to the unity of the church. So that we can know which of you has repented and received the word of life, raise your right hand to heaven as a sign of Catholic unity.' All raised their right hands in exultation, and so he brought his sermon to an end.

Henry had not been alone in finding a welcome in these parts. In 1119 a council at Toulouse, presided over by Pope Calixtus II, had ordered that 'those who, simulating the appearance of religion, reject the sacrament of the body and blood of the Lord, the baptism of children, the orders of priests and other clerics and the bonds of legitimate matrimony' were to be expelled from the church and handed over to the secular power for punishment. Hindsight has persistently connected this decree with the so-called 'Cathars' of later times, or with the recent arrival in the region of Henry or of another notorious preacher, Peter of Bruys, said to have been active for more than twenty years when he was killed at the end of the 1130s. The last two are certainly possible, in that Henry and Peter existed and may have been active in the region by this time, but there is no reason to assume that they were the only ones. This could have been simply a continuation of accusations exchanged during a bitter and pro-longed conflict between the bishops of Toulouse and the canons of St Sernin, both claiming to stand for reform.

Peter of Bruys took his name from a village in the Alpine diocese of Embrun, either because he was born there or because it was the parish in which he served as priest before being expelled for the heretical views that he continued to propagate for some twenty years. The news of his death was quite recent in 1139–40, when Abbot Peter the Venerable of Cluny wrote his treatise *Against the Petrobrusians*. Remarking that the heresy has been 'chased from Provence, and now makes ready its snares in Gascony and that neighbourhood', Peter the Venerable describes a strain of violence that goes well beyond anything we have encountered previously. Believers were rebaptised, he says, altars profaned and bon-fires made of crosses – on one of which Peter of Bruys himself met his death when faithful catholics at St Gilles-du-Gard threw him on to it as well. Priests were whipped, monks locked up and forced to marry, believers offered cooked meat to eat in public on Good Friday – some-thing of which, as it happens, Peter the Venerable also accused Jews, towards whom he was bitterly hostile.[10]

Against the Petrobrusians is our only source for the teaching of Peter of Bruys. It attributes five principal heresies to him: (i) 'that children who have not reached the age of understanding cannot be saved by Christian baptism' and cannot benefit from the faith of godparents on their behalf; (ii) 'that there should be no churches or temples in any kind of building, and that those which already exist should be pulled down. Christians do not need holy places in which to pray, because when God is called he hears, whether in a tavern or a church, in the street or in a temple, before an altar or in a stable, and he listens to those who deserve it;' (iii) 'that holy crosses should be broken and burned, because the instrument on which Christ was so horribly tortured and so cruelly killed is not worthy of adoration;' (iv) 'that they deny the truth that the body and blood of Christ is offered daily and continuously in church through the sacrament'; and (v) 'that they deride offerings by the faithful of sacrifices, prayers, alms, and other things for the dead, and say that nothing can help the dead in any way.' To his systematic rebuttal of these heresies Peter the Venerable adds that of another claim made by Peter of Bruys, that 'God laughs at ecclesiastical chants because he loves only the holy will, and is not to be summoned by high-pitched voices, or caressed by well-turned tunes.' This was not heretical, but to the abbot of Cluny, whose monks, in fulfilment of their ideal of the *vita angelica* (angelic life), had developed the singing of the liturgy to such a pitch of perfection that visitors thought themselves in a corner of heaven and they themselves had only two hours a day free from their choral duties, it verged on blasphemy.

To all this Peter the Venerable adds that Henry, 'the heir in wickedness' of Peter of Bruys, has added to his teaching. 'Recently indeed I have read in a book which is said to stem from him not only these five propositions but several others which he has added.' Henry's book has not survived, but a counter to it has, by Archbishop William of Arles, one of the addressees of *Against the Petrobrusians*.[11] William's responses show that Henry's attack was vigorously directed against the clergy, holding that 'bishops and priests should have no money or benefices' and 'have not the power of binding and loosing' – that is, of excommunication and hence of determining the membership of the church. Henry also maintained, consistently with his words and actions in Le Mans, that there was no need to go to priests for confession or penance, and that a marriage could not be ended for any reason other than fornication. He denied the necessity of infant baptism, maintaining (in contrast to the increasingly intolerant climate of the times) that the children not only of Christians but also of Jews or Muslims will be saved if they die before the age of reason – that is, before they are seven years old: old enough, it was thought, to understand what they were taught.

The constant tendency of the teaching of both Henry of Lausanne and Peter of Bruys was to reject everything for which they could not find direct scriptural authority and therefore, with special vehemence, the intermediary structure of the church, and especially the ever wider distinction between clergy and laity as it was represented and was being developed in their time, by the reformed papacy and its champions. If Peter the Venerable does not exaggerate (of which we cannot be sure), Peter of Bruys rejected the whole apparatus of the church and its sacraments more radically than anybody else in this period had been accused of doing. We have met before and will meet again the denial of the necessity of baptism and of prayers for the dead, of the penitential system and of church-building. The jibes against the liturgy, of no great theological significance, are of a piece with them. So is the hatred of the cross, which increasingly over the past century had become the symbol par excellence of the church militant and triumphant, most obviously in its use by crusaders.

The reason that Peter of Bruys gave for rejecting the eucharist, however, is his alone. It was neither the familiar one of the personal unworthiness of the ministers or the invalidity of their orders nor, apparently, denial of the doctrine of the real presence, a point that Peter the Venerable does not mention in his lengthy and thorough discussion of this issue. Peter of Bruys maintained that Christ shared the Last Supper only with the disciples, and that the words in which he offered himself were for them alone and had no application for later generations. In other words, he denied that Christ created, or intended to create, even a symbolic relationship between his life and any future followers or believers. The contrary belief was and has been of central spiritual importance to almost every tradition and strand even of (from a catholic perspective) the most radically heretical Christians; we will see in the next chapter that by this time some, at least, of those whose apostolic fervour had separated them from the church in the Rhineland had found their own means of catering for it. The position of Peter of Bruys amounted to a root-and-branch rejection not only of the catholic church but also of any idea of a church as a link between Christ and Christians, and between Christians themselves across the generations.

———

The hermits and holy men are generally seen as paving the way for the more systematic and comprehensive reforms that began to be put in place from around 1100, as bishops slowly acquired a new consciousness of their spiritual and pastoral responsibilities and the political and administrative skills to secure the co-operation of the laity in discharging them. Reform came very late to the lands between the Massif Central and the Pyrenees. It was not until well into the twelfth century that rural parishes began to be organised, priests appointed and tithes collected from the laymen who had previously appropriated them, and the services and disciplines of the church, including the regular administration of the sacraments, to be enforced. The success of Henry and Peter of Bruys in the 1120s and '30s shows that the process was not universally welcomed. There is no reason to attribute their influence to the novelty of their teaching. We can say with confidence that they were not theological dualists or subject to any such influence. On the contrary, since what they offered was a simple community-based theology and worship – in which, for example, the old practice of public confession and reconciliation was preferred to that of confession to priests, which the church was developing at this time – there is every reason to suppose that in the eyes of the villagers they appeared as champions of old and familiar ways against the newfangled, disruptive and expensive ones being pressed by the arrogant young clerks from the city. In this context their insistence that church buildings – let alone elaborate furnishings and fittings for them – were unnecessary because God could be worshipped in a field, or anywhere else where a few of the faithful were assembled, is particularly revealing if we pause to recall at whose expense the many hundreds of churches that are the glory of European architecture in this period were raised.

8

SHEEP IN THE MIDST OF WOLVES

Go your ways: behold, I send you forth as a lamb among
wolves. Carry neither purse nor scrip, nor shoes: and salute
no man by the way.

Luke 10: 3–4

At a council at Fritzlar in 1118 Norbert of Xanten was accused of 'claiming that he was entitled to wear the religious habit though he had not
entered the religious life properly, and was living in the world wearing
the skins of sheep and goats'. He replied with an apostolic quotation: 'he
who causeth a sinner to be converted from the error of his ways shall save
his soul from death and shall cover a multitude of sins' (James 5: 20). The
essence of religion, Norbert argued, lay in personal purity – had not John
the Baptist and St Cecilia worn hair shirts? – and in service to others,
visiting widows and children and helping them in their tribulations.[1]

Norbert became one of the most admired preachers of his time and
founder of the spectacularly successful religious order of Premonstratensians, the 'White Canons'. As befitted his high birth – he was probably
related to the German emperor – he had been destined for an eminent
place in the church. He was brought up in the household of Archbishop
Frederick of Cologne, a notable sympathiser of reform, and became at
an early age one of the wealthy and worldly canons of Xanten. In 1110–11

he went with the great expedition to Italy that Henry V mounted for his coronation as emperor. It was intended to secure a settlement of the long-running conflict between empire and papacy, and ended with the arrest of the pope and a number of cardinals. Three years later Norbert was nearly killed by a fall from his horse and resolved to dedicate himself to the religious life. He joined the Black Monks at the abbey of Siegburg but found their way of life insufficiently arduous and returned to Xanten to persuade his fellow canons to share his conversion. When they declined, he sold his goods, gave the money to the poor and embraced the life of a hermit preacher. The accusation at Fritzlar was probably the canons' retaliation for Norbert's criticism of them. Its outcome is unclear, but it was apparently unsatisfactory to Norbert, since he made his way, on foot, to St Gilles-du-Gard, where Pope Gelasius II, in exile after excommunicating the emperor, was happy to grant him permission to preach in the emperor's territories. This he did with the supporting warranty of abstinence so extreme that it killed the three loyal companions who had accompanied him.

Pope Gelasius died soon afterwards, however, and in 1119 Norbert appeared once again at a great church council, at Reims, before the new pope, Calixtus II. His licence to preach was renewed, but only on the condition that he placed himself under the direction of Bishop Bartholomew of Laon, ostensibly to moderate the dangerous rigour of his way of life. Bartholomew persuaded him to found a religious community for his followers in the forest of Prémontré, which was established in 1121. In 1126 Norbert became, reluctantly, archbishop of Magdeburg and narrowly escaped assassination when he tried to reform his cathedral by introducing canons from Prémontré. He became a conspicuous supporter of Innocent II during the papal schism that divided Europe throughout the 1130s, and an influential adviser of the emperor. By the time of his death in 1134 his order numbered more than a hundred houses and had become the principal instrument of reform and of the provision of pastoral services in the German lands.

———

These elementary facts contain a pattern very common among the many religious movements that began around this time under the inspiration of charismatic preachers of the apostolic life. We saw it in the career of Robert of Arbrissel. The success of the preachers in gathering around them devoted and often unruly followers, wandering through the countryside united by a vision of the common life and disenchantment with the existing state of the church, its services and its ministers, presented acute problems even to their admirers. Sooner or later they had to be fitted into the social order, found settled places to live and an orderly way of life, generally in the form of a monastery or religious house. This meant compromise, the acquisition of property and of worldly responsibilities, and the acceptance of hierarchy and authority. The architects of such settlements were seldom the original preachers. Typically the second generation of leaders were sterner, less inspiring figures who enforced rules, secured land and revenues, and established relations with the local clergy and aristocracy – often at the expense of dissension within the community from those who saw all this as a betrayal of the movement and the legacy of the founder.

In Norbert's case the foundation of Prémontré was such a crisis.[2] It was obviously insisted on by the Council of Reims (1119), 'in his own best interests', as it were, as a condition of the preaching that remained his chief activity. Beyond laying down that its rule should be based on that of the Cistercians, including the white (that is, undyed) habit, Norbert seems to have taken little interest in the new foundation, whose numbers grew rapidly, and to which further houses were soon added: there were said to be nearly a hundred of them in the first thirty years. When Norbert was elected to the archbishopric of Magdeburg some of the community wanted to go with him, but most preferred to remain at Prémontré and with Norbert's agreement elected Hugh de Fosses as abbot. It was Hugh who shaped the development of the order, and under him that the White Canons soon accepted the care of parishes, and the tithes and wordly contacts and responsibilities that went with it.

From the outset the bishops saw a distinctive role for the new order as a vehicle of reform and pastoral care. This was bound to be in tension with the ascetic ideal of withdrawal from the world. Norbert enjoined his followers 'to fear the company of men as a fish shuns dry land', but as early as 1121 Archbishop Frederick of Cologne ordered the canons of

Steinfeld, the first Premonstratensian house in his province, to undertake the service of two parishes from a chapel at their gate, where the
laity could come to receive the sacraments. Even more unacceptably,
from an apostolic point of view, he endowed them with the tithes of
two parishes to enable them to do so. Two years later Pope Calixtus II
permitted the canons of Springiersbach to preach, administer the sacraments and visit the sick. Many similar arrangements were made in the
following decades for Premonstratensian houses in Germany and the
Low Countries, though not in France or England. This development
was a source of division not only within the order but also between the
Premonstratensians and other religious, since those who accepted it not
only departed from the strictest understanding of apostolic poverty but
also took over substantial sources of revenue from older institutions,
including cathedral churches and Black Monk monasteries.

Another fundamental departure from Norbert's apostolic legacy followed soon after his death in 1134. His disciples had included women
as well as men, and, like those of several other great evangelists of his
generation his foundation and its many daughter houses were mixed
communities. In the late 1130s the general chapter – the group of
abbots that constituted the ruling body of the order – decreed segregation, which usually meant that the nuns were moved out. Little is
known of the manner in which this policy was carried out – of how, for
example, endowments were divided – but that it became progressively
harsher towards the women is suggested by the removal of the nuns 4
kilometres from Prémontré itself in 1141, and then to Bonneuil, 33 kilometres away, in 1148. Most of the nunneries formed by this separation
soon disappeared. This was part of a general movement against double
communities in these years, largely born of the traditional ascetic sen-
sitivity to sexual temptation so keenly felt by leaders such as Bernard
of Clairvaux.

To many of these apostolic communities banishing all worldly dis-
tinctions of rank, wealth and previous life, including that of gender, was
of fundamental spiritual importance. Further, many husbands and wives
had embraced the new life together and might justly resent enforced
separation. There is another reason for suspecting that segregation
was particularly resisted among the Premonstratensians. All their early

houses were double communities. This corresponded to a distinctive family structure, regarded by modern scholars as characteristic of northern Europe, which had already become apparent in the area where the order was established and experienced its extremely rapid early growth. In the Mediterranean regions, where historically Christian teaching and spirituality had been shaped, households normally comprised several siblings and their spouses, and women were married at puberty to much older men. In northern Francia, the Low Countries and the Rhineland couples were usually more equal in age and married later, when they could afford to set up an independent household. The much greater equality and independence of women that this implies is confirmed by abundant records of property transactions, especially from Cologne, which show that land was held equally by both spouses and inherited by their children of both sexes, and that women regularly appeared in court and in business deals as full participants. The prominence and equality, or near equality, of women in the religious movements of this region, and the willing acceptance of it by their male companions, therefore reflected everyday life and expectations.

———

Bitter struggles over appointments in the church, especially of cathedral canonries, were commonplace in the Rhineland and the Low Countries at least until the 1170s. The wealthy dioceses of Liège and Cologne, like pre-Patarene Milan, were ruled by great noble families who treated the lands and offices of the church as support for their sons and rewards for their followers. Marriage was normal among their higher as well as lower clergy. The bishops of Liège were chosen by an assembly of the cathedral and collegial clergy of the city, the abbots of the diocese, territorial princes and nobles, and even some bourgeois. The archbishops of Cologne were always among the emperor's most powerful supporters and closest advisers, their appointment an issue of the highest political importance and favour. In short, the higher clergy of both cities constituted solid, worldly and conspicuous ruling elites exactly designed to arouse the fury and scorn of the reformers, all the more since they naturally sided with the emperors, and with the imperially appointed anti-popes, against the Roman papacy in the long series of conflicts and schisms that dominated the twelfth century. On the other hand, those who considered themselves reformers were divided, sometimes bitterly, among the adherents of different traditions and understandings of the demands of the apostolic life and the acceptability of compromise with authority in its various aspects.

The reverberations of these conflicts surfaced from time to time in the form of accusations and counter-accusations of heresy, sometimes ending in burnings, whose relation to the actual beliefs and habits of the accused is hard to discern. This was the background to a letter written in 1147 to Bernard of Clairvaux by Eberwin, prior of the Premonstratensian house at Steinfeld, whose establishment had set the pattern for many more. Bernard had just completed a tour of preaching in the Rhineland, best known for its primary purpose of gathering support for the projected Second Crusade. In Cologne, however, he had also turned his attention to reform, and to the morals and lifestyle of the cathedral clergy, whom he denounced with all his usual eloquence, backed up by a slew of miracles. He had particularly attacked the private property that the rule currently followed by the canons permitted, and which he saw as the prime cause of their deviation from their apostolic heritage. Some of Bernard's admirers were anxious for him to return to the lands of the count of Toulouse, to spearhead a continuing campaign against heresy there. Eberwin's letter was ostensibly designed to encourage him to do so by alerting him to the scale of the danger that heresy now presented to the church. It also, however, tactfully implied that over-zealous criticism of the Cologne clergy might have dangers of its own. To this end Eberwin presented a lively account not of one group of heretics but of two, who had come to the attention of the authorities by quarrelling among themselves.[3]

Eberwin's story is that 'a group of heretics was found recently near Cologne, some of whom readily returned to the church', but that two of them – 'one who was called their bishop, with his companion' – refused to do so, defended their views for three days before 'a meeting of clerks and laymen, at which the archbishop and some great nobles were present', and, refusing to recant, were burned at the stake. They described themselves as 'wandering men, fleeing from city to city like sheep in the midst of wolves'. There were also 'other heretics in our area who are always quarrelling with them. It was through their perpetual wrangling and discord that we discovered them.'

Both of these groups claimed to live the apostolic life strictly in accordance with the gospels and the Acts, rejecting every innovation for which they found no warrant there. 'They say that all observances of the church which are not laid down by Christ or by the apostles after him are superstitions.' They were agreed in their contempt for the church and its ministers. As the second group put it,

> the body of Christ is not made on the altar because none of the priests of the church has been consecrated ... the apostolic dignity has been corrupted by involvement in secular affairs, and the throne of St Peter by failing to fight for God as Peter did, has deprived itself of the power of consecration which was given to Peter. Since the church no longer has that power, the archbishops who live in a worldly manner within the church cannot receive it and cannot consecrate others.

This is a stark proclamation of the Donatist position so common among reformers who made the fatal transition from denouncing clerical corruption or immorality and avoiding those guilty of it to holding that the orders and sacraments of such clergy were invalid. 'Thus they empty the church of priests, and condemn the sacraments, except for baptism', says Eberwin. 'Even that must be for adults, and they say that it is conferred by Christ and not by the minister of the sacraments.' Hence, it followed logically enough:

> they do not believe in the intercession of saints, and hold that fasts and other penances which are undertaken because of sin are unnecessary, because whenever the sinner repents all his sins will be forgiven ... They will not admit the existence of the fires of purgatory ... Consequently they condemn the prayers and offerings of the faithful for the dead.

The cult of saints was a sensitive point for both churchmen and heretics. Like every city in Europe, and even more spectacularly than most, Cologne was growing fast. It had become an important rendezvous, a natural point of convergence between the burgeoning markets of the north, from London to Novgorod, and those of the Mediterranean and Byzantine worlds, as well as of neighbouring Flanders and Champagne and the rapidly developing German east. In 1106 the area enclosed by its Roman walls was almost doubled, from 122 to 203 hectares. In 1180 it would double again. Migrants flooded in from the countryside to work the forges that produced widely exported swords and harnesses and the looms whose cloth, though less fine than that of Flanders, was in great demand, and to service the prosperous merchant community. In such conditions the cult of the dead, the penitential Masses, anniversaries and commemorations, the establishment of burial grounds, the veneration of relics, were not simply sources of profit to the clergy, though certainly they were that. They were also means by which a world in flux could find order, by which notables could display their ranks and dignities, neighbourhoods settle their status and assert their solidarities, and rich men find their places at the table, poor men theirs at the gate – and outsiders outside it.

Even change that is useful to many is seldom welcome to all. The extension of the church's services also made its role in the lives of families and communities more intimate. The organisation of burial grounds and the elaboration of services for the dead also made priests, rather than families, mediators between the living and the dead, and controllers of memory. The bones uncovered in vast quantities when a Roman cemetery was disturbed by the extension of the walls in 1106 were acclaimed as those of the princess Ursula, martyred by the Huns on her way to be married to a converted English prince, and the eleven thousand virgin companions who shared her fate. The new cult afforded splendid opportunities for the affirmation of civic pride and inspired many private devotions, but it also provided powerful ammunition for those who derided the booming cult of relics as a source of fraud, superstition and exploitation.

––––––

The spokesmen of Eberwin's first group of heretics insisted above all on their poverty:

We are the poor of Christ, wandering men; fleeing from city to city like sheep in the midst of wolves we suffer persecution with the apostles and martyrs. We lead a holy life, fasting, abstaining [from meat and milk in their diet, and from sex], working and praying by day and night, seeking in these things the necessities of life.

By contrast with the clerics who questioned them, their poverty was not only personal but collective: 'You join house to house and field to field and seek the things of this world. Those who are thought most perfect among you, monks and canons regular, possess things not individually, but in common: nevertheless they do possess all of these things.'

On this rested their claim to be the true followers of the apostolic life, in whom alone the heritage of Christ survived, in contrast to the 'false apostles [who] have corrupted the word of Christ for their own ends, and have led you and your fathers astray'. They went veiled to Mass but made their own communion by consecrating every meal with a recital of the Lord's prayer.

Eberwin does not say what the quarrels that had led to the arrests were about, but he describes somewhat differently the attitudes of the two groups to sexuality, and their forms of baptism. The first, which produced the martyrs, 'have women among them who are – so they say – chaste, widows or virgins, or their wives, alleging that they follow the apostles who permitted them to have women among them'. The second 'hold that all marriage is fornication, unless it is between two virgins, both the man and the woman', implying that on that condition they did not insist absolutely on sexual abstinence. This group insisted on adult baptism to satisfy the requirement that 'He that believeth and is baptised shall be saved.' The first group baptised by a laying-on of hands, not with water but in the fire and the spirit, as described in the gospels and the Acts. The greatest difference, however, as Eberwin saw it, was that the first group, distinguishing between leaders and followers, had a hierarchical organisation, and one that linked it to a wider heretical movement.

As a snapshot of the development of religious dissent in the most advanced parts of northern Europe in the turbulent three-quarters of a century since Gregory VII ascended the throne of St Peter, Eberwin's letter is revealing, if not always precise. The spokesmen for his first group insisted that they alone were the true followers of the apostolic life and emphatically rejected the possession of houses, property or land by monks and canons, even when held in common. This suggests strongly that they were followers of Norbert in his most radical phase, who had rejected the compromises entailed in the acceptance of parish responsibilities and revenues. In other words, they denounced as a betrayal the development in the Premonstratensian movement of which Eberwin himself and his house at Steinfeld had been the first example. The place of women among them shows that they were equally opposed to the separation of women from men and their expulsion from Premonstratensian houses, which had been pushed forward since around 1140. The description of some of these women as wives may have been no more than the truth, for (as Bernold of Constance had observed) it was not uncommon for married couples to join these movements together.

The fate of the losers in struggles like these can hardly be more than guesswork, but the satirist Walter Map, writing in the early 1180s, offers an unexpected hint. Commenting on a group of wandering Flemings condemned as heretics at Oxford in 1165, he remarks that the 'Publicans or Patarines', as he calls them, 'at first had single houses in the villages they lived in ... Men and women live together, but no sons or daughters result from their union.'[4]

The chronicle of Rolduc, another Premonstratensian house and originally a hermit community, albeit written some forty years later, seems to reflect this bitter division in the 1120s and '30s between advocates of the apostolic life and of the revised rule as a context for events at Liège in 1135. It says that some heretics were found who

> while appearing to observe the catholic faith and lead a holy life, denied legitimate matrimony, held that communities of women ought to be available to all, forbade infant baptism and maintained that the prayers of the living are of no use to the souls of the dead. When they could not deny these heresies the people wanted to stone them, but they were frightened and took flight during the night. Three of them were captured and imprisoned, of whom one was burned at the stake, while the other two made a confession of faith and returned to the church.[5]

There is nothing to point so clearly to a specific origin for the second group that Eberwin described at Cologne, except that they do not seem to have been itinerants and that their acceptance of sex in marriage suggests that they were lay people not under specific vows of chastity, or indeed of poverty, who had nevertheless been strongly influenced by reform preaching and anticlerical sentiment.

Eberwin's account raises questions about the evolution of apostolic communities over time, and about the internal development of what was, perhaps, becoming a sect. When the Cologne group was arrested, 'the one who was called their bishop and his companion' not only undertook to defend their beliefs but also

> asked for a day to be fixed on which they might bring forward men from among their followers who were expert in their faith. They promised that if they saw their masters refuted in argument they would be willing to rejoin the church, though otherwise they would rather die than abandon their views.

It does not seem that the masters appeared, but the challenge confirms that this was not an entirely isolated group – and that they were entirely willing to enter into reasonable debate.

Finally, Eberwin describes the form of baptism that this group used:

> Anyone who is baptised among them in this way is called *electus* [chosen], and has power to baptise others who are worthy of it, and to consecrate the body and blood of Christ at his table. But first he must be received by the laying-on of hands from among those whom they call *auditores* [hearers] into the *credentes* [believers]; he may then be present at their prayers until he has proved himself, when they make him an *electus*. They care nothing for our baptism.

He does not make it clear, however, whether he is quoting the heretics directly, as he has done previously, or whether this is his gloss on what they said, based on Augustine's description of the Manichees, whose terminology it uses, and which would have been familiar to Eberwin (as it was to Guibert of Nogent), and the obvious text for him to consult.

Either way, it confirms that the group had evolved a hierarchy and the rituals necessary to sustain and perpetuate itself. How had this come about? Eberwin offered his own conclusion in a peroration designed to confirm Bernard's worst fears:

> Those who were burned told us while they were defending themselves that their heresy had been hidden until now ever since the time of the martyrs, and persisted in Greece and other lands, and these are the heretics who call themselves apostles and have their own pope.

In 1143 a group of monks in Constantinople had been accused of being followers of the Bulgarian Bogomil heresy, which was said (also possibly by derivation from Augustine) to have a hierarchical organisation like that described by Eberwin, and which rejected the sacraments and authority of the church, embraced poverty and, on the basis of a dualist theology, prohibited procreation and the consumption of its products. Burnings and expulsions followed, and it is not impossible that some of the victims found their way to the west, along the well-established trade routes, and ended up in Cologne.

Eberwin, however, does not suggest any such exotic personal origin for the people he describes. His report permits a different conclusion, at least equally probable. It is perfectly consistent with the possibility that these were former Premonstratensians who had left or been expelled from the order as opponents of the changes that had overtaken it since Norbert's early preaching. As uncompromising devotees of the apostolic life driven to an itinerant existence by conflicts over many years with their religious superiors, whom they denounced as corrupt and traitors to the vision of their founder, including Eberwin himself, they would indeed have been members of a wider community. It would be perfectly natural that they should have masters among them – that is, men who had been educated in cathedral schools – whom they regarded as more learned or skilled in debate than themselves, and that leaders had emerged or been chosen (*electi*). It is in no way remarkable that such a group should have evolved ritual forms appropriate to their needs or that they should have looked to the Gospels for the means of doing so. These, after all, were people who had (or believed they had) been instructed by the pope to boycott the services of the regular clergy, the bishops and priests of their regions. What did the pope expect them to do instead? Preachers who had been mandated to issue such instructions must also have been authorised to give assurances that God would not punish those who obeyed them if in consequence their children, or the babies they were carrying, should die unbaptised, or they unshriven, without having received the eucharist or the last rites. That is at least a common reason, if possibly not the only one, why those who were described as heretics believed, or were thought by the clerics who examined them to believe, that the sacraments were not necessary to salvation.

————

Eberwin's letter was written against the background of two sets of religious conflicts, both of long standing, both extremely bitter and in both of which he was directly involved. The Premonstratensians, of one of whose senior houses Eberwin had been superior for more than thirty years, were the spearhead of the reform movement in the Low Countries and the Rhineland that had been launched by the reform papacy. One of its spectacular successes, in which Bernard of Clairvaux had played a prominent part, was the deposition as a simoniac of Bishop Alexander of Liège, at the Council of Pisa in 1135. After Bernard's visit some of the canons of Cologne levelled the same charge against their archbishop, Arnold, at the Council of Reims in 1148. In writing this letter to Bernard, however, Eberwin was reminding him that the unreformed clergy were not the only threat to the church. On the other side, and no less dangerous, were those among the hermit preachers and their followers and converts who believed that the reform had been betrayed by leaders such as Eberwin himself, leaders who had reached an accommodation not with the Alexanders of Liège and the Arnolds of Cologne, to be sure, but with the institutions and the ways of the world that in truly apostolic eyes were little better.

In these circumstances it is easy to imagine or to understand how regularly and vehemently accusations of heresy must have been traded in all directions during this half-century. Another surfaces in a much later source, the Annals of Brauweiler, under the year 1143, but written after 1179:

In this year an accusation was brought against heretics at Cologne, in the church of St Peter, in the presence of Archbishop Arnold. Most of them, captured and in chains, were cleared by the judgement of the water, but the others, conscious of their guilt, tried to escape. Three of them were burned at Bonn in the presence of Count Otto, preferring death to acceptance of the catholic faith.[6]

It is not obvious why some of those accusations ended in trials and burnings while others did not. We do not even know how many, but it does not seem to have been a very large number. We know almost nothing of the many that did not, but it is worth noting that Eberwin does not suggest that the second of his two groups had been persecuted or disciplined.

———

It may now be easier to see why among the many preachers and holy men considered in this and the last three chapters, who shared so much in their ideals, their inspiration, their way of life and their popular appeal, some came to be regarded as heretics while others were and still are venerated as saints of the church. Certainly the difference did not lie simply in loathing of clerical hypocrisy, avarice or corruption, which nobody denounced more passionately than Bernard of Clairvaux. His treatise *De consideratione*, a scathing denunciation of the shortcomings of the papal court, was composed during these same years when he was preaching against heresy and pursuing heretics both in the lands of the count of Toulouse and in the Rhineland. Nor does any of those we have considered seem initially to have been separated from the church by a question of doctrine. There were many, however, whether they ended as heretics or not, whose teachings became more radical in the face of the stubborn worldliness of the old guard. For such men a great deal must have depended on the sympathy and support that they found among their superiors. We have no way of knowing whether a Henry of Lausanne or a Peter of Bruys might have remained in the church if they had been handled as patiently or skilfully as were Norbert of Xanten and Robert of Arbrissel – or whether, when it came to it, Robert and Norbert were temperamentally prepared – as Henry and Peter were not – to submit to ecclesiastical authority.

Without denying the significance of personal qualities and circumstances, however, one crucial issue faced them all. We saw it most clearly in the choice that Robert of Arbrissel had to make between the traditions and values of his family and the world in which he grew up and those that he met as a student in Paris, 'at the time when Gregory VII held the papacy in Rome'. Robert chose the new world and suffered for it, but his sympathy for many of the victims of the changes that he himself was helping to bring about, his insistence on identifying with them, go a long way to explain the continuing ambivalence of his life and of his reputation. This reflects a contradiction in the business of reform that long remained unresolved. It owed both spiritual respectability and intellectual coherence to a universal ideal derived from the neoplatonist spirituality of the late Carolingian schools, expressed in the apostolic life and given programmatic form and Europe-wide circulation by the Gregorian papacy and its agents. But for practical support in local conflicts it appealed to popular indignation arising from grievances that, although very widely shared, were nonetheless to each community peculiarly its own – demands for tithes and payments for services, the fitness of priests for their positions and so on.

In the long run this alliance between the cosmopolitan and the local was bound to run into difficulty, not only or necessarily through a clash of material interests but because reform of its nature was centralising. 'Hang your reforms', says Mr Chichely in George Eliot's *Middlemarch*; 'You never hear of a reform but it means some trick to put in new men.' And not only new men, a subtler critic might have added, but new measures, new ways of doing things, new values. Hildebert of Le Mans and Henry of Lausanne, Bernard of Clairvaux and Peter of Bruys may have been united in their detestation of the entanglement of the church and churchmen in the structures of local power and the abuses that resulted, but the alternatives that they proposed were wholly different. And just as Hildebert the poet and Bernard the mystic were in their very different ways eloquent prophets of a new Jerusalem, so Henry and Peter were formidable spokesmen for the little community. They possessed an articulate and consistent theology, characterised by stark individualism and an uncompromising rejection of large and abstract structures of authority in favour of those firmly rooted in the community itself. They denounced clerical vice and avarice, and repudiated most sources of clerical income and power. They denied the authority of the church fathers to interpret the scriptures and insisted on their own right to do so. They maintained that marriage was a matter for those concerned and not a sacrament of the church. They advocated the baptism of adults, not of infants, and confession in public before the community, not in private to priests. In short, the faith they preached plainly affirmed the values of a world in which small groups of men and women stood together as equals, dependent on each other, suspicious of outsiders and hostile to every external claim on their obedience, allegiance or wealth. They represented a challenge increasingly difficult for the reformers to ignore.

9

MAKING ENEMIES

*The Lord said unto my Lord: Sit thou on my right hand
until I make thine enemies thy footstool.*

Psalm cx

In 1139 Pope Innocent II called the Second Lateran Council in Rome
to celebrate the end of the schism in the church which had arisen from
the circumstances of his elevation to the papacy in 1130. It had been a
bitter conflict, ended only by the death in 1138 of Innocent's rival, the
anti-pope Anacletus II (Peter Pierleone). The validity of the rival claims
had been far from clear, not least because a majority of the cardinals had
voted for Anacletus, who had been backed by King Roger of Sicily and
most of the Roman nobility. Innocent had become in effect an exile
in northern Europe, where he was supported by most of the leading
churchmen of the day, rallied by Bernard of Clairvaux, and through
them by the kings of France and Germany.

In opening the council, Innocent heralded a new phase of centralisation in the church by spelling out the supremacy of Rome in all its affairs,
and particularly in ecclesiastical appointments: 'Rome is the head of the
world', he is reported to have said; 'promotion to ecclesiastical dignity is
received from the Roman pontiff ... and is not legally held without his
permission.'[1] This council marked the end not only of the papal schism

of the 1130s but in many ways of the long period of upheaval, questioning and disorder in the church that had been inaugurated by Henry
III's dismissal of three popes in 1046 and the emergence of the Patarene
movement in Milan in the 1050s. In the decade between its summoning
in 1139 and the conclusion of its no less important (though not formally
ecumenical) sequel, the Council of Reims in 1148, the leaders of the
church settled many of the issues that had been contested so furiously
for so long, and put in place what can be recognised in retrospect as the
essential foundations of the church for the rest of the middle ages, both
governmentally and intellectually. In doing so, they effectively rejected
the most radical implications of the apostolic movement, settling (from
the apostolic point of view) for property rather than poverty, hierarchy
rather than fraternity, institutional authority rather than charisma based
on personal holiness of life. The apostolic ideal was not formally abandoned, of course, but it was firmly excluded as a practical model for the
life of the church in the world. In the eyes of its zealots, therefore, it was
betrayed.

So fateful a set of choices was not arrived at in any moment of clear
or conscious decision. It was the sum of the outcomes of many disputes
and debates, the settlements of many conflicts great and small. In some
of them the issues arose in the form of heresy, or accusations of heresy,
whose resolution helped to define the relationships that would thenceforth obtain within the body Christian and between that body and the
world. The several cases of heresy that arose in the 1140s differed greatly
from one another. Nevertheless, all were part of this wider process of
definition and pulling together of the church, and must be understood
in relation to it.

The twenty-third canon of Lateran II declared that

We condemn and cast out of the church as heretics those who, simulating a kind of religious zeal, reject the sacrament of the body and
blood of the Lord, the baptism of infants, the priesthood, and other
ecclesiastical orders, as well as matrimony, and ordain that they be

restrained by the civil power. For their partisans also we decree the same penalty.

This was a verbatim repetition of a resolution of a council at Toulouse in 1119. There is no reason to think that it was directed against or inspired by any particular heretic or group of heretics on either occasion. Rather, it presaged a considerably more active response to heresy accusations than had hitherto been the case. Between 1139 and 1148 two of the greatest in a stellar generation of scholars and teachers, Peter Abelard and Gilbert de la Porée, were charged with heresy in high-profile public trials; there were burnings in Provence, the Rhineland, the Low Countries and northern France; the two most influential churchmen of the age, Peter the Venerable, abbot of Cluny, and Bernard, abbot of Clairvaux, proclaimed heresy among the people a menace to the church, especially between the Alps and the Pyrenees, and wrote extensively against it; and the Council of Reims in 1148 dealt with at least four cases of heresy of quite different kinds and characters.

In retrospect it looks as though mounting anxiety about a trickle of heresy growing since early in the century ripened during the 1140s into a major preoccupation of the church. The appearance is deceptive. The fear of heresy among the people was not characteristic of early twelfth-century Europe, even though this was everywhere a time of acute political and social instability, of rebellions, risings and assassinations. 'The Catholic faith has fought, and has crushed, conquered and annihilated the blasphemies of the heretics, so that either there are no more heretics or they do not dare to show themselves', wrote Bishop Herbert Losinga of Norwich (1091–1119).[2] The young Guibert of Nogent, growing up in Picardy in the 1080s and '90s, formed, in the words of the latest and most acute study of his thought, 'a view of eleventh-century Europe that sees Christianization as complete, and senses no danger from heretics'.[3] This confidence had been shaken not by Guibert's encounter with the heretic Clement of Bucy but by his contacts with Jewish learning, and with the lively and unruly scholarly and urban communities of Laon and Soissons.

Guibert's younger contemporary Orderic Vitalis wrote sympathetically about the hermit preachers, despite their attacks on the ecclesiastical hierarchy and the traditional style of monasticism practised in his own house at St Evroul, but he had nothing to say about popular heresy or the threat of it. The rising that Henry of Lausanne fomented in Le Mans in 1116, 80 kilometres down the road from St Evroul and the centre of a region in which Orderic was keenly interested, does not rate a mention.

An obvious reason for this lack of widespread concern is that the cases of heresy in the 1120s, '30s, and '40s described in the last three chapters varied greatly in character and context. For the most part they had no connection with each other, and contemporary observers did not suggest that they had. What they had in common was derived from the movement to reform the church itself, from reactions to it and from the divisions that arose between different groups of reformers as to how, and how far, they should compromise with the world and with episcopal authority. Eloquent preachers could always get an enthusiastic hearing for attacks on clerical avarice and immorality, but only between the Loire and the Mediterranean, where Henry of Lausanne and Peter of Bruys, and perhaps others, had built up followings over several years, does it appear that there may have been something resembling a movement of popular heresy.

Even in that case the alarm of the churchmen has a certain air of artificiality. We know nothing of the origins of the expedition to the lands of the count of Toulouse in 1145, but it is not likely that preaching against popular heresy was its only, or even its primary, objective. It was led by a papal legate, Cardinal Alberic of Ostia, not by Bernard. The leading magnate of the region, Count Alphonse Jordan of Toulouse, did not lack rivals eager to stir up trouble (see Map 7, p. 186). As it happened, the activities of Peter of Bruys, and therefore Peter the Venerable's attack on them, drew attention to the eastern half of Alphonse Jordan's territories, where he was locked in rivalry with the count of Barcelona for control of Provence. The western part of his lands, whose overlordship King Louis VII of France, a firm supporter of the papacy through the long years of schism, now claimed by virtue of his marriage to Eleanor, daughter of Duke William IX of Aquitaine, was the focus, in complementary fashion, of Henry's activity and Bernard's preaching. Alphonse Jordan himself gained some political advantage from the 1145 mission, probably by directing its attention against some of the leading citizens of Toulouse, who were asserting the city's independence of his authority at just this time, and certainly by diverting it to Albi, the chief stronghold of his greatest rivals in the region, the family of Trencavel, vicomtes of Béziers.

Henry of Lausanne had been preaching for almost twenty years since he left Le Mans for Aquitaine before he was arrested and brought before the Council of Pisa in 1135, and for up to another ten before Bernard of Clairvaux went in pursuit of him in 1145, announcing his mission in letters, later widely circulated, that painted a lurid picture of a land ravaged by heresy. Peter of Bruys had been active over two decades or more when Peter the Venerable found it necessary to write against him around 1139; his reputation had been sufficient to earn a scathing reference from Peter Abelard (in a book that had itself been burned as heretical in 1121), including the assertion that he was re-baptising his followers.[4] It was, in short, rather late in the day when Bernard and Peter the Venerable issued their clarion calls. Heresy had not hitherto been a major preoccupation of either of them. Although Bernard led the attack in one of the most famous heresy trials of the middle ages, that of Abelard at Sens in 1141, heresy does not figure prominently in his extremely voluminous writings. Against Abelard, as in the Rhineland in 1147 and against Gilbert de la Porée in 1148, the initiative was taken by others, who had particular personal or political interests to pursue against those accused, and called Bernard's attention to real or alleged heresies with, indeed, a well-founded confidence in the vigour of his response. Bernard was not so much a hound of heaven as a blunderbuss that could be relied on to explode with a loud bang when aimed and primed by others.

———

For Peter the Venerable the identification and pursuit of heresy were only one part of a much larger enterprise that came to fulfilment in this decade of the 1140s.[5] His *Against the Petrobrusians* was the first of three treatises, followed in 1143–4 by *Against the Inveterate Obstinacy of the Jews* and in 1148–9, or perhaps 1154, *Against the Sect of the Saracens*. All three groups denied the fundamental propositions of catholic Christianity

– the Holy Trinity, the incarnation of Christ, his resurrection and real presence in the eucharist. Against each of them Peter mounted systematic rebuttals, using the technique of the disputation (*disputatio*) now being perfected in the schools of Paris, where Peter had been a student. A disputation set out the arguments for and against a set of propositions. Its object was to construct a logically complete case by refuting an equally complete set of contrary arguments. Those arguments were often attributed to a real opponent, but if that opponent had not provided a complete account of his position it was up to the disputant to do it for him, to ensure that his own case would be complete in its turn. Thus in rebutting five heresies attributed to Peter of Bruys, Peter the Venerable provided a systematic defence of catholic faith and practice at points crucial in this stage of its development – infant baptism, the building and use of properly consecrated churches, the adoration of the cross, holy communion from the hands of correctly ordained priests, and the penitential system, including offerings and prayers for the dead. The content and structure of *Against the Petrobrusians*, therefore, were determined by the requirements of Peter the Venerable's defence of contemporary catholic teaching rather than by what Peter of Bruys actually taught or believed. For this reason caution is necessary, and it becomes ever more so from the 1140s onwards in weighing statements in academic dissertations and by academically trained masters as evidence of the actual beliefs and practices of the heretics against whom they were ostensibly directed.

Peter the Venerable did not only debate the enemies of Christ. He demonised them. If Muslims rejected his appeal to convert, he said, they would show themselves to be, like the Jews, incapable of reason and the willing instruments of the Devil. He is deservedly remembered for commissioning the first translation of the Koran into Latin, arguing that reasoned rebuttal would be a better response to Islam than crusading – but in his introduction to the translation he claimed, in the most abusive terms, that Mohammed had been a vicious, devious and illiterate Arab who attained power and wealth by bloodshed and trickery, and constructed his heresy with the help of Nestorian heretics and Jews. In the same way, even the title of the treatise – not just 'Against the Jews', but against their 'inveterate obstinacy' – implicitly classified Jews as heretics, who were defined by pertinacity in adhering to beliefs that they knew to be contrary to catholic teaching. In this Peter complemented the teaching of Anselm of Laon that the Jews had known Christ to be the son of God when they crucified him. Earlier scholars such as Abelard and Gilbert Crispin had debated with Jews, in their writings and perhaps occasionally in reality, with a measure of scholarly curiosity and detachment. Peter's tone, and references to Jews in his other writings, make him the successor rather of Anselm of Laon and Guibert of Nogent. He was not only fundamentally opposed to Judaism intellectually, as of course Abelard and Gilbert Crispin had been, but also bitterly hostile to Jews personally and emotionally. He made much play, for example, with the suggestion that holy images and objects such as chalices, left with Jews as security for loans, were kept by them in privies and subjected to the foulest indignities. This was to become a recurrent motif of the anti-Semitism of the later twelfth century and beyond.

Professed Christians who would not acknowledge the authority of the church might occasionally undermine its popular support but had not hitherto aroused widespread anxiety. By treating Jews and Muslims as heretics, Peter the Venerable added to the list two enemies immeasurably more formidable than Tanchelm or Peter of Bruys. Jews denied fundamental propositions of catholic Christianity with the power and cogency of a much more ancient and sophisticated culture that Christians could not ignore. Christians were frequently at war with Muslims in Spain and the Middle East, but scholars who visited those lands encountered a civilisation whose prosperity and learning far eclipsed their own: the library at Córdoba had 100,000 volumes when in the Christian west a hundred amounted to a notable collection. Even more disconcertingly, Muslims were prosperous and influential subjects of the wealthiest and most glamorous monarch in Latin Christendom, Roger II of Sicily (d. 1153), prominent at his court and in his administration.

Peter the Venerable, like others of his generation in the monasteries and cathedral schools, was a casualty of the social revolution that was reshaping western society. As younger sons, they had had to give up their share of the estates to provide secure foundations for the family dynasties led by their elder brothers. What remained to them, apart from the spiritual consolations of the celibate life, was the task of shaping and defining a moral community to replace (though also to reinforce) the community of blood represented by those dynasties. That meant winning and securing the cultural hegemony on which the ability to confer legitimacy, and with it access to office and influence, must rest. Their only weapon was faith – a faith to be fought for, cherished as a gift, sustained by continual struggle, witnessed by hardship and sacrifice, as the writers of the twelfth century constantly insisted. Their sacrifice was well rewarded. In a society defined by faith the power of defining the faith itself was the key to every door.

———

It would be hard to decide which of Peter the Venerable's three targets in fact presented the smallest danger to Christian society in his time, for there was never the slightest possibility that the church would be overthrown by any of them. But in combination they gave him the means to define Latin Christendom with a new clarity by describing its enemies, though they had to be, if not invented, at any rate greatly magnified and reshaped for the purpose. In implying in *Against the Petrobrusians* that danger lurked among the common people, however, Peter struck a resonant chord. For four or five generations now, in the more prosperous parts of Europe, the systematic exploitation of agrarian wealth had become ever more harsh to the cultivators, while the increasing surplus that it generated supported the rapid growth of the towns and the conspicuous affluence of the privileged. The labour of the poor sustained a new variety of specialised activities, including most obviously teaching and learning, and all the arts and crafts associated with the building of the magnificent churches of this epoch, whose cost and splendour were one of the most regular grievances of those accused of preaching heresy. The tensions arising from rapid economic growth and the consequent widening of social differences were manifested not only in the widespread anticlerical unrest for which the language of religious reform provided expression but also in many revolts and rebellions, both in the towns and in the countryside. They were for the most part easily and ruthlessly suppressed, for in most conditions their desperate protagonists were helpless against armoured, mounted and highly trained knights.

Nevertheless, they were enough to prevent the mighty from always sleeping easily in their beds, as is vividly illustrated by the well-known manuscript illumination of the nightmare in which Henry I of England was assailed by peasants demanding justice.

Areas that had not yet experienced the upheavals of agrarian transformation and ecclesiastical reform – broadly speaking, the mountainous and the border regions – were also sources of unease. The stereotyping process was applied not only to heretics, Jews and Muslims but also to anybody from places that failed to conform to the mid-twelfth century's conception of a well-ordered society. In these decades we begin to be told by English chroniclers that Scotsmen wore kilts, Irishmen had tails and Welshmen were inveterate and incestuous liars. Another such region was the vast area between the Loire and the Mediterranean, which was also surrounded by ambitious rulers with more or less plausible claims to dominate it. What Bernard of Clairvaux took for the consequences of heresy there – 'churches without people, people without priests, and holy days deprived of their solemnities' – was, for the most part, simply the absence of the ecclesiastical developments that had taken place over the last century or so in areas he knew better. But in labelling this a land pervaded by heresy, 'in need of a great work of preaching', Bernard laid foundations that would be built on from the 1160s onwards, first by Henry II of England and later by the papacy and the French monarchy, to justify its conquest and subjugation.

————

The council convened by Pope Eugenius III at Reims in 1148, attended according to one estimate by 1,100 archbishops, bishops and abbots, presented an imposing image of the reordered and reinvigorated church. An important part of its business was to restate the measures of its predecessors relating to clerical discipline. The only note of dissension, it seems, was from a section of the German clergy, led by Rainhald of Dassel, soon to become a *bête noire* for reformers of every kind, who objected to the banning of furs for the clergy.[6] A notable reinforcement of the decrees against clerical marriage and concubinage insisted that marriages that had already taken place should be dissolved. This was to be applied not only to all those in holy orders of any kind ('even nuns') but also to those who had given up, or been removed from, their positions in the church and returned to the world. It is unlikely that the reiteration of these measures increased their effectiveness, but it served the purpose of the reformers in 'sending a message' (as their twenty-first-century counterparts like to put it) that the clergy was a separate order of society, and set firmly apart from the laity.

The conceptual basis of the distinction between clergy and laity, perhaps in the long run the most important result of the papal reform though by no means the unanimous intention of reformers, was also greatly clarified in the 1140s. The idea of ordination now came to designate a ritual in which an individual was permanently endowed with the power of conferring the sacraments, rather than simply being appointed to carry out certain functions in the community. That such power could not be vested in women or laymen was not ancient or firmly established doctrine. It emerged in the first decades of the twelfth century. Gratian of Bologna, who completed his authoritative compilation of canon law around 1140, gave it only as his personal opinion (an unusual indulgence for him), not as the authoritative ruling of the fathers and councils of the church, that 'women cannot be admitted to the priesthood nor even to the diaconate'. Yet there were many references to women deacons in the records of the early church. Followers of Anselm of Laon said that only heretics had ever held that this meant they had been ordained, but Peter Abelard disagreed. Abelard also said, citing other distinguished masters in his support, that in celebrating the Mass the words of consecration themselves were sufficient, regardless of who said them. Such a view threatened both to leave the way open for women to act as ministers and to blur the developing distinction between clergy and laity.[7] As we saw in the last chapter, this was one of the bitterest points of contention among the Premonstratensians between those who accepted episcopal discipline and the cure of parishes and the radicals who insisted on sticking to their original vision of the apostolic life. Eberwin of Steinfeld's accusation that 'these apostles of Satan have women among them who are – so they say – chaste, widows or virgins, or their wives, both among the believers and among the ministers' was regularly and often accurately levelled against dissenting groups. It was far from being an instance of heretical innovation.

The contrasting ways in which the Council of Reims dealt with two cases of heresy illustrates the implications of these developments. Eon (or Eudo) *de Stella* was a layman from Brittany who reportedly set up his own church, celebrating the Mass and ordaining bishops and archbishops from among his followers (or, in another version, designating them as angels or apostles). He claimed to be the son of God, convinced that the concluding words of the canon of the Mass, *per eundem dominum nostrum* ('through Our Lord himself') referred to him.[8] A very much later account of his trial, by William of Newburgh, writing in the 1190s, claimed that when the pope asked Eon to identify himself he replied, 'I am Eon, who will come to judge the quick and the dead.' 'In his hand', William continued,

> he held an oddly shaped stick, whose upper part was forked. Asked why he carried it he said, 'this is a most wonderful thing. When the stick is held as you see it now, with two points towards heaven, God possesses two parts of the world, leaving the third part to me. But if I hold the stick so that the two points which are now uppermost point towards the ground, and the lower part, which has only one point, towards the sky, I keep two parts of the world for myself and relinquish one to God.'

The council dissolved in laughter and, recognising Eon as a lunatic – correctly, for to a modern psychiatrist this is a textbook description of paranoid schizophrenia – ordered him to be kept in custody. He died soon afterwards.

It is difficult to know what to make of Eon. The council was obviously right in declining to take him seriously as a religious figure, and the bishop who brought him before it insisted that he should not be deprived of life or limb, presumably on the grounds of his madness. Yet several contemporary though fragmentary reports agree that Eon had attracted considerable support in Brittany, an example of the capacity even, or perhaps especially, of very eccentric preachers to win devoted followers among humble people. He may have been assisted by the fact that the later 1140s was a time of acute famine. Eon was alleged to have harrassed monasteries, which stored large quantities of food collected as tithes, and to have fed his followers, 'though not with true and solid food, but with food made of air', William of Newburgh insisted. William also says, though it is not mentioned by the more strictly contemporary sources, that some of Eon's followers who refused to repudiate his teaching and the ranks that he had conferred on them were burned at the stake. William does not say where or when these burnings took place, or whether it was on the authority of the council or of the Breton bishops.

––––––––

Gilbert de la Porée, the most celebrated master of the day and recently promoted to the bishopric of Poitiers, could hardly offer a greater contrast to Eon. He was accused by two of his archdeacons, who got Bernard of Clairvaux to take up the case, as he had done against Peter Abelard at Sens in 1141. Abelard's earlier trial at Soissons in 1121 and the eleventh-century trials of Berengar of Tours had been great public events before the assembled magnates of the kingdom, lay and ecclesiastical. These confrontations were inspired at one level by the great question of how far the issues of theology and the mysteries of the faith were to be subjected to the rumbustious and sceptical questioning of the dialectical method of the schools, as opposed to the authoritative exposition *ex cathedra* of the monastic tradition and of old-fashioned masters such as Anselm of Laon and William of Champeaux. But they were also episodes in the political struggles of the great men who, as patrons of the scholars involved, were implicitly threatened when their protégés were accused of heresy. Now, however, the character of these occasions was changing, reflecting a growing reluctance among churchmen to allow the mysteries of the faith to be debated before laymen, let alone decided by them. The result in 1141 had been calamitous for Abelard, the most daring and enormously popular exponent of the dialectic, who went to Sens anticipating an academic disputation in which he had no equal and found himself facing a trial in which Bernard had rigged the jury the night before. Rather than submit to certain conviction, Abelard had halted the proceedings by appealing to Rome. He set out immediately to defend himself at the papal court but was preceded by a storm of letters from Bernard urging the pope and cardinals to have no truck with him. He got no further than Cluny, where he passed the remaining year or so of his life under a vow of silence.

The outcome of Gilbert's trial was very different. It opened in Paris but after several days of discussion adjourned to Reims, where all those involved were due to attend the council. After further prolonged debate Gilbert was able to rally the cardinals to his defence, largely because it was suspected that Bernard was trying once again to prejudice the case in advance. Gilbert succeeded in rebutting the charges and disowned the book in which heretical views had been discovered by his accusers. This was a great triumph for Gilbert and the Parisian masters, and a great reverse for Bernard. It was the last time a noted master was held to account in this way before a public assembly of clerks and laymen. Henceforth, though a number of steps remained to be taken before the independence of the schools from external authority was formally established, it was effectively left to the masters themselves to regulate orthodoxy in their teaching and speculation. This was the beginning of the cherished European tradition of academic freedom. Its corollary, however, was that the distinction made by modern scholars between 'learned' and 'popular' heresy, until this time so thoroughly blurred as to be effectively meaningless, now became a real one. The way was opened for the rapid development of clerical ideas and expectations about heresy among the laity, and of measures for dealing with it.

The Council of Reims itself set that development in train with a canon against heretics and their protectors. It was intended for the remaining followers of Henry of Lausanne and Peter of Bruys, as its reference to 'heresiarchs and their followers in Gascony and Provence' makes clear, but it broke with precedent in neither naming them nor making any reference to the content or nature of their teaching and practice, thus leaving its provisions open for general application. Reflecting the character of the support that Henry at least had attracted, and perhaps more importantly what had enabled both men to flourish apparently unhindered for so long, it was specifically framed to deprive the heretics of the protection of the locally powerful, including the knights who had 'hated clerks and enjoyed Henry's jokes'. Those who embraced these unspecified errors were to be excommunicated, and 'the celebration of the holy offices in their lands forbidden'.

———

On 15 July 1148, on his way back from Reims, Eugenius III issued a bull forbidding the Roman clergy, on pain of the loss of their benefices and offices, to have anything to do with Arnold of Brescia, who had

> publicly denounced the cardinals, saying that their college, by its pride, avarice, hypocrisy and manifold shame was not the church of God but a place of business and a den of thieves, which took the place of the scribes and Pharisees amongst Christian peoples.

The pope himself, Arnold continued, in John of Salisbury's summary,

> was not what he professed to be – an apostolic man and shepherd of souls –but a man of blood who maintained his authority by fire and sword, a tormentor of churches and oppressor of the innocent, who did nothing in the world save gratify his lust and empty other men's coffers to fill his own.[9]

Wherever he went, at least since 1138, Arnold of Brescia had been making trouble, but he was no ordinary troublemaker. A well-educated son of the minor nobility of his city, he seems almost a throwback to the heroic age of reform, the days of Peter Damiani and Ariald of Milan. Brescia, the second city of Lombardy (after Milan), had been one of the main centres of Patarene activity since the Lateran Council of 1059 had outlawed simony and clerical marriage. In response, most of the Lombard bishops

> since they had received large sums of money from priests and deacons living in concubinage, concealed the pope's decrees, with one exception, namely the bishop of Brescia. On arrival in Brescia, after publicly reading out the pope's decrees, he was beaten by the clergy and almost killed. This event served in no small way to promote the growth of

the Pataria. For not only in Brescia but also in Cremona and Piacenza and in all the other provinces many people abstained from the communion of priests who lived in concubinage.[10]

Brescia's subsequent history up to Arnold's time is obscure, but it is clear that continuing conflict over religious reform was inextricably and perhaps indistinguishably linked to the bitter civil divisions that led to the emergence of the commune. Several bishops were deposed during that period, and so in the 1130s were several consuls, including two (at least) who were described as 'hypocrites and heretics'.[11] In an echo of Henry of Lausanne's stay in Le Mans in 1116, Arnold, who had become superior of one of Brescia's religious houses, 'so swayed the minds of the citizens when the bishop was absent on a short visit to Rome [in 1138] that they would scarcely open their gates to the bishop on his return', with the result that he was expelled from the city with his followers by Bishop Manfred, and his exile confirmed by Pope Innocent II.

After his expulsion Arnold went to Paris, where 'he became a disciple of Peter Abelard, and together with Master Hyacinth, who is now a cardinal, zealously fostered his cause against the abbot of Clairvaux'. Hyacinth Boboni, like Cardinal Guido de Castello, who also protected Arnold a few years later, belonged to one of the Roman noble families who had taken to sending their sons to Paris to finish their education before embarking on a high ecclesiastical career – to good effect in these cases, for they both became popes, Guido as Celestine II and Hyacinth as Celestine III. It may be that Arnold had been meant for the same path. After Abelard's fall in 1141 Arnold tried to teach in his place but secured only a handful of poor students, which suggests that his flair was evangelical rather than intellectual. He soon attracted the attention of Bernard of Clairvaux, who used his connections at the royal court to have Arnold expelled from France. He went to Zurich, where he won the approval of one of the emperor's closest counsellors, Count Ulrich of Lenzburg, and of two prominent local lords, counts Rudolf of Ravensburg and Eberhard of Bodmen. Zurich was in the diocese of Constance, which had been the recipient of some of Gregory VII's most incendiary exhortations to popular action against the bishop and local clergy, but the papacy had now become the defender of theocratic politics and the accumulation of ecclesiastical property. Zurich was also, though nothing like so advanced as its Lombard counterparts, a developing urban community which would later find itself in sharp conflict with the territorial aristocracy. That Arnold preached there for some time without arousing the hostility of the latter suggests that his message was religious rather than political. The reform of the clergy, and especially the married clergy, was the object of a papal mission to Bohemia in 1143, led by Cardinal Guido and accompanied by Arnold, to the fury of Bernard of Clairvaux.

Guido's succession to Innocent II in September 1143, as Celestine II, is the most likely reason for Arnold's reconciliation to the Roman papacy. Celestine died less than six months later. His successor, Lucius II, was confronted by a republican government which had taken control of the city. This was the latest stage of the determined struggle of some factions among the Roman aristocracy to maintain their grip on the city. If they could not do it through control of the papacy, the alternative was to revive Rome's ancient institutions, declaring a republic under the leadership of a restored senate. Lucius died in February 1145, allegedly from a wound received when he led an armed attack on its headquarters, the Capitol. Since Arnold immediately made his submission to Lucius's successor, Eugenius III, and embarked at his direction on a lengthy penance in the holy places of the city, he can hardly have played much part in these events, but that was soon to change. The deal that Eugenius made with the Romans to secure his succession quickly broke down, and within a year the pope had to flee the city. By 1148 Arnold's removal from Rome had become an absolute requirement of Eugenius's policy, and for the remainder of his pontificate he regarded Arnold as his greatest enemy in the city. So did his two successors. When the emperor Frederick Barbarossa chose to make peace with Hadrian IV in 1155, he signalled his amicable intentions by delivering Arnold, who had been captured by his troops, to the Prefect of Rome, in effect a papal functionary. He was condemned as schismatic by an ecclesiastical tribunal, returned to the prefect for punishment and sentenced to be hanged. On the scaffold he refused to abjure his sins or to make confession, saying that he believed that what he had taught was good and true and that he was not afraid to die for it. He knelt with raised arms to make his last prayer in silence.

His body was burned and his ashes thrown in the Tiber, to prevent him from becoming the object of a cult.

The fact that Arnold lived in a period not only of intense political conflict in Italy (with its accompanying miseries) but also at a time of rapid social change and increasing distance between rich and poor, and between clergy and people, helps to explain his ability to attract and maintain a popular following. 'He had disciples known as the heretical sect of the Lombards', John of Salisbury tells us, 'who imitated his austerities and won favour with the populace through outward decency and austerity of life, but found their chief supporters amongst pious women.' Their name, and Arnold's, persisted and would continue to be associated with pious dissent among the Italian laity, especially among the poor. At the bitter siege of Crema by the emperor Frederick Barbarossa in 1159 'a great gang of the poor and indigent' who did their best to hinder the attackers by pelting them with stones and rocks 'were derisorily known as the sons of Arnold'.[12]

The attempt to extinguish Arnold's memory was a hopeless failure. When Garibaldi overthrew the papal state in 1861, his triumph was celebrated by cries and posters that hailed 'The Pope no longer a king! The liberal clergy! Arnold of Brescia!' and as a hero of the Risorgimento Arnold has many statues in modern Italy, including one in his native city. To his contemporaries, however, he was not a political agitator or a champion of communal liberties but a prophet and a man of God. That is why a deep uneasiness pervades the records of his life and death. He was condemned, said Walter Map, no sympathiser with heretics, 'uncharged, undefended and in his absence'. According to a poet close to the court, even the ruthless and haughty Barbarossa 'lamented his death, but too late'.[13] His integrity, his austerity, his devotion and his idealism were undeniable. John of Salisbury says that he 'had mortified his flesh with fasting and coarse raiment: [he] was of keen intelligence, persevering in his study of the scriptures, eloquent in speech, and a vehement preacher against the vanities of the world.' Even his most furious enemy, Bernard of Clairvaux, who had not hesitated to exploit the personal lapses of many who aroused his wrath, including Peter Abelard and Henry of Lausanne, called Arnold 'a man whom I could wish was as praiseworthy for his doctrine as for his way of life', 'whose life is as sweet as honey and whose doctrine is as bitter as poison'. Yet although he flayed Arnold with his most extravagant invective for supporting Abelard, Bernard did not call him a heretic. That he denounced him, even in the aftermath of the Council of Sens, only as a schismatic (that is, as having caused division in the church but not as doctrinally in error) is compelling evidence that Arnold was not a heretic and that he was a sound and skilful enough theologian, and unimpeachable enough in his life and reputation, to be proof against the accusation. Wherein, then, lay the bitterness of his doctrine?

The answer to that question was terrifyingly clear. As John of Salisbury put it,

> He said things that were entirely consistent with the law accepted by Christian people, but not at all with the life they led. To the bishops he was merciless on account of their avarice and filthy lucre; most of all because of stains on their personal lives, and their striving to build the church of God in blood.

Many before him had said that the enjoyment of wealth and the exercise of temporal power by the church were unapostolic. Arnold did not shrink from spelling out the implications logically and in full, regardless of the practical consequences. When the Romans offered the imperial crown to Conrad III in 1148, they urged him, in words either written or inspired by Arnold, to take control of papal elections 'so that priests cannot make war and murder in the world. It is not permitted to them to bear the sword or the cup, but to preach, to affirm their preaching by good works, and not to cause war or strife in the world.'

A few years later a letter to Frederick Barbarossa written on behalf of the city by Arnold himself or a close follower claimed that

> the lie, the heretical fable which holds that Constantine simoniacally granted imperial property to [Pope] Sylvester I* is seen through in Rome so universally that the hirelings and whores confute the most

_____
*The reference is to the 'Donation of Constantine' to the church of extensive territories in Italy, the foundation of the temporal power of the papacy; it was indeed shown to be a forgery by Lorenzo Valla in 1440.

learned in argument upon it, and the so-called Apostolic and his cardinals dare not show their faces in the city for shame.

The church would be cleansed only when papal power was replaced by
the imperial authority that the Romans alone could legitimately confer.

As with many radical thinkers, Arnold's principal achievement was
to unite his enemies. However bitterly the pope, the emperor and the
Roman nobles might quarrel among themselves, they knew that in the
end they were locked together in a painfully constructed social, political and ecclesiastical order. The Roman nobles could no more afford
to abandon the wealth and power that accrued to them through their
close interconnections with the church than the church could give up
the resources indispensable to its mission in the world, or the emperor
place his crown at the disposal of the restless and venal citizens of a single
city. Frederick Barbarossa's uncle and biographer Otto, bishop of Freising, described Arnold with the rhetorical bluster of a seasoned politician
faced by arguments too near the bone to be directly confronted, calling
him 'a wolf in sheep's clothing [who] entered the city under the guise
of religion and inflamed to violence the minds of the simple people'.
More thoughtful observers were not so sure. Throughout his life Arnold
won admirers and supporters among the eminent as well as among the
humble. They included, as we have seen, two future popes and perhaps
Peter Abelard (the teacher of all three), who himself maintained that the
power of binding and loosing resided only in those bishops who were
worthy successors of the apostles.[103]

John of Salisbury was among the finest scholars of the age, an intimate of the English pope Hadrian IV and later one of Thomas Becket's
most loyal companions and supporters. His strikingly balanced and cau-
tious account of Arnold, although written after his arrest and death,
makes no mention of those events, or of Hadrian's part in them. John
gives his recital of Arnold's virtues as fact, of his faults as hearsay: 'he was
reputed [ut aiunt] to be factious and a leader of schism, who wherever he
lived prevented the citizens from living at peace with the clergy.' Unwa-
vering proponent of papal authority though he was, John did not think
that the questions that Arnold had raised were easily dismissed.

Part Two

THE DOGS OF WAR

EXPOSED TO CONTUMELY
AND PERSECUTION

Anyone prominent in affairs can always see when a man may
steal a horse and when a man may not look over a hedge.
Anthony Trollope, *Phineas Redux*, Chapter xliv

The burning at Cologne in 1163 with which we began was not an isolated event. The city's religious divisions had not diminished since the 1140s. The social differentiation that helped to make the area so lively a forum of dissension intensified as commercial growth continued more rapidly than ever and trading links became ever more extensive. The message of the Patarene papacy still reverberated. One of those whose enthusiasm for it got him into trouble was a parish priest named Albero, of the nearby village of Mercke, who certainly trod the boundary of heresy and may have crossed it. A pamphlet was written against his errors in the early 1160s by a monk of the Cistercian abbey of Altenberg, of which Albero's parish was a dependency.[1] Albero had been convicted of a series of errors that followed from the proposition that the Mass was invalid if the hands that performed it were unclean. The prayers of the corrupt priest, he had argued, would not be of assistance to the dead. In these depraved times the elevation of the host at the altar was surrounded more often by legions of demons than of angels. The sacrament would be valid only if those who received it did not know of the priest's depravity. That view, in the eyes of the church, was correct in relation to the validity of the priest's orders but heretical if applied, as apparently it was by Albero, to his morals.

Albero was not a simple parish priest, for he had developed his views not only from the gospels but also from the legislation of the popes, and especially the reformers Nicholas II, Alexander II and Gregory VII. We know nothing else about him except that his personal habits commanded the respect of his parishioners and lent weight to his dangerous opinions. He had been prepared, after his conviction, to put them to the test of ordeal by fire, which suggests some confidence in the support of the community.

Nothing had changed in the city itself to reassure doubters. It had a new archbishop in Rainhald of Dassel, whom we met at Reims insisting on his right to wear furs. Chancellor to the emperor Frederick Barbarossa since 1155, one of the richest and most powerful men in the empire, and one of the worldliest, he had been 'elected' archbishop in 1159 but was not consecrated until 1164. This was because he did not want to receive his office from a disputed pope, though he was himself an architect of the new and deep papal schism that had followed the death of Hadrian IV in 1159. So he did not come to Cologne until 1164, but he was already active in its affairs. His religious interests were slight but included a keen appreciation of the value of relics – in his case, of their political rather than their commercial value. One of his first acts as archbishop was to order fresh excavations at the site identified in 1106 as the burial place of St Ursula and the eleven thousand virgins. More bones were uncovered, in enormous numbers. Any scoffers so coarse as to attribute the fresh campaign to depletion of the first batch of relics by the briskness with which they had been traded were amply rebutted, and the pious excavators spared any doubts as to the authenticity of the new supply, by the fact that they were all neatly labelled with the names and ranks of the victims. Who but a heretic could doubt so plain a divine endorsement?

According to the earliest account of the 1163 trial, that of Dietrich of Deutz, the victims 'were condemned and excommunicated by the clergy and handed over to the judges and people of the city'.[2] This procedure conformed more precisely to canon law than that described by Eberwin in 1147, distinguishing clearly between the church court, which determined the guilt of the accused, and the civil one, which, sitting in the regular meeting place of the city council (*domus meliorum*), not on church premises, passed the sentence and carried it out. Since the archbishop was also the prince, both courts were presided over by his officers, but in practice they were usually absent, and by the middle of the century their deputies in the lay court would probably have been burghers. The choice of the site near the Jewish cemetery for the burnings was symptomatic of the growing tendency to associate all who were outside the church with one another. Dietrich's account neither confirms nor contradicts the assertion of the thirteenth-century version of the story that the heretics were newcomers to the city.

Dietrich's description of these people as 'Catafrigians or Cathars' indicates that the source of his information was Eckbert, of the Benedictine abbey of Schönau. Eckbert, who was writing his *Thirteen Sermons against the Cathars* at this time, had worked with Dietrich to publicise the revised version of the St Ursula legend called for by the recent relic discoveries. After being a student in Paris in the early 1140s, and a friend of Rainhald of Dassel, Eckbert became a canon of St Cassius in Bonn. He stepped aside from this path to high office in the church to become a monk at Schönau in 1155, and in effect secretary and interpreter to the outside world of his sister Elizabeth, a nun in that house, who had a growing reputation as a visionary. It was in this capacity that he described and circulated revelations of his sister's vindicating the authenticity of the newly discovered relics, though Elizabeth herself was deeply uncomfortable about them.

Eckbert's *Thirteen Sermons* were dedicated to Rainhald of Dassel (who died in 1167) 'for old acquaintance's sake and so that if any of these heretics happen to be examined before you, you will be provided with the means of stopping their evil mouths, and of strengthening the wavering souls of gullible men who have been deceived by their dreadful words'.[3] He mentions the Cologne trial as a recent event but says that the main source of his knowledge of the heretics is that 'when I was a canon at Bonn my friend Bertolf and I often used to argue with these people, and listen carefully to their opinions and arguments, and we also learned much from those who had left their groups.' The heresies that he attacks are by now familiar: condemnation of matrimony and of meat-eating, denial of infant baptism, and of the use of water in baptism, of purgatory, the penitential system and the cult of the dead, the eucharist and the validity of priestly orders. All of this had been described by Eberwin of Steinfeld and had grown from the history of the apostolic movement and of reform preaching in the region, its divisions and the dissensions and reactions that it evoked.

Eckbert adds, however, three claims that were new, that would be repeated regularly henceforth and that would be highly influential in shaping understanding of heresy and heretics both in the war on heresy of the next century and a half, and among historians in modern times. First, all these heretics are part of a single, widely disseminated sect: 'Among us in Germany they are called *Cathars*, in Flanders *Piphles*, and in France *Tisserands*, because of their connection with weaving.' Second, they are extremely secretive, 'hidden men, perverted and perverting, who have lain concealed through the ages, [and] have secretly corrupted the Christian faith of many foolish and simple men, so that they have multiplied in every land and the church is now greatly endangered by the foul poison which flows against it on every side'; their gravest heresies are concealed even from their own followers. Third, these include the beliefs 'that all flesh is made by the devil', that Christ 'was not truly born of the Virgin, and did not truly have human flesh, but a kind of simulated flesh; [and] that he did not rise from the dead, but simulated death and resurrection' and that 'human souls are apostate spirits which were expelled from heaven at the creation of the world; in human bodies they can come to deserve salvation through good works, but only if they belong to this sect.'

Eckbert is not an ideal witness. We have already seen good reason for suspecting him on other occasions – unless he was quite remarkably gullible or imaginative – of being ready to manipulate or even to create information in the interests of his patron Rainhald of Dassel, whose record, personality and current activities must have appalled and scandalised Cologne's apostolic dissenters. He acknowledges that the heretics 'say that they live the apostolic life' and mentions three different groups, each with its own leader: 'the followers of Hartwin', 'Arnold and his comrades' and 'Dietrich and his companions'. If these are the Arnold and Dietrich who were burned in 1163, as seems likely (although they are not uncommon names), it follows that the victims on that occasion belonged to more than one sect. According to Eckbert, the heretics he described differed among themselves on points of doctrine as well as in leadership. 'They hold various opinions about baptism', for instance, and 'there are indeed some among them who denounce and condemn marriage, and promise eternal damnation to those who remain in the married life until their death. Others approve of marriage between those of their number who come together as virgins.'

This last had been one of the key differences noted by Eberwin of Steinfeld between the two groups of heretics whose public disputes had attracted the attention of the authorities in 1145. Eckbert, therefore, had encountered a number of dissenting groups, including one or both of those described by Eberwin, and, while acknowledging differences between them, merged them in his description into a single sect.

This conflation of different, and sometimes mutually hostile, dissenting groups into a single heresy suggests that Eckbert's *Sermons* were only incidentally directed against the people he had encountered in Bonn and Cologne, who offered vivid illustrative material for what he intended to say in any case. This was a conventional rhetorical device. More importantly, by the 1140s, when Eckbert was a student there, the masters of Paris were perfecting the technique of expounding the essentials of the catholic faith by systematically rebutting propositions contrary to them, which were often placed in the mouths of fictitious opponents. A recent analysis of Eckbert's *Thirteen Sermons* demonstrates that this is just what he was doing.[4] His 'replies' to the heresies he refers to say almost nothing about how these heresies were defended by their alleged proponents. They simply serve as pegs for Eckbert to set out his own theological positions, with a fine display of his biblical and patristic learning and his prowess in debate. He is eager to deploy that learning to make up for the deficiencies in the heretics' account of themselves, and to show what a grave danger they presented: 'It should be known, and not kept from the ears of the common people, that this sect with which we are concerned undoubtedly owes its origin to the heresiarch Mani, whose teaching was poisonous and accursed, rooted in an evil people.' To this end he attached to his book an appendix of selections from the anti-Manichaean writings of Augustine of Hippo, 'so that my readers can understand the heresy properly from the beginning'.

This was not a new idea. Guibert of Nogent, for instance, had turned to Augustine for the same reason. Eckbert, however, went further than any of his predecessors in using Augustine to build an account of teachings and practices based on the belief that the material world was the creation of an evil deity, including the bodies in which he had imprisoned the souls of apostate or captive spirits. In doing so, he confused two of the sects that Augustine had described: the Novatians, also known in Augustine's time as *Cathari*, who were particularly obsessed with sexual purity and rejected marriage, and the dualist Manichees. Eckbert was followed by some of his medieval successors in conflating the two, but only in the nineteenth century did the equation come to be general and the name Cathars to be applied indiscriminately to anybody in the middle ages whose ascetic beliefs or practices were mentioned as evidence of heresy.

The paradoxical result of this scrutiny of the Cologne burning of 1163 is both to diminish and to enhance its importance. It was a less extraordinary event than it first appears, either as it was described by Eckbert and his collaborator Dietrich of Deutz or as it was remembered and polished for exemplary use in later generations. The victims did not, in all likelihood, include a beautiful young woman. Nor were they exiles from distant lands, bearers of exotic or extraordinary doctrines or members of a mysterious underground network. They belonged to one or more of the groups of devout believers that had multiplied in the Rhineland and the Low Countries throughout the twelfth century, many of them inspired by the legacy of the apostolic movement – some more, some less radical and anticlerical in their convictions; some more, some less evangelical in their enthusiasm. Some of them found themselves the objects of persecution. A few were made martyrs for their beliefs, for reasons that were largely incidental, the product of particular, local clashes of personality and circumstance that sometimes left revealing traces, but which can seldom now be fully explained. With respect to the case in 1163, there is nothing in the fragments of contemporary evidence to show what brought Arnold, Marsilius and Dietrich to the attention of the authorities. There is no anticipation, for instance, of the explanation offered by the *Chronica regia Coloniensis* in the 1220s that 'when they did not go to church on Sunday they were found out by their neighbours', although if it were the case there might have been many reasons for it – most obviously, a belief that Rainhald of Dassel or clergy under his authority had been simoniacally ordained. There was, however, a great deal in the current activity and tensions in the city and the personalities involved in them, as well as in the more general religious history of the region, to suggest possible sources of conflict between the cathedral clergy and their supporters and one or other group of pious believers.

———

Over the next twenty years or so the harrying of the remaining fragments of the apostolic movement continued, and the growth of piety among lay people, especially in the towns, stimulated the formation of religious associations and confraternities that occasionally fell foul of the authorities. An example of the first is the condemnation by a church council at Reims, in 1157, of

> the most wicked sect of the Manichees, who hide among the poor and under the veil of religion labour to undermine the faith of the simple, spread by the wretched weavers who move from place to place, and often change their names, accompanied by little women weighed down by the variety of their sin.

Imprisonment, branding and exile were prescribed for them and their followers.[5]

The story of the virgin of Reims who precipitated the discovery of a heretical sect in the 1170s by rebuffing the advances of Gervase of Tilbury looks like an example of the second. It also asserts that 'the blasphemous sect of *Publicani* was being searched out and destroyed all over France, especially by Count Philip of Flanders (1168–91), who punished them unmercifully with righteous cruelty.'[6] One of his victims may have been the Robert mentioned as having been condemned and executed at Arras in 1172. Like other even vaguer references relating to these years, the record is from a period several decades later, when memories and records of heresy were being constructed and reconstructed for all manner of reasons. Suggestions of heresy had cropped up regularly at Arras for many years, from Bishop Gerard's synod in 1025 to a letter from Eugenius III in 1153 to the clergy and people of the city in support of their bishop's condemnation of an unspecified heresy alleged to be spreading in the diocese.[7] Arras was one of the earliest centres of the cloth trade, and in the twelfth century its mint was one of the most active in the region. Its burghers had been among the first, early in the eleventh century, to emerge as a privileged urban elite and to form a sworn association among themselves. In 1163 Count Philip granted them a new code of laws, soon extended in its essentials to other Flemish towns, which increased the severity of the penalties for various criminal acts, but also the powers of the aldermen to investigate them and the town's share of the profits of justice.

In 1162–3 a group of people from Arras appealed to Pope Alexander III against Archbishop Henry of Reims.[8] They had been accused of being 'followers of a particularly vicious heresy' discovered by Henry on a recent visit. They offered him 600 marks to leave them alone. This was a considerable sum. A few years later a cardinal and papal legate won the admiration of one his colleagues by turning down an offer of 50 marks for a clerical appointment. When Henry refused, the accused appealed to the pope, and three men and a woman travelled to his court, insisting that they were 'free of any taint of heresy'. Alexander's position was delicate, since the church was in schism and he was an exile, largely dependent on the protection and support of Archbishop Henry's brother, King Louis VII of France, who joined him in pressing for 'severity against them which will be welcome to every lover of piety'. Nevertheless, Alexander delayed his verdict to consult more widely among the French bishops, asked Henry to 'make inquiries about (the accused) from people who will know about their manner of life and their beliefs, and report to us' and ordered that the petitioners should not be harmed in any way or suffer any loss of property until the matter had been decided.

According to Louis and Henry, these people had 'fallen into the errors of the Manichees, called *Populicani* in the vernacular', but 'some of their observances make them appear more virtuous than they really are.' They were not without powerful friends, for they were supported by 'many letters' and satisfied the pope sufficiently for him to insist, contrary to political expediency, on further investigation. No more is known about them or their fate, but the very fact of their appeal to the pope weighs powerfully against their being members of a radically anticlerical sect. It looks rather as though they belonged to some devout grouping within the church and had been denounced to Archbishop Henry – not, we may notice, the bishop of Arras, who is not mentioned in the letters – in consequence of some local grievance or rivalry not necessarily religious in origin. He seized the opportunity to assert his authority in a part of his province where it was often resented, or perhaps simply because, having begun his religious life as a novice at Clairvaux in the time of Bernard, he had been trained to suspect heresy wherever he might look. If that is speculative, the adventures of Lambert 'le Bègue', from the neighbouring diocese of Liège, will show just how such things could happen, but first we must consider one more case in the French kingdom.

———

Seven people – the largest number specified as having been burned on any occasion since Orléans in 1022 – were sent to the stake at Vézelay in 1167.[9] They were held in solitary confinement for two months, at the order of Abbot William, 'until they could be refuted by bishops or other eminent people who might happen to come our way', and eventually charged before the archbishops of Narbonne and Lyon, the bishop of Nevers and others. They were said to have denied

almost all the sacraments of the Catholic Church, including the baptism of children, the eucharist, the image of the living cross, the sprinkling of holy water, the building of churches, the efficacy of tithes and offerings, the cohabitation of husband and wife, the monastic order, and all the functions of clerks and priests.

Having heard that it would be decided that they should die at the stake, two of them demanded the ordeal by water, saying that they now believed in the church and its teachings and that they knew nothing more of secret errors, and would prove that they no longer subscribed to the error of the sect by undergoing the ordeal of water, willingly and without any other judgement ... One of them was judged by everybody to be saved by the water (though there were some who afterwards cast doubt on the verdict), but when the other had been immersed he was unanimously condemned. At the instance of many, including the priests, and by his own request, he was brought out from prison, and submitted to the judgement of the water again, but when he was thrown in for the second time the water once more refused to receive him. Since he had been twice condemned everybody sentenced him to the stake, but the abbot, giving consideration to his condition, ordered him to be publicly flogged, and banished from the town. The others, seven in number, were burned at the stake in the valley of Asquins.

This is a puzzling affair. We are told of it by Hugh of Poitiers in the last chapter of his *History of the Monastery of Vézelay*. It almost seems as though the story had been tacked on as an afterthought, for apart from a brief note immediately before it, recording the pilgrimage of Count William of Nevers to Jerusalem, the chronicle ends in 1166. Hugh is not habitually taciturn, but unusually among accounts of heresy cases this one says nothing whatsoever about the accused except that they were 'called *Deonarii* or *Poplicani*' – not even, as in so many such reports, that they were itinerants, or newcomers to the town. There is nothing about the examination of the accused, or how they answered the charges, and there is no indication of what 'secret errors' they were suspected of holding back. In all these respects Hugh's story differs noticeably from that of Guibert of Nogent about the Soissons burnings in 1114, which in other ways it markedly resembles.

The temptation must be to wonder whether this chapter, rather than being an unconnected afterthought of the chronicler, as it seems at first sight, is a discreet postscript to the story of the bitter struggle between Count William and the abbey which had dominated the previous sixty chapters. That story was itself the last act in a drama that had run for most of the century and constituted one of the central themes of Hugh's chronicle. The count had succeeded to his title in 1161. He believed, like his father and grandfather before him, that in the process that we now call reform he had been deprived by the abbey, with the assistance of the popes and other outside powers, of extensive hereditary rights over the abbey, its men and its revenues. His last ditch, as it were, was the right to demand hospitality for himself and his men, or money and provisions in lieu of it. In pursuit of this claim he waged war several times, entering and occupying the monastery by force, and even at last driving the monks out of it. Among those from whom they sought assistance, as it happens, were King Louis VII, Archbishop Henry of Reims and Pope Alexander III, by whose efforts an agreement was at last secured in 1166. The suspicion that the heresy accusations and trial represented a final defeat of the abbey's local enemies is increased by the victims' appeal to the ordeal. It should not have been necessary, since they had recanted. It also suggests that they had some hopes of support – not entirely without foundation, as it turned out – in a community in which opinion was evidently divided.

———

Lambert 'le Bègue' was a parish priest in a suburb of Liège who was imprisoned by his bishop on charges of heresy but secured his release by appealing successfully to Rome. The thirteenth-century nickname means 'the stammerer', but it has also been suggested erroneously that Lambert was the founder of the Béguine movement, which began in Liège half a century or so after his time.[10] His case uniquely reverses the chief difficulty with which we are constantly engaged in this book, for it is alone in being recorded only from the point of view of the accused, through the letters written by him and his supporters in pursuit of the appeal.

Lambert, the son of a smith and so from a solidly respectable background, but one far removed from the younger sons of the nobility who supplied the higher clergy of the prince–bishopric of Liège, was by his own account the very model of a reforming parish priest. When he was ordained by Bishop Henry, he was probably already the author of a pamphlet known as the *Antigraphum Petri*. Since it attacked simony and clerical incontinence in typically vigorous Gregorian style, Henry, who died in 1164, presumably knew what he was getting. Lambert served for three years in a small and dilapidated inner-city church. 'I painted it, made windows, filled in the holes in the walls, provided it with wax candles and everything else that was necessary to the conduct of services.' When he refused to pay the increased annual rent demanded by his ecclesiastical superiors on account of these improvements, he was moved to St Christophe, in the suburbs. At a diocesan synod in 1166 Lambert spoke up for Bishop Henry's reforming measures, including prohibition of the ordination of sons of the clergy, which had apparently been reversed by his successor, pointing out that

> according to decrees promulgated at the Council of Reims by Pope Eugenius III, priests and clerks ought not to have their clothes dyed in bright colours or slashed at front and rear; that in baptizing children no more than three should be brought to the font at a time, as the same council ordained; that omens and divinations should not be looked for in the celebration of the Mass, as they are by some false priests.

His enemies later claimed, but Lambert denied, that after this speech he was silenced by Bishop Alexander. At any rate he continued to preach in Liège and neighbouring cities, especially against excessive charges for the sacraments and services of the church, until Bishop Rudolf of Zahringen, who succeeded Alexander in 1167, accepted the accusations levelled against him by other clergy of the city and imprisoned him along with five other priests who shared his views. He was released when Calixtus III ruled in his favour in 1175, and died two years later.

The divisions revealed among the clergy by Lambert's story, including the reaction against the work of a reforming bishop under his unsympathetic successors, are obvious and by now familiar. The laity were similarly divided. Lambert, as might be expected, gathered ardent partisans among his parishoners, including

> poor clerks and many lay folk, who have seen my humble way of life, the meagreness of my diet, my contempt for glory and riches, my scrupulous attention to the conduct of worship and pastoral care, and – not very wisely I fear – have approached Christ through me, and come to observe his laws ...
>
> I saw them go frequently and regularly to church and pray with me with great devotion, conducting themselves most decently and

reverently. They listened avidly to the word of God, and during the mass they witnessed the Lord's renewed suffering for them with sobs and sighs ...

How can I describe with what contrition of heart, what out-pourings of tears, what reverence and trembling, without any of the common jostling and clamour they would receive the body and blood of their Saviour? They would come forward as though in military order, the seriousness of their faces terrible to the wicked ...

When they returned to their own homes they ate soberly and piously, and spent the rest of the day until Vespers – I am talking about Sundays – singing hymns, psalms and canticles, thinking over what they had heard in church, and encouraging each other to observe it.

Lambert made a rhythmical translation of the Acts of the Apostles for the use of his pious parishoners on these occasions. His descrip-tion evokes those groups of godly, serious people who appear so regu-larly in later European history, especially at periods of religious conflict and reformation. A clear strain of puritanism is apparent. Apart from the usual catalogue of clerical abuses, Lambert disapproved particularly vehemently not of pilgrimage itself (he insisted) but of the ostentation and distortion of proper values that often accompanied it – of shysters and fraudsters who bought respectability with their trip to Jerusalem, or people who had earned their money honestly enough but might better have used it on charity at home, or to help their aged parents. It is not extravagant to imagine behind these worthy views a substantial reser-voir of neighbourhood gossip and grievance, which would have had no difficulty in identifying, for instance, the one among Lambert's clerical accusers of whom 'I have heard that he went to Jerusalem, but never that he redeemed anybody from prison'.

The opposite side of the social face of reform lies behind Lambert's indignant rebuttal of another accusation, that he had encouraged his parishoners to work on the sabbath. His reply was that he had said only that it was a lesser evil than those that arose when

I saw that an infinite multitude of both sexes devoted the Lord's day not to restoring their negligence, but to multiplying their sins. They abstained from manual labour to watch mimes, plays and dancing girls, to take their holiday with drunkenness and gambling, to flock around armies of wicked women and eye them, or dance with them through the grounds of the churches and over the graves of their parents and relations singing obscene songs and indulging in lewd gestures.

The issue was not quite so simple. This is a reminder, like Henry's meetings in Le Mans, that the churchyard was historically and traditionally the preserve not of the church but of the community, and that bringing it under ecclesiastical control was a common (though not sufficiently researched) aspect of the reform. It involved not only questions of behaviour and the role of the churchyard as a forum for public meetings but also the commemoration of the dead, whom it was often customary to remember and to treat as still part of the community, by holding meals at their graves and by singing and dancing, thus binding the community itself together. Clerical opposition to such customs went back far beyond the twelfth century but was now strenuously pursued and bitterly resisted. This was another way in which the church was bringing under its sway fundamentals of family and social life that the community had been accustomed to manage for itself. That it was also socially divisive seems obvious; it is unlikely that many who cherished these customs were assiduous attenders of Lambert's Bible-reading circle.

This is what lies behind the most serious charges against Lambert, that he had created a personal following of *sectatores* – the word is effectively synonymous with heresy. Instead of going to church and taking communion his followers were conducting their own services at private gatherings. In making a translation of the Acts and other religious writings for their use Lambert had 'opened the holy scriptures to the unworthy'. While he denied that, his praise for the active devotion of his parishoners, even contrasting it favourably with his own, implicitly diminished the significance of his own status as an ordained priest while enhancing that of individual piety and collective practice. The use of Lambert's translation by his followers confirms that at least some of them were literate in the vernacular, and his defence shows that his opponents exemplified increasing nervousness among churchmen about potentially independent access to the scriptures on the part of the laity.

We do not know whether Lambert's followers actually formed a sect. The success of his appeal and the peaceful conclusion of the dispute and of his life suggest not. Nevertheless, his explanation shows what may have lain behind similar accusations that we have met before. It also brings out how and why the formation of a sect might take place, and how greatly whether or not it did so depended on the conduct and good sense of the ecclesiastical authorities.

———

In 1165 Roger of Worcester consulted his fellow bishop Gilbert Foliot about some people who had been found in his diocese and on being questioned refused to renounce unspecified heretical beliefs. Gilbert replied in two letters that, apart from referring to the people in question as *textores* (more probably meaning 'heretics' here than 'weavers'), tell us nothing about them.[11] Gilbert was a well-educated man and a leading figure among the English bishops; he had been widely expected to succeed to Canterbury in 1160, when the king shocked everybody by appointing his favourite, Thomas Becket. His advice to Roger shows an up-to-date knowledge of canon law but does not reflect the concerns of the recent Council of Tours, which will be discussed in the next chapter. His main concern was to insist that no decision could be made about the prisoners until 'the needs of the church and the business of the kingdom' allowed their case to be considered by a council 'of priests and other of the faithful'. Meanwhile he recommended that they should be kept apart from one another and urged by suitably reliable and educated warders to recant; these efforts should be reinforced by moderate floggings. He listed the punishments considered appropriate for heresy in Roman times, including scourging, imprisonment and burning, but did not recommend any of them.

Gilbert's tone is restrained, even academic, and though an experienced churchman – he had attended the Council of Reims in 1148 and became a bishop in that year of Hereford and in 1163 of London – he seems to be confronting the issue of heresy among the laity for the first time. The case must have been discussed in English monastic circles, for a few months later another reference to it turns up in a dialogue *On the Soul*, by the Yorkshire Cistercian abbot Ailred of Rievaulx. Ailred described the prisoners, once again, as *textrices et textores* – female and male heretics – and as *rustici*, uneducated and of humble station, and says that they condemn marriage and the eucharist and deny the resurrection of the flesh and the value of baptism, and that they are to be brought in chains for trial before a royal council.[12]

The hearing took place at Oxford, in the last days of 1165 or the first of 1166, presided over by King Henry himself.[13] The outcome is recorded in his Assize of Clarendon, issued a few months later, the first decree of a European monarch against heresy:

> Further, the lord king forbids anyone in the whole of England to receive in his land, or within his jurisdiction, or in a house under him, any of the sect of heretics who were excommunicated and branded at Oxford. If anyone receives them he shall be at the mercy of the lord king, and the house in which they have lived shall be carried outside the village and burned. And each sheriff is to swear that he will observe this, and make all his officers, and the stewards of the barons, and all the knights and freeholders of the county swear it.

Henry's action was a direct and ruthless application of the decree of the recent Council of Tours that heretics were not to be given shelter or protection. He had an obvious motive to show himself a stern defender of the faith in his quarrel with Thomas Becket, now in exile in France, and another in his designs on Toulouse, which will be discussed in the next chapter. In fact no special explanation is required. Secular rulers were no more inclined than ecclesiastical ones to be indulgent towards any kind of questioning of authority. The outcome is unknown, but the time of year and the general effectiveness of Henry's government lend plausibility to William of Newburgh's report, more than thirty years later, that 'their clothes were publicly cut off as far as their belts, and they were driven from the city with ringing blows into the intolerable cold, for it was winter. Nobody showed the slightest mercy towards them, and they died in misery.'

According to William, these unfortunates were Germans, rather more than thirty of them, led by their only educated member, whose name was Gerard and who spoke for them at their trial, saying that they were Christians and respected the apostolic teaching.

> Questioned in the proper order on the articles of faith, they answered correctly on the nature of Christ, but of the remedies with which he condescends to alleviate human infirmity, that is the sacraments, they spoke falsely. They attacked holy baptism, communion and matrimony, and wickedly dared to belittle the Catholic unity which is fostered by these divine aids. When they were confronted with evidence drawn from the holy scriptures, they replied that they believed what they had been taught, and did not want to argue about their faith.

Refusing the opportunity to repent and rejoin the church, they embraced their fate with fervour, 'laughing and abusing the words of the Lord, "Blessed are they which are persecuted for righteousness' sake, for theirs is the kingdom of Heaven."' They were sentenced to be branded on the forehead – and Gerard also on the chin, 'as a mark of his pre-eminence' – and whipped from the city, chanting 'Blessed are ye when men shall revile ye.'

Although he seems never to have gone far from his native Yorkshire, William of Newburgh was a careful and well-informed chronicler who took particular care to place his reports in a broad historical perspective. At Rievaulx he had a nearby source of strictly contemporary information about these heretics, and what he says about their teachings is consistent with Ailred's comment quoted above, as well as with what might be expected of devotees of the apostolic life from the Rhineland or Flanders. He would also have had access to information from another neighbour, Roger of Howden, who did not describe this incident in his own chronicle, which William used, but had been close to the royal court at the time.

Another commentator, the courtier Walter Map, writing in the early 1180s, differs from William on the number of people involved – 'no more than sixteen who, by order of King Henry II were branded and beaten with rods and have disappeared'. He identifies as their heresies denial of the eucharist and St John's gospel, the latter an assertion paralleled nowhere else. The context, a string of satirical lampoons on the claims of court magicians and the credulity of their audiences, cautions against taking Walter's comments at face value. Nevertheless, his remark that the 'Publicans or Patarenes', as he calls them, 'at first had single houses in the villages they lived in … Men and women live together, but no sons or daughters issue of the union' prompts the suspicion that this was another remnant of the primitive Norbertines, dispersed after refusing to submit to the reforms that would have regularised and segregated them.[14]

It is harder to assess how William of Newburgh's account was influenced by the very considerable development that had taken place between the 1160s and the 1190s in the perceptions of churchmen and others about heresy and heretics, and especially about the extent to which they were organised and proselytising, which will be the subject of the next three chapters. This may be reflected in his remark that 'they were believed to belong to the sect commonly known as *Publicani*, who undoubtedly originated in Germany from an unknown founder' and that 'they came here as though in peace to propagate their errors'. If so, it was an oddly constituted mission: an educated man with thirty illiterate followers sounds more like an apostolic community displaced by persecution. It may even be that the first descriptions of these people, as weavers, should be taken literally, for it was a trade well suited to fugitives. On the other hand, William's comment that 'they answered correctly on the nature of Christ' means that they did not subscribe to the docetist heresy – that Christ's human body was illusory – which was said by Eckbert of Schönau to be held by his 'Cathars' and by William's time was taken to be axiomatic among the dualist heresies with which the label *Publicani* would have associated these people. It confirms both his careful reporting and their innocence of that particular error, for they could have had no reason to deny it while proudly acknowledging so many others.

———

Fragmentary as they are, these incidents and accusations of heresy in northern Europe in the 1160s and '70s display both old-fashioned political expediency and the conventional use of heresy accusations to pursue rivalries and antagonisms among the clergy. They also show an increasing tendency for religious groupings and activities to reflect the growing diversity of lay society and its needs, though their very sparsity suggests that this development had not as yet aroused widespread interest or alarm among churchmen. Chapter 12 will show that, as might be expected, the tendency for the collective anxieties and aspirations of the unprivileged laity to seek religious expression was even more pronounced in the Italian cities. Between the Rhône and the Garonne rivers, however, more traditional preoccupations prevailed.

1 1

SOUNDING THE ALARM

Mistake me not, I count not War a Wrong:
War is the Trade of Kings, that fight for Empire;
And better be a Lyon than a Sheep.

John Dryden, *King Arthur*

If there was a moment when the war on heresy was formally declared, it was May 1163. A council of the church, meeting at Tours under the presidency of Pope Alexander III and the patronage of Henry II, king of England and duke of Aquitaine, declared that:

In the district of Toulouse a damnable heresy has recently arisen, which, like a cancer gradually diffusing itself over the neighbouring places, has already infected vast numbers throughout Gascony and other provinces, and hiding itself like a serpent in its own folds, undermines the vineyard of the Lord the more grievously as it spreads secretly among simple folk. Therefore we command the bishops, and all God's priests resident in those parts, to be vigilant, and to prohibit everybody, under pain of anathema, from sheltering the known followers of this heresy in their lands or presuming to protect them. Nor must they have dealings with them either in selling or buying, so that being excluded from all social transactions they will be compelled to renounce the errors of their ways. Anybody who contravenes this injunction will be included under its curse as an accomplice of their crime. If they are discovered by catholic princes, they are to be taken into custody and forfeit all their goods. And since they frequently assemble from different places at one hiding place, and have no reason to live together except their agreement in error, let all such hiding places be diligently sought out, and when discovered, forbidden under canonical censure.[1]

This was the most comprehensive measure that had yet been formulated against heresy. Previously it had been enough to direct that those who openly and pertinaciously rejected specified teachings or sacraments of the church should, in the words of Lateran II, be 'cast out of the church as heretics, and restrained by the civil power'. Now the Council of Reims (1148) was followed, and sharpened, its targets extended beyond the heretics themselves and their followers. Those who protect them (that is, their lords) or had dealings with them are to be treated as accomplices, and subject to the same penalties. The clergy are to be proactive. It is no longer enough to wait for heretics to reveal themselves by preaching or evangelism. They must be searched out in their meetings and meeting places. Their followers are to be identified by reputation ('known'). Any overt expression or sharing of heterodox views, however discreet or within however restricted a circle, is now to be treated as a declaration of dissent from the teaching of the church. Catholic princes who discover heretics must arrest them and confiscate their goods. Failure to uncover them will be proof not of their absence but of incompetence or connivance on the part of the ecclesiastical and civil authorities.

———————

The singling out of the area of Toulouse (*in partibus Tolosae*) as the epicentre of 'this damnable heresy' was an ominously specific amendment of the Reims canon's reference to 'Gascony and Provence'. There had been rumours and assertions of heresy in the area before, but most of them had arisen in the context of readily, or at least plausibly, identifiable

The wars against Toulouse

conflicts of one kind or another. Since Bernard's mission in 1145 the bishop of Agen, in the frontier region between Aquitaine and the *partes Tolosae,* had given a church to the monks of La Grande Sauve to help them restore the faith of the village of Gontaud, in what looks like a response to the conditions of which Bernard had complained. Around 1160 the bishop of Périgueux gave the heresy of its inhabitants as his reason for attacking the castle at Gavaudan, also in the Agenais. Like the welcome that had been accorded to Henry of Lausanne and Peter of Bruys in their time, these incidents tended to confirm what everybody knew already. Between the Rhône and the Dordogne lay a fragmented and unruly region in which neither secular nor ecclesiastical authority was easily asserted. This was also true of other mountainous regions that were not singled out in the same way. Here, however, the competing claims and constantly shifting rivalries of many lords, among whom the counts of Toulouse (of the family of St Gilles) and the vicomtes of Béziers (the Trencavels) had the greatest pretensions and were the most persistent in mutual hostility, offered a standing temptation to their neighbours in Aragon, Aquitaine, France and even the empire. The vulnerability of the region to such intervention increased throughout the twelfth century, and more rapidly from its mid-point, as in each of the neighbouring kingdoms and principalities internal order was gradually asserted and with it the wealth, military capacity and ambition of its ruler increased.

The circling vultures received a formidable addition in 1152, when Count Henry of Anjou, without the customary permission of his lord, King Louis VII of France, married Eleanor, duchess of Aquitaine, eight weeks after Louis himself had divorced her. Along with his wife Henry took over from Louis her hereditary claim to the county of Toulouse. Two years later he became king of England. Once he had established control over his new kingdom, Henry was in a position to pursue his claim on Toulouse. He struck up an alliance with Count Raymond Berengar of Barcelona, who was already at war with Raymond V of Toulouse and in league with Raymond Trencavel of Béziers. In 1159 he raised the largest army of his thirty-five-year reign and set out to seize Toulouse.

King Louis could hardly refuse to acknowledge a claim that he had himself asserted when Eleanor was his wife, but neither could he afford to ditch Raymond V, to whom he had married his sister in 1154, or allow Henry, already lord of Normandy, Anjou and (through Eleanor) Aquitaine, and in those capacities Louis's vassal, to add Toulouse to his dominions. He therefore took personal charge of the defence of the city, presenting Henry with the unpalatable alternatives of launching a direct attack on his lord – not an example he dared set his own vassals – or abandoning the expedition. Henry withdrew, accepting the thinnest of face-saving mediations, but he was not a graceful loser. The pursuit of revenge guided much of his policy for the rest of his reign and part of his son Richard's, in what William of Newburgh called 'the forty-year war against Toulouse'. One consequence of his vendetta is that almost everything we read of the development of heresy in the region of Toulouse over the next twenty years comes from English sources, and especially from the two great chronicles of Roger of Howden, who was not only a fine historian but a widely travelled and well-trusted courtier of King Henry, in whose service he participated in several diplomatic missions.

The council at Tours was intended to rally Pope Alexander's supporters against Frederick Barbarossa, who in turn was pressing Louis VII to withdraw his protection and recognition from Alexander. In preparing for it, the pope was equally in need of the co-operation of Henry II, who shared neither Louis's personal piety nor his respect for ecclesiastical authority. Nevertheless, Alexander was not disappointed. Tours was Henry's favourite city. He took an active interest in the preparation of the council, encouraging the bishops of all his lordships to be there, in marked contrast to his predecessor Stephen, who had forbidden English bishops to attend the Council of Reims in 1148. It is hardly fanciful to suspect his influence behind the pointed shaping of the canon against heresy to make it refer obviously and directly, though not quite explicitly, to the count of Toulouse. Henry's forebears had been well aware for the past century and a half, at least, how effectively a ruler could be undermined by the accusation of giving shelter to heresy, and how difficult it would be for a Capetian king whose own legitimacy was heavily dependent on his status as a defender of the faith to extend his protection to any of his vassals so accused.

———

Count Raymond could not afford to ignore, or be seen to ignore, the council's decree. That would have exposed him to its provisions against those who sheltered heretics. Instead he tried, as Alphonse Jordan had done in 1145, to turn it to his advantage against his most dangerous local rivals, the Trencavels. In 1165 a meeting was held in their territory, at the fortified village of Lombers, between Albi and Castres. It was attended by all the great magnates of the region, secular and ecclesiastical, including the countess of Toulouse, the vicomtes of Béziers (Roger Trencavel) and of Lavaur, the archbishop of Narbonne, the bishops of Albi, Nîmes,

Toulouse and Agde, several abbots and numerous other secular and ecclesiastical dignitaries. The record of the meeting is described as 'a final judgement pronounced upon the arguments, disputes and attacks on the catholic faith' which were pressed by 'certain men who caused themselves to be known as *boni homines* (good men), and who were supported by the men of Lombers'. At the conclusion of the meeting the bishop of Albi pronounced his verdict: the *boni homines* were heretics, and the lords of Lombers must give them no further support on pain of forfeiting the fines that they had deposited in the bishop's hands. His verdict was endorsed in turn by all the other grandees present, both laymen and clergy.[2]

Meetings such as this were normal in the region, but this is the only one of its kind known to have dealt with a heresy accusation. It was an arbitration, in which the case was laid before judges, or arbitrators, chosen by both sides in the dispute and mutually acceptable. It therefore reflects the absence of centralised power to investigate the business in question and compel the parties to accept the decision. This is not to be shrugged off as 'anarchy', still less as 'disorder'. It shows that developments in the centralisation of ecclesiastical authority that had been going on in much of western Europe – among which the exclusion of laymen from ecclesiastical courts was an important element – had not taken hold here. Neither had the parallel and more or less contemporaneous centralisation of secular justice, today seen as a crucial stage in state formation, and in the later twelfth century most visible in the English and French monarchies but also to varying degrees in many other lordships, especially in northern Europe. There was nothing inevitable about this development, but its absence tempts modern observers to echo uncritically the contemporary characterisation of the lands to the south of the Loire as backward and unruly which was used to justify their conquest and occupation. The truth is more simply that the region maintained a political and institutional regime of a kind that had quite recently been much more widely familiar – and which lent itself much less easily to the persecution of heresy.

The meeting was presided over by the bishop of Albi, who delivered his verdict 'after judges had been chosen and presented by each side'. Participation and attendance were voluntary – the *boni homines* came under safe conduct, and, they said, with the bishop's promise that they would not be required to swear any oath. The bishop denied this, but he would hardly have been content with their voluntary attendance, on their own terms, if he had had the means to compel it. Although the participation of the *boni homines* was no doubt secured by political pressure on their patrons, it remained essentially voluntary, a fact that lends a degree of credibility to what they said. They were questioned by Bishop Goslin of Lodève on a series of points designed to test their adherence to catholic teaching and discipline, from which it emerged that they did not accept the Old Testament as authoritative – only the gospels, the letters of Paul, the seven canonical epistles, the Acts and the Apocalypse; they would expound their faith only under compulsion; they were not prepared to discuss the necessity of infant baptism but would discuss the gospels and the epistles. On being asked where and by whom the body and blood of Christ should be consecrated and received, and if it mattered whether it was administered by a good or a bad man, they replied that 'whoever takes it worthily is saved, if unworthily damned' and that it might be consecrated by any worthy man, clerk or layman. To the question whether salvation was possible for the married they answered that 'men and women are joined because of lust and fornication, as Paul said.' They were questioned at length on penance and repentance – does repentance secure salvation, and in what circumstances? Is it enough to be contrite and confess? To whom should confession be made? Their reply: 'James says only "Confess your sins to one another", and confess to be saved. They did not wish to comment further.' Finally, 'they also said a good deal that they were not asked about', especially on the prohibition of oaths by Christ and James, and quoted Paul on what kind of men should be ordained priest, and against wealth and ostentation in priests and bishops.

These responses were evasive and not unskilful. On confession, for instance, the *boni homines* knew just how far they could go in criticising current practice without committing themselves to a heresy. This is one of several points at which they questioned the authority for the bishops' position, when they said that the gospels required only that sins should be confessed, not that confession should be followed by penance in the form of spiritual exercises and material gifts, as the church now

demanded. Their position on the eucharist was one that had been defini-
tively abandoned by the church only in the past twenty or thirty years.
It looks as though they were willing formally to co-operate with the
process but knew quite well that some of their views would be condemned if fully stated, and avoided giving that opportunity. In that case
they were, in the church's eyes, heretics, not simple believers who had
got it wrong. But it does not follow that they would not have claimed for
their faith the authority of traditional belief and practice, as opposed to
the teachings of the bishops. Everything they said is of a piece with what
had been preached by Henry of Lausanne and by Peter of Bruys. It had
been cordially received because it was consistent with customary belief
and practice in the region at the time, and indeed quite recently in many
parts of Europe. Much of the interrogation hinged on points at which
the church was innovating – especially here, where 'reform' had come,
or was coming, very recently. When Bishop Goslin denounced them as
heretics, the *boni homines* replied that 'it was not they who were heretical but the bishop who had pronounced judgment upon them', that he
was 'a ravening wolf, a hypocrite and a foe of God, and his judgement
was dishonest'. They then turned to the assembled people and made a
confession of faith that was wholly orthodox in respect of the trinity, the
incarnation, baptism, confession, penance, marriage and the eucharist.
But they refused to affirm this confession by oath as Goslin demanded
(which confirms that its content was satisfactory), 'because that would
be contrary to the gospels and the epistles' and their condemnation was
pronounced, and approved by all the ecclesiastical and secular authorities present.

———

Thirteen years later, in 1178, Pope Alexander dispatched a mission to
Toulouse, headed by his legate, Cardinal Peter of St Chrysogonus, and
the abbot of Clairvaux, Henri de Marci. It was staffed by a strong con-
tingent of experienced diplomats and administrators drawn largely from
the court of Henry II, headed by Bishops Reginald Fitzjocelin of Bath
and John 'of the Beautiful Hands' of Poitiers. Their military escort was
led by Raymond of Toulouse and included the vicomte of Turenne, a

vassal of Henry II and a powerful lord in the Limousin with a reputation for ferocity.

Henry and Louis VII were now acting in unison, if not exactly in harmony. Raymond of Toulouse had appealed to them, as his lords, to intervene, using the claim that heresy was rampant, to secure leverage against two rivals now threatening his position with renewed vigour. The city of Toulouse, which for much of the twelfth century had been asserting its independence of the count step by step, seeking to control its own revenues, its tolls and taxes, its administration and justice, had in 1176 taken the unprecedented step of electing its governing council (the *boni homines*, good men, now for the first time called consuls) without comital approval. One of them, Peter Maurand, was to be the most conspicuous casualty of the events that followed. Raymond's other rival, Roger Trencavel, vicomte of Béziers, was the most prominent of the lords being drawn into alliance with Alfonso of Aragon in furtherance of his designs on Provence. A letter from Count Raymond (of questionable authenticity, as we shall see) to the abbot of Cîteaux, in 1177, claimed that he needed help because 'my powers are inadequate to the task, for the more noble of my land are consumed with this heresy and with them a vast multitude of men, so that I dare not, nor am I able to, confront them'.[3]

This was an old game. It had recently been tried by the archbishop of Narbonne, who in 1173, threatened by a short-lived alliance between Henry II and Raymond of Toulouse, appealed to King Louis VII, unsuccessfully, for armed assistance because 'in our diocese the ship of St Peter is so broken with the oppression of heretics that it is in danger of sinking'.[4] But it was a dangerous one, and this time the results were catastrophic. The methods used by the mission to establish the presence and nature of heresy in Toulouse foreshadowed those that the inquisitors would later make familiar. The legates reported to the Lateran Council in the following year that

the plague was so strong in the land that the heretics had not only their own bishops and priests, but their own evangelists as well, who twisted and ignored the truth of the gospels, and made new gospels for themselves, who seduced the people and preached to them new doctrines drawn from their own evil hearts.[5]

This dramatically affirmed the region's reputation as a land dominated by uncontrollable heretics – the twelfth-century equivalent of a failed state. In doing so, it helped to shape new measures against heresy and a new conviction of its universal, underground presence, and set in train the events that led to the Albigensian Crusade, the establishment of the papal inquisition and the subjugation of the lands of the count of Toulouse to the French crown.

The expectations of the legates were confirmed by the predictable hostility that greeted their party in Toulouse. As Henri de Marci described it, 'as we entered the city [in late July or early August 1178], they mocked us as we travelled through the streets, making signs with their fingers, and calling us imposters, hypocrites and heretics.' The mission quickly gained purchase, however, through the *inquisitio*, a device of Roman law and familiar to several members of the party since it had been much used by Henry II in asserting his judicial authority in England over the past two decades. There witnesses were put on oath 'whether there be in their hundred or vill any man accused or notoriously supect of being a robber or murderer or thief, or anyone who is a receiver of robbers or murders or thieves'.[6] Now

> At the instruction of the legate the bishop and certain of the clergy, the consuls of the city and some other faithful men who had not been touched by any rumour of heresy were made to promise to give us in writing the names of everyone they knew who had been or might in the future become members or accomplices of the heresy, and to leave out nobody at all, for love or money ... After a few days a very large number of names entered this catalogue.

It must be doubtful whether they all did so simply on religious grounds. The chance to settle scores and undermine rivals is unlikely to have been missed in a community experiencing all the opportunities and all the stresses of rapid commercial growth, including rapidly rising land prices and diverging fortunes, as well as political conflict with Count Raymond.

From the names collected in this way Peter Maurand, 'great even among the ten greatest men of the city' – that is, the consuls – was singled out as the principal heretic, though a layman and uneducated, and summoned before the legates. Maurand was the head of a leading family of the burgh, the settlement that had grown around the church of St Sernin outside the old city: the two had become effectively united only in recent decades. His wealth had been greatly enhanced, if not originally created, by speculation in land and rents and by moneylending, in part at the expense of the older noble families of the old city, who would have been closer to the count, their incomes more dependent on stagnating customary dues from the countryside.

'Trusting in his riches and his relations Maurand refused the first summons, making a haughty and false excuse for delay', but under pressure from the count and others, 'using threats as well as arguments', he eventually appeared. He denied the accusation of heresy but was reluctant to swear to his denial – thus exposing himself to what would become a classic dilemma, for in the eyes of his accusers 'such a refusal would be characteristic of that heresy'. Accordingly,

> the relics of the saints were soon respectfully brought in and received with such solemn reverence and devotion that the faithful were moved to tears ... During the chant which we sang with copious tears to invoke the grace of the Holy Spirit, manifest fear and paleness overcame Peter, and colour of face and courage of mind alike forsook him. When the Holy Ghost approached how could any spirit remain among its enemies? You could see him shaken as though by some paralytic disease, and deprived of speech and sense, though everyone said that he was so eloquent that he usually overcame all others in argument.

Maurand broke down and swore on oath that he would answer the legates truthfully about his beliefs. 'Then an extraordinary thing happened, which gave great pleasure to the pious who were present', says Henri de Marci. The bible on which Maurand had sworn was opened at random, and a text turned up which could be read as a denunciation of heretics. It was indeed extraordinary, since in other circumstances the practice of divination in this way was routinely denounced as improper and superstitious, but it pleased the crowd and racked up the pressure on Maurand, who broke down and confessed 'that he held, by a new doctrine, that the holy bread of eternal life consecrated by a priest in the word of the Lord does not become the body of the Lord'.

The business was completed next day when Maurand, having negotiated through mediators the terms of his surrender, appeared at the church of St Sernin for sentence to be pronounced.

> The crowd was so large and so dense that the legate could hardly celebrate the Mass without a crush. Before that enormous crowd Peter, now our man, was led naked and barefoot from the doorway of the church, being scourged by the bishop of Toulouse and the abbot of St Sernin until he prostrated himself at the feet of the lord legate on the steps of the altar. There, in face of the church, he abjured all heresy and pronounced a curse on all heretics and was reconciled with the sacraments of the church. All his possessions were confiscated and taken from him, and the penance was laid on him that he should depart as an exile from his native land within forty days, and spend three years at Jerusalem in the service of the poor. In the meantime he was to go round every church in Toulouse on each Lord's day, naked and barefoot, with disciplinary scourges, to restore all the goods which he had taken from churches, to return all the interest which he had won by usury, to make amends for all the injuries that he had inflicted on the poor, and to rase to its foundations one of his castles which he had polluted with meetings of heretics.

The humiliation of Maurand served its immediate purpose, for 'after he had been dealt with the lord legate sent for others to be examined, for a great number were known to him either through public suspicion or private accusation.' It is not known whether Maurand carried out his promised pilgrimage, but he does not seem to have been permanently damaged. Certainly his family was not: his sons and their descendants continued to prosper and remained prominent in the affairs of the city throughout the thirteenth century despite regular condemnations as heretics and the losses that followed from them. 'Although there were undoubtedly difficulties,' their historian remarks, 'this family was anything but ruined' and by the end of the thirteenth century 'had successfully weathered the storm'.[7] Nor was the city's growing independence checked. By 1202–5 the powers of the consuls had developed to the point where they could launch a series of local wars to assert its control over the surrounding countryside, in the manner of its Italian counterparts.

Having dealt with Toulouse, the mission turned its attention to the Trencavels. The bishop of Albi had been imprisoned by Roger of Béziers, probably over a dispute about the temporal revenues of his see. Henri de Marci, now returning to Cîteaux, accompanied a detachment led by Reginald of Bath and the vicomte of Turenne into Roger's territory, which he saw, much as Bernard of Clairvaux had done before him, as 'a damnable region which is like a cess-pit of evil, with all the scum of heresy flowing into it'. Roger retired to one of his more remote strongholds, but the party found his wife and a number of his followers at Castres. In spite of Henry's forebodings, 'although we were there in their lands, in their power since we were surrounded by heretics on every side, the word of the Lord which we showered on them in continual rebuke and exhortation was not obstructed'. The bishop was released, and on behalf of the legate and the kings of France and England Roger was excommunicated as 'a traitor, a perjurer and a heretic, for having violated the peace and the personal safety of the bishop'. Thus the Trencavels were identified as the patrons *par excellence* of heresy, a reputation from which they would never recover, and their lands were exposed to the ambition of their enemies. As Henri put it, 'A fine door is open to Christian princes to avenge the wounds of Christ.'

———

On its way to Albi, Henri's party was approached by two men, Raymond de Baimac and Bernard Raymond, who said that they had been unjustly treated by Raymond of Toulouse and asked to be allowed to come under safe conduct to the city – from which, we must infer, they had been expelled as heretics – to defend their faith. It was agreed that they should do so and, whatever the outcome, would be allowed to return safely to their homes. The examination, presided over by Peter of St Chrysogonus, took place in the cathedral church of St Etienne, before the count of Toulouse and about three hundred other clerks and laymen. The two men had prepared a written statement, which they read aloud. It denied the usual charges, affirming their acceptance of the eucharist and the capacity of priests to confer it irrespective of their personal conduct, of baptism, marriage and the legitimacy of sex within marriage. It acknowledged that priests and the cult of the saints should be treated with respect, that tithes and first fruits should be paid and alms given to the church and the poor. In a handsomely comprehensive abjuration of anticlericalism that says a good deal about the state of opinion in the region Raymond and Bernard also 'agreed that archbishops, bishops, priests, monks, canons, hermits, Templars, and Hospitallers can be saved'. The new element in their statement, with which it opened, was that 'They said that there were not two principles, and confessed clearly and firmly, in public before us and the others we have mentioned, that one supreme God created everything, both visible and invisible, and that this was proved by the scriptures, the evangelists and the apostles.'

After the two men were questioned, with no result that Peter thought worth recording, the party adjourned to the nearby church of St Jacques, where 'an enormous crowd of people gathered, behaving as though they expected some great spectacle.' The two again read out their statement and affirmed 'in the hearing of all the people, that they believed in their hearts what they said with their lips, and had never preached anything against it'.

At this the count of Toulouse and many other clerks and laymen immediately convicted them as manifest liars. Some of those present steadfastly maintained that they had heard from some of the heretics that there are two gods, one good and one evil: the good god had created everything invisible and everything that could not be changed or corrupted, while the evil one created the sky, the earth, man, and other visible things. Others said that they had heard them preach that the body of Christ could not be conferred through the ministry of priests who were unworthy or guilty of any crime. Many testified that they had heard them deny that a man and his wife could be saved if they slept together. Others firmly said to their face that they had heard from them that the baptism of children is ineffectual, and heard them proclaim other blasphemies against God, the church and the catholic faith so appalling that we would prefer not to specify them.

The result was inevitable. 'Before the people, who applauded continually, and booed them vigorously, we lit candles, and with the bishop of Poitiers and the other clerics who had assisted us throughout declared them excommunicate, both them and their master the devil.'

———

'That there are two gods, one good and one evil: the good god had created everything invisible and everything that could not be changed or corrupted, while the evil one created the sky, the earth, man, and other visible things' is an unmistakable and unambiguous statement of theological dualism, the clearest and most uncompromising that we have yet encountered. Peter of St Chrysogonus and Henri de Marci were confident that they had amply confirmed the presence of a flourishing, well-entrenched and well-organised dualist heresy in what the council of Tours had called the *partes Tolosae*, that Peter Maurand, Raymond de Baimac and Bernard Raymond were among its leaders, and that it was gaining ground at an alarming pace. 'It was the general opinion in the city of Toulouse', concluded Henri, 'that if our visit had been three years later we would hardly have found anyone there who would call upon the name of Christ.'

This assessment played a large part in shaping the decisions of the Third Lateran Council in the following year (1179), and has been accepted effectively without question ever since. That acceptance, however, has owed a great deal to hindsight. The conviction that such a heresy existed, that it was well established and that its secret dissemination lay behind the most radical expressions of religious dissent, especially in the lands of the count of Toulouse, gained ground very rapidly after the Third Lateran Council. Yet the foundations on which it rested, and still rests, remain fragile. They must be carefully tested against the strictly contemporary evidence, not least because once the stereotype of a sinister, diabolically inspired underground movement had taken hold it distracted attention, then and now, from alternative sources of the dissent that it purported to account for.

There had been no trace of theological dualism in the answers of the *boni homines* at Lombers or, more importantly, in the questions put to them. Only the question about marriage could be thought even to hint at it, but the elevation of celibacy was probably the commonest single point of agreement in all ascetic and spiritual traditions. There was nothing about the eating of meat, an obvious traditional test of the 'Manichee', as with those who had been hanged at Goslar in 1052 for refusing to kill a chicken. They were not asked about Christ's assumption of human flesh, denial of which had been described by Eckbert of Schönau as a key 'Cathar' belief. This was a point of much contemporary interest because of the centrality of the eucharist to current catholic theological and pastoral preoccupations. The *publicani* examined at Oxford in the same year (1165) had been asked about it, and answered correctly. The question about the eucharist at Lombers, confined to the manner of its administration and the quality of the minister, seems to assume that the *boni homines* would not deny the incarnation of Christ per se. In short, there was nothing on that occasion to suggest that this interrogation was designed to detect or expose theological dualism, and there were surprising omissions if theological dualism was suspected. The *boni homines* echoed what had been preached a generation earlier by Henry and Peter of Bruys, a pre-Gregorian Christianity characterised by intense local loyalties, by resentment of the increased social distance between clergy and people that came with reform, of the growing demands for both money and deference as rural parishes began to be organised, for priests to be appointed and tithes collected from the laymen who had previously appropriated them, and for the services and disciplines of the church, including the regular administration of the sacraments, to be enforced.

Raymond V's letter of 1177 to the abbot of Cîteaux, as we have it from the English monk Gervase of Canterbury writing about ten years later, says that the heretics in Toulouse 'speak of two principles'. If the letter was authentic and unedited, however, it is surprising that neither the letter itself nor this point in it was mentioned by Roger of Howden, our fullest and best-informed source on these events, who was directly involved in the preparation of the mission of 1178 and may have accompanied it.

The assumption that dualist heresy was widespread in the region by this time, and that it had originated in the Balkans, was buttressed in the second half of the twentieth century by the conclusion of a distinguished scholar, ably reinforced by another, that despite many internal inconsistencies a document dating from the 1220s, at the earliest, contained an authentic account of a 'council' held by the heretics at St Félix de Caraman (now St Félix de Lauragais), 20 kilometres south-east of Toulouse, ostensibly in 1167. It describes how, under the direction of an emissary from Constantinople, they appointed bishops – including the Bernard Raymond who was excommunicated in 1178 – to lead their followers in dioceses coterminous with the catholic ones. Since the document in question is, at best, a product of the years after the Albigensian Crusade, when the religious history of the region was largely rewritten, or at any rate re-imagined, by the heretics as well as by their persecutors, it will be considered and its testimony evaluated at the appropriate point below (see p. 289).

The reports of Henri de Marci and Peter of St Chrysogonus assume, although they do not say, that Peter Maurand's heresy was the same as that of Raymond de Baimac and Bernard Raymond. The most serious heresy of which Maurand was convicted was denial of the eucharist, and that is what the oath he took (which has been discovered and identified) required him to abjure. If the legate did not require Maurand to abjure belief in two principles, it was because he saw no reason to. Conversely, that Raymond and Bernard found it necessary to deny it suggests that they were conscious of the accusation. Yet in describing how the indignant witnesses who had heard them preach 'convicted them as manifest liars', Peter of St Chrysogonus made a clear though unobtrusive distinction between the general assertion, that 'some of those present steadfastly maintained that they had heard from *some of the heretics* that there are two gods' (my emphasis) and what was specifically testified against Raymond and Bernard themselves, namely:

> Others said that they had heard them preach that the body of Christ could not be conferred through the ministry of priests who were unworthy or guilty of any crime. Many testified that they had heard them deny that a man and his wife could be saved if they slept together. Others firmly said to their face that they had heard from them that the baptism of children is ineffectual.

While it may be the case that the doctrine of the two principles had been preached or professed in Toulouse, none of those examined in 1178 was directly accused or convicted of doing either. We certainly cannot exclude the possibility that the spectre, by now regularly deployed as target practice in the classrooms of Paris, had been raised by the legate's party itself. As at Lombers, the propositions actually attributed to particular people were the ones most commonly advanced by all those accused of heresy in Latin Europe for the previous 150 years, with emphasis on the points that had become increasingly prominent and controversial with recent theological and pastoral developments – extreme personal abstinence, the eucharist, infant baptism, the role and purity of the clergy, the penitential system and the building and maintenance of churches.

———

Henri de Marci remarked in passing that the heretics in Toulouse 'had not only their bishops and priests, but their own evangelists as well'. Neither legate refers to such organisation again, but it does appear that there had been a crystallisation of religious leadership since 1145. Nothing suggests that it came from outside the communities themselves. The fact that the spokesmen at Lombers are described as *boni homines* (*bons oms*, good men) has encouraged speculation that they already belonged to what became known in the region as 'the heresy of the good men', the ostensible objective of the Albigensian Crusade which was investigated by the inquisitors of the 1230s and '40s. But the phrase was used of a great many others. When King Henry II fell ill in 1170 and believed that he was about to die, he demanded to be carried to the priory of Grandmont, in the Limousin, and buried at the feet of its founder, Stephen of Muret, because his sins were too lurid to be offset by the prayers of any guardians less holy than the *boni homines* of Grandmont. The writer who quotes Henry several times as referring in this way to these famous catholic monks is Roger of Howden, within a few pages of his careful summary of the meeting at Lombers and of his account of the papal mission to Toulouse in 1178. The phrase *bonus homo* (and correspondingly, if much less often, *bona mulier* or *bona femina*, good woman) crops up throughout the middle ages, and in many contexts. In the towns of our period, including Toulouse, it was a common synonym for *consul* – that is, the (often twelve) people chosen each year to oversee the government of the city – and for phrases like *legalis homo*, signifying a man in good legal standing, whose evidence would carry weight and who might be entrusted with civic responsibilities. Similar usages go back to the ninth century at least. During the eleventh century, in the villages of the south, the phrase lost its specific association with lordship and the conduct of legal business. It reappeared precisely in the period we are concerned with as a general honorific, which came to be used of almost anybody who was acting or being referred to in his capacity as a member of a group, including the village community itself. This does not mean that the *boni homines* constituted some sort of settled village elite. On the contrary, the phrase might refer to different people in different contexts, of varying degrees of formality. Its use of the spokesmen at Lombers tells us nothing whatever about them, though the confidence with which they stood up to the bishops may suggest that they were of some standing in their own communities.

The position in the city of Toulouse was rather different. As a consul, Peter Maurand was indeed a *bonus homo* in the most formal sense, and as a man of wealth and head of a leading bourgeois family he must have carried great weight in any group to which he belonged. It is too obvious that he was singled out for political reasons for any inference about his religious role, if he had one, to be justifiable. Nor is it certain that his beliefs were the same as those of Raymond de Baimac and Bernard Raymond. He was convicted of denying the real presence in the eucharist (that the consecrated bread became the body of Christ) altogether, they of holding that it would not be so in the hands of unworthy ministers. The distinction may seem a fine one to many modern readers, but it was not to twelfth-century catholics, and we may not assume that the legates overlooked it. It was quite as important, for example, as that between denying matrimony altogether and permitting it only between virgins which Eberwin of Steinfeld described between quarrelling sects in Cologne.

Raymond de Baimac and Bernard Raymond themselves were described by Peter of St Chrysogonus as *falsi fratres* (false brothers), implying that they were or had been members of a religious order

– perhaps canons of St Sernin, which had been regularly involved in disputes with the count, and with other factions in the city. Anywhere else in Europe they would be described as enthusiastic reformers who had overstepped the mark, either politically or theologically. There is no reason to take a different view here, and no reason to doubt the judgement of the appalled Henri de Marci that 'heretics ruled the people and lorded it over the clergy' – that is, that religious affiliation was various and religious debate vigorous and open. Certainly the bishop lacked the power, if he had the inclination, to prevent it. It was in that, and in the venom with which accusations of heresy were exchanged among its bitterly competing factions and levelled against it by the predatory neighbours who meant to profit from those divisions, rather than in the 'heresy' itself, that the *partes Tolosae* differed from the more developed and more closely governed territories around them.

1 2

DRAWING THE LINES

'It's too late to correct it,' said the Red Queen: 'When you've once said a thing that fixes it, and you must take the consequences.'

Lewis Carroll, *Through the Looking Glass*

At Venice in July 1177, following his defeat at Legnano by the forces of the Lombard League of Italian cities in the previous year, the emperor Frederick Barbarossa formally acknowledged Alexander III as pope and abandoned his own anti-pope, Calixtus III. The eighteen-year schism in the papacy was over. As part of the peace it was agreed that the end of the schism should be marked, like that of its predecessor in the 1130s, by an ecumenical council to settle the accumulated problems of the church. In September 1178 some one thousand prelates, including more than three hundred bishops of the Latin church, met at the Lateran Palace in Rome.

The first resolution of this council, Lateran III, that to prevent future schisms only cardinals might participate in the election of a pope, which would henceforth require a two-thirds majority, was of lasting importance. Otherwise, in accordance with the essentially celebratory nature of the occasion, its canons for the most part affirmed and clarified uncontroversial decisions of earlier councils in respect of the discipline of the clergy, the prompt filling of vacant positions in the church, the protection of ecclesiastical property and so on. But the papal and imperial officials who prepared the council's business had been able to agree, if not on much else, on the perfidy of heresy and the urgency of action against it. Accordingly it was resolved that

> since in Gascony and the regions of Albi and Toulouse and in other places the loathsome heresy of those whom some call the Cathars, others the Patarenes, others the Publicani, and others by different names, has grown so strong that they no longer practise their wickedness in secret, as others do, but proclaim their error publicly and draw the simple and weak to join them, we declare that they and their defenders and those who receive them are under anathema, and we forbid under pain of anathema that anyone should keep or support them in their houses or lands or should trade with them. If anyone dies in this sin, then neither under cover of our privileges granted to anyone, nor for any other reason, is Mass to be offered for them or are they to receive burial among Christians.[1]

In 1184 the mechanisms for enforcing this resolution were completed by the bull *Ad abolendam* ('To bring an end to the depravity of various heresies'), issued at a council at Verona by Pope Lucius III, 'supported by the power and presence' of the emperor. Heretics and anybody who supported or protected them were to be excommunicated and handed over to the secular power for punishment; bishops who were insufficiently energetic in pursuing them would be suspended for three years. Once or twice a year any parish reported to have heretics living in it was to be visited by the bishop of the diocese or his officers, and

> two or three men of good credit, or, if need be, the whole neighbourhood, [are] to swear, that if they know of any heretics there, or any who go to private meetings, or differ from the normal habits of the faithful in their demeanour or way of life, they will point them out to the bishop or the archdeacon.[2]

This was the *inquisitio*, the technique that had been used so effectively to identify and convict Peter Maurand in Toulouse. It was to be the church's main weapon against heresy for the rest of the middle ages, but it was already widely employed in secular matters, even where justice was not based on the Roman law from which it derived. It effectively extended the scope of the law beyond the personal injuries and disputes that give rise to accusations by one known party against another by creating a new category of offences against an abstract public good, defined as such by the public authorities themselves. In pursuit of such offences officials were empowered to put individuals or groups of people on oath to identify malefactors, without being liable to the penalties otherwise attached to bringing a false accusation – normally, the punishment that the guilty party would have suffered if convicted. These assumptions and procedures opened the way to the ever-widening circles of denunciation and accusation that would lie behind the mass burnings of the next century and the culture of innu-endo, of conspiracy and betrayal, of guilt by association, that flourished in their shadows.

Ad abolendam meant that inquisition was now to be regularly and universally employed to enforce conformity in religious belief and practice. Like all legislation, it was an expression of aspiration, not a description of what would actually happen. Translation of the aspiration into reality would always be slow, patchy and uncertain; there would be many places that inquisitors never reached and many communities that successfully refused to admit them. Nevertheless, *Ad abolendam* was promulgated at a time when the scale, variety and effectiveness of mechanisms of government of every kind and at every level, and of the number of men trained and available to operate them, taking full advantage of the consequent opportunities to develop their careers, line their pockets and undermine their rivals, were increasing exponentially. To ensure the vigilance of such officials *Ad abolendam* added that 'all counts, barons, governors and consuls of cities, and other places' must undertake on oath to give the church every support and assistance in its endeavours, on pain of losing their lands and offices, being excom-municated and having their goods confiscated for the use of the church. Those convicted of favouring heresy were to lose their civic rights and be excluded from public office. Cities that failed to execute the decree were to lose their bishop and be excluded from all commerce with other cities.

———

Lateran III had described those against whom its legislation was directed as a single body of heretics, 'whom some call the Cathars, others the Patarenes, others the Publicani, and others by different names'. In fact there was no basis for the assumption that all these names had described the same set either of people or beliefs. 'The regions of Toulouse and Albi' – the latter specified here for the first time in a conciliar decree, in another ominous narrowing of the geographical focus – owed their prominence in it to the reports of Peter of St Chrysogonus and Henri de Marci, who had been influential in preparing the ground for this council, but none of these names had ever been attached to the heresies supposed to thrive there. Although *Publicani* and its apparent variants (*popelicani, piphiles*) had been used of a number of groups in the Low Countries and northern France, Patarenes had not been heard of outside Italy, or Cathars, except in the lively imagination of Eckbert of Schönau, outside the classroom. The use of this last term is probably attributable to the prominence in the preparations on the imperial side of the archbishop of Cologne, Philip of Heinsberg, who as dean of Cologne had been a colleague of Eckbert of Schönau and had presided over the heresy trial there in 1163. Thus the council had drawn together into one menacing spectre all the manifestations of dissent real and imaginary, so various in their origins, nature, expression and support, that the assembled prelates had encountered, had heard rumours of or were prepared to believe in.

The readiness of prelates from all over Latin Christendom, meeting as a body for the first time in a generation, to attribute to a single cause the dissent that several of them had encountered in various forms is not difficult to understand. The twelfth century was not the last time in European history when leading political figures confronted by simultaneous manifestations of social change beyond their comprehension attributed them to the machinations of hidden subversive organisations. The prelates at Verona in 1184 were better informed, or cast their net wider. In extending the application of *Ad abolendam* to 'the Cathari, the Patarini and those who falsely call themselves Humiliati or Poor Men of Lyon, Passagini, Josepini and Arnaldistae', they dropped Lateran III's equation of 'Cathars' and 'Patarenes' and made no suggestion that all or any of the groups named were to be identified with one another. They perceived heresy as a many-headed hydra rather than a single, widely diffused movement. As far as recent posterity has been concerned, regrettably, the damage had been done, and in the twentieth century 'Cathars' would be found lurking beneath an ever more exotic array of ill-assorted beds.

In using these names, 'Cathars', 'Patarenes' and *'Publicani'* in Lateran III the medieval church laid claim to a heresy of its own. The use of contemporary names, for the first time in a formal ecumenical pronouncement, here and in *Ad abolendam* implicitly described a contemporary phenomenon, not simply a revival of ancient error. Previous condemnations had been directed in general terms against 'those who' held certain beliefs, or were the followers of certain unnamed persons. Narrative and literary sources had been similarly disinclined to coin names for new heresies and sects. The only significant exceptions are the *simoniaca haeresis*, which was not a sect, the Patarini of eleventh-century Milan, who were not heretics, or at any rate never formally condemned as such, and the Petrobrusians. Nor, in spite of a few well-known examples, had those who preached heresy, or their followers, commonly been described as reviving or renewing ancient heresies. When ancient heresies were invoked, it had been not to describe doctrine but to threaten or justify particular disciplinary measures, as when Wazo of Liège had insisted on describing the people about whom Roger of Châlons had written to him in the 1040s as Arians rather than Manichees. By giving modern names to the heresies it anathematised, Lateran III acknowledged heresy as inherently present in Christian society, at least until it could be eradicated. It was thereby transformed from a general but amorphous danger into a specific and universal threat, requiring sustained disciplinary action.

In twelfth-century Italy heresy among the laity (strictly defined as openly avowed, formally condemned and stubbornly maintained heterodox opinion) had been conspicuous chiefly by its absence. There had been no recorded case of it since the burning in Milan in 1028. The heresies of which we hear much in the second half of the eleventh century are those of simony and nicolaitism, by definition charges directed against clergy, not lay people. The Milanese *Pataria* of the eleventh century is not usually included in the list of heretical movements, though perhaps it should be. But the tensions that the *Pataria* had created or revealed persisted for decades in the Lombard cities, and the name continued to be associated both with heresy and with political faction. In 1111 the enemies of Ambrogio de Mozzo objected to his nomination as bishop of Bergamo on the ground that he was a Patarene. Since he was the patron of Astino, a daughter monastery of Vallombrosa, which had close connections with the Patarenes in Florence, they probably had a point. In the 1130s a number of consuls in Brescia, once a Patarene stronghold, were deposed as heretics.[3]

There is every reason to suppose that the word 'Patarene' had retained its ambivalent association with insistence on apostolic purity, hostility to clerical worldliness and contempt for ecclesiastical authority, but documentation in the middle decades of the century is lacking. It crops up again, probably just before Lateran III, not in Italy but in the brief treatise *Contra Patarenos* (*Against the Patarenes*), written by an Italian resident of Constantinople, Hugh Eteriano, from a noble family in Pisa.[4] His work was apparently directed against a group of western Christians living in Constantinople who, according to Hugh, denied the authority of the Old Testament, the validity of the sacraments of unworthy priests, the real presence in the eucharist and the sanctity of marriage, and objected to the veneration of the cross – the same charges regularly levelled against apostolic enthusiasts in the west, and subject to the same reservations as to the accuracy with which they describe the beliefs of the accused. Indeed Hugh, who was a layman but had been a student in Paris in the late 1130s or early '40s, shows just the same lack of interest as Eckbert of Schönau in the arguments by which his 'heretics' defended their contentions, and just the same enthusiasm for showing off his own skill in argumentation.

At around the same time, shortly before Lateran III, Hugo Speroni, another noble and a consul of Piacenza in 1165–7, sent a copy of his book on theology to his friend Vacarius, with whom he had shared lodgings as a student in Bologna in the mid-1140s. The book does not survive, but the reply of Vacarius, who had become a canonist and a teacher of law in England, does. Vacarius's response was moderate and thoughtful in tone, as befitted a discussion between old friends. It shows that in revulsion against the lifestyle of the clergy Speroni had arrived at a radical and typically Patarene rejection of the sacraments and of clerical authority, and implies that he had a following and had been engaged in public controversy.

If Hugh Eteriano called his opponents in Constantinople 'Patarenes', it must be because that is what he would have called their counterparts in Italy. The *Patarini* of Lateran III and *Ad abolendam* were groups like this. Similarly, according to John of Salisbury, Arnold of Brescia had 'had disciples who imitated his austerities and won favour with the populace through outward decency and austerity of life', although there is no record of the formal condemnation that would strictly justify John's description of them as 'the heretical sect of the Lombards'. It is reasonable to guess that Arnold's memory and legacy also lay behind the 'Arnaldistae' condemned by *Ad abolendam* in 1184, although there is no indication that any of them were formally organised or of how widely they were distributed. The '*Passagians*' referred to in *Ad abolendam* seem, according to a single obscure source, to have been a Lombard group anxious to observe literally the legal requirements of the Old Testament, including that of circumcision.

———

These fragments of information confirm that the growing need of twelfth-century lay people north of the Alps to express their shared convictions and aspirations through religious association was also felt in Italy. We can see more of it among the Lombard Humiliati, condemned by *Ad abolendam* but recognised as a religious order by Pope Innocent III in 1201. They had originated from 'certain inhabitants of the Lombard towns living at home with their families, choosing a particular form of religious life, refraining from oaths, lies and lawsuits, content with plain clothing, committing themselves to the Catholic faith'.[5]

The name 'Humiliati' was something of a portmanteau label, used of a number of rather diverse groups, which seem to have appeared in the 1170s and early '80s. They were mostly to be found along important roads and at river crossings rather than in the cities, and seem often to have had connections with the wool trade and other artisan occupations. The first we know of, in the Brera district of Milan and at Viboldone a few kilometres outside that city, enjoyed clerical support. Some of them secured the protection of Pope Alexander III, apparently on condition that they would not preach. A breach of that stipulation probably accounts for the condemnation of 1184, but there is no reason to suppose that it was directed at all those who became known as Humiliati, or indeed that all of them had taken to preaching. In 1199 some of them approached Innocent III asking to be reconciled with the church. He set up a commission to examine their proposals as to the basis on which they wished to do so, and in 1201 recognised them as a religious order in three strands, of men and of women living in communities under a rule, and of married couples living with their familes. The number of communities embraced by the new order was very large – perhaps 150 or so – and they possessed a good deal of property, administered churches and had set up hospitals. It is not clear how many of these communities of Humiliati had been associated with one another before this formalisation or, outside the diocese of Verona, how many of them had been excluded from the church. This is a good illustration of the difficulty of knowing whether or how groups of believers that had formed independently of one another, though often in similar ways and for similar reasons, were drawn together in these years, either of their own volition or under official pressure.[6]

———

The absence of heresy accusations against lay people in Italy between 1028 and 1179 plainly does not mean that they entertained no heterodox ideas. Such a conclusion would be absurd. Whatever may be the reason for the long silence, it was not the absence of public dissent from the teaching and discipline of the church. On any view of what the causes of heresy might have been, Lombardy and Tuscany at that time displayed them in abundance: a world-rejecting religious movement active since the millennium; associated with it, preaching enthusiastically received and often luridly anticlerical; both the fragmentation and the reassertion of ecclesiastical authority; rapid economic and demographic growth accompanied by greater and more visible extremes of wealth and poverty and increasing social differentiation and conflict in town and countryside; high levels of pedagogic activity, of lay literacy and of social mobility; all the miseries of oppression and war.

What the absence of formal accusations and trials shows is that the Italian bishops were not particularly nervous of the circulation of such ideas during these years and did not identify them as a potential source of popular unrest, or of the many other difficulties with which they had to cope. Vacarius's response to Hugo Speroni, firm in substance but measured and temperate in tone, may have been more typical of Italian churchmen of his background and generation than our preoccupation with heresy and heresy hunters leads us to expect. In calling for the persecution of the 'Cathars or Patarenes' on the ground that 'they no longer practise their wickedness in secret, as others do', after all, Lateran III might be read as having acknowledged, and implicitly condoned, the existence of private heterodoxy. If so, however, attitudes now changed sharply. The elaboration of the machinery of prosecution in *Ad abolendam* was largely the fruit of pressure from Italian bishops. As soon as the bull had been issued, those of Rimini and Ferrara called on the secular power to expel heretics from their cities, and others quickly followed their example, inaugurating a long tale of the pursuit of heresy in Italy and its inextricable entanglement with political conflict at every level.

The city of Verona dramatically illustrates the magnitude of the changes that followed *Ad abolendam*. Before 1184 its history, so far as the concerns of this book go, had been singularly uneventful. It had no record of heresy, accusations of heresy or religious violence, had offered no forum that we know of even to hermit preachers, still less the Patarenes, and was not visibly disturbed by the mighty upheavals of the eleventh and early twelfth centuries. But in 1199, in an action that Pope Innocent III himself thought indiscriminate, a large group of lay people was excommunicated by the bishop of Verona after being accused of belonging to the sect of the Humiliati anathematised by *Ad abolendam*, and in 1233 Verona was the scene of a mass burning, a terrible landmark in the systematic repression of heresy in Italy.

The deterioration of relations between bishop and city after the 1180s was less sudden than this chronology makes it look. Verona's absence from the turbulent record of eleventh-century religious politics is both a reminder that the storms that raged in Milan and Florence did not blow everywhere and a tribute to the success of its church in coping with the demands of the economic and social transformation that all these cities shared. The pastoral needs of a rapidly expanding urban population and of new and growing communities in the countryside had been catered for with energy and flexibility. The number of churches and places of worship in the diocese of Verona almost doubled between 1000 and 1150, most of the new foundations being in new settlements or in older ones where economic activity was particularly vigorous. Old churches were enlarged, new ones built on a larger scale, hospitals established on the outskirts of the city, where its poorest inhabitants were found. The building work itself provided employment and nurtured skills. The cathedral clergy did not dominate the city's religious life; a number of the new churches established in the later tenth and early eleventh centuries seem to have been intended as training centres for parish clergy. In those years, in fact, the bishops of Verona provided on a considerable scale services and innovations of very much the kind that the Patarenes later brought to Milan in revolt against the archbishop and his allies. Bishop Ratherius (931–74) was demanding, and to some extent securing, celibacy from his priests and conscientiousness in the discharge of parochial services long before the hermit preachers went into action in that cause in Milan and Florence.

All this was possible because Verona throughout this period had been securely under imperial control. Until the settlement between pope and emperor, the Concordat of Worms of 1122, its bishops were imperial nominees with imperial backing. This did not always work to the disadvantage of the city. Their regular absences encouraged the bishops to develop consistent diocesan administration through competent deputies; when present or concerned, they had clout and wealth to put behind their projects. After the concordat the cathedral chapter elected the bishop, who no longer enjoyed the support of an emperor now much more remote from Italian affairs. Both election to the episcopal office and the manner in which it was exercised became part of the politics of the city, at a time when factional rivalries were becoming more intense than ever. In the middle decades of the twelfth century the authority that the bishops had established over the clergy and churches of the diocese in the previous two hundred years, the concentration of property and patronage in their hands, the incomes, offices and resources that they had developed, became fuel for the flames of competition for resources and power.

The emergence of the commune in these years, and the consolidation of control over the city and its affairs by noble families at the expense of outsiders, both imperial and papal, further politicised the functions of the bishops while diminishing their power. Their position was further eroded by the Peace of Constance, in 1183, when Frederick Barbarossa, after two decades of bitter warfare, was forced to acknowledge the legitimacy of communal government. Over the previous sixty years the bishops had lost a great deal of power and influence. They now found themelves very much in need of a role.[7]

13

SPEAKING OF PRINCIPLES

When Statesmen gravely say 'We must be realistic'
The chances are they're weak, and therefore pacifistic:
But when they speak of Principles, look out: perhaps
Their generals are already poring over maps.
W. H. Auden, Collected Shorter Poems

The Lateran Council over, Henri de Marci, now a cardinal, crossed the Alps in the spring of 1181 to take up again the struggle against heresy. He came as a papal legate, the first in history to raise and lead an army on a military expedition in a Christian territory. Henri had taken his vows at Clairvaux in 1156, three years after the death of Bernard, became abbot of one of its important daughter houses (Hautecombe in the Savoy) only four years later and returned to Clairvaux as abbot in 1176. What he had seen in 1178 in Toulouse — to him 'the mother of heresy and the fountain-head of error' — gave substance to the nightmare that he had inherited from Bernard of 'the order of heretics, an army of apostates, irreverently reviling the troops of the living God, impiously presuming to blaspheme against the majesty of the Lord'. Henri had been influential in preparing the Lateran decree against heresy, and he and his successors continued to regard the campaign against it in this region as a special responsibility, and popes to entrust them with it. In consequence the Cistercians largely moulded both the church's perception of the nature of heresy in the region at the end of the twelfth century and, through their letters and reports, modern understandings of it.

The mission of 1178 had been dispatched in response to an appeal for help from Raymond V of Toulouse against those whom he called heretics and their patrons. His real target was a political alliance formed against him after his occupation of Narbonne the previous year. The war that he had triggered by this action had raged intermittently ever since, and would continue until the mid-1190s. It was conducted by mercenary soldiers employed on all sides:

> the Brabanters, Aragonese, Navarrese, Basques, Cotereaux and Tria-
> verdins, who practise such cruelty upon Christians that they respect
> neither churches nor monasteries, and spare neither widows, orphans,
> old or young nor any age or sex, but like pagans destroy and lay every-
> thing waste.[1]

Thus Lateran III had condemned these mercenaries in the same canon as the heretics and imposed the same penalties on 'those who hire, keep or support them'. According to Stephen of Tournai, travelling through the region on his way to meet the papal legate, 'we see nothing but the burned villages and ruined houses; we find no refuge; all threatens our safety and lays ambush for our lives.' Afterwards he remembered how 'passing there not long ago I saw the terrible fiery image of death, churches half destroyed, holy places in ashes, their foundations dug up. The houses of men had become the dwellings of beasts.'[2]

The misery and devastation that Stephen witnessed were real and his horror genuine, but by this time the armies of every king and prince in Europe were made up of mercenaries like these. Armies were no longer composed, if they ever had been, of gallant knights giving loyal service to their lords. What Stephen saw and the council had condemned was not a new evil but the sight of familiar forces out of what they regarded as proper control, compounding the miseries of the countless petty wars and feuds endemic in a deeply fragmented society, too many of whose young men had nothing to lose but their 'honour'.

Cardinal Henri's army laid siege to Lavaur, a stronghold of Vicomte Roger Trencavel of Béziers currently under the command of his wife, Adelaide. Roger immediately agreed to stop protecting heretics and made a start by handing over Bernard Raymond and Raymond de Baimac, who had taken refuge in Lavaur after their encounter with Peter of St Chrysogonus in Toulouse in 1178. Brought before a council of the church at Le Puy, they were so moved by the eloquence of Henri de Marci (he recounted) that they broke down, undertook to reveal the secrets of their sect and were allowed to return to Toulouse as canons respectively of St Etienne and St Sernin. Both were reported still to be leading praiseworthily religious lives in those positions six or seven years later; Bernard Raymond witnessed several acts of the chapter of St Etienne between 1184 and 1197.

These events, including the confession, were described by Henri de Marci in a letter now lost but used by the Limousin chronicler Geoffrey of Vigeois, who died in 1184, and another Cistercian abbot, Geoffrey of Auxerre, three or four years later.[3] The account of Geoffrey of Vigeois contains two important novelties. He was the first to describe the heretics as Albigensians, meaning specifically heretics living in the area of Albi. After the Albigensian Crusade was launched in 1209, this became the name commonly used by northerners for all adherents of the (supposedly) dualist heresy against whose protectors it was directed, and by historians until the term 'Cathar' came into vogue in the second half of the twentieth century.

Geoffrey of Vigeois's report of the confession itself is more sensational. Having described the heresy which the two converts recanted at Le Puy as rejecting, predictably enough, the teaching of the Roman church on the sacrifice of the Mass, the baptism of infants, marriage and the other sacraments, he quotes them as saying that it taught that

Satan, the Great Lucifer, who because of his pride and wickedness had fallen from the throne of the good angels, is the creator of heaven and earth, of all things visible and invisible, and of the evil spirits. It was he who had given the law of Moses. Christ had only the appearance of humanity; he did not experience hunger, thirst or other bodily needs; he did not undergo the passion, was not crucified, did not die and has not risen again. Everything claimed by the Gospels and the apostles is fantasy.

Raymond and Bernard also claimed that the heretics indulged in sexual orgies and justified abortion and infanticide on the ground that giving life was the work of the devil. For good measure Geoffrey of Vigeois throws in the story that the wife of a local noble who had left her husband to join the heretics was initiated by being vigorously debauched by fifty of their senior members. Geoffrey of Auxerre adds that, according to Bernard and Raymond, the heretics dismissed infant baptism as valueless because adults must undergo their own ritual imposition of hands from their elect, and that they attacked alms to churches and condemned prayers for the dead as a mercenary racket invented by clerks.

Thus far Bernard and Raymond had reiterated for the most part a familiar combination of anticlerical and anti-ecclesiastical sentiments deriving from literally understood biblical precepts whose implications were exaggerated either by the heretics themselves or their accusers. It was embellished by the routine monastic invective that Henri de Marci had used to describe the Toulouse he entered in 1178, in which every form of pollution, from heresy to leprosy, sodomy and bestiality, was merged into a single diabolically inspired menace to the divine and social order.

In its vivid and explicit description of Satan as the creator of the earth and the giver of the law of Moses, on the other hand, the confession made a major contribution to the emerging account of the heresy as not merely another set of doctrinal errors springing from apostolic enthusiasm and anticlericalism but a counter-church with its own ritual and hierarchy and a theology and mythology based on the belief in two principles. That such a counter-church indeed existed in the lands between the Rhône and the Garonne has often been inferred, with varying plausibility, from some of the earlier accusations discussed in this book. It is here asserted directly and explicitly for the first time. It became henceforth the model for Cistercian accounts of the Albigensian heresy and was eventually taken up by the inquisitors of the thirteenth century. But it is not clear where it came from. It is possible that as repentant heretics Raymond and Bernard were simply reporting what they knew from experience to be true, but it is also possible that they hoped to win pardon and favour (as, in fact, they did) by confirming the expectations of their interrogators. If so, they would have been neither the first nor the last converts to do so.

It was not the tradition of Bernard of Clairvaux, whose interest was in the moral and sacramental consequences of heresy rather than its theological basis, that led Henri de Marci to look for dualism. Nor are the rumours of dualist preaching in Toulouse before 1178 substantiated by the accounts of the mission of that year, though they had been reported, as rumours, by Peter of St Chrysogonus. It would have been in Peter's retinue, rather than that of Henri de Marci, that we would expect to find clerks from the Paris schools, where rebuttal of the 'Manichaean' heresy, based on the descriptions of it by St Augustine and other early fathers of the church, was by now a routine academic exercise. Be that as it may, it looks as though it was from the mission in 1178, though not directly from his own experience or observation during it, that Henri de Marci learned to anticipate the abomination that in 1181 he confirmed to his own satisfaction and fed into a regular place in the rhetoric of his order.

A direct link between the Paris schools and developing Cistercian insistence on the dualism of the heretics was provided by a famous master and teacher who joined the order towards the end of his life, Alan of Lille. Alan was a prolific author, whose treatise *On the Catholic Faith* is thought to have been written around 1190. Its first book, purportedly addressed to 'the heretics of our time [who] say that there are two principles of things, the principle of light and the principle of darkness',[4] has often been taken as describing the Albigensians from direct experience, largely because it was dedicated to Count William VIII of Montpellier. This does not follow. William had spent most of the 1180s resisting the claim of Raymond of Toulouse to the lordship of Montpellier and, after reaching a reluctant settlement with Raymond in 1190, was very much in need of legitimisation for his bastard sons. Both circumstances provided him with excellent reasons to show himself a good catholic, as the patron of a comprehensive defence of the faith by one of the most celebrated Parisian masters of the day. There is nothing in Alan of Lille's disappointingly undocumented life to connect him with the Languedoc or to confirm that he ever visited the region in any capacity. His treatise is directed not only against heretics but against Jews and infidels, and attributes to the 'heretics' of the first book not a coherent set of beliefs but a series of propositions that Alan rebuts, in the standard order established by his teacher Peter Lombard, in such a way as to construct his own statement of catholic orthodoxy. Like the *Summa against the Heretics* that he had written as a young man, it is a scholastic exercise, based on the writings of the church fathers, in a tradition of disputation going back to the days of Peter Abelard of which Alan was a famed exponent. The 'heretics' it describes are another example of ivory-tower dualism.

Whether he wrote *On the Catholic Faith* before or after he left Paris for Cîteaux, Alan of Lille was ideally equipped to provide the intellectual buttressing that would show how the rumours and reports circulating so disturbingly among his new or future brethren fitted into the ageless struggle between the church and its eternal adversary. There is, however, no basis for supposing that he had been in direct contact with the Evil One's current representatives. Nor does Alan represent the only contact between the Cistercians and the schools. Recent studies of manuscripts from Cîteaux show that the order's early distrust of scholastic theology had by 1200 given way to a realisation that academic sermons and commentaries on the Bible, as well as collections of *quaestiones* – model discussions of theological issues – could form part of their armoury against irreligion and unbelief. Or, to put it another way, they could provide spectacles through which to view and interpret the theological errors found in circulation among uneducated people.

———

Henri de Marci and Geoffrey of Auxerre played a major role in making another substantial religious movement that began in this region into a heresy. The Waldensians worried them less than the one deserted by Bernard Raymond and Raymond de Baimac, but the manner in which they dealt with them, and the consequences of their doing so, were in some respects more typical of the way in which the thirteenth-century war on heresy came about. The Waldensians began, like the Humiliati in Lombardy with whom the bull *Ad abolendam* confused them, as a group of pious catholic laymen:

> At the Roman council under Pope Alexander [i.e., Lateran III] I saw some Waldensians, simple illiterate men, called after their leader Waldo [or Valdès], who was a citizen of Lyon, on the Rhône. They offered the pope a book written in French in which was contained, with a gloss, the Psalter and many of the books of the two Testaments. They pressed very earnestly that the right of preaching should be confirmed to them, for in their own eyes they were learned, though in reality they were barely beginners.

The request was refused, and Walter Map, whose account this is, was satisified that as one of those who questioned them on behalf of the council he had assisted in a conclusive demonstration of the palpable ignorance of these presumptuous laymen. Nevertheless, he saw them as a threat to the clerical order. 'These people have no settled abodes', he continues; 'they go about two and two, barefoot, clad in woollen, owning nothing but having all things in common, like the apostles nakedly following the naked Christ. They are now beginning in a very humble guise, because they cannot get their foot in; but if we let them in we shall be turned out.'[5]

Writing forty years later, another chronicler described Valdès as a rich usurer who, inspired by the story of St Alexis (the son of a Roman noble who fled his wife and inheritance to devote himself to the Christian life, living disguised as a beggar in his father's house[6]), gave away his considerable property, to the understandable dismay of his wife. Thenceforth he lived on alms, gathering disciples with whom he took to preaching 'both against their own sins and those of others' – that is, of course, the clergy. It was a story sure to appeal to the age of Francis of Assisi, and became famous. Scrutiny of the strictly contemporary circumstances, however, suggests something much more reminiscent of the conflicts of the earlier twelfth century, and more consonant with a Lyon still relatively backward and commercially undeveloped. Archbishop Guichard, like the city, was old-fashioned – in fact, the oldest surviving Cistercian abbot, having become abbot of Pontigny in 1137. He had been elected in 1167 to an archbishopric long plagued by conflict between noble factions for control of its lands and revenues. When his attempt to introduce the common life – that is, to reform the cathedral chapter – was bitterly opposed, he turned for help to the pious lay people who had so often provided the impetus to reform in those circumstances. One of them was Valdès, who employed a young scribe named Bernard Ydros to copy translations of the scriptures that he had commissioned from a teacher and canon of the cathedral named Stephen of Anse, the books that were later produced in Rome.[7]

The Lateran Council approved the Waldensians' way of life but permitted them to preach only with the approval of local clergy. In 1181, however, Valdès was summoned before a council at Lyon and required to make a profession of faith. The council was presided over by his patron, Archbishop Guichard, but it had been summoned at the initiative of Henri de Marci and Geoffrey of Auxerre. Although both were Cistercian abbots, Guichard and Geoffrey were old adversaries, having clashed many years before over Guichard's willingness to give refuge at Pontigny to Thomas Becket, in exile from the wrath of King Henry II. Geoffrey had been the loser; he had resigned his abbacy of Clairvaux in consequence, and made himself thereafter custodian of the legend of St Bernard, and especially of St Bernard as a prophet against heretics. Hence the suspicion that the oath administered to Valdès was a defensive move on Guichard's part, to vindicate his sponsorship of the preaching of Valdès and his companions. The zealous outsiders' contempt for the local clergy was also shown in the deposition at this time of Archbishop Pons d'Arsac of Narbonne and several senior members of his cathedral chapter. There is no reason to think of Pons as a particularly incompetent or scandalous prelate; on the contrary, unlike most in the region, he had remained on good terms with the lord of his city, the Countess Ermengard, and her ally Roger of Béziers, keeping the peace and winning patronage for his church from both of them by doing so. Perhaps that was the problem. Or perhaps, as the only member of the 1178 mission who actually knew the region and understood its politics, his view of what really lay behind the heresy accusations and counter-accusations of that year had failed to conform to the expectations of its leaders.[8]

Guichard's protection availed Valdès little, for a year later both Guichard and Pope Alexander were dead, and Guichard had been replaced as archbishop of Lyon by John 'of the Beautiful Hands', bishop of Poitiers. John had been a member of the mission to Toulouse in 1178 and had also been offered, but declined, the vacancy at Narbonne following the removal of Pons d'Arsac; he died a Cistercian. One of his first actions in Lyon was to expel Valdès and his followers, presumably because they had refused to give up preaching. Certainly, dispersed through Provence and Lombardy, they continued to preach, maintaining that they were required to do so by the command of the apostle James that 'the man who knows the good he can do and does not do it is a sinner' (James 4: 17). They still travelled in pairs, as Walter Map had described them, at first barefoot but later wearing sandals, living in apostolic poverty and simplicity, and were reported as far afield as Toul in 1192 and Metz in 1200. They were condemned by the archbishop of Narbonne in or soon after 1185, and by the archbishop of Montpellier before 1200, and were the object of legislation by King Alfonso II of Aragon in 1194 and his successor, Pedro II, in 1197. Pedro's was the first to prescribe death by fire for convicted heretics.

The Waldensians' success in Lombardy was reputedly considerable, but obscure. It was reported much later to papal inquisitors that in 1218 a meeting of representatives of French (Leonist) and Lombard 'Poor Men' at Bergamo had failed to repair a long-standing division between them. They had agreed to the election of a single superior and to the ordination of ministers among them, that baptism in water was necessary for salvation, and that marriages could not be dissolved without mutual consent. The Lombards, however, would not accept that Valdès and one of his companions were certainly in heaven, or that the Mass could be consecrated by a lawfully ordained but sinful priest.[9]

The traditional acceptance, by both catholics and Waldensians, that all these incidents and accounts refer to the same people, members of a single movement in which the modern Waldensian church originated, is bedevilled by the familiar problem of establishing how far they were lumped together by the terminology of *Ad abolendam* – which lumped them also with the Lombard Humiliati, with whom they were clearly not identical – the perceptions of the authorities, and hindsight in the sources. Scholarly opinion is sharply divided.[10] More relevant here is the extent to which the followers of Valdès remained free of doctrinal heresy in spite of their exclusion from the church and consequent persecution. The confession of faith avowed by Valdès himself in 1181 added to the template on which it was based an affirmation of the unity of God and the humanity of Christ, a sign of the anxieties of those who administered it. The fact that Valdès subscribed to it without demur merely confirms his freedom from a variety of errors and his obedience to the church. Their refusal of the church's authority to license preaching long remained the only charge against him and his followers, of whom a group led by Durand of Osca (either Osques in the Rouergue or Huesca in Aragon) returned to the church in 1205 and continued their mission as Poor Catholics. In the light of their experience the bitter hostility to the church of Rome and its hierarchy always reported of the Waldensians is hardly surprising. Even so, as late as 1218, it would appear, the Poor of Lyon (as they continued to be called, at least by the inquisitors) refused to take so early a step along the heretical road that we have regularly travelled in these pages as to deny the ability of sinful priests to confer the sacraments.

———

In proclaiming the depth and depravity of the heresies that they uncovered in and around the lands of the count of Toulouse, Henri de Marci and his successors spoke to a world willing to listen. Bernard of Clairvaux had been shocked in 1145 to find a land of 'churches without people and Christians without Christ' where the changes that had been bringing more regular and better-organised parochial services to the parts of Europe that he knew best had hardly begun to take hold. In the fifty years after Bernard's visit the disparities with the much more rapidly developing lowland regions of western Europe became still greater, in secular as well as in religious life. It was in the second half of the twelfth century that the social transformation that had been gathering since the millennium and before really took off. More intensively and efficiently cultivated fields in cleared forests and on drained marshes supported rising agricultural productivity, the volume and variety of trade grew apace, both locally and over long distances, markets proliferated, the scale and quality of building soared, towns mushroomed, and the number of their inhabitants and the diversity of their skills and occupations multiplied accordingly. Slowly and fitfully, but inexorably, the authority of kings and princes was being translated into effectively exercised power, peace more regularly secured, order better maintained. By the 1180s the transformation – including the stresses and tensions revealed in the last chapter – was visible everywhere, and most spectacularly in Lombardy and Tuscany, in the Low Countries and the valleys of the Rhine, the Seine and the Thames.

The lands between the Rhône and the Dordogne were not untouched. Toulouse, Narbonne and Montpellier had grown, and their citizens had become somewhat more inclined to assert themselves. But they were still small towns dominated by their territorial lords – lords whose flamboyant splendour belied the fact that their estates were far less ample and their followers far less effectively controlled and deployed than those of their northern counterparts. Even more important in setting the region apart was its lack of participation in the common developments that were building in Europe a common culture under the direction of an increasingly cohesive clerical elite. Superficially that is not obvious. The gaze of posterity – like the age itself – is easily distracted by the glamour of the warrior aristocracy and its amusements. The southern nobles were prominent in the crusades and supported their share, or more than their share, of courtly culture, especially in the songs of the troubadours, which rank in any valuation among the greatest artistic achievements of one of Europe's most creative centuries. But by the harsher measure of what directly changed the world, what constituted usable power, the warriors were no longer dominant. Military power still ruled, of course, and always would, as we shall have grim occasion to observe. But it no longer resided in the valour and courtesy of the perfect knights who rode their magnificent chargers so valiantly through the nostalgic pages of the romances. It rested on the steady streams of revenue secured by the ruthless, limitless ingenuity of the clerks who flocked to the courts of princes and great lords, spiritual and temporal. That was how the mercenaries everywhere so bitterly complained of were paid for.

The advance in the dominance of the clerks is reflected in the contrast between the two missions from the outside world that had done so much in 1145 and again in 1178 to construct the image of the *partes Tolosae* as a seat of heresy and disorder. The mission of 1145 was led by a papal legate, but its directing force was the ragged and emaciated Bernard of Clairvaux, the most famous holy man of the day, its weapons against the heretics his eloquence and the fame of his miracles. The expedition of 1178 was also led by a papal legate and also starred the abbot of Clairvaux, but it was staffed by bureaucrats who turned against the heretics, to much greater effect, the administrative techniques that they had been honing in the service of their royal masters. In the intervening three decades clerks like these had multiplied in number and influence throughout northern Europe precisely for the reason illustrated by that contrast, because they could offer better solutions to the problems of their lords.* These included maximising traditional sources of revenue and identifying new ones (such as the fines that could be levied on heretics and their supporters) certainly, but the process of change went much deeper, to a subtler and more flexible understanding of the nature and use of power itself.

The great engines of this change were the schools of Paris and Bologna. Not yet formally constituted as universities (this would come in the early years of the thirteenth century), they had established in essentials their curricula and teaching methods by the 1140s, and as we saw in Chapter 9 their masters had secured effective intellectual autonomy at Reims in 1148. The students who flocked to them from all over Europe went on to become in effect members of an international managerial elite, able to move easily between different countries and between secular and ecclesiastical courts, carrying with them shared outlooks as well as shared skills, common habits of thought and common values. Their opportunities were greatest, their mobility and influence maximised, in the great national and international political structures that now flourished. In the greatest, the church, the end of the papal schism in 1178 opened the way for the clerks to carry their ambitions and ideals to ever higher levels

---

* Mrs Thatcher explained that she valued the self-made businessman Lord Young of Graffham, who was mistrusted by the traditional grandees of her Conservative party, because 'the others bring me problems; he brings me solutions'.

of aspiration and opportunity. It now became true once again that all roads led to Rome.

Of course, graduates of Paris and Bologna did not fill all the key positions, but their ways of thinking shaped the new forms of power. Neither Henry II's treasurer, Richard Fitzneal, nor his chief justice, Ranulf Glanvill, builders of the most developed secular government in northern Europe, was educated in the schools, although the unidentified author of the great treatise on *The Laws and Customs of England* that goes under Ranulf's name may have been. Nevertheless, both Richard's *Dialogue on the Exchequer* and 'Glanvill' show the influence of the dialectical reasoning that was the hallmark of the schools, and both men in their work approached the everyday problems of government in a consistently analytical fashion that clearly reflects scholastic assumptions and habits of mind. 'A case is either criminal or civil' says 'Glanvill'; a thing is either *a* or not *a*. Upon such logical polarities the new world of the clerks was constructed, leaving little room for the fuzzier traditions of compromise and negotiation through which the community had established its boundaries of acceptability. Trial by ordeal was now despised and soon to be abolished as superstition; miracles were performed not by living, breathing holy men but by the bones of the saints at authorised and carefully regulated shrines.

All this had largely bypassed 'the world of the troubadours'. The mighty though short-lived empire created by the marriage of Henry of Anjou and Eleanor of Aquitaine brought English clerks to Toulouse in 1178. We do not find clerks from Toulouse on missions to England, or men from this region rising to prominence in the schools of Paris or the papal curia, as many of them would do a hundred years later. The anomalies perceived by outsiders became correspondingly more acute, the appearance correspondingly more sinister, of a land without rule or religion, riven by heresy and disorder, prey to the forces of chaos that the world beyond was painfully and still precariously striving to overcome. That such perceptions could so readily be made to justify its subordination to the political, religious or cultural hegemony of the new order in Latin Europe did nothing to diminish the sincerity and fervour with which they were embraced.

1 4

THE ENEMY AT THE GATE

If the earth should rise up against you, and the stars of the heavens should reveal your iniquity and manifest your sins to the whole world, so that not only humans but the very elements themselves should join together for your destruction and ruin and wipe you from the face of the earth, sparing neither sex nor age, even that punishment laid upon you would still not be sufficient and worthy.

Innocent III to the citizens of Viterbo[1]

As Innocent III, Lothar Segni, the outstanding talent in a new generation of leaders, became pope in 1198. At thirty-seven he was probably the youngest man ever to do so. The son of a well-connected family of the Roman Campagna, he had been educated in Paris and active in the papal curia since his elevation to the cardinalate in 1189 or 1190. It was this experience that gave him a reputation as a lawyer and a man of business, for there is no evidence that he had a legal education. As pope he brought several masters from Paris to his court, and theology rather than law pervaded his thought. During the 1190s he wrote two works of devotional theology, *On the Mystery of the Mass* and *On the Contempt of the World*, which remained influential for several centuries, the latter surviving in more than 700 medieval manuscripts.

Innocent III had charm, dynamism and vision. He also had a loftier conception of the powers of his office than any pope since Gregory VII.

> It is to me that the words of the prophet apply: I have established thee above peoples and kingdoms, that thou mightest uproot and destroy, and also that thou mightest build and plant. It is to me that it was said: I will give thee the keys of the kingdom of heaven, and whatsoever thou shalt bind on earth shall be bound in heaven.

On this basis he claimed 'fullness of power' (*plenitudo potestatis*) over the lives and business of the Christian people and used it to excommunicate two emperors, seven kings and many lesser lords, and to suspend catholic services in their lands. Holding himself bound to intervene vigorously in the affairs of the world because 'We who are, unworthily, the vicar of Christ on earth, following his example and imitating the custom of our predecessors, wish and are obliged to attend to the restoration of true peace and concord between those who are in dispute', he presided over two of European history's infamous atrocities.[2] In 1204 Constantinople, the greatest Christian city in the world, was besieged and looted by an army of crusaders initially raised to recover Jerusalem from the Muslims. In 1208 Innocent launched another crusade, ostensibly against the Albigensian heretics of the lands between the Rhône and the Garonne, whose relentless succession of sieges, lootings and burnings set a new level of savagery in wars between Christians. Posterity has generally supposed that in both cases Innocent did what he thought was right.

———

Two years before Innocent's accession the city of Orvieto had seized control of the stronghold of Acquapendente, which commanded a road bridge crucial to its trade, and over which the papacy had long claimed jurisdiction. One of Innocent's first actions was to demand its return. When the Orvietans refused, he placed the city under interdict, recalled the bishop to Rome and sent a Roman noble named Pietro Parenzo to take over its government as papal rector. The events that followed, as

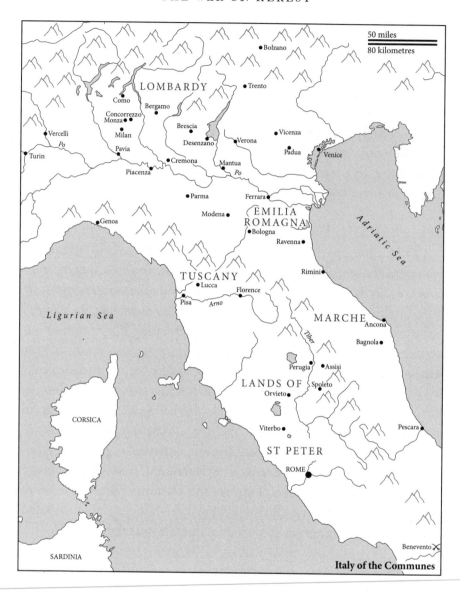

50 miles
80 kilometres

Bolzano

LOMBARDY
Como
Trento
Bergamo
Concorrezzo
Monza
Brescia
Vercelli
Milan
Desenzano
Verona
Vicenza
Po
Pavia
Padua
Turin
Cremona
Venice
Mantua
Piacenza
Po

Parma
Ferrara
Modena
EMILIA
ROMAGNA
Genoa
Bologna
Ravenna

Adriatic Sea

TUSCANY
Rimini
Lucca
Florence
Pisa
Arno

Ligurian Sea

MARCHE
Ancona
Bagnola

Tiber
Perugia
Assisi
LANDS OF
Spoleto
Orvieto

CORSICA

Viterbo
Pescara

ST PETER
ROME

SARDINIA

Benevento

Italy of the Communes

described immediately after Pietro's murder less than a year later, by Master John, a canon of the cathedral who himself became bishop of Orvieto in 1211, offer a unique cameo of the place of heresy in Italian life and politics at the end of the twelfth century.[3] John's tale of Pietro's heroic confrontation with the heretics, the hatching of a plot against him, his bloody death and the reaction that followed, sealed by miracles at his tomb, would have given Verdi the material of a superb libretto.

In Act I Orvieto's heretics were so emboldened by the bishop's absence that

> the notion began to grow upon them of confiscating the goods of any catholics who would not join their sect, and expel them or kill them, so that they could turn the city, with its impregnable fortifications, into a citadel for heretics from all over the world to hold against the catholic church.

The terrified catholics,

> afraid that the tunic of Christ would be irreparably torn, met together under divine inspiration and sent some of their number to Rome to find a rector who would acquire the pope's favour for the Orvietans, make peace with the Romans and extirpate the heresy from the city.

The pope ordered Pietro Parenzo, 'young in years, but old in wisdom, constant, intelligent, eloquent and clear-headed', to cleanse Orvieto of heresy, with the comforting reassurance that 'if he died in the attempt he would be assured of eternal glory'.

In Act II Pietro 'was received in Orvieto with joy and honour, with laurels and olive branches, by all the citizens, high and low'. He inaugurated his regime by forbidding jousting at the Lent carnival, 'since at that time many murders had been committed under the cover of sport'. On the first day of Lent the heretics, pretending to be playing a game, started a brawl and soon

> the whole city was fighting in the piazza with swords and lances, stones were thrown from the towers and palaces around it and the peace was shattered. Pietro mounted a horse and broke up the fight by riding between the sides, exposing himself to the danger of death. By divine protection he passed through their ranks unharmed.

Sadly, John neglected to record his aria.

Condign punishment of the heretics followed. Pietro

had the towers and palaces from which the skirmishing had been con-ducted razed to the ground so that everybody was punished in pro-portion to his wealth and without regard to persons. From the many who had fought, with great bloodshed, he exacted lawful recompense with severity.

In conjunction with the bishop Pietro then issued an ultimatum:

> Anyone who returned to the church before a stated day would be received with mercy and good will; anyone who refused to return before the day fixed would be liable to the penalties laid down by civil and canon law. The recalcitrants were bound in iron fetters, and some were sentenced to be publicly flogged, some exiled from the city, and some fined, which was bitterly lamented by the greedy; he exacted large recog-nisances* from others, and had the houses of many of them destroyed.

At the beginning of Act III Pietro returned to Rome to spend Easter with his family, reporting to the pope that he had acted against the her-etics with such severity that they were publicly threatening to kill him. Innocent accepted this news with equanimity, promising that 'by the authority of God, and of the apostles St Peter and St Paul I absolve you from all your sins if you die at the hands of the heretics.' Pietro went home, made his will and bade farewell to his weeping mother and sisters. Meanwhile in Orvieto the heretics laid their plot, bribing one of Pietro's servants to betray him. Pietro returned, once more to be 'received by the Orvietans with garlands, flowers and great joy'. 'Far from giving up his persecution of the heretics, he bravely ignored their threats and warnings and visited them with the full penalties of the law.'

On 20 May, as Pietro was preparing for bed, a gang of heretics called at his palazzo, asking to see him. With the help of the bribed servant they seized and gagged him, and took him to a mill in the *contado*, where they demanded that he return their recognisances, promise to stop har-assing them, and resign his lordship of the city. Pietro was willing to give back their money from his own resources, but

---

*Money deposited as a pledge of good behaviour.

he would rather submit to any torture than stray from the path of the catholic faith by consenting to their heresy. He would not evade his orders, or ensnare himself in the web of perjury, for the government of Orvieto had been entrusted to him, on oath, for one year.

In this he persisted until

one of them growled, 'Why are we wasting words on this scoundrel?' He raised his fist and struck Pietro in the mouth, knocking out a tooth and leaving his face streaming with blood. Another, seized by the same fury, grabbed a millstone and hit Pietro on the back of the head, so that he fell to the ground and got a mouthful of dust, which he received as a holy sacrament. Others killed Pietro with swords and knives. He was stabbed four times. They tried to get rid of the body in an old well overgrown with vegetation, but they could neither move the body nor open the well. The body remained immovable so they fled, leaving it under a walnut tree which had formerly been sterile, but that year by God's will produced two heavy crops in witness of the martyrdom.

Next morning Pietro's body was found by monks on their way to the mill, and Act V describes the distress of the Orvietans and their reaction, in which some of the heretics were lynched, others were brought to trial and some escaped from the city, but not from the plague that followed, a sign of divine vengeance. Pietro was buried in the cathedral, but only after a good deal of argument, because

the great church was deprived of attendance and respect, and there were scarcely three lamps inside to provide light ... the place where his tomb rests had almost no protection from the rain, given the poor condition of the roof above it. As a result that deserted place, with the rain irrigating it and the grass growing appeared like a meadow.

As the resting place of the martyr, however, the cathedral became once more a place of pilgrimage and the centre of the life of the city, not the least of the miracles that Pietro worked being to call down fire from heaven, 'burning scarlet and gold, to light the lamps, candles and lanterns whenever their own flames had burnt out'.[4]

It is, of course, quite anachronistic to retell the story of Pietro Parenzo in the shape of a five-act opera. Apart from anything else, Verdi, a fervent supporter of the nineteenth-century Italian Risorgimento, would have sided with the heretics. Master John's story was directly, and equally self-consciously, modelled on the passion of Christ. It is deliberately and carefully crafted, designed to consolidate the supporters in Orvieto of papal lordship and of the recovery by the bishopric of lands and revenues lost, largely to lords of the *contado*, during the turbulent 1160s and '70s. In neither respect was it entirely successful. The cathedral was still dilapidated and the episcopal property wretchedly depleted when Bishop Rainerio made an inventory of it in 1228, and the attitude even of catholic Orvietans to papal lordship remained ambivalent. Master John himself, when he became bishop, found it necessary to defy Innocent III by renewing a feudal contract with Count Bulgarello of Parrano, at a time when Bulgarello was under sentence of excommunication as a supporter of the emperor Otto IV. Innocent's refusal when he preached in Orvieto in 1216 to give a hearing to fifty Orvietans who wanted to testify to miracles at Peter's tomb is another indication that the story was not quite so straightforward as John makes it appear. Passionately committed though he was to the fight against heresy, it did not suit the pope to give a saint to a Roman family with which his own relations were distinctly strained.

————

Even for so clear-headed a man as Innocent III it was not easy to distinguish between heresy as a religious force and as a political one. Of all the problems that confronted him the most dangerous had been created by the death of King William II of Sicily, without a legitimate male heir, in 1189. Its consequences reshaped and dominated the affairs of the Italian peninsula, and therefore of the papacy, for the rest of the period considered by this book. The succession was fiercely contested by William's able and well-supported but illegitimate nephew Tancred and by the emperor Henry VI, who claimed it through his wife, Constance, a daughter of

Roger II of Sicily. The Sicilian kingdom was a papal fief, and though their relations were often uneasy, it had provided the papacy throughout the twelfth century with an essential counter-balance to imperial power in Italy – essential, at any rate, if the papacy was to preserve any measure of political independence, and still more so if it was to exercise political power on its own account.

The pope could hardly view the prospect of empire and kingdom in the same hands with equanimity, or welcome Henry's victory, after a series of exceptionally cruel campaigns, in 1194. Henry's early death in 1197 precipitated another succession dispute. The empire was claimed by his brother Philip of Swabia and by Otto of Brunswick, hereditary enemy of the Hohenstaufen. The championship of Philip's cause by Henry's most trusted lieutenant, Markward of Anweiler, precipitated a renewed and bitter struggle throughout the peninsula. In May 1198 Innocent crowned Frederick, the three-year-old son of Henry and Constance, as king of Sicily, but not as king of the Romans, the title that normally designated the heir apparent to the empire. In return Constance reaffirmed that Sicily was a papal fief. When she died in November 1198, Innocent accordingly assumed the guardianship of Frederick and the regency of Sicily. These events framed the conditions in which the papacy acquired the habit of using every weapon in its spiritual armoury – crusading, privileges for its allies, excommunication and anathematisation as heretics for its enemies – in defence of its territorial interests. Henceforth every rebellion, every factional conflict, every project of domination, could be assimilated to the cause, or at least adorned with the label, of the Guelfs (Welf being the family name of Otto IV), who upheld the temporal power of the papacy, or the Ghibellines, the supporters of the Hohenstaufen. The drama of Pietro Parenzo's governorship of Orvieto was not only the simple story of heroic piety pitted against heretical depravity that we heard from Master John. In the circumstances that gave rise to it, the manner in which it was played out and its aftermath it contained almost all the elements that came together in the 1190s to transform Italian politics. The tensions and divisions that multiplied in its course, at every level of society, created an environment in which accusations of heresy and their consequences multiplied and flourished.

Whatever their relations, both pope and emperor faced another power that both despised, but which was potentially greater than either of them. The towns were now growing explosively in size and wealth, and ever more vigorously engaged in dominating and enlarging their *contados*, often in rivalry with one another. Tensions that had long been building between towns and their lords and between different factions of citizens surfaced in the 1190s to make the first half of the thirteenth century, a time of even more rapid growth and development than the twelfth had been, also one of constant and violent civic conflict. The communes had been established by the factions of noble families that dominated them for most of the twelfth century, conducting their vendettas from their networks of fortified towers. Merchants too banded together to defend their common interests and win a share in civic government. Little is known of the early history of the merchant guilds because, when possible, they were ferociously suppressed by the noble communes. From about the 1150s, however, they fragmented and multiplied as particular trades and specialisms, and the inhabitants of particular quarters, began in their turn to claim and seek to advance their collective identities and to form armed associations to defend their common interests. These were the groups that became known collectively as the *popolo*, whose ferocious conflicts with the noble communes reverberated through the thirteenth century, eventually to deliver the cities to the rule of despots. The contest broke into the open at Brescia in 1196, at Piacenza in 1198, at Milan between 1198 and 1201, at Assisi between 1198 and 1202, Padua in 1200, Cremona in 1201, Lucca in 1203 ... and at Orvieto in 1199. The particular combination of grievance and alliance between different groups and interests, between those within the city and in the *contado*, between the factions in the city and the claims and claimants of rival cities, of wider lordship, of empire or papacy, was unique in every case, but all were drawn from the same list of ingredients.

Innocent confronted the towns directly when, in April 1198, a council at Verona, instructed by him to deal with the problem of heresy in northern Italy, decreed that heretics should be excluded from all participation in municipal elections and from every official position.[5] Thus within a few weeks of his accession Innocent gratified the ambition of every political agent and every would-be tyrant for a handy way to disqualify his opponents, before or after the event. The message was received well beyond Lombardy. Within a few months Zukan, lord of Dioclea (modern Montenegro), in rebellion against his elder brother the ruler of Serbia, saw an opportunity to find favour both with the pope and with King Imre of Hungary. He claimed that his neighbour and rival lord (*ban*) Kulin of Bosnia, an underling of Imre's own rebellious younger brother, had become a heretic, along with ten thousand others, and suggested that the pope might urge Imre to expel them. So it continued.

Reputation must be confirmed by due process, of course, and Innocent did his best, on occasion, to see that those accused – a clerk at Nevers in 1200, a group of laymen and women from La Charité-sur-Loire and another from Bologna, in 1205 – had a proper, legal opportunity to defend themselves. On the other hand, convinced that he was surrounded on all sides by the enemies of the faith, he was always ready to identify opposition to his designs with hostility to the Christian religion itself, and to deploy the full panoply of spiritual sanctions against every opponent. Among those enemies Innocent, at heart more theologian than lawyer, saw heretics as the most dangerous, and their danger greatest in the theological dualism for which his generation of students had been taught to look out. He warned especially against

> the impious Manichaeans, who call themselves Cathars or Patarenes, and whose madness the apostle Paul foresaw, 'giving heed to seducing spirits and doctrines of devils ... forbidding to marry and commanding to abstain from meats ...' created not by God but by the Devil, by whom all corporeal and visible things were created ... more to be detested than Simon Magus.[6]

It is a revealing comparison. It was of the sin of Simon Magus, which they regarded as the root of the evils that beset the church, that the first Patarenes had accused Innocent's predecessors, and it was this sin that their successors in his time continued to denounce.

In pursuing the heretics whom he so fervently believed to menace the souls of the Christian people, Innocent could not, or would not, refrain from advancing simultaneously the political interests of the Roman see and the centralisation of ecclesiastical policy and of appointments in the papal court. One of his first actions was to issue, in March 1199, the bull *Vergentis in senium*, addressed to the clergy and people of Viterbo. In this decree he described heresy as lèse-majesté, equating it with the crime of high treason and subject to the same penalties in Roman law, which was cited extensively. The property of heretics was to be confiscated. They were to be declared infamous, incapable of holding office and denied access to the courts, and these penalties were to be extended even to their catholic descendants: 'Life only is to be allowed to their children, and only as an exercise of mercy.' It was another huge step in the papacy's embrace of the model of secular monarchy that appalled its critics, and another huge incentive to princes everywhere to discover and convict heretics among their subjects. It was this policy that brought the citizens of both Viterbo and Orvieto into confrontation with papal authority.

———

According to Master John, heresy had been introduced to Orvieto in the time of Bishop Rustico – that is, before 1175 – by a Florentine named Diotesalvo.

> He denied the sacrament of the body and blood of Christ, and the efficacy of catholic baptism; he said that alms and prayers do not help the dead to attain absolution; that St Sylvester* and all his successors are suffering the tortures of the damned; that all visible things are the creation of the devil and subject to his power; that any good man has the same merits and prerogatives as St Peter, the chief of the apostles, while any evil man suffers the same punishment as the traitor Judas, and a number of other pernicious doctrines which may readily be found in the book *Contra haereticos*.

'That all visible things are the creation of the devil and subject to his power' is one of the earliest surviving assertions of theological dualism

---

* Pope from 314 to 335.

among Italian heretics, and is consistent with Master John's characterisation of the heresy as Manicheeism. It is not, however, consistent with the other teachings he lists, for to those who believed that the material world was the creation of the devil it was the only hell their theology required: there was no place in it for the post-mortem tortures of the damned. This suggests that Master John borrowed his description from the pope, or found it in the *Contra haereticos* to which he refers – apparently an academic treatise of unknown authorship that survives in a number of thirteenth-century Italian manuscripts.

After Bishop Riccardo (1178–1202) threw Diotesalvo out of the city, the latter's place was taken by two women,

> Milita of Monte-Meato and Julieta of Florence, both daughters of iniquity. They adopted the semblance of religion, so that by appearing eager to hear the holy offices they seemed to be sheep though in reality they were wolves. The bishop was deceived by their religious disguise, and advised their admission into the confraternity of the clergy for regular prayers. Milita, like another Martha, feigned anxiety about the state of repair of the cathedral roof, while Julieta, like Mary, pretended to embrace the contemplative life. Many of the ladies of our city and their relations began to respect them as very holy women. So, as beloved enemies or highly virulent germs these snakes in the grass drew many men and women into the labyrinth of their heresy under the pretext of piety.

We have met such women before, often prominent in varied expressions of lay piety, often involved in good works around the church. It is an interesting coincidence, though perhaps no more, that in Florence, where Milita and Julia came from, the clothworkers' guild had been taking responsibility for looking after the fabric of the baptistry for the past fifteen or twenty years, and that there, though not until well into the thirteenth century, accusations of heresy did arise from tensions between clergy and laity involved in such arrangements.[7] The condition of the cathedral roof was a sensitive point in Orvieto. A canon of the cathedral might easily have concluded after the event that lay activity in the cause of repairing it, coupled with accusations of avarice or neglect against the clergy, was no more than a cover for heresy. Master John placed a similar interpretation on the arrival of an emissary from Viterbo, 'a doctor of the Manichees named Peter the Lombard who began to hold secret conclaves in Orvieto with other heretical leaders' after Innocent III's interdict in 1198 had withdrawn Bishop Riccardo from the city. Viterbo was at this time engaged in precisely the same dispute with the pope about the nature of his jurisdiction over it as Orvieto. In both cases, that is, those who resisted the consolidation of papal authority in their respective cities were identified and condemned as heretics.

15

TO WAR AND ARMS

They burned them with joy in their hearts.
Peter of Les Vaux de Cernay, *History of the Albigensian Crusade*

After the sensational revelations of Henri de Marci's 'pre-crusade' in 1181–2 we hear little more about heresy in the lands of the count of Toulouse for almost two decades. As always, the level of anxiety reflected the political preoccupations of the outsiders who expressed it. During those years the papacy was absorbed in resistance to the claims of the emperor and the communes in Italy, while the kings of England and France played out their rivalry on other stages, including the Holy Land. Soon after his election in 1198, however, Innocent III appointed as legates to the archiepiscopal province of Narbonne two Cistercian monks, Guy and his own confessor, Rainer of Ponza. They were empowered to excommunicate heretics, place lands under interdict, order the confiscation of property and correct clerical abuses. Rainer and Guy were the first of a succession of Cistercian legates to the region, of whom Peter of Castelnau, appointed in 1203, was the most energetic and uncompromising. As Innocent's legates, they harried and replaced the senior clergy of the region, denounced its lords as protectors of heresy and occasionally and reluctantly engaged in debate with prominent good men, as the 'heretics' were known.

Innocent's intention was not only to attack heretics and their supporters but also to revive catholicism through a great campaign of preaching.
In 1203 he renewed that objective by appointing as an additional legate
the abbot of Cîteaux himself, Arnold Amalric, and instructing the order
to provide monks to accompany him. In doing so, he brought to the
region a figure of legendary determination and intransigence, one of the
most influential in working out its fate in the years to come.

There is no sign that the renewed evangelism was particularly effective, even when the efforts of the Cistercians were supplemented in 1206
and 1207 by Bishop Diego of Osma and Dominic Guzman of Calaruega.
The newcomers, observing the failure of the well-equipped and amply
provisioned entourages of the legates to undermine the influence of the
good men, took to the roads barefoot and in pairs, in the apostolic
tradition of their adversaries. They engaged the good men in public
debate, sometimes for prolonged periods – eight days at Servian, fifteeen
at Montréal – as the Waldensians and the Poor Catholics led by Durand
of Osca were also doing. This was a sharp break from the Cistercian
style. A precedent had been set in 1204, however, when King Pedro II of
Aragon arranged for both good men and Waldensians to dispute with
catholics before him and the legates at Carcassonne, and pronounced
both heretical. The new approach won Dominic the admiration of his
fellow catholics and made him the founder of an important and influential religious order. It is doubtful whether it had much immediate
impact, however, beyond confirming to the offended Cistercians their
stereotype of the region as one in which heresy was preached openly, and
catholics subjected thereby to persecution.

———

The efforts of the legates included an ecclesiastical purge. Between 1204
and 1213 two archbishops and seven bishops were deposed or suspended
as insufficiently active against the heretics, or unduly sympathetic to
those who protected them. Several of them were replaced by Cistercians. This repeated the pattern set by Henri de Marci's removal of Pons
d'Arsac in 1181, of replacing local men by outsiders, on pretexts of varying
plausibility as to their fitness for their positions. Innocent III promoted

and justified this policy, reviling the bishops of the Languedoc as 'dogs that no longer bark' and denouncing their avarice, morals, slothfulness and neglect of their flocks in language that the most embittered heretic would have been hard put to match. His rhetoric was squarely in the Gregorian tradition of exploiting resentment of the shortcomings of the clergy to break down local solidarities in the interests of papal sovereignty. Innocent's sincere personal conviction of the danger that heresy represented to the church, intensified by his ready acceptance of the reports and recommendations of his Cistercian legates, is not in doubt. Here, as in Italy, it sat comfortably with his political ambition.

Innocent's greatest frustration in bringing the recalcitrant inhabitants of the Languedoc to heel was the indifference to his project of Europe's secular rulers. The English kings' long-standing feud with the counts of Toulouse had been dramatically reversed when Richard I made peace with Raymond VI in 1196 and, the following year, gave him his sister Joanna in marriage. Both Richard and his successor, John, were tied down by the bitter and eventually unsuccessful defence of their continental territories, in occasional alliance with the emperor Otto IV, against Philip Augustus of France. Philip's own energies were also fully engaged in this struggle until he defeated these enemies in a great victory at Bouvines in 1214.

Pedro II of Aragon, the representative from 1196 of Raymond's oldest and most persistent dynastic rivals, was more than ready to fill the gap for the papacy. (See Map 7, p. 186.) In 1198 he advertised himself as a pillar of orthodoxy by becoming the first monarch to decree burning for heretics in his own lands, though there is nothing to show that he enforced it. He sought to enhance his position in the region by marrying Maria, the daughter and successor of Count William VIII of Montpellier. William, who died in 1202, had conducted a long campaign to legitimate his sons by his second marriage and thus disinherit Maria, but Innocent refused to oblige him, even though he had recently found it possible to grant the same favour to Philip Augustus. In 1204, a few months after his marriage to Maria (handed over without demur, it seems, by her first husband, the count of Comminges), Pedro was crowned by the pope in a magnificent ceremony in Rome, swearing fealty to him and promising an annual tribute from Aragon.

It was convenient for Innocent that no small-minded consistency in the matters of matrimony and legitimacy stood in the way of his acquisition, through these manoeuvres, of a champion of the anti-heretical cause. As lord of extensive territories in the archbishopric of Narbonne, Pedro could assert the right – indeed, the duty – to enforce the decrees and decisions of the papal legates. He remained, however, the pope's second string. In May 1204 Innocent made the first of several appeals to Philip of France to launch a crusade against the count of Toulouse, offering him the confiscated lands of protectors of heresy, and his troops the same indulgences that they would gain by service in the Holy Land. He received the reply that the king's relations with royal vassals were none of his business, and that there was no legal basis for the action he proposed.

———

In 1205 Raymond of Toulouse undertook to expel heretics and mercenaries from his lands. But, understandably (we might think) anxious to avoid the threatened invasion without setting off yet another bout of internecine warfare, he did not deliver. In 1207 Arnold Amalric and Peter of Castelnau demanded that Raymond join an armed league against his own vassals, swear to keep peace with his enemies in the Rhône valley, dismiss his mercenaries and the Jewish officials on whom, like other lords in the region, he relied for much of his routine administration, and stop fortifying churches. Hypocrisy apart – for, it has often been pointed out, Raymond must have been perfectly aware that both mercenaries and the fortification of churches and monasteries were extensively used in military campaigns organised by Innocent III in southern Italy and Sicily – it is hard to imagine that Raymond could possibly have accepted such terms and defended his lands or his position, or that the legates could have supposed otherwise. He refused, and was excommunicated. This fact was to be proclaimed in churches throughout the region every Sunday until Raymond submitted. It meant that religious services were forbidden anywhere where he might be staying; his men were released from homage and his subjects from obedience; judges, notaries, even tradesmen, were forbidden to serve him.

In principle it was terrifying. In practice, as Raymond (like everybody else) knew, Philip of France had recently ignored excommunication for two years without suffering any noticeable damage. He did not know that John of England would soon do so for five, but he certainly understood that even in lands that were not alleged to be riddled with heresy the spiritual sanctions of the church were no more effective than the nobles chose to make them. But Raymond was much more vulnerable than either Philip or John (both formidably powerful within their own kingdoms) to the ultimate threat that excommunication carried of confiscation and deposition. In November 1207 Innocent once more demanded that Philip Augustus should act against Raymond. The terms on which he was invited to do so – crusading indulgences for everybody who took part, and the confiscation and redistribution of the lands and revenues of those who resisted – were also made known and available to 'all the counts, barons and soldiers, and all the believers in Christ established in the kingdom of France'.[1] To put it less elegantly, the lands between the Rhône and the Dordogne were up for grabs.

Philip's reply was not encouraging. He could not, he said, fight two wars at once. He would undertake to campaign in the south only if the pope would ensure that the French clergy would contribute to the cost, and if he could arrange a truce with King John of England, whose allies were giving Philip serious trouble in Poitou; even then, he would return immediately if John should break the truce. Since Innocent was at loggerheads with John – would very shortly excommunicate him – over the appointment of an archbishop of Canterbury, this amounted for practical purposes to a refusal. Meanwhile Raymond VI, probably unaware of Philip's intentions and certainly desperate to avert invasion, informed Peter of Castelnau that he was ready to surrender. They met at St Gilles-du-Gard on 13 January 1208. Raymond tried to negotiate, the legate was unyielding, and the meeting broke up with the usual ill-tempered exchanges.

As Peter of Castelnau was crossing the Rhône next morning, he was ambushed by an unknown knight and murdered. Whoever inspired it – and there is no reason to suppose that Raymond, after his experience of the last ten years, was so naïve as to imagine either that one legate more or less would make much difference to his situation, or that his enemies would fail to exploit all the possibilities the outrage would present – the murder of Peter of Castelnau was a disaster for the count. Innocent cried scandal to the heavens and demanded the confiscation of Raymond's lands. Philip Augustus, pointing out that Raymond had not been convicted or shown to be guilty of any crime, including heresy, still declined to take part himself, but he could no longer prevent his vassals from answering the pope's call for a crusade. The duke of Burgundy and the count of Nevers were quick to respond and promised five hundred knights. The crusade was formally proclaimed by Arnold Amalric at Cîteaux in September 1208, and preached throughout the winter by his monks, offering their noble hearers the remission at least of interest on their frequently substantial debts, and at best of their sins in eternal glory. Some were willing to settle for the intermediate prospect of the spoils and lands of the heretics.

In vain Raymond of Toulouse sought help at the courts of Philip Augustus and of Otto IV; in vain he knelt at Arnold Amalric's feet to beg forgiveness; in vain he offered an alliance, or at least a truce, to his nephew and rival Raymond-Roger of Trencavel, vicomte of Béziers. By January 1209 he saw no recourse left but to send an emissary to Rome with instructions to offer the pope seven crucial castles and the county of Melgueil, and to accept any terms in return for a new, more flexible legate. Innocent appointed two, Milo and Thedisius, secretly instructing them to take their orders from Arnold Amalric 'because the count suspects him but not you'. In June Raymond was ordered to St Gilles-du-Gard, where Milo led him, stripped to the waist, through the streets to the great church. There he was required to swear obedience to the legates in all matters and to promise redress for a long list of complaints real and alleged against him – employing Jews and protecting heretics, using mercenaries, fortifying churches and taking various exactions from them, being suspected of having ordered the murder of Peter of Castelnau. Milo wrapped his stole around Raymond's neck and, flogging him as they went, led him on his knees the length of the church to the altar. There he was absolved, and spent the next four days giving the orders necessary to fulfil his undertakings and hand control of his territories to the legates.

It was far too late to halt the crusade, if anyone had wanted to. Even before Raymond's humiliation at St Gilles-du-Gard an army led by Guy of Clermont and the archbishop of Bordeaux had laid siege, unsuccessfully, to Casseneuil (on the Lot north of Agen), ravaged some nearby villages and vanished from the only source that mentions it, Guilhem of Tudela's *Canzo de la crosada*, as abruptly as it had appeared. The 'many heretics' it condemned to be burned and 'the many fair women thrown into the flames, for they refused to recant, however much they were begged to do so' were the first of the many hundreds who would meet that fate in the next twenty years.[2] On 24 June 1209 what Arnold Amalric called 'the greatest Christian army ever' mustered at Lyon, from every part of France, from Germany north and south, from Provence and Lombardy – 20,000 horsemen and 200,000 others, foot soldiers, camp followers and all, said Guilhem of Tudela. The 3,000 horsemen – four times as many as Philip Augustus ever commanded – 8,000 foot soldiers and 10,000–12,000 auxiliaries and camp followers of a more sober modern estimate[3] were still astonishing numbers.

Without hope of repelling such a force, the only move left to Raymond was to join it, earn the crusader's immunity for his own lands and turn the storm against the vicomte of Béziers. Raymond-Roger, grasping at last the depth of his danger, met the army at Montpellier with protestations of innocence and regret and offered to submit on the same terms as Raymond of Toulouse had done. Arnold Amalric declined to hear him and proceeded to Béziers, which on 21 July was sacked, plundered and destroyed by fire. The entire population was massacred, including women, children and the priests of the churches in which they had taken refuge. Almost 20,000 people were put to the sword, Arnold Amalric reported to Innocent III, without regard to rank or sex or age. 'After this great slaughter the whole city was despoiled and burned as divine vengeance raged marvellously.'

The sack of Béziers, hailed by some as a miracle, was not planned, and in his enthusiasm the legate probably exaggerated the number of dead, by perhaps a third. The victorious commanders had been taken by surprise when, the siege barely begun, the defences were breached by a mob of servants and camp followers in spontaneous retaliation against a foolish sortie by ill-disciplined youths from the town. It must be doubtful whether the leaders could have restrained a rabble whose excitement, ambitions and appetites had been built up on the long trek from so many corners of Europe against an enemy demonised by propaganda and dehumanised by ignorance. Equally, there is no sign that they wished to do so, or that they saw the least reason to minimise the horrors, let alone regret them, after the event; no reason to think that Arnold Amalric would have disowned the words put into his mouth a decade later by an admiring fellow Cistercian, fixing his memory for posterity: 'Kill them. The Lord will know his own.'[4]

The leaders quickly decided to put their triumph to maximum use.

> All agreed that at every castle approached by the army a garrison that refused to surrender should be slaughtered wholesale. They would then meet with no resistance anywhere, as men would be so terrified at what had already happened. That is how they took Montréal and Fanjeaux and all that country.[5]

The greatest prize, Carcassonne, to which Raymond-Roger had retreated after his rebuff by Arnold Amalric, taking with him the Jewish community of Béziers, surrendered after a three-week siege. The inhabitants, heretics and all, were allowed to leave in safety after it had been decided to avoid a sack and preserve the city as the headquarters of the successor to Raymond-Roger who would be needed to rule the captured territory. Raymond-Roger himself was seized and chained, despite the safe conduct he had been promised, and died in prison three months later, to be remembered as youthful – twenty-four years old when he died – handsome, gallant and foolish, or betrayed. All that he may have been, but he was also the unfortunate legatee of the long and bitter rivalry between the counts of Toulouse and of Barcelona, now kings of Aragon, in which the Trencavel lands were strategically pivotal. There is no real reason to think that the region was especially given to heresy, but it had repeatedly been portrayed as such by those who hoped to dominate it, at least since Count Alphonse Jordan of Toulouse pointed St Bernard in that direction in 1145. The Trencavels, while no more hostile to the church than the ordinary tensions of lordship dictated, had neglected to offset this reputation by building strong links of patronage with the religious orders, notably the Cistercians.

———

Since none of the great lords who had accompanied the crusade felt his sins in need of further expiation, the lordship of Béziers and Carcassonne fell to Simon de Montfort, a minor lord from the Île de France with close ties to the Cistercian order, a record of military competence and unbending piety, and a claim through his wife to the English earldom of Leicester, which in due course brought fame to his youngest son. The bulk of the army, having performed the forty days' service required to earn indulgences and seeing little expectation of further plunder, quickly faded back whence it came. Simon was left with perhaps thirty knights to defend the ruins of Béziers, the huge treasure looted from Carcassonne and the two hundred or so villages and minor castles that surrendered in the aftermath of those victories. This set the pattern of his rule. A large part of each summer's conquests was lost or abandoned by the small force that remained when the spring flood of reinforcements mustered by ambitious lordlings and incited by Cistercian preachers across Europe ebbed with the approach of winter. Nevertheless, through ruthless singleness of purpose, abundance of energy and inspirational military leadership, greatly assisted by the divisions and incompetence of his enemies, Simon gradually imposed control.

Raymond of Toulouse, ever desperate to calm the storm by appealing to the pope's persistent if ineffectual sense of legality, constantly hesitated to give a firm lead or to take the initiative against the crusaders. He knew that no victory could be secure so long as his lands were trumpeted through the world as fair game for outsiders. Frantic lobbying in Rome was a constant backdrop that made no practical difference to the slaughter. Innocent vacillated between the protestations of Raymond's emissaries that he was no heretic and had done and would do everything in his power to satisfy the pope's demands and the implacable determination of the legates – who in any case represented Innocent's authority on the spot and interpreted it as they chose – to confiscate Raymond's lands and replace him by Simon de Montfort. It is not obvious that the excommunication, when it finally came, in February 1211, made things much worse.

Pedro of Aragon, havering between preserving his standing as a favourite of the papacy and retaining his independence as overlord of the former Trencavel lands, avoided accepting de Montfort's homage for Béziers and Carcassonne. Simon suffered a serious reverse when Pedro found his attempts to mediate between Raymond and Innocent frustrated by the intransigence of the legates, announced that he was taking the county of Toulouse under his protection and, in September 1213, crossed the Pyrenees with a large army. Simon's reverse became a triumph when Pedro, having surrounded the greatly outnumbered crusaders in the village of Muret but holding it unworthy of his honour to await their inevitable surrender, contrived to expose himself to an unexpected charge from the desperate defenders and was killed. By the end of the year Simon was master of the territories between the Rhône and the Garonne, apart from the important but now isolated cities of Toulouse and Montauban.

———

The most notorious of the events and atrocities that have given the Albigensian wars the reputation of reaching new levels of savagery and destructiveness took place during this first phase of the campaigns and triumphs of Simon de Montfort. That reputation is founded on the chillingly exuberant triumphalism with which the clerical leaders of the crusade celebrated the holocausts that they ordered, admiringly recorded by the principal catholic chronicler, Peter of Les Vaux de Cernay, and the bitter partisanship that has shaped the history and memory of these wars ever since. Above all, it is founded on the facts. The marked superiority of defensive over offensive capacity meant that campaigning turned on taking and holding strong points, not only the cities but also the forti- fied villages with which the countryside was dotted and the castles that provided remote, almost impregnable, refuges in the mountains. Every siege began by laying waste the surrounding countryside, burning crops, uprooting trees and destroying buildings, dykes and dams, and ended more often than not with burning and looting, and the dispersal – at best – of the defeated population. The people were, as ever, astonishingly resilient, and recovery often surprisingly rapid, but the accumulated cost in desolation and destruction of twenty years' campaigns in which almost every settlement of any size changed hands several times remains beyond calculation.

Prolonged warfare would have brought that fate to any region that suffered it, and frequently did. This war had the additional horrors to be expected when a hugely outnumbered alien force struggled to occupy hostile and inhospitable territory. The intention of the crusaders to conquer and rule by terror, exacerbated by the mutual demonisation of ideological confrontation, was regularly re-emphasised. When Simon de Montfort took Bram in the spring of 1210, he allowed the garrison to retreat to Cabaret with all their noses cut off and all their eyes put out, except for one left to a leader, to guide them. The resisters, when they could, replied in kind. Towards the end of 1209 two Cistercians of the legate's entourage were found stabbed to death near Carcassonne, and two captured knights were taken to Minerve, where their ears, noses and upper lips were cut off, and they were left naked, in bitter weather, to find their way back to Carcassonne. When de Montfort took Lavaur, which yielded great booty, in May 1211, the entire garrison was put to the sword to revenge the massacre of a party of crusaders from Germany ambushed on their way to reinforce Montgey. The lady of Lavaur, Girauda de Laurac, a woman 'whose presence no one ever left without having eaten' but reputedly a heretic or a sympathiser, was thrown into a well and crushed to death by the rocks piled on her at de Montfort's orders. Three or four hundred presumed heretics found in the town were taken to a meadow outside the walls where 'our crusaders burned them alive with great joy'. The same rejoicing attended the burning of sixty more at Cassès a few days later.[6]

In describing these holocausts Peter of Les Vaux de Cernay uses the Latin phrase *cum ingenti gaudio* ('with great joy'), frequently quoted in liturgical contexts and originally evoking the biblical offering of burned sacrifices on an enormous scale at the consecration of the temple at Jerusalem (I Chr. 29: 14). The burning had begun at Casseneuil, almost before the crusade itself, and de Montfort made a point of watching the first two people burned under his aegis at Castres, in September 1209. After the fall of Carcassonne the greatest lords and their followers had dispersed to the remote strongholds of Minerve, Termes and Cabaret, ideal bases for resistance. Minerve was the first of them to be taken, in July 1210, after a six-week siege in which both sides suffered greatly. Among the captives was a large number of heretics who had fled for safety to this apparently impregnable stronghold. What followed stamped the character of the Albigensian Crusade on every succeeding memory.

On 22 July William, the lord of Minerve, sought to negotiate an honourable surrender with Simon de Montfort. This would have meant, as at Carcassonne, allowing the occupants of the fortress to leave in safety. As they talked, Arnold Amalric and his fellow legate Thedisius arrived on the scene, and Simon promptly said that any agreement must be subject to the abbot's approval. The abbot was not best pleased. 'He wanted the enemies of Christ to die', according to the wholly admiring and quite unironic Peter of Les Vaux de Cernay, 'but as a monk and priest he did not dare condemn them to death.'[7] He therefore suggested that William should write down the surrender terms he would offer and Simon those he would accept, 'hoping that one or other of them would find the proposals unacceptable and revoke his agreement to accept arbitration'. In this way the siege would be continued to the bitter end, the defenders would meet the fate of Béziers rather than of Carcassonne, and the Lord's, or at least the legate's, will would be done.

William unsportingly frustrated this ruse by declaring that he would accept any terms that were required of him.

The abbot therefore ordered that all the inhabitants of Minerve, including the heretical believers, should be allowed to live, provided that they agreed to be reconciled and to obey the orders of the church. The perfected heretics would also be spared if they agreed to be converted to the catholic faith.

To this, one of Simon's closest lieutenants, a sturdy hero of the army and 'a noble and dedicated catholic' named Robert Mauvoisin ('bad neighbour' – coincidentally or not also the nickname given to the enormous catapult that broke Minerve's defences) objected vigorously that the army would not stand for it. He and his comrades had come to kill heretics, he said, not to let them off with conversion. Arnold Amalric reassured him. 'Don't worry. I believe that very few of them will accept conversion.'

It seems that Arnold Amalric had learned more about his adversaries during his years in pursuit of them than his singularly inflexible cast of mind might have led us to expect. The army entered the town. Abbot Guy of Les Vaux de Cernay, who had taken a prominent role in the siege, went to a house where a large number of heretics had gathered and tried to convert them. 'They interrupted him and said with one accord, "Why do you preach to us? We will have none of your faith. You labour in vain. Neither death nor life can separate us from the faith we hold."' Guy then went to another house 'where the heretics' women folk were gathered, but he found the women heretics even more obstinate and determined than the men'. His efforts to win repentance were seconded by Simon de Montfort himself, who 'as a true catholic wished them all to win salvation and come to know the way of truth'. When they declined, he had them all, 'at least a hundred and forty perfected heretics', taken outside the castle, to where a huge pyre had been built. 'All were thrown on it, though indeed there was no need for our soldiers to throw them on it, since they were so hardened in their wickedness that they rushed into the fire of their own accord.' Three women were rescued at the last moment and reconciled to the church with the remaining inhabitants of the town. Mud was shovelled over the remains of the rest, 'so that no stench from these foul things should annoy our foreign forces'.[8]

———

The holocausts at Minerve and Lavaur were by far the largest that had happened anywhere in Europe up to this time.* It is inescapable from the

---

* The slaughter of some 150 Jews at York in 1190 by murder and mass suicide was hardly less savage, but it was the result of incompetence on the part of royal officers and manipulated mass hysteria rather than deliberate policy.

exultant description of Peter of Les Vaux de Cernay that the 140 people who perished at Minerve, refusing the opportunity of recantation, did so by choice. They have left us therefore with a stark and unequivocal statement of their faith, to be set against the unrelenting recitals of their enemies upon which we otherwise depend. It was fortified, no doubt, by resentment of the invasion and the solidarity of the first stages of resistance, but still unfiltered by the perceptions and preconceptions of outsiders or by memories that had had to cope with twenty years of devastating, transformative warfare. As such, the sacrifice at Minerve is the last testament we have of the nature in this countryside before the crusade of what others described as heretical belief. But what does it say? What was it that brought these people to embrace their terrible fate?

Peter of Les Vaux de Cernay, in effect the official historian of the Albigensian Crusade, writing between 1212 and 1218 and dedicating his book to Innocent III, had no doubt. Peter was the nephew of Guy, abbot since 1181 of the Cistercian house of Les Vaux de Cernay, some 35 kilometres south-west of Paris, which had close links with the family of Simon de Montfort, the leader of the crusading army. He had accompanied Guy and Simon on the disastrous Fourth Crusade of 1203–4, where by Peter's account they had tried to convey, at some personal risk to themselves, the pope's unsuccessful attempt to prevent the crusaders from pillaging Constantinople.[9] In 1212 Guy, an energetic preacher of the Albigensian Crusade, was appointed bishop of Carcassonne, and took his nephew with him as his personal assistant. Peter's *History* is unfinished; since it speaks in the present tense of Simon de Montfort, who died in 1218, it is supposed that Peter himself died at about that time.

Peter of Les Vaux de Cernay was therefore extremely well informed about the leading personalities and events of the Albigensian Crusade, as well as being an intelligent observer and an accomplished historian. His view of the world had been moulded not only by his uncle and Simon de Montfort, both heroes to him, but also by his Cistercian vocation. He tells us nothing of his personal life beyond mentioning that Guy, like most senior Cistercians, was of noble family, but he had probably been brought up in Les Vaux de Cernay under his uncle's direction. His description of the Albigensian heresy is obviously derived – with a generous helping of conventional monastic invective – from the account put together in the 1180s by Henri de Marci and Geoffrey of Auxerre. Its development has been traced in these pages from the time of Bernard of Clairvaux. It had been used by Eberwin of Steinfeld and others to demonise those who criticised their conduct and impugned their authority from the perspective of apostolic fundamentalism, and been placed by Eckbert of Schönau and Alan of Lille in the theological framework of scholastic disputation perfected in Paris since the 1140s. It is immediately recognisable today as the basis not only of standard textbook descriptions of the heresy but also of numerous sensational accounts of an alleged secret history of the Roman Catholic Church, of a great many novels and films and of a flourishing tourist trade in the 'Cathar country' of modern France.

'The barons of the South almost all became defenders and hosts of the heretics, welcomed them to their hearts and defended them against God and the church', Peter begins.

The heretics maintained the existence of two creators, one of things invisible, whom they called the 'benign' God, and one of the things visible, whom they called the 'malign' God. They attributed the New Testament to the benign God and the Old Testament to the malign God, and rejected the whole of the latter except for certain passages quoted in the New Testament ...

In their secret meetings they said that the Christ who was born in the earthly and visible Bethlehem and crucified was 'evil'; and that Mary Magdalene was his concubine, and that she was the woman taken in adultery who is referred to in the Scriptures; the 'good' Christ, they said, neither ate nor drank nor assumed the true flesh, and was never in the world except spiritually, in the body of St Paul. I have used the term 'earthly and visible Bethlehem' because the heretics believe there is a different and invisible earth in which – according to some of them – the 'good' Christ was born and crucified ...

These people had infected almost the whole of the province of Narbonne with the poison of their perfidy. They said that the Roman church was a den of thieves and the harlot spoken of in the Book of Revelations. They ridiculed the sacraments of the church, arguing publicly that the holy water of baptism was no better than river water,

that the consecrated host of the holy body of Christ was no different from common bread ... that confirmation, extreme unction and
confession were trivial and empty ceremonies ... that holy matrimony
was mere harlotry ... They denied the resurrection of the body, and
invented new myths, claiming that our souls were really those angelic
spirits who were driven from heaven through their rebellious pride
and ... that these souls, after successively inhabiting any seven earthly
bodies will then return to their original bodies ...

It should be understood that some of the heretics were called 'perfected heretics' or 'good men', others 'believers' of the heretics. The
'perfected' heretics wore a black robe, claimed (falsely) to practise
chastity and renounced meat, eggs and cheese ... They also said that
no one should take oaths for any reason ... Those called 'believers'
were dedicated to usury, robbery, murder and illicit love ... they felt
they could sin in safety and without confession and penitence so long
as they were able to recite the Lord's prayer and ensure a 'laying-on of
hands' by their masters in the final moments of their lives.

They selected from the 'perfected' heretics officials whom they
called 'deacons' and 'bishops', and the believers held that no one of
them could attain salvation without the laying-on of hands by these
clergy just before death; indeed, they considered that however sinful
a man might have been, then provided he had undergone this laying-
on of hands on his death-bed, and so long as he was able to recite the
Lord's prayer, he would gain salvation and (to use their own expression) 'consolation' to the extent that he would immediately fly up to
heaven without making any reparations for wrongs he had committed
...

Some of the heretics declared that no one could sin from the navel
downwards; they characterised images in churches as idolatry; they
maintained that church bells were the trumpets of devils; and they
said it was no greater sin for a man to sleep with his mother or his
sister than any other woman.[10]

9. Durand of Bredon, abbot of Moissac 1047–72, commemorated *c.* 1100 in the cloister of his beautiful church. Thanks to him, 'where the boar once roamed the woods churches now stand' – but his acquisition of property for his monastery aroused conflict and resentment.

10. (a) A Christian knight slays a monster – heresy? – on the west front of the cathedral of St Pierre, Angoulême, built *c.* 1110–28 to the design of Gerard de Blaye, reforming bishop and papal legate, but heavily restored in the nineteenth century.

(b) A monster – heresy again? – consumes a soul: St Pierre, Chauvigny, mid-twelfth century.

11. A processional cross from Castile or Leon, c. 1120. Henry of Lausanne pointedly preferred one made of plain iron for his entry to Le Mans.

12. Lambert le Bègue, remembered (mistakenly) *c.* 1255–65 as the founder of the Béguines. Uniquely, he was the subject of heresy accusations of which we know only his version.

13. Pierre Maurand was scourged from west door to altar of the great pilgrimage church of St Sernin, Toulouse, in 1178. The cloister where Bernard de Caux and Jean de St Pierre interrogated more than 5,000 people was demolished at the beginning of the nineteenth century.

14. (a) The tombs of Henry II and Eleanor of Aquitaine at Fontevraud. Robert of Arbrissel did not intend to found a royal mausoleum – but Henry would rather have been buried among the *good men* at Grandmont.

(b) Oldrado da Tresseno, *podesta* of Milan, who ordered the construction of this palazzo, the Broletto nuovo, between 1229 and 1233 and, according to the inscription, 'burned the Cathars as he ought to.'

15. (a), (b), (c) The fantasies licensed by the war on heresy continued to haunt the European imagination and fuel persecution for centuries to come. In these images, from fifteenth-century Germany and seventeenth-century Italy, witches turn into animals as they fly to a coven, Satan is adored in the customary fashion, and protestants and Jews are burned as witches.

AD ARNALDO
AL PRECURSORE AL MARTIRE
DEL LIBERO ITALICO PENSIERO
BRESCIA SUA DECRETAVA
TOSTO RIVENDICATA IN LIBERTA
ΦDCCCLX

16. The memory of Arnold of Brescia lingered long after his death, and was revived in the nineteenth century, when he became a hero of the *risorgimento*. The inscription on this statue in his native city reads 'To Arnold, precursor and martyr of Italian free thought, by order of his liberated city of Brescia, to vindicate the victim of the flames. 1860.'

This is what Guy of Les Vaux de Cernay believed to lie behind the obduracy of the people who were burned at Minerve. Stripped of everything that might have been only his uncle's interpretation based on the account developed by his Cistercian predecessors, such as the description of those who chose to be burned as 'perfected heretics', Peter's account still tells us a great deal. The people who had sought refuge in Minerve were known and recognisable; they could not, or would not, simply fade into the landscape as the crusading army advanced. Without speculation as to how many others might already have perished in the war or fled or taken refuge in other places, their number was not negligible: they represented, in some sense, a sizeable body of the population. Their uncompromising and unhesitating acceptance of their fate suggests, though it does not prove, acknowledgement of the obligations of public standing as well as private conviction.

This accords with the stories of recognised spokesmen for the heretics engaging in debate with catholics and Waldensians in the years before the crusade. It accords also with the memories that the inquisitors Bernard de Caux and Jean de St Pierre collected at Toulouse more than thirty years later, of the 'good men' (*bons omes*) or 'friends of God' (*amickx de Dieu*) of the Lauragais, between Toulouse and Carcassonne. Bernart Gasc, more than seventy years old in 1242, not only remembered meeting several of them in and around the village of Caraman in 1205, but as a child in Fanjeaux around 1180 had lived next door to one, Guilhem de Carlipac, who often gave him bread, wine and nuts. Guilhem de la Grassa went to live with his father, Bernart, and other good men in 1195, and himself became a good man, 'a clothed heretic', at some time in his adolescence; many others told similar stories. According to these memories, the good men were mostly but not exclusively noble. The extent of their goodness was carefully and exactly graded by observation, reputation and recollection, and their standing varied accordingly, but (contrary to the understandable presumption of catholic outsiders) there was no settled hierarchy among them.[11]

The good women (*bonas femnas*), at Minerve 'even more obstinate and determined than the men', were, according to these later memories of the time before the crusade, not exactly equivalent. They lived in seclusion in shared houses, and all of them were noble. Their status, directly contrary to what was assumed and asserted by the catholic model of 'Catharism', was not permanent. It not only could be, but normally was, laid aside and resumed. Girls became good women – again, 'clothed heretics' – a few years before puberty, were married as soon as they reached it and became good women again as matrons or widows when their years of fertility were over, now to preside over and supervise those who awaited marriage.[12] In other words, whatever religious beliefs lay behind or underpinned it, this was an institution whose function was to protect the chastity of nubile females.

The imposition of comparably strict control over young women, keeping competition for them within bounds and protecting the 'honour' of their fathers, brothers and prospective husbands, has particularly been observed in societies where male prestige is even more than usually dependent on control over sexual access to women and the property rights associated with it. This was just such a society. Its social climate and the rhythms of its daily life were shaped by the extreme fragmentation of every kind of property and of the rights it conferred. Every strip of land, every vineyard, every mill, every olive or walnut grove, every wood and marsh, every pasture and fishpond, was parcelled and reparcelled into tiny shares, each the subject of competing claims and counter-claims, long-nourished grievances, secretly harboured ambitions. For a century or more the population had been increasingly concentrated in the fortified villages that had become so typical of the region. They were presided over by a petty aristocracy whose impoverishment by the demands of constant warfare was unalleviated by the restriction of inheritance to a single heir that had come to protect patrimonies in most of north-west Europe. Every village was shared between a myriad of petty lords – Montréal and Mirepoix each had thirty-six, Lombers fifty on the eve of the crusade – and every lord subsisted precariously on a multitude of minute, widely dispersed incomes.

In these tiny, tightly constrained and intensely competitive worlds of perhaps 200 to 500 inhabitants each, civility and survival demanded the daily observance of an elaborate and scrupulously precise code of behaviour – *cortezia* – to secure modesty of demeanour and the avoidance of offence, deceit and ostentation. Such were the values celebrated by the troubadours of the region, and embodied by its *bons oms*. It is no coincidence that the emergence of both is visible from the middle decades of the twelfth century, when the crisis of the villages, exacerbated from around 1100 by rapid inflation, became acute. On the other hand, the growing claims of the churches and monasteries represented new demands on an overburdened economy. The services they pressed more determinedly in return – for a more intrusive sacramental life and more elaborate ritual, notably through the elevation of matrimony, closer control over burial rights, the multiplication of penance and prayers for the dead – in the north suited the interests of the nobles by buttressing the elevation of the dynastic family but here ran against its grain. The religious style needed by these village lords was precisely the modest demeanour and low profile, the freedom from material and sexual demands and interests, the daily embodiment of courtesy and restraint, that the good men offered.

As we have seen in earlier chapters, it is not clear when or how the leadership of the good men crystallised, though the anticlericalism of the village lordlings had been noisily demonstrated to Bernard of Clairvaux in 1145. *Bons homs* had appeared as the securely acknowledged spokesmen of such lordlings at Lombers in 1165, where they publicly professed before their supporters a simple statement of Christian faith based on the New Testament and marked by the avoidance of oaths. To this we have no later addition except the assertions of their catholic enemies from outside the region. We cannot tell whether the good men were the legatees of simple country priests of the pre-reform era, or (like so many who were branded as heretics elsewhere) of apostolic preachers from beyond the region, such as Robert of Arbrissel, Gerald of Salles, Peter of Bruys or Henry of Lausanne, who had been active in the first decades of the twelfth century. Here, as elsewhere in Europe, patterns of religious allegiance and expression were evolving to fit the needs of a diversifying population. In Lombardy or the Rhineland, that was most obvious among the beneficiaries of change: craftsmen, merchants and shopkeepers, notaries. Here we see it among the casualties. Because the needs were very different, so too was the pattern. That is why the 'heresy' most characteristic of the region appeared to outsiders not as a recognisable, though reprehensible, variation on their own catholic faith, or even a deviation from it, but as terrifyingly, diabolically alien.

Innocent III and his legates attributed their failure to win support, or even more than minimal and reluctant co-operation, from the lords of the lands between the Rhône and the Garonne, lay and ecclesiastical, at best to indifference to heresy and at worst to belief in it or even active adherence to it. Yet that the legates were not cordially welcomed by any section of society, catholics included, is not in the least surprising. Their demands for action against heretics and protectors of heretics might occasionally offer a convenient ploy against a current rival, but in general they could scarcely appear as anything other than meddling and arrogant outsiders, ignorant of local conditions and traditions, stirring up unnecessary and indeed dangerous trouble. Much that they complained of reflected quite ordinary tensions and conflicts. In other parts of Europe, for instance, the complaint of the abbot of St Gilles-du-Gard that his territorial rights were infringed by one of Raymond VI's fortifications would not have seemed to have any special religious significance. Similar and probably justified complaints against other great lords of the region, including the count of Foix and the vicomte of Béziers, bolstered their representation as supporters of heresy. Such incursions, and the accusations of irreligion backed up by spiritual sanctions, were perfectly commonplace – but elsewhere now less common than they would have been thirty or forty years earlier. Like so much else about this region, by the 1190s such episodes have a somewhat old-fashioned appearance. Not everywhere, to be sure, but in the best-governed parts of Europe it was now held that disputes like these ought to be settled by courts of law or by arbitration, and increasingly often they were.

Such rhetoric aside, it is not easy to estimate the extent or the depth of support for the good men, and impossible to assess how far such support entailed acceptance of their teaching, whatever it may have been. The outsiders, naturally enough, presumed that their enemies were organised in much the same way as themselves. That is not confirmed by the memories of those among whom the good men had lived before the crusade. Peter of Les Vaux de Cernay thought that the victims of Minerve were 'perfected' heretics, who had attained that status by means of a ritual that he called the *consolamentum*, as described by Eckbert of

Schönau, but Guilhem de la Grassa and others, men and women, spoke only of having been made 'clothed' heretics. This suggests some formal occasion, certainly, but not one, as we have noticed, that necessarily entailed a permanent or irrevocable change of condition. Similarly, the inquisitors in 1246 attached great significance to body language, and to behaviour in meetings, always asking whether people had 'adored' the good men, and usually being answered in the affirmative. They were looking for evidence of a ritual of which they had read in their scholastic texts, called the *melioramentum*. Theoretically, participation in it would have placed those involved among the *credentes*, believers and acknowledged followers of the heresy. But those who were questioned merely described what they knew as the formal but everyday gestures of respect whose exchange was simply a matter of *cortezia*. If there was indeed such a category as that of acknowledged 'believers' in the heresy – and nothing in those recollections requires it – it was not denoted or betrayed by routine good manners.

The yawning chasm of mutual incomprehension between Occitanians and outsiders makes nonsense of the natural questions of how many heretics there were and what proportion of the population supported them. Historians have come up with wildly differing estimates, ranging from a few hundreds to many thousands of heretics, from a very low percentage of sympathisers to a very high one. This is partly, but only partly, because some count as 'heretics' only so-called 'perfects' while others include all 'believers' – which is akin to the difference between counting only black cats in an unlighted cellar while blindfold, or dark grey ones as well. Both procedures beg the question – that is, assume an answer to a question that has not been confronted, or perhaps even formulated – whether there was in fact any division in the society of the lands between the Rhône and the Garonne that corresponded in the eyes of its inhabitants to the distinction between catholics and heretics. To Innocent III it was so fundamental that he could not conceive of a world without it. Yet to ask how many of these heretics, however designated, there were before the Albigensian Crusade is rather like asking how many witches there were in Europe on the eve of the great witch craze of the sixteenth and seventeenth centuries. It assumes the objective, measurable existence of a category that was actually in the process of being constructed by the interrogators themselves, and which in that process was described in language that meant different things to different people.

This is not simply a question of nomenclature, of whether we ought to speak of 'the Provençal heretics' (*provinciales heretici*), as Innocent III did, or of Albigensians, like Peter of Les Vaux de Cernay, or of 'Cathars' as the late twentieth century preferred. Nor is it to deny the existence of religious difference. Whatever they were called or called themselves, some people agreed with the good men and some did not. Both groups were aware of that difference between them, and aware of other such differences, for example with the Waldensians, who shared the beliefs of the catholics and opposed the heretics, but themselves were regarded by many catholics as heretics.

What is entirely lacking is any indication that within the lands between the Rhône and the Dordogne before 1209 those differences of faith or opinion either gave rise in themselves to enduring antagonism between those who held them, or corresponded to other social or cultural divisions that did so. Thus, Peter of Les Vaux de Cernay was scandalised by, and recorded as scandalous, innumerable stories that great lords of the region, and still more their wives, permitted heretics at their courts and treated them with respect. This was what brought Girauda de Laurac to her dreadful death at Lavaur. To outside eyes it was an obvious contempt of the church, epitomised in the famous reply of a catholic knight years later to the bishop of Toulouse who asked him why he would not expel the heretics from his lands. 'How can we? We have been brought up side by side with them. Our closest kinsmen are numbered among them. Every day we see them living worthy and honourable lives in our midst.' To the bishop this was a flagrant contempt of the many prohibitions that had been repeated with increasing force and precision, and with specific reference to this region, for almost a century past. To the knight those prohibitions made no sense, not because he was unaware of the difference between his views and those of the heretics, but because it simply did not appear to him as a division that need, or should, override the ordinary obligations and loyalties of kinship, neighbourliness and courtesy. The world as he saw it was not divided by a stark polarity between catholic and heretic, between the realm of God and the realm of Satan. It was to Innocent III and those who thought, as he did, that Manichean dichotomy had become so instinctive as to make it impossible to envisage a creation without it. They could not do other than presume that their victims were similarly afflicted.

1 6

POLITICS BY
OTHER MEANS

'I don't know what you mean by "glory",' Alice said. Humpty Dumpty smiled contemptuously. 'Of course you don't – till I tell you.'

Lewis Carroll, *Through the Looking Glass*

Innocent's pontificate was crowned by the great council, known as Lateran IV, which he summoned in 1215. It was attended by more than 1,200 prelates from all over Latin Christendom and beyond, as well as the representatives of many secular rulers. In seventy canons the document issued with its authority drew together the reforming initiatives of the past century and a half to shape the church for the rest of the middle ages, consolidating and greatly extending the role of the clergy in every aspect of personal life and public affairs. The war on heresy was presented as the primary rationale for these measures.

The official statement of the council's conclusions opened with a confession of faith.[1] It was couched in the terminology of the Paris schools, a number of whose masters had been prominent in the preparation of the council. It emphatically disavowed the theological dualism now held to be the basis of the most pernicious heresies, insisting on the unity of creation, the incarnation, the resurrection of the body, the real presence in the Mass. The influence of the Paris masters was reaffirmed in the second canon, which vindicated at some length the teaching on the trinity of their emblematic figure and author of their essential textbook, Peter Lombard (d. 1160), against the criticism of the Calabrian visionary and prophet Joachim of Flora. It also condemned in a single sentence, but did not specify, the teachings of another Paris master, the charismatic Amalric of Bène (d. 1206). Amalric had been tutor to Louis, heir to the French crown. His teachings, which seem to have undermined the distinction between clergy and laity, had been widely disseminated in a number of northern French dioceses by students of his who had become parish priests. In 1210 ten of them were burned at Paris and four others imprisoned for life; another was burned at Amiens two years later. Amalric himself was exhumed and posthumously excommunicated and his bones thrown on a dungheap.

This second canon, at first sight somewhat parochial, even personal, in the context of a grand promulgation of regulations for the church universal, served (like the vindication of Gilbert de la Porée at Reims in 1148) to underline the essential autonomy of the masters as the definers of catholic doctrine. This was emphasised rather than qualified by the brusque acknowledgement of Amalric's error in what amounts to a postscript. It constituted an essential preface to the unstated (and largely unforeseen) consequence of all the elaborate measures spelled out by this council for the better governance of the church, firmer control over its offices and revenues, and the better education and more effective disciplining of its clergy. Provision for the closer and more regular pastoral care of the laity included the famous requirement that every mature catholic should confess to a priest at least once a year, an institution without parallel in any other world religion. Like all sweeping and visionary measures of administrative reform, the implementation of the decrees would entail vastly increased responsibilities and opportunities for the administrators themselves. Lateran IV was a charter for the clericalisation of society.

The third canon was a firm assertion of the necessity for such a programme. It was a comprehensive restatement of existing provisions for the detection, trial and punishment of heretics, and of those who gave credence to their teaching or gave them hospitality, protection or support. They were to be excluded from public affairs and commercial and professional activity, and deprived of civic rights, including those of testifying in court and making a will; their property was to be confiscated and their children disinherited. The provisions of *Ad abolendam* against office-holders, secular and ecclesiastical, who acted with insufficient vigour against heretics and their supporters were repeated and elaborated. A secular ruler who failed to act within a year against heretics pointed out by the church was to be reported to the pope, who would release his vassals from their allegiance and offer his lands to catholics, whose indulgences and privileges were confirmed.

The terrible force of these sanctions, if not perhaps the awful menace of the dangers they were designed to avert, was driven home by the appearance on their knees before a full session of the council of Count Raymond VI of Toulouse and Count Raymond-Roger of Foix. Neither had been formally convicted of heresy or of supporting heretics, and both had undertaken to obey papal demands, but their appeals for the restoration of their confiscated lands were refused by vote, seemingly against the wishes of the pope. Raymond VI was to lose all the lands that had been conquered by the crusaders and live in exile with a modest pension. He was permitted to retain his wife's dowry, and his son, when he came of age, to inherit the unconquered family lands east of the Rhône. The case of the count of Foix was referred to a commission of inquiry, which in due course declared him a catholic.

———

Innocent III died at Perugia in July 1116. His body was stripped overnight of his magnificent funeral garments as it lay unguarded in the cathedral, to be found next morning 'putrid and almost naked'.[2] The Lateran settlement was already unwinding. A few weeks later the capture of Beaucaire on the Rhône by the younger Raymond of Toulouse launched a campaign to recover the conquered lands, in conjunction with forces led from the Pyrenees by his father and Raymond-Roger of Foix. Simon de Montfort responded with his usual energy and ferocity until, in June 1218, as he was about to take Toulouse after a prolonged and bitter siege, he was struck on the head by a rock from a trebuchet. His body was taken back to Carcassonne. When his son and successor Amaury finally abandoned the south in 1225, it was sewn into an ox-hide and taken back to his estate near Paris for burial. Raymond VI survived until 1222, though effective leadership of the resistance had passed to his son. He died in the habit of a knight of St John and a generous benefactor of the church – but still excommunicate and therefore unburied. Since Popes Honorius III, Gregory IX and Innocent IV refused in turn to reverse the sentence, his coffin lay outside the priory of the Templars at Toulouse for as many decades as it took for the rot and the rodents to do their work.

The slaughter continued as pious and mercenary adventurers responded to the calls of frantic papal legates for aid against the Raymonds' attempts to restore their land and position, but without Innocent III and Simon de Montfort the crusading enterprise lacked shape and direction. Philip of France still resisted appeals from all sides to fill the vacuum, but his son Louis was steadily, though at first reluctantly, drawn into doing so. In 1219 Philip ordered him to assume the leadership, to forestall a suggestion that Thibaud of Champagne, who would have made a formidable rival, might do so instead. Louis showed himself a true crusader by presiding to the last woman and child over the massacre of the inhabitants of the small town of Marmande, which had rashly failed to surrender. He laid menacing siege to Toulouse but, to the astonishment and relief of its citizens, packed his bags and went home when the forty days required by his vow were up. But in 1224, his father dead, Louis VIII, as he now was, accepted from the hapless Amaury de Montfort the transfer of his rights and claims in the south which Philip had refused. Louis possessed the fanaticism lacking in his father. In his eyes this was still a holy enterprise. In 1226 he took the cross once more and assembled the largest force gathered since the first invasion of 1209. His death of a wasting disease at Montpensier in November 1226, with most of the region already in his hands, is attributed by the worldly to dysentery, but one chronicler blamed it on his refusal to avail himself of a young woman thoughtfully placed in his bed by a solicitous courtier who feared that an excess of chastity had undermined his constitution. Whether Louis's 'Madame, it shall not be' portended a triumph or a failure of the will, the story is an early example of the supreme skill with which the thirteenth-century expansion and elevation of the French monarchy was bathed in the odour of sanctity.[3]

In the following year Raymond VII, who had shown himself a vigor-ous and resourceful leader, recovered most of the lost territory. Towns and lords all across the region, desperate to avoid yet another round of laying waste, of devastated crops, ruined orchards and uprooted vine-yards, sieges and burnings, flocked to his banner as they had to Louis's, and to Raymond's own before that. Their fervour only brought it home yet again that neither side had a basis for unconditional victory. For twenty long years one had lacked the resources to repel invasion, the other to sustain a military occupation – but the French monarchy, unlike the de Montforts, would always be able to come back. In November 1228 Raymond accepted that he could not indefinitely withstand papally legitimated Capetian ambition and sued for peace. The guardians of the twelve-year-old Louis IX saw the wisdom of allowing Raymond terms that, harsh though they were, were not impossible to accept. By the peace concluded at Paris in 1229 Raymond remained count of Toulouse and lord of what had in effect been its core territories. His eastern provinces, along with the Trencavel lands, passed to the French. His nine-year-old daughter Joanne was betrothed to Louis's younger brother Alphonse of Poiters, with the stipulation that they and their children would be Ray-mond's heirs. As it transpired they had none, so Toulouse passed directly to the French crown when both Alphonse and Joanne died in 1271. In addition Raymond not only offered substantial sums to various churches by way of reparations for the damages alleged against him and his father but also paid for the foundation of a university to bring sound Parisian theology to Toulouse. He also undertook that his officials (among whom there would be no Jews or heretics) would seek out heretics and punish them as the church required.

The first secular ruler to make positive provision for the enforcement of the anti-heretical decrees of Lateran IV was the mightiest. Frederick II was crowned emperor in Rome in 1220, twelve years after assuming the Sicilian throne on reaching his majority (when he was fourteen) and five after his election as king of the Romans by German princes opposed to Otto IV. At a diet in Frankfurt earlier that year Frederick had acted against heresy in his German lands, though without specifying it as his objective, by proclaiming severe curtailments of the legal rights of the excommunicate. Pope Honorius III now took the opportunity to demand 'something worthy of the royal dignity against heretics and their supporters', and the observation of the Lateran provisions in all Frederick's lands was duly proclaimed. In 1224 at Catania, Frederick stipulated that convicted heretics were to be seized by his officers and delivered to the flames, unless the ecclesiastical judges wanted them to be kept alive to secure the conviction of others. In that case their tongues were to be cut out, presumably after they had been persuaded to vouchsafe the requisite information.

In 1231 Frederick's comprehensive legal code, the Constitutions of Melfi, opened with a statement of full and elaborate measures against heretics and their supporters, equating their offence with treason and laying down that anybody tainted with the slightest suspicion was to be examined by an ecclesiastical tribunal, and if convicted burned alive 'in the sight of the people'. The property of their supporters and of their supporters' children was to be confiscated and their civic rights denied, though the children might recover their positions by denouncing others.[4] The substance of these provisions is by now familiar, though here presented with extreme thoroughness and ferocity. The language and rhetoric, however, did not follow those of the ecclesiastical pronouncements and conciliar canons of the previous century and more. They constituted an assertion of royal authority, containing no reference to the papacy, with which Frederick was by this time at loggerheads. The streams of heresy, he said, had been diverted from 'the region of Lombardy, in which we know for certain that their wickedness is widespread' – and where, as it happens, Frederick was ruthlessly bent on consolidating his power.

————

In principle the systematic detection and eradication of heresy would have required the constant vigilance of appropriately trained clergy in every diocese. Over time the measures prescribed by Lateran IV greatly improved the training and organisation of the parochial clergy. The higher clergy became better disciplined and – though always with many and conspicuous exceptions – less thoroughly entangled in the world. The ability of the papacy to control ecclesiastical appointments and through them to provide emoluments and promotion for its function-aries as well as advancement of its policies was greatly extended, though at a heavy cost in political resentment. Nevertheless, local clergy would always be more vulnerable, and often more sympathetic, to local inter-ests and traditions than seemed desirable from a Roman perspective. The conditions that had made the Cistercians appear necessary as the advance guard and shock troops of the war on heresy had been especially visible in the lands of the count of Toulouse. They were present every-where in Latin Christendom, though in varying degrees.

A solution to this problem, as indeed to many others, was supplied by the most dramatic development in the church since the days of the papal revolution, the appearance of the friars (from the Latin *frater*, 'brother'). The conviction of Dominic Guzman of Calaruega that the influence of the good men might be more effectively contested by those who could match their austerity of life and humility of demeanour bore little fruit under the shadow of the Albigensian wars. By 1215 Dominic was established with sixteen companions in a house in Toulouse, and had vowed to follow the rule of St Augustine for canons regular, to possess no property and to combat heresy by preaching and pastoral solicitude. He had no visible results to show for it. Two years later, after a visit to Rome, he experienced some kind of crisis, and despite the protests of Simon de Montfort and the papal legate, dispersed his companions with instructions to preach the gospel and carry the fight against heresy across the world. At Bologna in 1220 Dominic confirmed in a general chapter of his followers that preaching was the main business of their order. His insistence that the best available academic training in theol-ogy and disputation was an essential foundation for this task not only took Dominican friars to the newly established universities of Paris and Bologna but quickly attracted recruits among the students and masters. By 1224, 120 Dominicans were studying theology at Paris; by 1234 their 20 houses had become 100, and by 1277 they had 400 houses, dispersed throughout Europe.

Francis of Assisi is one of the most familiar and, to many, most attractive personalities of the entire medieval period. Controversy surrounded his convictions and intentions almost from the beginning and became a major inspiration both of heresy and of persecution in the second half of the thirteenth century. Francis converted in 1205, from the soldier and would-be crusader son of a wealthy merchant to a hermit embracing the most extreme personal abstinence in the pursuit of poverty. He emerged three years later as a preacher of spectacular charismatic force and a minister to the poorest and most wretched of the world. The number of followers he gathered and the power of his life and preaching to arouse intense excitement and devotion in the teeming cities supplied the church with a new and immensely potent source of religious fervour, and the papacy with a force of energetic though unruly auxiliaries who spread rapidly in Italy from early in the thirteenth century, and then over Europe. The conversion was squarely in the apostolic tradition of John Gualberti and Peter Damiani. Francis differed from them, perhaps, in personal deference to every form of authority (apart from that of his father). He and his immediate followers, approved as a religious order by Innocent III in 1209, did not attack the ecclesiastical hierarchy by precept, however eloquently they may have seemed to do so by example.

The friars differed from the monks of the traditional orders not only in renouncing all property, living by begging (and for that reason being known as mendicants) and devoting themselves to activity in the world rather than withdrawal from it, but also in embracing not stability but mobility. They had no affiliation to a particular house and owed obedience not to an abbot or prior but to the superiors of their order and through them directly to the papacy, at whose disposal they always remained.

In 1221 Honorius III followed up the anti-heretical legislation that he had secured from the emperor by directing his legate Cardinal Ugolino of Ostia to have its provisions inserted, together with those of Lateran IV, into the municipal statutes of the Lombard and Tuscan cities. In 1227 Honorius and Ugolino, who in that year succeeded him as Gregory IX, demanded the incorporation in municipal statutes of both ecclesiastical and imperial legislation against heresy, specifically including that of Frederick II. The church thus offered, for the first time, its explicit endorsement of the death penalty for heresy. Since the death was to be by fire, the ancient prohibition of the shedding of blood was not infringed. In 1231 Gregory laid down that condemned heretics remitted to the secular power should be punished by 'the debt of hatred' – that is, put to death – and that the excommunication of their supporters and protectors should in itself incur permanent legal infamy – the loss of civic rights including that of election to public office, the power to make a will or to receive an inheritance, and access to the courts. At the same time the Roman senator (chief magistrate) Annibaldo issued a decree confirming these penalties, and the confiscation of the property of all condemned heretics, even if their heirs were catholic. One third of it would go to those who had denounced the heretics, one to the Senator's treasury and one to the maintenance of the city walls. Denunciations and burnings duly followed.

Although reinforced by preaching missions conducted by Dominican and Franciscan friars, these measures seem to have had, in general, little immediate result. They were often accepted by the cities without objection but not actually implemented, while more pressing problems militated against sustained pressure from the papal side. In 1221 only Bergamo, Mantua and Piacenza responded promptly to Ugolino's demands, and in Piacenza at least the effect was slight, for heresy in many guises was active, openly acknowledged and debated there well into the next decade. In 1230 Bergamo elected a Ghibelline *podestà*, who promptly released a number of heretics from prison. The pope retaliated by prohibiting its citizens from being elected as *podestàs* in other cities. There was a change of political allegiance in the opposite direction when, in 1228, Milan (traditionally the capital of heresy) temporarily transferred its alliance from emperor to pope. Heretics were expelled from the city and its territories on pain of the usual penalties and fines.

The nature of heresy in the Italian cities, and the difficulty (from the papal point of view) of dealing with it, was clearly expressed by the leaders of the defeated faction in Brescia in 1224. After several years of bitter conflict with the bishop and his allies, they were forced to seek terms from the pope. 'Brescia', they explained, 'has been divided into factions for a long time, as everyone knows', and they had defended their towers 'not so much as heretics, but as members of their party'. And yet they did not deny that they were heretics, as indeed they might be thought to have demonstrated by burning several churches, and by conducting a parody of the ritual of anathema in which they solemnly excommunicated all members of the church of Rome.[5] The point they were anxious to clarify was that their political rivalries existed independently of the religious difference and indeed, at least by implication, pre-dated it. By this time political conflict and religious rivalry had been inextricably interwoven in Brescia, and probably in most other cities of any size in northern and central Italy, for a century and a half or more. For most of that period the opponents of the bishop and his allies had been called Patarenes. This need not mean either that they had been organised as a sect or that their beliefs or religious practices had remained unchanged, any more than those of the catholics had done. The accusation of heresy was a very old weapon. It gained greatly in power and manoeuvrability in the decades following Lateran IV, but it did not necessarily describe the beliefs of its targets more accurately.

THE SLEEP OF REASON

Were such things here as we do speak about?
Or have we eaten on the insane root
That takes the reason prisoner?

Macbeth I.iii

The evil spirit with God's permission uses his power to make some people believe that things really happen to their bodies which they imagine (through their own error) to occur ... that a Queen of the Night summons nocturnal gatherings at which feasting and all kinds of riotous exercises take place ... that children are sacrificed, being cut up into small pieces and greedily devoured. Who can be so blind as not to realise that this is the deceit of the Devil? It must be remembered that those who have such experiences are but a few poor women and ignorant men with no real faith in God.[1]

In dismissing tales such as these as the superstition of the ignorant, John of Salisbury stated in 1159 what had long been the orthodox view. At the beginning of the eleventh century Burchard of Worms had prescribed penance for those who assisted the devil's work by repeating foolish stories of the kind, and his ruling was endorsed in the twelfth century's most authoritative statements of canon law, by Ivo of Chartres and Gratian. Gregory VII (not usually thought one of the most level-headed of popes), in warning the king of Denmark against the 'cruel and barbarous practice' of holding blameless women responsible for bad weather or personal injuries, similarly upheld a long tradition of ecclesiastical opposition to the scapegoating of those held to be witches or cunning folk.[2]

In 1233 Pope Gregory IX, in a famous letter beginning *Vox in Rama* ('A voice in Rama'), demanded action from the archbishop of Mainz against heretics who had been reported to him by friar Conrad of Marburg. 'When a novice is to be initiated and is brought before the assembly of the wicked for the first time,' he wrote,

> a sort of frog appears to him; a toad according to some. Some bestow a kiss on his hind parts, others on his mouth, sucking the animal's tongue, and slaver. Sometimes the toad is of a normal size, but at others it is as large as a goose or a duck. Usually it is the size of the mouth of an oven. The novice comes forward and stands before a man of fearful pallor. His eyes are black and his body is so thin and emaciated that he seems to have no flesh and only skin and bone. The novice kisses him, and he is as cold as ice. After kissing him every remnant of faith in the catholic church that lingers in the novice's heart leaves him.

The pope went on to describe how the banquet that followed was presided over by a black cat 'as large as a fair-sized dog,' whose anus was kissed in turn by all those present, beginning with the initiate, the lights were extinguished and a general orgy followed.

> Then, from a dark corner, the figure of a man emerges. The upper part of his body from the hips upward shines as brightly as the sun. Below that his skin is coarse and covered with fur like a cat. The presiding heretic presents him with a piece of the novice's clothing, saying, 'Master I have been given this and I in my turn give it to you.' These people describe themselves as devotees of Lucifer, who they say was temporarily expelled from heaven, and will return.[3]

We have heard stories like this before, from Paul of St Père and Guibert of Nogent, who had inherited them ultimately from tales circulated about early Christians by their pagan enemies. They cannot be shrugged off either as 'medieval superstition' or as in some way a natural or necessary concomitant of the catholic Christianity of the high middle ages. Such fantasies have been circulated in every century, and probably still are, about heretics, Jews and many other marginalised people and groups. The variation has been in who believes them and in how seriously they have been taken by cultural and religious leaders and by those who exercise power. In the early middle ages they were certainly repeated in more monastic cloisters and other places than we know of, but among serious people the rational scepticism of Burchard of Worms and John of Salisbury prevailed until the thirteenth century. As the first official document of any kind, let alone a papal decretal, to accept and repeat as facts the invocation, appearance and sexual engagement of the devil, Lucifer, at secret meetings, *Vox in Rama* marks the reception into high culture of belief in the reality of such practices and phenomena. Its baleful influence was to persist for half a millennium.

———

The official descent into superstition is not solely attributable to the temperamental or intellectual deficiencies of Gregory IX. The connection between the allegations of licentious behaviour, belief in the independence of the evil principle and access to supernatural powers and spirits had been made by the Cistercians Henri de Marci and Geoffrey of Auxerre in the 1180s. Year in and year out from the early 1200s their nightmare had been broadcast through Europe by increasingly strident preachers recruiting for the Albigensian Crusade. They painted a menace to all that was valued by God-fearing people in the most lurid colours the mass medium of the age could command, with all the mass media's regard for accuracy and perspective. In the 1220s another Cistercian, Caesarius of Heisterbach, in his *Dialogue on Miracles*, a widely circulated collection of improving anecdotes, fashioned a vivid account of a universal diabolic conspiracy against the faith. Caesarius was close to Conrad of Marburg, on whose report to Gregory IX *Vox in Rama* was based. The cat had been brought to the party by Walter Map, who usually had his tongue in his cheek, describing in the early 1180s the excesses of those whom he called 'Publicani' or 'Patarini', who 'have lain low since the days of the Lord's passion, wandering among Christians everywhere'. It was stirred into the Cistercian stew by their star recruit from the Paris schools, Alan of Lille. For Alan the cat provided a source for the name 'Cathar'. He used the feeble lecture-room pun to fix the label which his fellow schoolmen had taken from the church fathers, along with the dualist theology, ritual and ecclesiastical hierarchy of Manicheeism. For three-quarters of a century by now students had been leaving their classrooms thoroughly exercised in the detection and rebuttal of this spectre. Small wonder if most of them had become persuaded that such beliefs were widely entertained in the real world beyond their classrooms. It was now fast becoming true that the more learned a man was in the traditional scholarship of his time, the more likely he was to believe in Cathars.[4] By this time graduates predominated in responsible positions, pastoral as well as administrative, at almost every level in the church.

———

A potent brew emerged from this blend of the growing concentration of scholastic theology on the devil and his works with the fevered preoccupation of the monastic imagination with human sinfulness. Proclaimed to the world by the impassioned eloquence and ascetic lives of the friars, it rapidly permeated the public discourse and private devotions of thirteenth-century Europe. It was vividly captured in two sumptuously illustrated bibles, equipped with commentaries designed for the use of laymen – *bibles moralisées*, as the genre is known – prepared in Paris at just this moment, in the 1220s. The first, in Latin, was commissioned by or for a king, probably the pious and well-educated Louis VIII; the second, in French, for an unknown patron closely connected to the royal court.[5]

Eleventh- and twelfth-century manuscripts did not carry illuminations of contemporary heretics, even to illustrate attacks on them. The famous heretics of the ancient world – Arius, Faustus the Manichee

– were occasionally depicted, commonly in debate with the fathers of the church. Unnamed, generic heretics were occasionally shown threatening the faith or morals of monks, as in the vividly illustrated Bible of Stephen Harding, the early leader of the Cistercian order. In none of these cases, however, were the heretics given special characteristics, associated with particular symbols, or made identifiable as heretics simply by their appearance. The Paris *bibles moralisées* inaugurated a very different tradition. They contain a great many representations of contemporary heretics in a variety of contexts, illustrating every aspect of the stereotype whose construction we have followed in these pages: heretics in confrontation with the righteous, denying the sacraments and refusing to acknowledge the authority of priests; meretriciously representing themselves as barefoot, poor and humble, 'naked following the naked Christ'; in sexual, including homosexual, embraces; engaging in obscene rituals presided over by the devil in the form of a cat; offering him homage and the obscene kiss. The burning of heretics – a subject that soon became popular and would long remain so – is illustrated here for the first time, 200 years after the first actual burning at Orléans. This is not the past being drawn upon to admonish the present. It is hot news about the *publicani*, or *poplicanz*, with direct reference to both Albigensians and Waldensians. They are linked by subject matter and iconography with Jews, also being systematically demonised at this time. Both Jews and heretics are associated with sexual debauchery to show them not only as enemies of the faith but also as conscious agents of the devil, embodiments of evil. The nightmare world of the *bibles moralisées* and of *Vox in Rama* is one and the same, firmly installed in the two decades following Lateran IV to haunt the imaginations of the masters of Europe for centuries to come.

Conrad of Marburg, whose report to Gregory IX inspired *Vox in Rama*, was one of the thirteenth century's most remarkable spiritual heroes. Of obscure but apparently not noble background, he earned prominence from around 1213 as an itinerant preacher of the crusade, including (it must be supposed) the Albigensian Crusade. He refused many offers of preferment but became confessor to Elizabeth, daughter of the king of Hungary and wife of her childhood sweetheart, Count Ludwig of Thuringia, who in 1227 died of plague en route for the Holy Land. On hearing the news, the twenty-year-old Elizabeth embraced the religious life, abandoning on Conrad's instructions the three children whom she loved dearly, and moved to Marburg to build a hospital where she devoted herself to the care of lepers and the destitute. She also submitted herself to Conrad's spiritual direction, which largely consisted of ordering not only Elizabeth herself but also her maids to strip to their shifts and submit to prolonged and repeated beatings, administered by him or by others under his supervision. This was punishment for her failure to carry out his capricous and contradictory instructions, 'in order to break her will and allow her to direct her whole desire to God'.[6] When, for example, Elizabeth, with Conrad's permission, visited the convent in which her infant daughter had been placed, he had a Franciscan friar flagellate her and the maid who had opened the door for her with a long and heavy rod, while Conrad chanted *miserere me Deus* ('Lord have pity on me'). She still bore the marks three weeks later.

Shortly after his accession to the papacy in 1227 Gregory IX commissioned this virtuoso of the spiritual life to take up the war on heretics by denouncing them to ecclesiastical judges who would launch prosecutions. When Elizabeth, debilitated by her austerities, died in 1231, Conrad was free to devote all his energies to the task. Gregory authorised him not simply to denounce but also to arrest and try heretics, and to demand the aid of the secular authorities. He was assisted by two henchmen already proficient in the work: Conrad Tors, a Dominican lay brother, and a layman named John, who had but one hand and one eye – with which, however, he claimed a special ability to recognise heretics, of whose guilt the pair maintained that their word was proof enough, on the basis that 'we like to burn one hundred innocent people among whom there is one guilty person'.[7] On this principle time was not wasted on trials. The accused were given no opportunity to offer a defence or call witnesses but forced instantly to confess their guilt and choose between the flames and renunciation. The heads of the penitents were shaved and they were required, again on pain of burning, to prove the sincerity of their repentance by denouncing their co-religionists.

This technique generated an ever-widening circle of 'heretics'. Spiritual benefits apart, it was not without advantages for those involved. A young woman named Adelheid was enabled to send to the stake the entire tribe of relatives with whom she was in dispute over an inheritance, and it was said that many heretics, happy to die for their faith, were happier still to take with them even more good catholics whose pleas to Jesus, Mary and the saints might be heard issuing from the pyre.

From October 1231 until July 1233, 'on account of heresy both real and imagined many nobles and non-nobles, clerks, monks, hermits, townsmen and peasants were sent to the flames', in the Rhenish archbishoprics of Cologne, Mainz and Trier. It ended only when Conrad made the mistake of turning on Count Henry of Sayn and it was rumoured that other powerful nobles would follow. Instead of submitting, Sayn rallied the higher clergy and nobility, who until now had stood aside. He demanded to be heard before his peers by the traditional accusatorial procedure, in which witnesses testified openly and false accusations incurred penalties on the accuser, as opposed to Conrad's inquisition (*inquisitio*), in which the prosecutor was also judge and found evidence where he thought fit. The archbishop of Mainz summoned a synod to hear the case, which Conrad failed to prove when 'the accusers and witnesses withdrew. Some claimed that they had been forced or goaded into saying wicked things about the count, and others were branded with presumptive hatred of him.' Sayn was cleared and Conrad told to conduct himself with more discretion. On 30 July he was murdered by a band of Sayn's knights. Conrad Tors was stabbed and One-Eyed John hanged soon after.[8]

It is not known how far the rage against heresy in Germany had extended, or for how long it had already lasted before this phase, which is described in a handful of brief and general chronicle entries, let alone how many victims there were. Conrad of Marburg himself had secured the burning of two alleged Waldensians in Strasbourg in 1229, and one chronicle implies that he had been active for much longer. Conrad Tors and One-Eyed John had certainly been at work before they became his assistants. They had not acted without official sanction. The fevered Gregory IX thought the German bishops insufficiently zealous and denounced them in language even more lurid than that which Gregory

VII had directed at their predecessors, or Innocent III at the prelates of the Languedoc. Nevertheless the archbishops of Mainz and Trier had been active in the pursuit of heresy, though we have no particulars, and it was under the auspices of the former that Conrad had acted before he received the papal commission. There is a certain flavour of retrospective self-justification in the deprecation of Conrad's methods that followed his death; its authors, after all, had stood by for a year and a half while both secular and ecclesiastical law were blatantly flouted. According to a decree of King Henry VII in 1231, the property of condemned heretics was divided among their lords (including, of course, the bishops), with a proportion for the king himself. The suggestion that this contributed to the acquiescence of those lords until the threat came too close to home does not seem unduly cynical.

For this reason the claims of the chroniclers that popular support for the heresy hunters made it impossible to restrain them must be taken with a large pinch of salt. Considerable social tensions, and so quite possibly an element of mass hysteria or mob rule, must have lain behind these events, but there is nothing to show what they were. There were doubtless real heretics among the victims, but we cannot discern who they were or what they believed. The Trier chronicler says that three different heretical sects were uncovered in that city, but the hotch-potch of beliefs he lists suggests an even greater variety, not unexpectedly given the profusion apparent in the Rhineland already in the previous century:

> many of them were versed in the holy scriptures, of which they had a German translation; some performed a second baptism; some did not believe in the sacrament of the Lord's body; some held that the body of the Lord could not be consecrated by evil priests; some that it could be consecrated in silver and chalice in any place whatsoever … some refused to keep holidays and fasts and thus worked on feast days and ate meat on Good Friday …[9]

and so on. The demonising elements apart, this is strongly reminiscent of the apostolic traditions that had proliferated at that time and is consistent with their persistence.

Another favourite of Gregory IX, the northern French counterpart of Conrad of Marburg, is even less satisfactorily documented. In February 1233 Gregory, as usual suspecting the bishops and local secular authorities of insufficent zeal, entrusted the pursuit of heretics in the French kingdom to the Dominican order. In April he commissioned the friar Robert Bulgarus (conventionally translated as *bougre*, 'bugger') to inquire into heresy at La Charité-sur-Loire. Robert was said to have defected from a 'Manichaean' sect in Milan at about the time of Lateran IV, after twenty years' membership. Hence his nickname, which was beginning to be used of heretics in northern France around this time and acquired its pejorative sexual connotation from the tales of orgies conducted by the heretics and their alleged condemnation of procreative sex.

Robert reported that La Charité was a nest of heresy, from which missionaries spread all over France, from Flanders to Brittany. He assured Gregory that the heretics were far more numerous than the bishops would admit, and pursued them and their converts with the same ruthlessness as Conrad, although not all his victims were burned. Some were buried alive. Robert's methods and his disregard for the authority of the bishops in whose dioceses he operated provoked vigorous protests to the papal court, and he was suspended for eighteen months. But his commission was renewed and the pattern repeated, for Robert enjoyed the confidence not only of the pope but also of King Louis, who provided him with an armed escort. In 1236 a sweep through Champagne and the Low Countries yielded some sixty burnings, attended according to the chroniclers by great crowds of people of all ranks and conditions. Robert's greatest triumph, however, came on 13 May 1239, at Mont-Aimé in Champagne, when the count of Flanders presided over 'a holocaust pleasing to the Lord', as Aubri of Trois Fontaines put it, of 180 'Manichaean' heretics. Also present were the archbishop of Reims and all twelve of the bishops of his province, together with three from the neighbouring province of Sens, a great many lords from the neighbouring regions and a crowd of spectators assessed by Aubri at 700,000.

It need hardly be said that Aubri of Trois Fontaines was a Cistercian. His fanciful and inconsistent account of the holocaust at Mont-Aimé does not help us to know who the victims were or, if any of them were heretics, in what their heresy consisted. In remarking that a woman named Gisla saved herself by agreeing to name others, he confirms that the number of victims was swollen in the manner associated with inquisition, by demanding denunciation as a sign of contrition. He added that Gisla confessed to having been carried many times by night to Milan, the capital of the heretics, to serve at banquets presided over by Satan. Whether it was necessary to torture or only to terrify Gisla to elicit this information, it clearly satisfied the needs and expectations of her interrogators.

This was not Gisla's first encounter with Robert. In 1234 she had been arrested and imprisoned on suspicion of heresy by Count Thibaud of Champagne. The action was contested by the abbot of St Quiriace, in the wealthy market town of Provins, who claimed that he was entitled to jurisdiction in the case. He was supported by Robert and a fellow Dominican, Jacob, representing the papacy. Both count and abbot claimed to be Gisla's lord, and therefore custodian of her property and beneficiary of the confiscation that would follow a conviction of heresy. The property, it is reasonable to infer, must have been valuable enough to be worth the trouble and expense of the dispute. Since Gisla 'was called abbess', it is equally reasonable to infer that it was the property of the community that she headed. But what community was that? Not, the vagueness about her title suggests, an established house of one of the regular religious orders. The likeliest answer is one of the sisterhoods of pious women devoted to the apostolic life, known as Filles-Dieu ('daughters of God') that had appeared in Champagne during the twelfth century. They were mostly to be found along the main trade routes, and on the outskirts of the fair towns, including Provins. In due course some of them adopted the Cistercian rule and placed themselves under the authority of that order, while others clung to their independence. In the early decades of the thirteenth century it seems that they came under increasing pressure to regularise their position; their historian remarks that the affair at Mont-Aimé 'made clear the necessity of regulated and sanctioned belief and profession'.[10] In the Rhineland and the Low Countries, as we saw in Chapter 7, many communities of this kind had originated in the dispersal of the mixed houses of the original followers of Norbert, including some whose loyalty to their apostolic vocation exposed them to accusations of heresy and brought them to the stake.

The involvement of Count Thibaud in Gisla's troubles was no coincidence, and his responsibility for the burnings, as lord of Champagne, no empty technicality. Mont-Aimé was one of his most important castles (and so an improbable headquarters for the international heretical network of the Cistercian imagination), and the gathering of lords spiritual and temporal assembled there for the occasion a tribute to his power and prestige. He came of a line of loyal sons of the church, always prominent among leaders of the crusades, but by 1239 he was seriously embarrassed by his failure to carry out his own crusading vow, and under heavy pressure from Gregory IX to do so. A spectacular assault on heresy was a fitting preliminary to crusade and an opportunity to show himself a zealous catholic prince. It would also help to resolve a practical problem. Thibaud was having great difficulty in raising money for his crusade and, as his earlier attempt on Gisla's property illustrates, had been eager for some time to claim much smaller amounts than would be yielded by confiscations following the conviction and burning of 180 people as heretics. Nothing is known of who they were, or their condition, but it is worth noticing that the English chronicler Matthew Paris attributed the scale of this conflagration to popular hatred of merchants and bankers. The attack that led to the deaths of 150 Jews at York in 1190 had been led by knights who owed them money.

———

On 19 April 1233 the bishop and commune of Bologna formally undertook to accept the arbitration of a Dominican preacher, John of Vicenza, in their long and bitter dispute over the bishop's claim to the rights of justice in ten villages of the *contado*. John had been preaching in the city for several weeks at least, and had resolved many property disputes. Now he organised for Saturday 14 May a penitential procession that everybody in the city was to join, in readiness for the celebration of Pentecost, when the Holy Spirit descended to the Apostles 'to teach them all things' (John 13: 13). On Monday the bell was rung in the Piazza

Communale, and messengers proclaimed through the city that John was about to address the council. As he spoke, a luminous cross appeared on his forehead, visible to all, and his audience was moved to tears by the beauty of his words. He had demanded full powers to rewrite the laws of the city, and now cancelled all oaths that had been sworn in Bologna and its *contado* – the oaths by which men swore to protect each other and take vengeance on each others' enemies, thus sustaining and perpetuating the vendettas that had plagued the city for decades. He lectured the citizens on how they must avoid such conflict in future, and ordered the release from prison and the return from exile of its past victims. At the end of that week John left Bologna to intercept the advancing armies of its traditional enemies, Modena, Parma and Cremona, and persuaded them to disperse and go home. On 20 June he promulgated his final settlement between the bishop and the commune, which was heavily in favour of the city. The bishop lost almost all his judicial rights in the disputed villages, the officials responsible for those that remained were to pledge loyalty to the commune, and officers of the commune to have full powers to supervise weights and measures, raise a militia and ban rebels.

Meanwhile John embarked on a still more ambitious venture of reform and reconciliation, designed to bring peace to the even more turbulent and violent territories to the north-east, the Veneto and the marches of Verona and Treviso. There the universal afflictions of civic strife and inter-communal rivalry were compounded by the struggle between shifting groupings of cities under the leadership of powerful families or clans such as the da Romano and the d'Este. John was greeted with the usual ecstatic fervour, especially when he persuaded the five cities allied against Verona to return as a gesture of good will the *caroccio** that they had captured in battle the year before. He was carried in triumph into the city, seized the opportunity to propose himself as *podestà*, was joyously proclaimed *dux et rector* – Doge and governor – and demanded oaths from every citizen that they would accept his arbitration and carry out its provisions. Some sixty, including 'men and women from the leading families of the city', refused. They were condemned as heretics, and for three days, from 22 to 24 July, John presided over their burning.

---

* An ox-drawn cart or platform carrying the standard (*vexillum*) of the city; its loss was an intense humiliation.

There is no immediate background history to explain the actions or the fate of the victims, but Verona was not free of the tensions and disputes familiar everywhere, or of the charges and counter-charges that accompanied them. The cathedral chapter, for example, had been engaged for the past forty years in a series of attempts to extend its jurisdiction in the commune of Cerea and the villages around it, most recently by claiming to enforce the anti-heretical decree of 1221. They had encountered considerable local resistance, and had repeatedly characterised their opponents, including the family of Cerea's first *podestà*, as supporters of 'Cathars', apparently people described by their neighbours as Patarenes or Humiliati. Even if the refusal of the oath by those who went to the flames in 1233 stemmed directly from religious conviction, as certainly it may have done, it would be difficult to avoid the suspicion that something more like mob hysteria, fuelled by long-standing conflicts of that kind, demanded their sacrifice as enemies of the peace.

John of Vicenza was one of the leading figures, and his settlement in Bologna one of the most striking and best-documented achievements, of the Great Alleluia, a religious upheaval that swept through Lombardy and Emilia Romagna in 1233. It brought to a head the miseries of decades of civil conflict, compounded by the intermittent but increasingly bitter dispute between empire and papacy, by the extortionate and savage ambitions of regional tyrants thrown up in its train, such as the infamous Ezzelino da Romano, and by several seasons of dreadful weather, failed harvests, famine and disease. During this spring and summer Dominican and Franciscan preachers appeared in one city after another, attracting immense crowds. They were hailed as miracle workers, and begged to bring peace between families and factions within the city, and between the city and its enemies. To that end they demanded, and were granted, the power to rewrite the municipal statutes. John of Vicenza did so in Padua, Verona and his native Vicenza as well as Bologna; Gerard of Modena in Padua and Parma; Peter of Verona in Milan; Leo de Valvass- sori in Monza and Henry of Cominciano in Vercelli.

Because in some cases – probably in all – the preachers' revisions of the municipal statutes incorporated provisions against heresy, and because of the holocaust over which John of Vicenza presided at Verona, the Alleluia was for long regarded as an anti-heretical movement. That view has not survived the most recent analysis.[11] Preaching was broadly directed at all sources of division in communities. Heresy, of course, was generally supposed to be one of them, but it does not seem to have ranked as high on the agenda as several others, such as the oaths and sworn associations that perpetuated vendettas, or behaviour that flaunted wealth in hard times and seemed to invite divine chastisement, such as prostitution or ostentation in dress. Sorcerers, whose manuals had been publicly burned in Bologna in 1232, and soothsayers, exploiters of the poor and credulous, were also attacked. The cancellation of debt and release of debtors from prison was always prominent in the friars' peace prescriptions. Moneylenders, as often in hard times, were popularly scapegoated: one of the first responses of the Bolognese to the preaching of John of Vicenza was to burn the house and records of a prominent moneylender, who was almost lynched before he escaped from the city. Regularly though the popes demanded the incorporation of laws against heresy into municipal statutes, it actually happened very slowly and did not become general until the second half of the century. The Alleluia preachers may have revised or reinforced existing legislation, but it does not seem that they either introduced such legislation for the first time or proposed more savage penalties to enforce it.

The Great Alleluia exhibited in intensified form many of the ways in which religion articulated the responses of thirteenth-century Italians to the problems of their world and its transformation. The preachers won great influence, as the friars in general had already done in the previous decade, because without property and far from their homes and families, austere in their lives and manifestly free of the ties and interests from which quarrels and conflicts arose, they could be entrusted with the desperately needed business of arbitration and reconciliation. They lost their position just as surely when it became apparent that they could not, or would not, exercise the powers that had been vested in them with the expected impartiality. John of Vicenza was thrown into gaol when the Paduans concluded that he had subverted their interests in favour of the da Romano clan. He was soon released, but by the end of September 1233 had in effect retired into a long obscurity. Whether or not he or others succumbed personally to the corruption of the great power that they wielded so briefly, the simplistic solutions that had swept them to that power were quite incapable of offering enduring answers to the nightmare of endlessly tangled and interwoven conflicts in which their erstwhile supporters were trapped. The spectacular success of the Alleluia preachers testified to the urgency of the need for pastoral services and religious consolation. This the friars would address in the next decades as they set up permanent settlements in the cities, establishing themselves as new centres of social power alongside and in tension with both bishop and commune. Their failures, in their turn, would be a firm reminder of the impossibility that those needs would ever be wholly met by even the boldest, most visionary, institutional solutions. In one way or another the search for alternatives would continue.

———

In Toulouse reason slept in the aftermath of military defeat. It would be a romantic delusion to think of the twenty years of savage conflict as a source of social solidarity. Even without religious difference the hardships and opportunities of war and disruption were as likely to aggravate as to heal old divisions, and to open new ones. If many catholics thought the cruelties of invasion a greater evil than the divergent beliefs of their relations and neighbours, to others it proved the wickedness of dissent and intensified resentment of the heretics. The arrangements for peace provided abundant opportunity to settle old scores, but the prominence of natives of the region on every side in the savage conflicts of the 1230s points to divisions deeper and longer-standing than mere scores, an implosion of the constraints of civility represented by the code of *cortezia*.

In 1229 Louis IX ordered his officials to seek out and destroy heretics in all his lands, and Raymond of Toulouse followed suit, offering a reward for voluntary exposure and denunciation of heretics and their supporters of 2 marks (about 20 ounces) of silver per head for two years, and 1 mark thereafter. There are some grounds for thinking that the good men had been able to take advantage of Raymond's successes to resume public activity in the 1220s. In 1223 the papal legate Conrad of Porto, formerly abbot of Clairvaux and Cîteaux and much admired by Caesarius of Heisterbach, had circulated a lengthy account of their latest enormities whose most sensational claim was that they had their own pope, located 'near Hungary, on the borders of Bulgaria, Croatia and Dalmatia', at whose command leadership of the southern heretics had been ceded to Bartholomew of Carcassonne by their 'bishop' Vigorosus of la Bacone. Bartholomew, describing himself in an echo of the papal title as 'servant of the servants of the holy faith', was said to have convened a great council of the heretics, appointing and consecrating bishops among them.

Conrad of Porto's letter is rightly discounted as a florid specimen of Cistercian invective. It reiterated all the old nightmares and reinforced them with a new stereotype of the Balkans (which in the aftermath of the Latin conquest of Constantinople in 1204 had become a focus of the growing tensions between the Roman and Greek churches) as a centre of heresy and subversion. But the rumour of greater local activity that sparked Conrad's tirade has a degree of corroboration. 'Bishop' or not, Vigorosus had been active in the region of Quercy for many years. Raymond de Perelha, lord of Montségur, testified after its fall in 1244 that Guilhabert of Castres (whom he described as the 'bishop' of the heretics, and who had indeed been a leading figure among them since the great public debates before the crusade) had carried out ordinations there and consecrated two others as bishops, 'fifteen years or more ago'. The strange document that purports to be the record of a meeting held at St Félix de Caraman in 1167, at which heretical bishops were consecrated and the boundaries of their 'dioceses' defined, may be, if it is anything at all, a straw in the same wind. There is no doubt that it is a forgery. The only questions are whether it is by the seventeenth-century antiquary Guillaume Besse, in whose alleged transcription alone it survives, or whether it dates from the 1220s, and if the latter, whether it was produced by someone among the heretics themselves, to lend authority to the case for adopting a more hierarchical organisation, or by a catholic, probably in the entourage of the bishop of Toulouse, to underscore the danger that the heretics represented.[12] The details it describes may reflect no more than the habitual assumption of catholics that the world picture of the heretics was a negative image of their own. On the other hand, it is quite credible that the calamities of the first ten years of the war, the destruction of many of their local bases and institutions and the enormous casualties inflicted on them had driven the good men to adopt a supra-communal and more hierarchical organisation.

Later in 1229 a council of the church at Toulouse under the presidency of a papal legate forbade lay people to possess either the Old or the New Testament; they might have breviaries, psalters and books of hours to assist in catholic devotion, but only in the Latin language.[13] 'Those will be considered heretics who are so designated by public reputation', it decreed, 'who have been classified as such by the bishop on the denunciation of honourable and serious people' or who fail to take communion or confess three times a year. On reaching their majority both men (at fourteen years old) and women (at twelve) must take an oath abjuring heresy and proving their sincerity by naming the heretics known to them; a written record was to be kept. In every parish a team of two laymen and a priest was to be set up to search for heretics in houses, villages and woods; any house in which a heretic was found would be destroyed. Those who converted through fear of death would be imprisoned for life, in solitary confinement; those who confessed freely to heretical beliefs and gave the names of others would receive penances such as shorter terms of imprisonment, wearing a yellow cross, pilgrimage, fines or occasionally flogging. The men who implemented these directives and created the secular and ecclesiastical institutions that embodied them were not, for the most part, outsiders, though many of them, the churchmen especially, owed their positions to outside authority.

———

To set the ball rolling, a former good man, William of Solier, was brought before the Council of Toulouse to denounce his former associates. Those he named were summoned to name others in their turn, and the presiding legate set an important precedent by refusing to identify witnesses. In the previous year a sermon of William of Solier's at Lagarde had provoked a great dispute between catholics and followers of the good men. This was one of the last occasions on which a heretic preached in public. Henceforth they did so in the houses of believers and then increasingly out of doors, in woods and secret places, usually at night.

The necessity for concealment entailed a crucial transition in the relations between the followers of the good men and others and among themselves. It demanded a defining commitment. One might listen to a public debate or attend an open meeting without necessarily sharing the beliefs or sympathies of those who conducted it. To go to a secret meeting, incurring severe penalties by the very fact of doing so, was to declare oneself a follower of the heretics. To arrange such meetings, and to ensure that the arrangement would be known to believers and kept from the authorities and their officers and informers, necessitated more elaborate organisation and thereby enhanced whatever internal hierarchy the sect had developed. It meant knowing who the believers were, and at least suggested the prudence of testing their sincerity and commitment before admitting them to knowledge of the group and its doings. In other words, to whatever extent the good men and their followers had constituted an organised body before this time – a difficult and contentious question – the provisions of the Peace of 1229 and the Council of Toulouse forced them to complete the process.

Secrecy did not save the twenty or so who were burned in 1232 after being caught worshipping at night in the forest near Labécède. Nevertheless the decrees against heretics were more easily proclaimed than carried out and regularly provoked resistance, as when the lord of Laurac refused to hand over good men to the archbishop of Narbonne and a French knight who came to arrest them was ambushed and killed. Gregory IX did not rest content to leave enforcement in local hands. In 1232 he informed the archbishops of Bourges, Bordeaux, Narbonne and Auch that responsibility for inquisition into heretical depravity was to be entrusted to specially selected Dominican friars. The first standing tribunals to be established on this authority, at Toulouse and Carcassonne, soon acquired staffs of notaries and the habit of keeping written records of the confessions they received, the names revealed to them and the penances they imposed. Despite enormous losses through the vagaries of the centuries, these records constitute a massive and still far from mastered source of information not only on the activities of the inquisitors themselves but also on the places in which and the people among whom they operated.

The Dominicans of Toulouse, provided by a wealthy citizen with a substantial new site in the city and another in the bourg, had already distinguished themselves in the struggle against heresy under the leadership of Raymond of Le Fauga, soon to become bishop, and Roland of Cremona, a famous Parisian scholar brought in to teach at the new university. Their efforts were recorded in heroic terms by another fresh recruit, Guilhem Pelhisson, a Toulousain who believed that 'the heretics were doing more harm by far in Toulouse and that region than they had even during the war'.[14] Roland lost no time in denouncing them from the pulpit, to the wrath of the consuls, who summoned the prior to the town hall and told him that such preaching must stop, for 'they would take it very ill if it were said that there were heretics there, since no one among them was any such thing'. Roland, no mere ivory-tower intellectual content with fine words, heard that a benefactor of St Sernin had been buried in the cloister there after becoming a heretic on his death-bed and led a mob to dig up the body and drag it to the fire to be burned. Shortly afterwards, with fine impartiality, he led another through the town to perform the same office on the corpse of a prominent Waldensian. Bishop Raymond did even better when he hastened to the death-bed of an old woman rumoured to be a believer. In her fever she mistook him for the good man come to give her the last rites, and he secured her confession in time to have her 'carried on the bed in which she lay to the count's meadow and burned at once'.

Digging up and burning the bodies of posthumously denounced or condemned heretics was a regular tactic of inquisitors in the following years. It provoked universal revulsion, even among catholics, and was often vigorously resisted, not least because it accused the families of its victims and threatened them with confiscation. A particular triumph was the voluntary conversion of a good man named Raymond Gros. Through his revelations

prominent burghers, noble lords and other persons were condemned by sentences, exhumed and ignominiously cast out of the cemeteries of the town by the friars in the presence of the people. Their bones and stinking bodies were dragged through the town; their names were proclaimed through the streets by the herald, crying 'Who behaves thus shall perish thus', and finally they were burned in the count's meadow, to the honour of God and the Blessed Virgin his mother, and the Blessed Dominic his servant.

It took several days to write down the names that came out as those denounced by Raymond tried, or were forced, to save themselves by naming others in their turn. Of the living at least twenty were burned, and scores of others fled the city.

Similar scenes took place at Cahors, at Albi, at Moissac and throughout the region. Lesser penalties were handed out in abundance. In retaliation two inquisitors were lynched at Cordes and another beaten up in Albi. A priest at Cahors was driven from his parish after reporting three women as heretics to the bishop. In Narbonne, not previously alleged to be an important centre of heresy, a prolonged confrontation over several years between the inquisitor, Friar Ferrier, and the people of the bourg was provoked not only by Ferrier's arbitrary severity but also by the belief that the archbishop was using his activities as a cover to attack the trade guilds and the emerging consular government. Eventually the royal seneschal, though finding formally in the archbishop's favour, restored a number of confiscations, charged only a handful of citizens with the deaths that had occurred in a series of armed clashes and punished them only lightly. In Toulouse too the Dominicans consistently targeted consular families, who were their most determined opponents. In 1235, after opening proceedings against a dozen such people as believers, the inquisitors were run out of town, 'seized by the heads and feet and carried through the gate by force'. Soon afterwards the consuls ordered a boycott of the Dominicans, who were blockaded in their convent for three weeks, living on what food their supporters could throw over the wall at night.

Opposition was not wholly ineffective. Count Raymond complained to the pope of the secrecy of the friars' methods, their refusal to allow any opportunity of defence or appeal and their receptiveness to accusations arising out of personal enmity, not least against himself. He secured a three-year suspension, largely because Gregory – for even he was capable of trimming the war against heresy to the political needs of the moment – needed Raymond's help against Frederick II. But that pendulum soon swung again. Raymond's involvement in a failed military alliance against

Louis IX left the rural nobles who had protected the good men weaker and more impoverished than ever, and Raymond politically too feeble to avoid at least the appearance of collaboration. In 1241–2 a hopeless rebellion was raised by the son of Roger Trencavel to win back his family lands. The work of inquisition resumed in Toulouse and Quercy, and continued apace in Carcassonne and Narbonne, where Ferrier's energy led the council to complain that they had run out of prison space, and of the materials to build new prisons. In 1242 at Avignonet a small army of knights led by Pier Roger of Mirepoix murdered Guilhem Arnaut with three brother inquisitors and their retinues and destroyed their increasingly feared registers. The royal seneschal of Carcassonne, Hugh d'Arcis, now took over the long-running but hitherto ineffective siege of the Pyreneean stronghold of Montségur. From this refuge the good men had for many years continued to minister to their harried flock. It surrendered in March 1244, and more than 200 were burned. A few years later Raymond of Toulouse found eighty more at Agen to send to the flames on his own account.

———

We do not know enough about these contemporaneous spasms of overtly religious violence to compare at all closely the impulses that inspired or sustained them. Their common context (Montségur apart) was the extremely rapid growth of the cities in the early decades of the thirteenth century, and correspondingly of the extremes of both wealth and poverty. It was most clearly visible in Italy, but at least equally dramatic in the Rhineland and the Low Countries and hardly less so in the developing parts of northern France. The new population was gained not by natural increase but by migration from the countryside, often from considerable distances. It was therefore disproportionately male and youthful, rootless, without ties of family or culture, desperately dependent on casual employment, if necessary of the most demeaning kinds – and subject, especially in hard times, to all the obloquy and resentment usually directed at impoverished immigrants. The misery of the new masses, their craving for consolation, conciliation and respect, their vulnerability and volatility, are the constant backdrop to the history

– especially the religious history – of these decades, most obviously and universally in the welcome and influence accorded to the friars in every corner of Europe.

The tribulations and passions of the urban poor had their part in the cataclysmic events described in this chapter. Nevertheless, we should remember that studies of ostensibly religious riots in the developing world today have shown that they are seldom as spontaneous as they seem: they tend rather to be carefully organised in the interest of political factions. The crowds who flocked to the preachers of the Great Alleluia may have been the necessary fuel of its combustions, but by far the most general and persistent conflict in the Italian cities was that between the old nobility who dominated the communes and the upwardly mobile merchants and artisans who constituted the *popolo*. The vendettas whose cessation was so central an objective of the Alleluia were conducted within and between those groups, not by the poor. There is no reason to doubt the claims of the chroniclers that the burnings carried out by Conrad of Marburg and Robert *le bougre* were attended by large and enthusiastic crowds of spectators, if hardly the 700,000 at Mont-Aimé alleged by Aubri of Trois Fontaines. Nevertheless, that these descriptions are heavily conventional in character and markedly lacking in specifics suggests that they owe more to rhetoric than observation.

On the other hand, there are frequent though shadowy reminders in all four cases that the traditional function of heresy accusations as a vehicle for the rivalries of the powerful, and for the extension of their power, was far from being exhausted. After all, it was in the end the secular rulers who decided whether and how ferociously heresy would be persecuted, as Count Thibaud's role at Mont-Aimé and the frequent frustration of repeated papal demands for the implementation of anti-heretical measures underline. It is impossible to overlook the increasingly precise and comprehensive insistence, from Innocent III's *Vergentis in senium* of 1199 to Frederick II's Constitutions of Melfi, Gregory IX's bull *Excommunicamus* and the decree of Annibaldi of Rome, all in 1231, that the property of heretics should be confiscated and their families disinherited. This unleashed, or at any rate legitimated, a widespread assault on those who lacked the means to protect their property, whether old families in decline as rampant inflation eroded customary rents and revenues, or upstarts as yet insufficiently entrenched to secure their winnings against the resentment of the old guard. It was an ordinary if unappetising sign of a widespread realignment of social and political power resulting from extremely rapid economic growth, punctuated but not interrupted by moments of great adversity and hardship. In that respect the Albigensian Crusade, extinguishing the possibility of independent state formation between the Rhône and the Garonne, securing what turned out to be the permanent subordination of the region to the French crown and ending Aragonese ambitions beyond the Pyrenees, was the most far-reaching and brazenly trumpeted precursor of the shape of Europe to come.

———

The evidence for the ubiquity and peculiar malevolence of the heresy that was, and often still is, blamed for these events is scarcely adequate to bear the weight. It is entirely to be expected that once the authorities began to look for heretics they would have no difficulty in finding them. An exuberant variety of religious belief and practice existed more or less everywhere in Europe, difficult though it usually is to discern its real nature and dimensions through the fog of incomprehension, misrepresentation and hysteria generated by its opponents. A great deal of it was accommodated within the church in movements such as the Lombard Humiliati and the quite similar Béguines, houses of devout women that spread rapidly through the Low Countries in the early 1200s. It was contained and expressed in the promotion of confraternities and guilds of the pious, the cult of saints and other forms of popular devotion, and above all in the parish system now in place almost everywhere and the growth in quantity and quality of the pastoral services provided through it. But much was overtly opposed to the church and to ecclesiastical interests, most obviously in the lands that suffered the Albigensian Crusade and in the Italian cities, where the most prominent anti-catholics, traditionally called Patarenes but increasingly also Cathars, were regularly aligned to long-standing political divisions and factional rivalries. From other regions, especially the Rhineland and the Low Countries, enough survives, fragmentary though it is, to show that accusations of heresy often ran along similar fault-lines in the social fabric. Yet the evidence for what lay behind those accusations, for the origins, composition and teachings of the heretical sects so stridently blamed for so many ills, is, up to this point, strikingly insubstantial. It is certainly incapable, without the generous application of hindsight that the account presented in this book has striven to avoid, of sustaining any coherent general description of their beliefs or organisation. It would be the task of the inquisitors in the next generation to remedy that deficiency.

THE VINEYARD OF
THE LORD

*Miss Prism: Memory, my dear Cecily, is the diary that we all
carry about with us.
Cecily: Yes, but it usually chronicles the things that have
never happened and couldn't possibly have happened.*
Oscar Wilde, *The Importance of Being Ernest*, II.i

Denunciations and burnings were not the whole story. After the inquisition carried out by Pier Seilha in 1235–6 penances for heresy were
imposed on 653 people from a number of towns in the Quercy. Among
them were 163 men and 93 women from Montauban, who had confessed
'spontaneously' in April 1236, after a lengthy period of non-cooperation
in the town, and immediately after the installation of new consuls in
March. The suspension of the Toulouse inquisition prevented Seilha
from prescribing penances until 1241. When he did so, they were relatively light. Almost everyone was told to go on pilgrimage, some to
Constantinople, Compostela, Rome or Canterbury but most to make
several visits to much less distant shrines. Even these penalties were not
exacted in full, for many of those sentenced to lengthy absences were
still in Montauban in 1242–3. The implication is that the sentences had
been commuted to fines.

Pier Seilha came from a family that had risen in the service of Count

Raymond V. His father had been the count's vicar for Toulouse in the early 1180s, so he dealt with the consuls on Raymond's behalf at a time when relations between the count and the city were particularly difficult. Pier had been one of the first companions of Dominic, to whom he turned over his inheritance as the first Dominican house in Toulouse, and was a senior and experienced member of the order when he became an inquisitor in 1233. The lightness of the sentences handed down in Montauban is not attributable to any lack of zeal on Seilha's part. His arbitrary severity elsewhere was attested with admiration by his younger colleague Guilhem Pelhisson, and with indignation by Raymond VII, whose complaint of it to Gregory IX secured his suspension.

What made the difference in Montauban has been revealed by the survival, in addition to the list of penances, of a register of the town's thirteenth-century charters (the 'Red Book'), which contains details of the dominant families. Some fine historical detective work has cor-related the two.[1] It shows that virtually all of those who confessed to being associated with the heresy of the good men belonged to consular families. Conversely, all ten of the families that provided Montauban's consuls during this period numbered followers of the heresy among their members. Evidently the political elite had decided in 1236 to make terms with Seilha, and had been able to secure agreement in the town to do so. Equally, Seilha had been willing to reciprocate. The contrast with Toulouse and Narbonne, where the pursuit and denunciation of heresy were so clearly interwoven with other divisions in the commu-nity, is marked. No riots, no widening circles of denunciation here. It seems that the money from the fines was used in Montauban itself, to rebuild the church of St Jacques. Similar arrangements appear to have been reached later at Lavaur (1254), Najac (1258) and Gaillac (1271). Even the most brutal victory must be followed sooner or later by negotiation, overt or covert, if its fruits are to be durable.

The way in which the inquisitors went about their business was authori-tatively codified by Raymond of Peñafort, Dominican minister-general and leading canon lawyer, at the Council of Tarragona in 1242. Bernard de Caux and Jean de St Pierre described it in the first of what soon became a well-established genre, the inquisitor's handbook:[2]

> We choose a suitable place from which to conduct an inquisition. Calling the clergy and people together there we deliver a general sermon and make whatever explanation is necessary; then we issue a general summons, either orally or by letter: 'To so and so, parish priest. We enjoin and strictly instruct you, in virtue of the authority we wield, to summon in our name and by our authority all the parishoners of [church], or inhabitants of [place], men from the age of fourteen or women from the age of twelve, or younger if they have been guilty of an offence, to appear before us on [day] at [place] to answer for acts which they may have committed against the faith and to abjure heresy.
>
> … the person is diligently questioned about whether he saw a heretic or Waldensian, where and when, how often and with whom, and about others who were present; whether he listened to their preaching or exhortation and whether he gave them lodging or arranged shelter for them; whether he conducted them from place to place or otherwise consorted with them or arranged for them to be guided or escorted; whether he ate or drank with them or ate bread blessed by them; whether he acted as their financial agent or messenger or assistant; whether he held any deposit or anything else of theirs; whether he received the touch of peace from their book, mouth, shoulder or elbow;* whether he adored a heretic or bowed his head or genuflected and said, 'Bless us' before heretics, or whether he was present at their baptisms or confessions; whether he was present at a Waldensian Lord's Supper, confessed his sins to them, accepted penance or learned anything from them; whether he was otherwise on familiar terms with, or associated with, heretics or Waldensians in any way; whether he made an agreement, heeded requests or received gifts in exchange for not telling the truth about himself or others; whether he advised or persuaded anyone, or caused anyone to be advised or persuaded to do any of the foregoing; whether he knows any other

---

* In the kiss of peace women touched men only on the elbow.

man or woman to have done any of the foregoing; whether he believed
in the heretics or Waldensians or their errors.

These were not procedures designed to elicit information about
the beliefs, rituals or organisational principles of the heretics. That was
assumed to be known already. The focus was firmly and minutely on
behaviour, and specifically on establishing whether the witness was either
a confirmed heretic or one of seven categories of associates (believers,
concealers, defenders etc.), and ensuring that no shred of information
was overlooked that might help to track down others. Bernard and Jean
were careful to set out the nature and extent of the inquisitors' authority,
the punishments (or strictly, penances) to be imposed and the correct
legal forms for each step in the process, including turning people over
to the secular authorities. An official record of the condemnations and
penances, sealed and witnessed, was to be kept. Scrupulous legality is the
hallmark. 'To no one do we deny a legitimate defence, except that we
do not make public the names of witnesses' and 'we do not proceed to
the condemnation of anyone without clear and evident proof or without
his own confession ... holding in all things to the letter of the law, or to
specific apostolic ordinances.'

All this was in line with the best practice of the most advanced
secular courts, and of the revived Roman law which such courts were
now adopting. Confession, currently at the forefront of pastoral development in the church, was also increasingly sought in civil law. It was
seen as the remedy for the frailty of traditional procedures. Unless the
defendant had been caught red-handed by responsible officers before
reliable witnesses, 'clear and evident proof' was seldom available. Conviction depended on circumstantial evidence, reputation, hearsay or testimony all too easily fallible, corrupt or partisan. To secure a confession
judges might use torture. Inquisitors were licensed to do so by Pope
Innocent IV in 1252, though only as a last resort, and in strictly defined
conditions. In this the inquisitors were not innovators. They resorted to
torture less readily and employed it less indiscriminately than many of
their counterparts in secular courts. Nevertheless its use meant that the
expectations of a prosecutor who sincerely believed that he confronted
a terrible and urgent danger would always be confirmed. To understand

why, it is necessary only to ask how he concluded, in the absence of other evidence, that the truth had at last been elicited and the torture might cease.

———

Bernard de Caux and Jean de St Pierre were well qualified to write their handbook, for they had recently completed the largest inquisition of the entire medieval period. The district of the Lauragais, to the south-east of Toulouse, was thought so deeply infected by heresy that every man and woman in thirty-nine parishes had to be questioned. It was considered so dangerous (Avignonet, the scene of the murders of Guilhem Arnaut and his party in 1242, is in the middle of it) that, instead of being visited in their villages by the inquisitors, the witnesses had to be summoned to the church of St Sernin in Toulouse, up to 90 kilometres away. There on 201 days between May 1245 and August 1246 Bernard and Jean questioned 5,471 people. The two surviving volumes of the ten into which their reports were copied about twenty years later, if read with the technical skills of the medieval historian and an anthropologist's grasp of the workings of religion in small pre-modern societies, bring us closer than any other body of evidence to what this faith meant to the people among whom it was lived.[3]

This register does not show the people of the Lauragais using the academic and monastic terminology of the dualist heresy that their interrogators feared so greatly. There are no 'Cathars' here (or indeed in any other medieval sources from this region), and none of the *parfaits* (*perfecti*) who abound in modern accounts. There was, in fact, no collective name for this faith and its followers. Even to the inquisitors its ministers were simply 'the heretics'. Later in the thirteenth century they were sometimes referred to as Albigensians or Manichaeans. The latter name betrays the real source of catholic descriptions of them, in scholarly debate rather than real encounters. There is no mention of 'bishops' among them before the crusade and very few after it, or of their travelling companions, 'elder' and 'younger sons' of whom the inquisitors in Italy had a good deal to say. There are references to 'deacons', who until after 1230 had taken the lead in the ritual known to the inquisitors as 'heretication' or the *consolamentum* (becoming a good man or woman), which was always performed by men. It was the cherished hope of most believers to receive this rite at the point of death, when they could still speak but were beyond hope – or danger – of recovery, attended, at least until it became too dangerous, by family and friends. The good men and their followers were not generally buried separately from other Christians before the crusade, though they did have some burial grounds of their own. After 1230 they and their believers were buried in haste and secrecy, to avoid the exhumation on which the inquisitors were so zealously determined.

The status of good man or woman might be conferred even on children, though before the crusade it was not necessarily, or for girls normally, permanent. 'Clothed heretics', as they became, were usually known to one another as 'friends of God', and to others as 'good men' and 'good women', an honorific that they shared with many others. Those who considered them holy were referred to as believers by themselves and others, but there is no evidence that the description corresponded to any formal category until such a category was created by the danger of associating with the good men or attending their meetings. Before the crusade, as we have seen, good men lived and worked openly and as celibates, in known houses where they regularly practised and taught crafts, notably leatherwork, dressed in sober colours and avoided meat, cheese and eggs – the fruits of procreation – in their diet. Their mild and gentle demeanour was recalled many decades later by those who remembered, as children do, small treats of food and acts of kindness. To their followers the good men and women were points of contact with the holy. They were routinely accorded gestures of respect – bows, respectful nods, requests for a blessing – which the inquisitors took for 'adoration' and counted as incriminating signs of 'believer' status, but – at least, again, until it became too dangerous – it was by no means only believers who offered these courtesies. For believers to be in the company of good men, to eat with them, or to eat bread blessed by them, to receive the kiss of peace from them, were memorable, cherished occasions, most intense at the regular meeting for common worship that the inquisitors called the *apparalamentum*. On these occasions holy men, women, even children, would sit among rapt, even ecstatic followers, in adoration perhaps not so much *of* as *through* them.

After the crusade, with a brief respite in the 1220s, the houses of good men and women disappeared, replaced in the confessions by innumerable references to the hazards and services, the guides and messengers, the food, money and hiding places, necessary to support a fugitive ministry. This was not an absolute change: heretics, like other people, had always had many reasons to travel and had built up their networks of contacts and places to stay, often and naturally with like-minded people. Neverthless, the contrast between the solid, firmly rooted village worthies of the pre-crusade period and the will-o'-the-wisps lurking in woods and caves in the 1230s, fed and guided by anxious, tenacious followers and helpers, represents a transformation whose ramifications for their community and faith firmly prohibits any glib assumption of continuity either of organisation or belief.

———

Were it not for the screen of terrible suffering and lurid accusations through which we view all this in retrospect, the good men and their followers might not appear so very different from many other pious sectaries in the Europe of that time and since. What structure of belief lay behind their influence is difficult to discern from the depositions at St Sernin. Dualism is certainly suggested by occasional comments incidental to the inquisitors' immediate concerns – that God did not make the world, that the devil did, that a man who slept with his wife could not be saved (and so might just as well sleep with somebody else) or that, conversely, a former believer's marriage showed the authenticity of her repentance. Testimony presented before Bernard de Caux and Jean de St Pierre by a group of Franciscan friars a year after their great inquisition was more revealing.[4] One of their brethren, William Garcias, had been visited in their convent by a relative, Pier Garcias, a believer and a citizen of Toulouse, and the pair had argued about religion; once Pier brought another believer, Raymond Pier of Plan, to back him up. Since, along with two of his brothers and six others, Raymond Pier was sentenced to life imprisonment for his heresy three days after the first appearance of these friars before the inquisitors, it looks as though his trial had triggered their testimony. Perhaps it was intended to clear William Garcias of suspicion, for their story was that it was at his suggestion that on at least two occasions they had hidden in a balcony or loft above the common-room where he met Pier, to listen in to the conversation.

The unique value of the friars' stories, which differ in detail but are the same in substance, is that they record a spontaneous account of Pier's beliefs, given of his own volition. It was edited, of course, by the friars' own presumptions and memories, compared and discussed among them, but it was not initially shaped by the questions or preconceptions of anyone else. Pier did not feel that he was in danger, or under pressure either to divulge or to disguise his opinions, which he expressed with some vigour. The God who had given the law to Moses, he said, was a malevolent scoundrel, who would damn nine hundred and ninety-nine out of every thousand men he had made; Pier, if he got hold of him, would spit in his face, bite and scratch him, break him in pieces, 'May he die of gout!' He expressed the anticlerical sentiments and anti-ecclesiastical views that had been current in the region – and not only in this region – for a century or more with the same vehemence: the church should have no property; its sacraments were invalid and its alms and penances worthless, since there was no purgatory; its buildings were not churches, but mere structures in which falsity and nonsense were spoken; its liturgy unintelligible, meant to deceive simple people; and the cross merely a piece of wood. Nobody should be condemned to death, and officials who pronounced such sentences, such as preachers of the crusade, were murderers. Marriage was prostitution, and nobody who slept with a woman, even his own wife, could be saved; Pier himself had not done so for two years, though his wife was not a believer but 'an idiot like you'.

Pier Garcias did not answer the summons to respond to the friars' testimony and was excommunicated. His property was confiscated, and no more is heard of him. Although much that he said suggests theo-logical dualism, none proves it; it could have been merely Pier's own conclusions from reading the translation of the New Testament that he admitted he had at home. Nonetheless, his assertions that God had not created visible things, that (interrupting William) his creation was 'visible to the heart and invisible to the eyes of the flesh', that only angels who had fallen from heaven would be saved, that the flesh would not be resurrected and that Christ, the Virgin and John the Evangelist had come directly from heaven and did not have human bodies, show that Pier was familiar with a body of dualist teaching and legend in some form. Yet the witnesses deposed that, when William had asked him whether he believed in two gods, Pier replied that 'he could in no way reach certainty about this.' Striking as they are, his views hardly amount to a coherent body of doctrine, any more than the occasional comments of the same kind dropped to Bernard de Caux at St Sernin had done. Rather, they warn that even the most ardent votaries of any faith do not necessarily understand or endorse what theologians, or historians, may regard as the obvious, necessary corollaries of what they say. Pons Estoz, a believer since 1215, told Bernard and Jean at St Sernin that he had left the good men at once when he heard one of them say 'that God did not make visible things, that the sacred Host is not the body of Christ, that baptism, like marriage, is no salvation, and that the bodies of the dead will not be resurrected' – in 1233. Was he just another old lag desperately denying all knowledge of the crime, or does the astonishment that he professed at this revelation, after eighteen years, suggest that the theological abstractions that were everything to the inquisitor (and, for all we know, to the good man) meant little to ordinary devotees, whose faith was rooted in the power of lived holiness to temper by example rather than precept the conflicts and anxieties of daily life?

———

In Italy the efforts of the inquisitors continued to be hamstrung by the lack of unified political backing. Religious differences were correspondingly open and exuberantly debated, though without leaving the record that more systematic persecution might have created. A glimpse remains in the *Superstar** of Salvo Burci, a catholic notary and a native of Piacenza, completed in 1235, in the house of a nobleman named Monaco di Cario.[5] The di Cario were one of Piacenza's leading families, on the record since the middle of the tenth century and vassals of the bishop since the middle of the eleventh, and had extensive commercial interests,

* *Liber supra stella*: the curious title refers to a heretical *liber de stella* which has not survived.

notably in the cloth trade, that gave them a network of contacts in the Languedoc, Flanders and Champagne. Despite the breadth of information thus available to him about areas notorious for heresy, however, Salvo's focus and preoccupations were firmly Piacenzan. Together with its great length – more than 400 pages in the modern edition – and lack of orderly structure, this suggests that *Superstar*, which was not widely circulated and survives in only one manuscript, was meant as background or briefing material for the private or political use of Salvo's patrons rather than as a direct contribution to public debate. Even by Lombard standards Piacenza was a city bitterly divided by the enmity between the commune – which Innocent III had declared tainted with heresy when it tried to tax the bishop – and the emerging *popolo*. It had incorporated Frederick II's decrees in its statutes in 1221 and burned two heretics in 1230. Three years later it was the scene of a rare failure of the Alleluia movement when one of the most celebrated Dominican preachers, Roland of Cremona, had to beat a hasty retreat, badly injured, when he and his entourage were pelted with stones.

For Salvo Burci the most important heretics by far were the Cathars and the Waldensians. He saw neither as a unified body. On the contrary, he insists that the faction and division that characterised heretics were a clear sign that theirs was not the church of God. He was well informed about the Waldensians, stating clearly the differences and divisions outlined above between the Poor Men of Lyon and of Lombardy (to which he adds that the Lombards considered that 'a husband may be separated from his wife against his will, or a wife from her husband') and recounting their unsuccessful attempts at unification. His account of Cathars in Lombardy goes beyond the stereotypical descriptions of pernicious doctrines and scandalous behaviour. The greatest difference among them, he says, 'so sharp that each damns the other to death', is between the Concorezzans, who believe that God is good, and the Albanenses, who hold that he is not; other groups include the Caloianni and the Francigene (French-born) 'who in general do not share the beliefs of the Albanenses or the Concorezzans', and the Bagnolenses, who like the others reject the sacraments of the church and have only two of their own – the imposition of hands and the breaking of bread, to which they all, but especially the Albanenses, attach less importance. 'It is well known, however, that

the Albanenses and Concorezzans have met together many times and
have often taken counsel together to discuss how they might agree on
one faith.' Salvo insists that 'it is an evident fact that the Cathars were
once members of the Roman church, and in that faith received baptism
and confirmation and the other sacraments, and in it they remained for
a time.' He does not say when this schism or schisms occurred, whereas
he dates the appearance of the Waldensians and Speronists accurately to
the 1170s.

Salvo Burci's chief concern, however, was the defence of public order
and institutions against the subversive implications of heretical teaching. Kings, princes and secular or temporal authority were the work of a
benevolent God, not of the devil. The rich man who asked Jesus how he
could be saved was *not* told to give away all he had: it was perfectly possible to be both wealthy and virtuous. He returns repeatedly to sex and,
more particularly, marriage. His reiteration of the common assertion
that the heretics, condemning all intercourse, make no discrimination in
their lusts between the women who come to hand, mothers and sisters
included, reflects the darkest male anxieties of the tiny, introverted world
of the noble families for whose domestic authority and political strate-
gies unfailing control of women's sexuality was imperative. Secret marriage, outlawed by Lateran IV but always an acute problem in the Italy of
the communes, was even more dangerous than promiscuity. The longest
sustained discussion in *Superstar* defends, with many references to vendetta, the swearing of oaths as essential to the maintenance of civic order.

———

Who, then, were the Cathars? In Italy, unlike the Languedoc, the term
was widely used about, if not by, followers of what was believed to be the
most dangerous deviation from the teachings of the church. From the
time of Innocent III it was effectively interchangeable with 'Patarene', an
epithet that embodied the memories of those who clung to the radical
apostolic and anti-hierarchical vision of the eleventh-century reformers,
and sometimes with 'Manichee', the academic epitome of dualism.

Imperial territorial authority in Italy, of which shelter and support
for heretics had so often been a by-product, was effectively ended when

Charles of Anjou defeated Manfred of Sicily at Benevento in 1266. This victory tilted the balance of local power in Lombardy and central Italy significantly towards the inquisitors. Even then they rarely enjoyed consistent political support and never operated on the scale that produced the massive series of registers compiled by their counterparts in the Languedoc. In 1268 an inquisition at Orvieto sentenced sixty-seven living people and eighteen dead. The bones of the dead were ordered to be exhumed and burned, their ashes scattered, the goods of their heirs confiscated and their houses destroyed. The living, some of whom were old enough to carry the memory of offences back into the 1230s, were dealt with less harshly. The Franciscan inquisitors, local men, were sensitive enough to avoid overt hostility. The sentences ranged from fines and pilgrimages to wearing the yellow cross, imprisonment and excommunication, but there were no burnings. The most severe penalty, because it permanently undermined the families affected, was the confiscation of property, which was divided between the church and the commune; at least some of these confiscations were carried out.

These events and comparable inquisitions at Florence and Bologna are well enough documented to leave no doubt that in Italy Catharism, whatever else it may have been, was a social fact. That the people sentenced in Orvieto were in some sense supporters or believers was a matter of public knowledge. Many of them were connected with one another, and had been for generations, by marriage, by business and professional association, and by political allegiance to the popular movement that had contested power in the city since the 1190s and won it by the 1240s. Several public officials of the 1240s and '50s were from Cathar families. They often came from the newer nobility that had emerged since the middle of the twelfth century, the relative upstarts who had been prominent in the rise of the *popolo*, but also from a wide social spectrum, including bankers and notaries, and many skilled craftsmen. One indication that they were winners rather than losers from social change is the presence among them of many engaged in the fur trade, which was now developing the skills to make clothing with fur turned inwards, symbolic of a world that saw itself as a civilisation triumphing over the barbarism that had worn its fur on the outside since the days of Attila the Hun.

Armanno Punzilupo died in his native Ferrara in 1268. He had been a gentle, kindly man, a regular prison visitor, remembered for his generosity and the simplicity of his life. A large crowd carried his body to the cathedral for burial. Miracles were reported at his tomb, which soon became a place of pilgrimage, festooned with the offerings of the devout. This was how saints had always been made until Rome took firm control of the process at the end of the twelfth century. But in the years that followed several abjuring heretics identified Armanno as someone who had met many well-known Cathar and Waldensian ministers, had been seen to take off his hat to them, bow and exchange blessings. He had publicly condemned the burning of a 'good man' and often been heard to make jokes at the expense of the catholic clergy, to question their morals and beliefs, to query their sacraments. One penitent swore that Armanno was a believer of the Bagnolan sect, another that he had died a Cathar. Eventually the case was taken up by inquisitors, and though many testified to his catholic piety – including seven priests who swore, contrary to one of the charges against him, that he had attended church regularly and that they had heard his confession and given him absolution – Armanno was condemned as a heretic in 1301, his body exhumed and burned, his tomb in the cathedral broken up and the offerings piled around it destroyed.

In 1299 a similar dispute raged in Bologna when Bompietro di Giovanni and Giuliano were burned as heretics, together with the exhumed bones of the widow Rosafiore. Rosafiore's husband had died at the stake some years earlier, and she had been sentenced to wear the yellow cross. Her parish priest, believing her sincerely penitent before she died, had absolved her, given her the last unction and allowed her to be buried in the cemetery. As Bompietro, who came of a Cathar family, was being taken to the stake, he asked for absolution and the sacrament. It was refused and he was burned. Riots followed, and the rioters were in turn excommunicated for defying the inquisitors, who were accused of cruelty and injustice, of acting out of corruption and greed for Bompietro's property or, others said, because his sister had refused the inquisitor her favours. People were especially bitter against the Carmelite friars to whom Bompietro had regularly given wine for the Mass. The angry protests involved people from every part of the community, including the clergy, for Rosafiore's parish priest had been made to dig up her bones with his own hands and punished, along with an archdeacon who had acted as Giuliano's legal adviser, for granting her absolution without the inquisitor's approval.

Asked during his interrogation 'what faith and belief and which heretical faith he held', Bompietro replied that 'he could not differentiate well among the beliefs and sects of the heretics, but he believed that the heretics were the best men in the world and that true salvation was in them and in their faith, and damnation in the faith of the Roman church'.

Now as ever, the voice of the ordinary layman or woman – Bompietro was a pursemaker by trade – tells us that faith is vested in personal conduct and demeanour, not in doctrines. Bompietro's house served as a meeting place for heretics, but he attended the services of the Carmelites as well as giving them wine, and his charity embraced both Cathar and catholic. Armanno Punzilupo paid his respects to all he regarded as good men and criticised the avarice and hypocrisy of bad ones, irrespective of their theological differences, of which he probably knew little and certainly cared less. Neither his beliefs nor those of his admirers prevented him from becoming the object of a cult of the most uninhibitedly catholic piety, repellent in principle to the flesh-hating dualists the inquisitors were so determined to find and root out.[6]

So again, who were the Cathars? Until believing in or supporting them became criminal in itself, the only 'heretics' were the people who preached heresy, or who, without the approval of the church, performed religious rites for those who desired them, among which the most important for Lombard Cathars was the death-bed blessing that the inquisitors called consolation (consolamentum). For most people it was then, and only then, that they actually became Cathars. Until that moment those who accepted the preachers' message and believed them to be evangelists of the true faith were not categorically distinguished from the many who merely turned up to listen, or were inclined to think that there might be a good deal in what the heretics said, or without agreeing with them admired their self-denial and modesty of demeanour, or simply accorded them the ordinary courtesies of daily life. In principle such shades of heretical grey had been outlawed with increasing firmness since the Council of Tours in 1163. In practice the Albigensian wars had not been enough to banish them from the Languedoc. They lingered even after the Council of Toulouse in 1229 finally drove the good men underground and forced those who assisted them or attended their meetings to declare themselves by doing so members of a clandestine sect.

The stories of Armanno Punzilupo and of Bompietro show how remote was the black-and-white world picture of the official church from the religious life of Italian cities, even by the end of the thirteenth century. The faith of those who were outraged when Bompietro was denied the sacrament and who worshipped at Armanno's tomb was vested in the two men's personal character and conduct, not in systems of belief. There was no clear line between Cathars and catholics. People accounted Cathars by the inquisitors, or even by their neighbours, routinely attended catholic services and participated in catholic religious practices, including (for instance) the veneration of relics which in theory should have been repugnant to them. Conversely, scepticism of the powers and claims of the catholic clergy was widespread. The imperfections of their lives, relished in the telling and deeply resented, were openly, not to say exultantly, discussed and easily led to doubt of their teaching. The question that so profoundly exercised the bishop and chapter of Ferrara, the Dominican inquisition and the papal court, whether Armanno was a catholic or a heretic, was of no interest to the people who had prayed and left offerings at his shrine. Whether it mattered to Armanno himself there is no telling. It was the inquisitors who insisted that he must be one or the other.

―――――――

The Dominican inquisitors were, as Dominic had insisted, products of the schools, where everything began with the elementary precept of Aristotle that a thing could not be both *a* and *not a*. They were also men of passion and dedication, living in poverty and at the disposal of their superiors, without the consolations of freedom, of sex, of companionship except each others', regularly beaten up by angry crowds and revelling in the prospect of maryrdom that the beatings foreshadowed. 'Let me hear from you whether you are prepared to die for the faith of our Lord Jesus Christ', cried the prior at Toulouse when he called the brothers together to ask for volunteers to go to Carcassonne, where nobody was willing to confront the heretics. 'I want those who are so prepared to prostrate themselves, as for pardon.' 'At this all, acting as one, prostrated themselves in the chapter', wrote Guilhem Pelhisson, himself one of the volunteers.[7] The appeal for help had come from Guilhem Arnaut, soon to be murdered at Avignonet.

The prototypical martyr of inquisition was Peter of Verona. His assassination near Milan in April 1252 provided a promptly and successfully cultivated image of the Dominicans as the church's valiant defenders against the ravaging monster of heresy. He was canonised by Pope Innocent IV within a year, in the fastest official saint-making ever; in 1254 the General Chapter ordered his portrait to be hung alongside Dominic's in every Dominican house and church, and his death became a popular subject for the greatest painters of the Renaissance.

Peter, who once almost died after fasting so rigorously that he became too weak to open his mouth for food, was a hugely successful preacher throughout northern Italy in the violent 1230s and '40s. He was also an energetic and successful organiser of lay fraternities in many cities, seeing them as vehicles of solidarity among the pious and militant organisations for the suppression of heresy. That as an inquisitor he caused nobody to be burned (as far as we know) vindicates the conventional depiction of him as a gentle and peaceable man, but like many inquisitors he came from a Cathar family, and one equally conventional story of his childhood evokes the violence that lay close behind every conversion. When Peter was seven years old, his uncle, a Cathar, collecting him from school, asked what he had learned that day. The creed, Peter replied, beginning to recite 'I believe in God Almighty, Creator of heaven and earth.' His uncle objected, 'Don't say "creator of heaven and earth" because God is not the creator of visible things', citing the scriptural authorities read in that way by the heretics. Peter 'turned them against the uncle and slew the man with his own sword, so to speak, leaving him disarmed and unable to parry'. Peter was able to see his uncle, another hagiographer suggests, 'not just as his uncle, but as a poisonous snake and a rabid wolf'.[8] The language is a reminder that religion (Latin *religio:* from *ligere*, 'to tie or bind') meant not personal faith but the most sacred tie that bound a group together. When everyone's identity, security and fortune were almost exclusively rooted in the family thus bound, to break with one's family religion was not only traumatic but devastatingly and disruptively violent in itself. That is why the idea of conversion – or, from the other point of view, apostasy – is commonly associated with the language of treason and perfidy. This is another reason for caution in weighing the testimony of converts.

————

Peter Martyr of Verona was probably the author, around 1235, of the earliest of a series of treatises on heresy produced by the Italian Dominicans. Where their brethren of Toulouse and Carcassonne took the teachings of the heretics for granted and concentrated on the activities of their supporters and believers, the Italians went in for long and systematic rebuttals of heretical teachings rather in the manner of the schools, while concrete information about the heretics themselves and their doings sometimes appears almost incidental. Indeed the agenda of the longest and most comprehensive of these treatises, by Moneta of Cremona (*c.* 1240), is so thoroughly governed by the requirements of academic exposition of catholic orthodoxy that it is doubtful whether it addressed any real heresy at all. It was a classroom exercise, designed to equip its students systematically with rebuttals of every shade of heretical opinion that they might conceivably encounter, rather than those they actually would.

Peter's treatise, lengthy but incomplete, has much of this character, but it also shows a good deal of practical knowledge of heretics and their doings in such places as Milan, Como, Bergamo and Piacenza. One result is that, though its first book (of five) is devoted to errors peculiar to the 'Patarenes or Cathars', it goes on to name and sometimes to discuss a long list of other heresies mentioned barely or not at all by others, including Predestinarians, Circumcisers, Speronists, Rebaptisers, Arnaldones, Corrucani, Milui, Levantes, Cappelletti 'and the like'.[9] Here the progressive narrowing of focus on to the Cathars and to a much lesser extent the Waldensians typical of these treatises (and of modern historiography) has not obscured the point made repeatedly above, that these cities were teeming with an infinite, even a bizarre, variety of religious opinions and ideas, and of more or less enduring groupings of people around them. Peter's first concern, as any rational observer's would be, was to make sense of them by relating them to an ordered context. He did so as a theologian, not as a historian or a sociologist. What mattered to him were the ideas themselves and their relation to catholic doctrine, viewed not historically but in the light of eternity, and therefore unchanging. The ephemeral, temporal circumstances of who held these beliefs, where they came from and when, were of no importance. Thus the Predestinarians 'are second only to the Patarenes in the seriousness of their deviation' – which says nothing about how many of either there are, where they are to be found, how long they have been around. Rather, in the systematic, scholastic way Peter divided the Predestinarians into four types, according to nuances of doctrine that he associated respectively with various ancient and biblical sources and rebuttals accordingly.

The most influential of these inquisitorial treatises, by Rainier Sacchoni, wastes no time on minnows: 'Once there were many sects of heretics but they have now been almost destroyed. Two of importance, however, are still to be found, the Cathars or Patarini and the Leonistae or Poor Men of Lyon.'[10] Rainier, yet another Piacenzan, had been a Cathar for seventeen years and occupied a leading position among them – he does not say of which persuasion – before joining the Dominicans. He had been the companion of Peter Martyr and narrowly escaped sharing his fate. His book, written in 1250 and widely circulated, survives in more than fifty manuscripts. His treatment of the Waldensians is brief and unimportant, but his account of the Cathars has been and remains more influential than any other. The essential point is stated promptly and unequivocally:

All Cathars believe that the devil made the world and everything in it, and that all the sacraments of the church, both that of baptism by water, which is material, and the others, do not help us to salvation, and are not true sacraments of Christ and his church but devilish frauds of a church of the wicked; they regard as mortal sins reproductive sex, the consumption of its fruits, meat, eggs and cheese, and the swearing of oaths; they deny purgatory.

They have four sacraments: the *consolamentum* or laying-on of hands, the breaking of bread, penance, and ordination.

There were several Cathar 'churches' whose followers could be identified by their differences from one another on details of these essential principles, which are therefore set out with great care. 'Blame not me, dear readers, for giving them the name of churches,' says Rainier, 'but rather those who do so.' He lists seven in Italy, three in the Languedoc, and six in Greece and the Balkans. The most numerous were the Albanenses, the Concorezzans and the Bagnolans. Theologically the crucial difference between them was that the Albanenses considered Satan to be an independent principle, like God eternal and uncreated, while the others thought, with variations on the theme, that he had been created by God and subsequently rebelled against him. Each 'church' had a bishop; the bishop had two assistants, his 'elder and younger sons', who might perform all his functions; succession from younger son to elder and from elder to bishop was automatic. These three were itinerant, but there was also a deacon in each city where they had followers. This is an organisation designed to withstand persecution: continuity can be maintained even if two of the three leaders are apprehended simultaneously. It is not a territorial organisation: the bishop's authority is over all of his sect, wherever they may be, while followers of several sects may be found in the same city.

The nature of the bishop's office as described by Rainier was different from that of his catholic counterpart. When a new younger son was needed, he was 'chosen by all the prelates and their followers who are present at the meeting where the choice is made, and ordained by the bishop'. He was not appointed by his seniors, that is to say, but elected by the community, without distinction between prelates and others. While there were some differences between the 'churches' in consecrating the bishop himself, all of them replaced the 'younger son' in the same way. This confirms both the autonomy of these sects and the radical difference between the nature of their office and that of the catholic priesthood. It is, says Rainier, 'a form of ordination obviously wrong'. Salvo Burci tells us why:

> Your terms include 'bishops', 'elder sons', 'younger sons' and 'deacons'. Where is the name of priest? The title priest is wanting among you … Therefore it does not seem that you are of the church of God.

In the early church bishops had been chosen by their communities. The principle that they still were had been used with considerable effect by the eleventh-century reformers but in practice soon evaporated thereafter. The election of the 'younger son' among the Cathars echoes the apostolic tradition of the early reform period to which Italian 'Patarenes' had clung so obstinately. It also implies that they rejected the crucial distinction that had become entrenched in the 1140s, when ordination was firmly defined as permanently endowing an individual with the power of conferring the sacraments and not simply appointing him to administer them, or to carry out other functions in the community. Cathar spiritual leaders were ministers, not priests.

———

'All the Cathar churches accept one another, even though they hold different and contradictory doctrines, except the Albanensians and Concorezzans who damn one another in turn', says Rainier Sacchoni, echoing Salvo Burci. Rainier's list of Cathar churches includes that of France, 'to be found in Verona and Lombardy', and those of 'Toulouse, Albi and Carcassonne, with what was once the church of Agen, but is now almost destroyed'. By his time the church of France included many refugees, but it probably had not started that way; there had always been frequent and recently greatly increasing movement across the Alps, and migrants or itinerants naturally collected in communities based on religious as on other affinities. Persecution greatly increased the extent to which heretics in the Languedoc looked to Italy for shelter and support, and the need for secrecy enhanced self-consciousness and promoted formality of organisation.

Wherever they looked, the inquisitors found confirmation of their expectation that despite their acknowledged divisions the Cathars constituted a single enemy. 'The inquisition' of popular legend did not exist at any time in the middle ages. Each inquisitor was personally appointed and operated independently, at first for particular occasions, later with general responsibility in a designated area. There was no formal co-ordination between inquisitions, no central office or registry. But the mobility of the friars fostered the exchange of ideas and experience among them, and they habitually read and used each other's records and treatises (or, as we might say, case notes). The uniformity of their procedures fostered a uniformity of observation. The same questions, posed in the same prescribed words, often evoked the same answers. Their common intellectual formation in the theology of the schools, with its growing emphasis on the reality of evil, nourished by the dedication of their order to the eradication of heresy and the cult of their martyred brethren, gave the Dominican inquisitors a formidable coherence of outlook and expectation soon matched by their Franciscan counterparts. In any case it was natural, if not inevitable, that there should have been many real resemblances between the innumerable bodies of believers that formed and re-formed throughout our period – for the most part, we must never forget, to be reintegrated in one way or another into the church. Since there is only a limited number of ways in which sects can operate, they tended to have a distinct family resemblance, stressing the story and teaching of the gospels and of St Paul, and favouring what they believed to be a literal adherence to their precepts, valuing simplicity of life and ritual, of which they needed to develop at least a minimum to express their community and mark the great transitions of life and death.

Heretics sought to imitate the lives and obey the teachings of the apostles, and a basis for everything they said and believed may be found in the New Testament. An Eckbert in Cologne, a Pier Seilha in Montauban, a Rainier Sacchoni in Piacenza, were quick to see in the laying-on of hands and the breaking of bread the heretical practices of which they had been warned by the church fathers, and especially by Augustine of Hippo. A long tradition of deeply erudite scholarship has traced those practices through the mists of late antiquity and the hidden valleys of the Balkans to emerge in our period as the *consolamentum* and the *apparalamentum* of a mythical 'Cathar church', the legatee and ultimate expression of a 'dualist' or 'gnostic' tradition. In its simplest forms (though certainly capable of endless elaboration by its devotees as well as its historians) it amounted to little more than obvious answers to frequently recurring questions, beginning with how a benevolent god could be responsible for evil. It was, and is, necessary to look no further than the opening chapters of the Acts of the Apostles to find perfectly innocent precedents for how simple, comradely gestures may become the rituals through which the members of almost any community – certainly any spiritual community – express their fellowship and renew their solidarity.

One of the commonest impulses in the emergence of these heretical communities was scepticism of the holiness of sacraments performed by manifestly unholy priests and of the validity of orders conferred by even less holy bishops. The earliest leaders of the reform, including the greatest reforming pope, had forbidden their followers to accept the sacraments from unworthy or improperly ordained priests. It is to be expected that the most serious of those who heeded these prohibitions should have evolved substitutes for the catholic sacraments, and that those substitutes often looked very much alike. The similarities among the heretics that catholic observers attributed to a common doctrine and organisation can be at least as well explained by common experience, and by a common history that began not in the mists of antiquity but in the upheavals of their own quite recent past.

———

The heretics too had their reasons for perceiving kinship rather than mere resemblance among themselves. All Christians are bound to believe that theirs is the one true church from which others have deviated, whether it is maintained by an unbroken succession of bishops from the apostles, as the catholic church insists, or in the spiritual sense preferred by those who hold that this church has betrayed, and thereby forfeited, its mandate. Whether their sense of kinship draws them together against the common foe, especially under the threat of persecution, or brings fratricidal bitterness to small but perceivedly crucial differences of doctrine or practice must depend a good deal on chance and personality.

An anonymous tract from the 1220s or '30s, *The Cathars of Lombardy,* describes how its subjects tried, repeatedly but unsuccessfully, to heal the divisions among themselves.[11] Their troubles began, it says, when Mark, their bishop over 'the whole of Lombardy, Tuscany and the Marches', accepted a fresh *consolamentum* from a visitor from Constantinople, named Nicetas, who told him that his original *consolamentum,* which he had received from Bulgarian heretics, was invalid. After Mark's death, however, his followers heard from another visitor from 'across the sea' that Nicetas's own *consolamentum* had not been valid because the man from whom he received it had been found with a woman. This caused some of them to withdraw their allegiance from Mark's successor and choose a new leader. The two parties agreed to draw lots between their respective bishops. After much wrangling, including the deposition of one bishop who said he would not accept the result and the resignation of another because he thought that if chosen he would not be accepted, candidates were selected from each side and the lot fell upon Garattus – who was promptly reported by two witnesses to have slept with a woman. 'Because of this there were many who maintained that he was unworthy of his rank, and therefore they no longer considered themselves bound by their promise of obedience to him.' Followers of the heretics in several cities lost patience and chose their own bishops, so that 'the community which had been divided into two parties was now dispersed into six.' Another Dominican inquisitor, Anselm of Alessandria, provides further details.[12] Mark, he says, was a gravedigger, a native of Colognio, near Concorezzo, who had originally been converted by a French notary and had converted others. It was the recommendation of Nicetas that they ought to have a bishop, and Mark died on the way to Bulgaria to be ordained by a bishop there. Yet further fragmentation was caused by a report that reached Lombardy that Nicetas also had been found to have slept with a woman, as indeed, said Nicholas of the March, who wanted to become a bishop, had Mark himself.

Only after rehearsing all this do these texts go on to describe the theological differences between the various factions that emerged from these disputes. They evoke the vulnerability to intrigue, or mere human frailty, of faith vested in personal sanctity, and the intensity of the quarrels by which groups founded on such faith (seeing at stake not just personal ambition but eternal salvation) are constantly riven. This volatility makes any description misleading because it must be momentary. Surviving texts, accurate or not, can never represent more than random stills from an endlessly complicated and rapidly moving film. *The Cathars of Lombardy* and the introductory part of Anselm of Alessandria's treatise are neither precise nor consistent, internally or with each other, but they are informative. Their stories constitute not a historical record but a body of anecdote, founded on a myth of original unity, that circulated among these communities, growing more, not less, circumstantial and precise with the passage of time: Anselm wrote around 1270. They are contributions to a foundation legend, or origin myth, a genre that flourished in the twelfth and thirteenth centuries with the multiplication of new communities of every kind – families, cities, monasteries, devotees of particular shrines, as well as religious sects. Such stories often open in the mists of time, and in a distant, exotic place, to be plausibly if vaguely linked to the present with acknowledged fact – 'A Persian named Mani once asked himself, "If there is a God, where does evil come from?"' Anselm of Alessandria begins. 'He preached around Dragovitsa, Bulgaria and Philadelphia ... later the Greeks went there to trade ... later the Franks went to Constantinople to conquer the land ... and were converted.'

Origin myths blend memory with imagination, but also adapt it to present needs and expectations. Thus the anonymous treatise confirms that the various Cathar sects grew from the influence of many particular, local leaders and preachers. It describes them at a time when some of them were trying to cope with the problems characteristic of such groups – most obviously of succession to the original leaders or their chosen successors – and to join together in the face of persecution. In response more regular procedures were devised and memories were elaborated to legitimate both the procedures themselves and the leaders they produced. Anselm of Alessandria's more sophisticated account draws on the familiar scholastic description of the nature and origin of the Manichaean heresy to place the hierarchy of the Cathars in a line of succession from very early times, mirroring that of the catholic church. In this it reflects recent development among the sects themselves, some of which do appear to have evolved an episcopal hierarchy and an articulate dualist theology by the second half of the thirteenth century. Greater precision would be illusory. The blend is too finely mixed and too volatile to lend itself to retrospective distinction between a kernel of truth and a husk of legend. Nor can we make a clear distinction between the contributions to it of heretics and inquisitors – several of whom were heretics turned inquisitors. It served the needs of both and emerged not so much from conscious invention or even direct interrogation as from the confrontation, but also the convergence, of their respective cultures.

———

The place of Bulgaria and Constantinople in the origin myth raises the question of the extent and nature of relations between heresy in the Latin and Greek worlds. We cannot say how far these memories were real or invented, how far they preserved or reflected real contacts, momentary or continuing, between real people. Conscious as we are of the lack of mobility in the early medieval world, of the constraints that bound the great majority of the population to the land, the very low levels of exchange and urbanisation, the difficulties and dangers of travel, it is easy to forget how much movement there actually was. Some of the most important historical research and thinking of recent years has shown that we have greatly underestimated the extent and influence of long-distance contacts, especially across and around the Mediterranean but also between the Mediterranean lands and northern Europe, in the centuries between the waning of Roman power and the beginning of this book. From around the millennium such contacts grew exponentially in number, variety and regularity. A great many – missionary work, letters and visits between churches and ecclesiastical authorities, pilgrimage, the exchange of relics – were wholly or partly religious in nature. It is hardly possible to exaggerate the importance of evangelism in the dissemination of ideas, and of the itinerant preacher, the archetypal outsider, in prompting the questioning of habits of life and deference long accepted as simply how things are.

For just the same reasons outsiders were easily blamed when things went wrong, and the distance from which they had come and the obscurity of their origins were easily inflated by gossip and memory. That a heresy that had appeared in the west originated 'in Greece and other lands' was first asserted by Eberwin of Steinfeld in 1147. The claim is by no means impossible – but there is no evidence to corroborate it, and Eberwin had his own reasons for making it, and for obscuring rather than clarifying the real origins and inspiration of the 'heretics' he was describing. The plausibility of his assertion was enhanced by the fact that for almost a century since one of the great architects of the papal reform, Cardinal Humbert, had excommunicated the patriarch of Constantinople in 1054, the Byzantine world had been represented in the west as a source of heresy and corruption. The intensity of such propaganda was ratcheted up again in the aftermath of the sack of Constantinople by crusaders in 1204 and the subsequent imposition of papal authority on the Greek church. By the 1220s, when Conrad of Porto repeated Eberwin's story of a heretical pope in the Balkans, heretics in the west were occasionally called 'Bulgars'. *The Cathars of Lombardy* gave western dualism a Bulgarian source and introduced a disruptive visitor from Constantinople to renew the connection. Manuscripts containing legends and rituals associated with the Bulgarian Bogomil heretics circulated in northern Italy and in Provence, but none can be confidently dated before the middle of the thirteenth century. This tends to confirm that the interest of some western heretics in the legends or teachings of their eastern counterparts was not simply an invention of inquisitors or schoolmen, but it says nothing about the nature or extent of relations between the two, still less how they had arisen, or how long ago. The earliest and best evidence we have of the actual presence of heretics from one side on the soil of the other is that for Italian heretics in Constantinople in the 1170s.[13]

'The Cathars of Toulouse, Albi and Carcassonne subscribe to the errors of Balasinanza and the old Albanenses', says Rainier Sacchoni, referring to the Lombard sect which believed that the devil was absolute, eternal and uncreated, and to one of their recent leaders. In saying that the Lombards sent for advice on how to resolve their differences from a heretical bishop 'beyond the mountains' *The Cathars of Lombardy* suggests identity between Cathars in Italy and the good men in the Languedoc. This is the first such explicit assertion since the Lateran decree of 1179. The identity it asserts is of belief, not of history, organisation or association. To the inquisitors, of course, belief was what mattered, but historians cannot take it for granted that these were in any other sense 'the same heresy'. As we have seen, there are good reasons for doubting the accuracy of the inquisitors' assumptions about the beliefs of the good men and their followers. Even if Rainier was right about their doctrines, it is perfectly possible for similar, even identical beliefs, based ultimately on the same passages of the same scriptures, to arise quite independently of one another. They are not by themselves evidence of connection, either in space or time, between the people who held them.

Communication there was. The inquisitors of Toulouse questioned people systematically about how good men were concealed and contrived to move from place to place. Their registers record that heretics travelled constantly between the two regions for many reasons, and that some of them shared a good deal in the way of contacts and networks of support, and had been doing so for some time. How often such arrangements overrode the doctrinal difference that led the French exiles in Italy (who did not agree with the Albanensians) and those whom Rainier called the 'Cathars' of the Languedoc to 'damn one another in turn' we can only guess. Such contacts and connections offer a vivid account of an active heretical underground, or undergrounds, in the middle of the thirteenth century and suggest that it had a longer history, but they say nothing about either the structures or the formation of the various groups of believers on either side of the Alps, and not that they had a common origin.

The inquisitorial registers tend to confirm the conclusions of earlier chapters about the emergence of the good men. In the 1230s they were still firmly entrenched among the noble families of the ruling elites of the cities, the crusade notwithstanding. In Montauban those families had demonstrably maintained their positions since the foundation of the town in the 1140s, and in Toulouse probably from about the same time. It seems likely that this was the outcome of a regrouping of noble families prompted by the fragmentation of landholdings and the rapid inflation of the first half of the twelfth century, which combined drastically to erode incomes from land and rents from rural property. In the larger towns this regrouping produced the patrician elites from which the consulates arose, in the fortified villages the petty knighthood of whose constraints and difficulties we have heard so much. The disparity between the two would have been much less at first than it became with time and growth.

Clear signs of religious division also appeared in the 1140s, both in Toulouse and in the villages. It would be naïve to deny a connection with the crisis of the noble families, although we cannot discern its nature. Its most obvious source is resentment, articulated by apostolic preachers, of the increasing material demands and social intrusiveness of the church that resulted from reforming initiatives. Durand of Bredon was installed as abbot of Moissac when it was placed under Cluny in 1048. Under him and his successors Moissac acquired extensive territories as far afield as Roussillon, Catalonia and the Périgord, and undertook extensive building programmes so that, as a later abbot wrote, 'churches now stand where the boar once roamed the woods'. A new abbey church was consecrated in 1063, and rebuilt in the latest style between 1115 and 1130. The cloister, its sculptures among the great masterpieces of Romanesque art, was completed in 1100. Correspondingly, even inescapably, the abbey was continually and bitterly embroiled in disputes over property with other churches and with the regional nobility. Even more divisive were the new monastic foundations. Grandeselve and Bellesperche, probably founded by Gerald of Salles, were incorporated in the 1140s into the Cistercian order, which by the 1170s had acquired or founded some forty houses between the Rhône and the Garonne. Contrary to the image promoted by their origin myth, which presented them as accepting only unoccupied land, the Cistercians disrupted existing patterns of cultivation and livestock management throughout the region in order to impose their own.[14]

In this context the religious thrust of apostolic preaching such as that of Henry of Lausanne was conservative, especially in the countryside – to resist the growing demands and pretensions, the sacramental innovations and the liturgical elaborations of the monks and urban clergy and stick with traditional patterns of simple communal piety. At what point persistence in doing so became what the monks and later the inquisitors identified as heresy, and as dualist heresy, it is impossible to say. There was probably no sudden moment of intrusion or conversion. We have no origin myth for heresy in this region that might reflect such an episode or turning point earlier than the one manufactured in the 1220s which is described above. More likely is a gradual polarisation, leading to the emergence of the good men as spokesmen of the recalcitrant, first visible at Lombers in 1166. The crystallisation of the ritual expression of their values and leadership, still more of its theological underpinning (if there was one) in the progressive demonisation of catholic power and material wealth, is beyond our view. That is not a reason to accept at face value the construction put upon it by their enemies.

A WINTER JOURNEY

'I generally hit everything I can see – when I get really
excited.'
'And I hit everything within reach', cried Tweedledum,
'whether I can see it or not!'

Lewis Carroll, *Through the Looking Glass*

By 1300 there was no sanctuary for heresy in western Europe, and very few hiding places. Between 1318 and 1325 Jacques Fournier, bishop of Pamiers, formerly abbot of the Cistercian house of Fontfroide and later Pope Benedict XII, investigated 98 cases of heresy involving 114 people (66 men and 48 women), of whom 94 actually appeared before him and 25 were convicted. Those examined included a handful of nobles and priests, but most were peasants, artisans or small shopkeepers from the highland region of Sabarthès, 28 of them from among the 250 or so inhabitants of Montaillou, high in the Pyrenees near the present border between France and Spain. Montaillou had already been turned over in 1308, when the inquisitor Geoffrey d'Ablis arrested its entire adult population. This had been part of a campaign in which Geoffrey and Bernard Gui interrogated 650 people (who named around 300 more) in some of the areas that had been most persistently associated with the heresy of the good men. The region was thought to have been evangelised by up to sixteen good men led by Pierre Autier, a well-connected notary from Ax, and his brother Guillem, who had given up a flourishing business and their wives and families to be trained in Lombardy for the mission that they began around 1300. They went to the stake in 1310, and the last known of their followers in 1321.

Fournier was a skilful interrogator who did not use torture. He knew that if he let ordinary people talk for long enough they would eventually tell him what he wanted to know. His meticulous records have allowed the lives and feelings of the villagers of Montaillou – the villainous and lecherous heretic priest and village boss Pierre Clergue, the lady of the castle Béatrice de Planissoles, one of Clergue's many lovers, the thoughtful and courageous shepherd Pierre Maury – to be recovered with unique intimacy and vividness. But brilliantly conducted though it was, this was only a mopping-up operation. In the half-century before Fournier's time the influence of the good men had worn away. Inflation and the continuing fragmentation of estates progressively reduced the lords who had supported them in the countryside to poverty and obscurity. In the cities the firm control exercised by the French monarchy undermined the prestige and independence of the consular families in which the good men's heresy had been rooted but also opened up career opportunities for their sons in the royal and ecclesiastical bureaucracies that now ruled without challenge. The faith and memory of the good men might linger still among simple people in remote places, but there was no longer a role for them in what was now the Languedoc.

This did not mean that the war on heresy was over. In the perspective of European history it had only just begun. In the two more centuries before it became so general as to tear all Europe and most of Europe's communities apart in the Protestant Reformation its victims included Spiritual Franciscans in Italy, Waldensians in Germany, Hussites in Bohemia, Lollards in England and many more. Its infinite adaptability to the uses of power was sensationally illustrated, if further illustration is needed, when in the early hours of Friday 13 October 1307 agents of King Philip IV arrested the Knights Templar in the houses of their order throughout France and seized their property. They were charged with a long list of heresies and blasphemies, including denying the divinity of Christ, spitting on the crucifix, obscene kissing, sodomy and idol worship. Pope Clement V (born in Villandraut, between Agen and Bordeaux) protested at first but soon settled for a share of the proceeds and ordered the confiscation of the Templars' lands throughout Christendom and the suppression of their order. In France the charges were sustained by 198 confessions in a five-year trial that culminated in the burning of fifty-four Templars outside Paris in 1310, and of the master of the order, Jacques de Molay, still protesting his innocence, in 1314. There is no doubt that the confessions were secured by prolonged and repeated torture, or that the charges were wholly without foundation.

The war on heresy continued, but the incorporation of the lands between the Rhône and the Garonne into the French kingdom and the end of imperial rule in Italy in the second half of the thirteenth century had effectively completed the alignment between the structures of secular and religious authority. Epic confrontations of church and state lay ahead, but however violently their representatives might disagree on how power should be distributed between them, they were united in the determination that it should be shared, at the highest levels, by nobody else. Recognising their mutual dependence, each affirmed the authority of the other in principle and habitually supported it in practice. Under their auspices the armoury of repression to whose development the war on heresy had contributed so much was maintained and diversified.

Among the weapons forged during this war two in particular remained invaluable to the centralisation of power. First, inquisition had a formidable capacity to break down the instinctive resistance of small communities to the demands of outsiders. Second, the representation of any set of human characteristics as constituting a community, real or imagined, could readily provide a basis for demonising the defence of local customs or the expression of particular grievances as manifestations of universal conspiracies that menaced human society and the divine order. These were instruments that could be turned to many uses, of which the most general was to extend the reach of governmental institutions and the penetration of society by the culture of the literate minority. Those ends have been served regularly down the centuries by the persecution of people defined as deviant in their religious convictions, their culture, ethnicity, sexuality, manner of life – victims of the whims or necessities of others, from the highest reasons of state to the pettiest neighbourhood grudge. From time to time, especially in the eighteenth and nineteenth centuries, the cultural and legal protections which also had roots in the twelfth and thirteenth centuries, and indeed in some of the responses to the war on heresy, gained ground, only to be forced into retreat again by the barbarities of the twentieth and twenty-first.

The war on heresy, however, also had a more specific role. The persecution of heretics secured progressively clearer definition of catholic faith and practice by squeezing out from an infinitely diverse array of belief and believers those whose stubborn insistence on avowing particular doctrines, adhering to particular practices or following particular leaders seemed in one way or another to frustrate the ideals or obstruct the ambitions of secular or ecclesiastical power. Such groups were always likeliest to be those most tightly bound together by other ties (*religio*), whether of material or political interest or of custom, values and way of life. They were often the beneficiaries or the casualties of social change. The former were easier to deal with. Aspiration could be fruitfully accommodated. Despair made martyrs. Among the upwardly mobile the frustrations that might feed heresy could often be channelled into the expansion and elaboration of the church's provision for lay piety, and thence to social acknowledgement and respectability. Conversely, a striking proportion of those who went willingly to the holocausts described in these pages did so as the defenders of values, a community or a way of life under unrelenting threat, clinging to the apostolic vision of a Norbert of Xanten or an Arnold of Brescia, or to the courtly identity and vanished pre-eminence of an obsolescent nobility.

Useful though it occasionally was as an instrument of terror, the war on heresy was not directed chiefly against the mass of the population. Most heresy accusations arose from sectional conflict among the elites, sometimes on an epic scale, as in the religious revolution of the eleventh century or the Albigensian Crusade. The spectre of heresy among the people was a disturbing symbol of the unease aroused in the privileged by those on whom their privilege rested so heavily. This was one of the things that made the accusation of spreading it so deadly a weapon in disputes among courtiers, scholars or preachers. The imperative of maintaining 'unity' – that is, of refraining from questioning the authority of current office-holders and the conventional wisdom that sustains it – can almost always be made to trump the merits of any issue. Accordingly, the most enduring legacy of the war on heresy has been to entrench heresy itself as the crime of crimes, and the heretic – the person who in his or her heart does not subscribe to the prevailing ideology – as the most untrustworthy of people, a habitual liar and a secret plotter, the most dangerous and insidious of traitors. The accusation of being a sympathiser with such people remains powerfully de-legitimising.

All this arose not from any master plan or conscious intention but step by step from exclusive preoccupation with what often seemed the urgent necessities of the moment. The men who transformed every aspect of European government and society in the twelfth and thirteenth centuries did so very largely, as their successors have done ever since, by entering small communities and converting or replacing their leaders – including married priests in the eleventh century and 'Cathars' in the thirteenth. They became adept at convincing themselves and each other that resistance to their authority, and to their noble and sincerely held ideal of Christian unity under the leadership of the church universal, was the work of the devil. The measure of their achievement is that so many still believe it.

A f t e r w o r d

THE WAR AMONG THE SCHOLARS

'Yes, I am fond of history.'
'I wish I were too. I read it a little as a duty, but it tells me
nothing that does not either vex or weary me. – it is very
tiresome: and yet I often think it odd that it should be so
dull, for a great deal of it must be invention.'

Jane Austen, *Northanger Abbey*, Chapter xiv

From *c.* 1250 until *c.* 2000 it was almost universally believed that most
of the people who were accused of heresy in western Europe during the
period covered by this book were preachers or followers of an organised
dualist movement that had originated in the Greek-speaking world, most
probably in the Balkans. With the few recent exceptions mentioned in
the section on Further Reading, all current histories of heresy before 1250
and virtually all references to it in textbooks and other general works are
still based on this assumption. Specialist scholars, however, now reject
it, though in varying degrees. They have come increasingly to doubt
whether changing religious attitudes are best explained by the passage
of neatly wrapped packages of ideas from generation to generation, like
batons in a relay race. They have increasingly wondered whether this
particular package lurked in the minds of the clerics who interrogated
suspected heretics or wrote the reports about them, rather than in covert

gatherings of often illiterate suspects. Finally, in the last twenty years or so the circumstances of the composition, circulation and survival of the comparatively small body of Latin texts on which the generally accepted interpretation was based, their relationships to one another, the understanding, aims and motives of their authors, and in some cases their authenticity, have been more closely and expertly questioned than ever before. As a result the traditional story of 'medieval heresy' in which 'the Cathars' played a starring role is now authoritatively challenged at almost every point.

The parts have gradually worn away, but the dilapidated old vehicle is still on the road. No attempt has yet been made to retell as a whole the story of the emergence and growth of heresy and accusations of heresy in eleventh- and twelfth-century Europe in the light of new and often radically different understandings of the sources, either in English or (as far as I know) any other language. To do so is the aim of this book. That is why it is based on what must often seem a pedantically painstaking text-by-text examination of each reported episode. Only by scrutinising each piece of evidence afresh, and as far as possible without hindsight and without taking anything for granted, is it possible to see what was really going on. It has become necessary to do this because, astonishingly, almost everybody who has written on the subject until very recently, myself included, has overlooked the elementary principle that historical research must begin by establishing the order and circumstances in which the sources were produced.

When this is done it becomes obvious, as we have seen repeatedly in these pages, that the traditional account has depended at crucial points not on the earliest or best informed sources but on texts constructed often long after the events they describe, and often with the expectation, and even the intention, of confirming the presence of an organised dualist heresy.

When this is pointed out to academic conferences, with the suggestion that it exposes the 'dualist tradition' and 'the Cathars of the Languedoc' as largely mythical, the question is sometimes asked, 'How could so many good scholars have got it so wrong?' There was a time when the same question was asked about the sixteenth- and seventeenth-century belief in organised witchcraft. As Hugh Trevor-Roper remarked, 'the more learned a man was in the traditional scholarship of his time, the more likely he was to support the witch-doctors.'[1]

The reasons, now as then, lie deep in the political and religious history of modern Europe as well as in the history of history itself. There has been a long tradition of separation between the study of secular and religious history. It is visible today in the existence both in European and in North American universities of separate departments, often in different faculties, of History and of Religion or Church History, and of separate (though nowadays overlapping) academic journals to publish their research. This division was part of the nineteenth century's great unfinished battle between faith and reason, and of the tentatively forged and still uneasy truce that now obtains. It meant that church historians were slow to adopt the critical techniques developed since the middle of the nineteenth century by mainstream historians, in part because that development was itself intimately associated with religious scepticism, and with overt hostility to the social and political influence of the churches. Conversely, secular historians have tended to steer clear of issues closely relating to personal faith, and to accept the assertion of religious belief, individual or collective, as sufficient explanation for actions – mass murder or mass suicide, for example – that might otherwise seem to call for further investigation. Since the late twentieth century both groups have begun to outgrow the legacy of mutual suspicion, but there are still many areas, including the study of medieval heresy, in which the two traditions remain clearly visible.

This separation fostered a certain readiness on both sides to accept at face value not only the reports and observations of the thirteenth-century inquisitors but also their interpretation of what they found – that is, as they believed, an organised dualist church or churches, with ramifications almost everywhere, but especially in southern France and northern Italy. The authority of the inquisitors in academic eyes was reinforced by the fact that their registers and writings had long been edited in accordance with the highest scholarly standards, though for the most part by scholars who shared their assumptions. The inquisitors, without reaching any precise conclusion as to dates, took it for granted (in the case of the 'Cathars') that their quarry had been lurking in the undergrowth for a long time. Consequently, the scattered and fragmentary indications, or allegations, of heretical activity in the eleventh and twelfth centuries were long regarded as early traces, left in the sources more or less by chance, of a widespread but hidden phenomenon, the dualist movement that would surface in the thirteenth century.

The assumption that almost every accusation of heresy from the burning at Orléans in 1022 onwards should be accounted for in this way was not seriously challenged until after the Second World War. By the 1970s it was widely accepted that there was no compelling evidence of a dualist movement in the West before the 1140s, but nobody seriously questioned the appearance and wide diffusion of such an influence after that point. This was the consensus represented in the books by Lambert (in his second edition of 1992), Fichtenau and myself mentioned in Further Reading. It had arisen from questioning the reasoning of the traditional interpretation of what the texts contained, rather than from fresh scrutiny of the genesis of the texts themselves and their relationships to one another. With the exception of Arsenio Frugoni's study of Arnold of Brescia (1954; translated, influentially, into French in 1993) those questions were not applied to pre-inquisitorial descriptions of heresy until 1975, when Robert-Henri Bautier – not a historian of religion or the church but a distinguished expert on the study of documents, and on the early history of the Capetian monarchy – published his conclusions about the Orléans affair. In transforming the clerks of Orléans from a coterie of obscure intellectuals dabbling on the fringes of mysticism and magic into the highly placed victims of the ruthlessly organised show trial described in Chapters 1 and 2 of this book, Bautier pointed the way to transforming the study of medieval heresy itself.

Since the 1980s a number of scholars trained in the same tradition of the French historical profession have turned their attention to several other aspects of the subject. Naturally, they have paid particular attention to heresy in the Languedoc, which – again for deep-seated cultural and historical reasons – had hitherto been left largely to the attention of amateurs, often very gifted but variously motivated and not invariably abreast of the most rigorous techniques of historical research. Two volumes by members of this group, inspired, organised and edited by

Monique Zerner — *Inventer l'hérésie?** (Nice, 1998) and *L'histoire du catharisme en discussion* (Nice, 2001) — subjected the documentary basis of the accepted understanding of 'Catharism' and its repression to close and searching analysis. They showed how fragile were the foundations on which that towering historical landmark was built, and how limited the perspectives in which the evidence for it had been evaluated and interpreted. For me the attempt to apply the same principles case by case to the whole story has been an exhilarating and thought-provoking experience. I hope that I have succeeded in sharing it with my readers.

---

*English-speaking readers should bear in mind that in French *inventer* means both 'to invent' and 'to discover'.

CHRONOLOGY

Date	War on heresy	*Popes* and the church	Other rulers and events
987			Hugh Capet becomes king of the Franks
996–1031			Robert II of France
999–1003		**Sylvester II** (Gerbert of Aurillac)	
1002–24			Emperor Henry II
a. 1014	Leutard of Vertus		
1022	Burning at Orléans		
1024	Trial at Arras		
1028	Burning at Milan		
1024–39			Emperor Conrad II
1039–56			Emperor Henry III
c. 1030–c. 1060			Norman conquests in southern Italy
1046		Synod of Sutri	
1049–54		**Leo IX**	

Date	War on heresy	*Popes* and the church	Other rulers and events
1050	First condemnation of Berengar of Tours		
1052	Hanging at Goslar		
1054		Patriarch of Constantinople excommunicated	
1056–1106			Emperor Henry IV
c. 1057–75	Patarenes active in Milan		
1058–61		**Nicholas II**	
1060–91			Norman conquest of Sicily
1061–73		**Alexander II**	
1066			Norman conquest of England
1073–85		**Gregory VII**	
1077	Burning of Ramihrd at Cambrai		
1085			Christians take Toledo
1088–99		**Urban II**	
1095			First crusade launched
c. 1095–c. 1115	Preaching of Robert of Arbrissel and others		
1098		Foundation of Citeaux	
1100–35			Henry I of England
1108–37			Louis VI of France
1114	Burning at Soissons		

Date	War on heresy	**Popes** and the church	Other rulers and events
1115	Murder of Tanchelm		
1116	Henry of Lausanne at le Mans		
1119–24		**Calixtus II**	
1121	Council of Soissons: condemnation of Abelard		
1122			Concordat of Worms
1123		First Lateran Council	
1130–43		**Innocent II**	
1130–53			Roger II of Sicily
1135	Burning at Liège	Council of Pisa	
1137–80			Louis VII of France
1138–52			Emperor Conrad III
1139	(approx.) burning of Peter of Bruys	Second Lateran Council	
1143	burning at Bonn		
1145–53		**Eugenius III**	
1147	burning at Cologne		
1148		Council of Reims	
1148–94			Raymond V of Toulouse
1152–90			Emperor Frederick I Barbarossa
1154–59		**Hadrian IV**	
1154–89			Henry II of England

Date	War on heresy	*Popes* and the church	Other rulers and events
1155	Execution of Arnold of Brescia		
1159–81		**Alexander III**	
1162–96			Alfonso II of Aragon
1163	Burning at Cologne	Council of Tours	
1165	Trial at Oxford		
1166	Meeting at Lombers		
1175	Lambert le Bègue freed		
1170			Murder of Becket
1176			Battle of Legnano
c. 1178	Burning at Reims		
1178	Papal mission to Toulouse		
1179		Third Lateran Council	
1180–1220			Philip II (Augustus) of France
1184	Bull *ad abolendam*	Council of Verona	
1189–99			Richard I of England
1189			d. of William II of Sicily
1190–97			Emperor Henry VI
1194–1222			Raymond VI of Toulouse
1196–1213			Peter II of Aragon
1198–1216		**Innocent III**	
1198–1250			Emperor Frederick II

Date	War on heresy	*Popes* and the church	Other rulers and events
1199–1216			John of England
1199	Murder of Peter Parenzo Bull *Vergentis in senium*		
1204			Sack of Constantinople
1209–29			Albigensian Crusade
1210	Burning at Minerve Burning in Paris		
1213	Battle of Muret		
1213–76			James I of Aragon
1214			Battle of Bouvines
1215		Fourth Lateran Council	Magna Carta
1216–27		**Honorius III**	
1216–72			Henry III of England
1217		Dominicans and Franciscans launch universal missions	
1220–26			Louis VIII of France
1222–1249			Raymond VII of Toulouse
1220s	Papal and imperial legislation		
1224			
1226–70			Louis IX of France
1227–41		**Gregory IX**	
1229		Council of Toulouse	

Date	War on heresy	*Popes* and the church	Other rulers and events
1229–33	Conrad of Marburg active in Rhineland		
1231	Burnings in Rome		Constitutions of Melfi
1233	Bull *Vox in Rama* Appointment of inquisitors at Toulouse Burning at Verona	Great Alleluia	
1233–39	Robert le Bougre active in France		
1239	Burning at Mont-Aimé		
1243–54		**Innocent IV**	
1244	Montségur		
1249	Burning at Agen		
1249–51			Alphonse of Poitiers inherits Toulouse
1265–73		Thomas Aquinas, *Summa theologiae*	
1285–1314			Philip IV of France
1307–14	Trial of the Templars		

FURTHER READING

Outstanding among introductions to medieval Europe are R. H. C. Davis, *Medieval Europe from Constantine to St Louis* (3rd edn, London, 2006), Friedrich Heer, *The Medieval World* (London, 1963), Barbara Rosenwein, *A Short History of the Middle Ages* (3rd edn, Toronto, 2009) and William C. Jordan, *Europe in the High Middle Ages* (London, 2001). My own view of the transformation of Europe between the eleventh and thirteenth centuries which framed the changes discussed in this book is set out in R. I. Moore, *The First European Revolution* (Oxford, 2001). Part IV of Diarmaid MacCulloch, *A History of Christianity* (London, 2010) is a riveting survey of medieval Christianity, and Colin Morris, *The Papal Monarchy 1050–1250* (Oxford, 1989) a masterly account of change in the church.

The standard English-language accounts of heresy in our period are Malcolm Lambert, *Medieval Heresy* (Oxford 1977; 3rd edn, 2002), Heinrich Fichtenau, *Heretics and Scholars in the High Middle Ages* (University Park, PA, 1998; originally in German, 1992), and my own *The Origins of European Dissent* (London, 1977; 2nd edn, Oxford, 1985). All three, however, as explained in the Afterword, are radically flawed by their failure to take sufficient account of the order and circumstances in which the sources they used were produced. Among the scholars who have made this apparent I have particularly drawn on the work of Jean Louis-Biget and Monique Zerner on early claims of heresy in the region and the genesis and preparation of the Albigensian Crusade (in Chapters 7, 11, 13 and 15–18), Dominique Iogna Prat on Peter the Venerable's demonisation of heresy (Chapter 9), Uwe Brunn on heresy and heresy accusations in the archdiocese of Cologne (Chapters 6, 8, 10), Alessia Trivellone on the representation of heretics in manuscripts (Chapter 17) and a number of others for more specific points.

Other aspects of the story can be explored further in the works mentioned below.

The motto at the head of the Prologue is from the opening of J. M. Roberts, *The Mythology of the Secret Societies* (London, 1974), an exemplary study of the growth and influence of irrational belief in a widespread and sinister conspiracy. Another is Norman Cohn's study of the origins of the European witch craze of the sixteenth and seventeenth centuries, *Europe's Inner Demons* (London, 1975), which includes an important discussion of the demonisation of heretics in the thirteenth century and shows how the traditional acceptance of continuity between heresy and witch beliefs was largely based on forged documents. My discussion of the burning at Reims follows Edward L. Peters, *The Magician, the Witch and the Law* (Philadelphia, PA, 1978), a pioneer of sophisticated (but very readable) source criticism. For a superb study of the European witch craze see Robin Briggs, *Witches and Neighbours* (London, 1996), and for the emergence of systematic persecution as a peculiarly European phenomenon R. I. Moore, *The Formation of a Persecuting Society* (2nd edn, Oxford, 2007).

For the politics of marriage, including the marriages of King Robert II, (Chapters 1, 2) see Georges Duby, *The Knight, the Lady and the Priest* (London, 1983), and for masters, teaching and learning C. Stephen Jaeger, *The Envy of Angels* (Philadelphia, PA, 1994). The *Letters and Poems of Fulbert of Chartres* are translated by Fredrick Behrends (Oxford, 1976). For the apostolic tradition and the movements inspired by it and the religious repercussions of social change (Chapters 3–8) see Herbert Grundmann's immensely influential *Religious Movements of the High Middle Ages* (Notre Dame, 1995; from the 2nd German edn of 1961),Henrietta Leyser, *Hermits and the New Monasticism* (London, 1984), Lester K. Little, *Religious Poverty and the Profit Economy in Medieval Europe* (London, 1978), and M. D. Chenu, *Nature, Man and Society in the Twelfth Century* (Chicago, IL, 1968). On the emergence of the masters as a cultural elite (Chapter 9) see R. W. Southern, *Scholastic Humanism and the Unification of Europe,* vol. I, *Foundations* (Oxford, 1995), and of the clerks as a dominant caste, Alexander Murray, *Reason and Society in Medieval Europe* (Oxford, 1978), Dominique Iogna Prat, *Order and Exclusion: Cluny and Christendom Face Heresy, Judaism and Islam (1000–1150)* (Ithaca, NY, 1998), and Gary Macy, *The Hidden History of Women's Ordination* (Oxford, 2008). For the background to the events of Chapters 11 and 13, see John Gillingham, *The Angevin Empire* (2nd edn, London, 2001), and Frederic L. Cheyette, *Ermengard of Narbonne and the World of the Troubadours* (Ithaca, NY, 2001); on the progressive isolation and demonisation of the region Jean-Louis Biget, *Hérésie et inquisition dans le midi de la France* (Paris, 2007) and for Cistercian invective Beverley Mayne Kienzle, *Cistercians, Heresy and Crusade in Occitania, 1145–1229* (York, 2001). On changing relations between church and society in twelfth-century Italy (Chapters 12, 14) see Maureen C. Miller, *The Bishop's Palace: Architecture and Authority in Medieval Italy* (Ithaca, NY, 2000), on Italian heresy Carol Lansing, *Power and Purity: The Cathar Heresy in Medieval Italy* (New York, 1998), and on Innocent III, John C. Moore, *Innocent III: To Root up and to Plant* (Notre Dame, IN, 2009).

Mark Pegg's fine *A Most Holy War* (New York, 2008) is now the best of many introductions to the Albigensian Crusade (Chapters 14, 15) and the only one to take full account of recent scholarship on heresy, although Jonathan Sumption, *The Albigensian Crusade* (London, 1978) and Walter L. Wakefield, *Heresy, Crusade and Inquisition in Southern France, 1100–1250* (London, 1974) remain useful. For the background and influence of *Vox in Rama* (Chapter 17) see Peters, *The Magician, the Witch and the Law*, and Norman Cohn, *Europe's Inner Demons*; on images of heretics, see Alessia Trivellone, *L'hérétique imaginé* (Turnholt, 2009) and Sarah Lipton, *Images of Intolerance* (Berkeley, CA, 1999); on Conrad of Marburg and Robert *le Bougre*, see Karen Sullivan, *The Inner Lives of the Medieval Inquisitors* (Chicago, IL, 2011); on the Great Alleluia, Augustine Thompson, *Revival Preachers and Politics in Thirteenth-Century Italy* (Oxford, 1992).

Edward Peters, *Inquisition* (New York, 1988), is the best introduction to an enormous literature, and James Given, *Inquisition and Medieval Society* (Ithaca, NY, 2007) to its daily working (Chapter 18); valuable recent additions that prefer new insights to routine denunciation are Christine Caldwell Ames, *Righteous Persecution* (Philadelphia, PA, 2009) and Karen Sullivan, *Inner Lives*. The literature on the findings of the inquisitors in southern France (especially) and Italy is even larger and more diverse. Malcolm Lambert, *The Cathars* (Oxford, 1998), and Malcolm Barber *The Cathars: Dualist Heretics in Languedoc* (London, 2000) are admirable statements of the traditional view, and Caterina Bruschi, *The Wandering Heretics of the Languedoc* (Cambridge, 2009) is rich in insight. All of them, however, are superseded in varying degrees by Mark Pegg's brilliant *The Corruption of Angels: The Great Inquisition of 1245–46* (Princeton, NJ, 2001), which offers a devastating critique of the methods of his predecessors and an entirely fresh understanding of the religion of the good men.

Montaillou (Epilogue) is the subject of two fascinating and contrasting reconstructions: Emmanuel Leroy Ladurie, *Montaillou: Cathars and Catholics in a French Village* (London, 1978), and René Weis, *The Yellow Cross* (London, 2000). Stephen O'Shea, *The Friar of Carcassonne* (London, 2011) is a lively and revealing account of resistance to the excesses of the inquisitors. Karen Sullivan, *Truth and the Heretic* (Chicago, IL, 2005), shows how the heretic became the model of the secret traitor. Malcolm Barber's fine study of *The Trial of the Templars* (Cambridge, 1978) laid many myths to rest. The same cannot be said for Umberto Eco's novel *The Name of the Rose* (London, 1983), based on the pursuit of the Spiritual Franciscans, but it is a uniquely compelling evocation of the world whose genesis this book has tried to explain.

NOTES

The following abbreviations are used in the Notes:

Bouquet	M. Bouquet et al., *Receuil des historiens des Gaules et de la France,* 24 vols (Paris, 1738–)
BPH	R. I. Moore, *The Birth of Popular Heresy* (London, 1975)
H&A	Edward Peters, *Heresy and Authority in Medieval Europe* (Philadelphia, PA, 1980)
Mansi	J. D. Mansi, *Sacrorum conciliorum nova et amplissima collectio* (Florence and Venice, 1758–98)
MGH	*Monumenta Germaniae Historica*:
	L de L Libelli de lite
	SRG Scriptores rerum Germanicum in usum scholarum
	SS Scriptores in folio
PL	J. P. Migne, *Patrologia Latina*, 221 vols (Paris, 1844–5)
RS	Rolls series (London, 1858–1911)
W&E	Walter L. Wakefield and A. P. Evans, *Heresies of the High Middle Ages* (New York, 1969)
Wakefield	Walter L. Wakefield, *Heresy, Crusade and Inquisition in Southern France, 1100–1250* (London, 1974)

Prologue: death and a maiden

1   *Chronica regia Coloniensis, MGH SRG,* XVIII, 114; *BPH,* 88–9.

2   *MGH SS,* VIII, 65–6; *BPH,* 21.

3   *MGH SS,* XIII, 286–7.

4   *Chronicon Anglicanum,* ed. J. Stevenson, RS (London, 1875), 121–5; *BPH,* 86–8.

5   Walter Simon, *Cities of Ladies: Beguine Communities in the Medieval Low Countries, 1200–1565* (Philadelphia, PA, 2001), 23.

6   Graham Robb, *The Discovery of France* (London, 2007), 35.

7   William of Newburgh, *Historia rerum Anglicarum,* II, xiii, ed. R. Howlett, *Chronicles of the Reigns of Stephen etc.,* RS (London 1884–5); *BPH,* 131–4.

1: The avenging flames

1   *Rodulfus Glaber Opera,* ed. John France, Nithard Bulst and Paul Reynolds (Oxford, 1989), 138–51.

2   John of Ripoll, in *André: vie de Gauzlin, abbé de Fleury,* ed. R. H. Bautier and Gillette Labory (Paris, 1969), 181.

3   *André: vie de Gauzlin,* 99.

4   For a clear exposition of this inheritance, David Luscombe, *Medieval Thought* (Oxford, 1997), 9–38.

5   *Chronicon,* ed. J. Chavanon (Paris, 1897), 184–5; *cf.* Richard Landes, *Relics, Apocalypse and the Deceits of History: Ademar of Chabannes, 989–1034* (Cambridge, MA, 1995), 130–53.

6   Norman Cohn, *Europe's Inner Demons* (London, 1975), 1–15; Stephen Benko, *Pagan Rome and the Early Christians* (London, 1985), 54–79.

7   Paul of St Père of Chartres, *Gesta synodi Aurelianensis,* Bouquet, X, 536–9; *BPH,* 10–15.

8   Landes, *Relics,* 178–93.

9   For what follows, R. I. Moore, 'Heresy as Politics and the Politics of Heresy', in *Law and the Illicit in Medieval Europe,* ed. Ruth Mazo Karras, Joel Kaye and E. Ann Matter (Philadelphia, PA, 2008), 33–46.

10   *The Letters of Abelard and Heloise,* trans. Betty Radice, 2nd edn (London, 2003), 20.

11   M. T. Clanchy, *Abelard: A Medieval Life* (Oxford, 1997), 289–90.

2: The gift of the Holy Spirit

1   *BPH,* 14.

2   *André: vie de Gauzlin,* 97–8.

3   *Rodulfus Glaber,* 92–3.

4   Landolf Senior, *Historia mediolanensis,* II, *MGH SS,* VIII, 65–6; *BPH,* 19–21. *Rodulfus Glaber,* 177–81, has a story apparently related but even by his standards too bizarre to be worth discussing.

5   Huguette Taviani, 'Naissance d'une hérésie en Italie du Nord en XIe. siècle', *Annales ESC* 29:5 (1974), 1224–52.

6   'What was essential to a textual community was not a written version of a text, although that was sometimes present, but an individual who, having mastered it, then utilized it for reforming a group's thought and action.' Brian Stock (the originator of this extremely important idea), *The Impact of Literacy* (Princeton, NJ, 1983), 90.

7   *Acta synodi Atrebatensis, PL,* 142, col. 1271–1312; *BPH,* 15–19.

3: The apostolic life

1   *Acta synodi Atrebatensis, PL,* 142, col. 1271–1312; *BPH,* 15–19.

2   *Rodulfus Glaber,* 88–91.

3   *Gesta episcoporum Leodiensis, MGH SS,* VII, 226–8; *BPH,* 21–4.

4   Baldri of Dol, *Vita B. Roberti, PL,* 162, col. 1043–58, Chapters 11, 23; trans. Bruce L. Venarde, *Robert of Arbrissel: A Medieval Religious Life* (Washington, DC, 2003).

4: Monks, miracles and Manichees

1   *Chronicon,* ed. Chavanon, 173; *BPH,* 9. On Adémar see Landes, *Relics.*

2   *BPH,* 79, where it is wrongly dated *c.* 1160: see Guy Lobrichon, 'The Chiaroscuro of Heresy', in *The Peace of God: Social Violence and Religious Response around the Year 1000,* ed. Thomas Head and Richard Landes (Ithaca, NY, 1992), 80–103.

3   'Chronicle of St Pierre du Puy', in C. Devic and J. Vaissette, *Histoire générale du Languedoc,* V, col. 15.

4   *Chronicon,* ed. Chavanon, 184.

5   P. Bonnassie and R. Landes, in *Les sociétés méridionales autour de l'an Mil,* ed. M. Zimmermann (Paris, 1992), 435–59.

6   *PL* 137, col. 823–6; trans. Thomas Head, 'The Translation of the Body of St Junianus', in Miri Rubin (ed.), *Medieval Christianity in Practice* (Princeton, 2009), 218.

7   E. E. Evans-Pritchard, *Witchcraft, Oracles and Magic among the Azande* (Oxford, 1937); abridged edn (Oxford, 1976), 18.

8   Patrick Geary, *Living with the Dead in the Middle Ages* (Ithaca, NY, 1994), 95–124.

9   Oxford, Corpus MS 157; Edmund King, *Medieval England* (London, 1988), 34–5.

5: The simoniac heresy

1   Orderic Vitalis, *Ecclesiastical History,* viii, 26, ed. Marjorie Chibnall, 6 vols (Oxford, 1968–80), IV, 312–5.

2   *Vita Romualdi, PL,* 144, cols 965, 1005.

3   See p. 63.

4   John of Lodi, *Vita B. Petri Damiani, PL,* 144, col. 115.

5   Odo of Cluny, *Life of Gerald,* trans. Gerard Sitwell, *St Odo of Cluny* (London, 1958), 102–3.

6   *Vita B. Arialdi, MGH SS, XXX,* ii, 1050; *Vita S. I. Gualberti, MGH SS, XXX,* ii, 1091.

7   Arnulf, *Gesta episcoporum … mediolanensium,* III, xi, *MGH SS,* VIII, 18.

8   Bonizo of Sutri, 'To a Friend', trans. I. S. Robinson, *The Papal Reform of the Eleventh Century* (Manchester, 2004), 196.

9   *MGH SS,* XXX, 1057.

10 Odo of Cluny, III, 9, trans. Sitwell, 80–81.

11 Trans. Robinson, *Papal Reform,* 83.

12 Robinson, *Papal Reform,* 137.

13 *Enarrationes in Psalmos,* X.v.

14 Bonizo of Sutri, trans. Robinson, *Papal Reform,* 212–14.

6: Routing out these detestable plagues

1   *Life of Anselm of Lucca, MGH SS,* XII, 24.

2   *The Register of Pope Gregory VII, 1075–1083,* 2.55; trans. H. E. J. Cowdrey (Oxford, 2002), 148–9; *The 'Epistolae Vagantes' of Pope Gregory VII,* trans. H. E. J. Cowdrey (Oxford, 1972), 26–7.

3   *MGH L de L,* II, 438.

4   *BPH,* 24–5; *Register,* 231–4.

5   *PL,* 172, 1398–9.

6   *A Monk's Confession* III, 17, trans. Paul J. Archambault (University Park, PA, 1996), 195–8. Guibert's memoir is also translated, less accurately but with an excellent introduction and notes, by John F. Benton, in *Self and Society in Medieval France* (New York, 1970).

7   See below, p. 102–3 (Lambert), p. 94 (Waldensians), p. 177–8, 221–2 (Bernard Raymond).

8   Cf. pp. 177–9, 221–2 (Vézalay) below.

9   *A Monk's Confession,* III, 16, trans. Archambault, 193–5.

10 *A Monk's Confession,* I, 26, trans. Archambault, 89–91.

11 Beryl Smalley, *The Study of the Bible in the Middle Ages* (Oxford, 1941), 55.

12 Jay Rubinstein, *Guibert of Nogent: Portrait of a Medieval Mind* (New York, 2002), 111–24, 132–75.

13 Bernard of St Blasien (Bernard of Constance), *Chronicle,* trans. I. S. Robinson, *Eleventh-Century Germany* (Manchester, 2008), 305–6.

14 *BPH,* 32–3.

15 *PL,* 182, col. 52.

16   Paul Frédéricq, *Corpus documentorum inquisitionis haeretica parvitatis neerlandicae* (Ghent, 1889–1906), I, 15–18; *BPH*, 29–31.

17   *BPH*, 31–2; Gregory of Tours, *History of the Franks,* trans. Lewis Thorpe (Harmondsworth, 1974), X, 25.

18   See p. 50.

7: Sowers of the word

1   Bruce L. Venarde, *Robert of Arbrissel: A Medieval Religious Life* (Washington, DC, 2003), 75.

2   Venarde, 92–100.

3   Wendy Davies, *Small Worlds: The Village Community in Early Medieval Brittany* (London, 1988), esp. 100–102.

4   Baldri of Dol, *First Life of Robert of Arbrissel*, in Venarde, 1–21.

5   Geoffrey Grossus, *The Life of Blessed Bernard of Tiron,* trans. Ruth Harwood Cline (Washington, DC, 2009).

6   Baldri of Dol, Chapter 15.

7   Andreas, *Second Life,* in Venarde, 22–67; the recently discovered portion is at 50–67.

8   *Gesta pontificum Cenomannensium,* Bouquet, XII, 547–51; *BPH*, 34–8.

9   *PL*, 182, col. 184–6; *BPH*, 39–46.

10   *Tractatus contra Petrobrusianos,* ed. James V. Fearns, *Corpus christianorum continuatio medievalis,* X (Turnhout, 1968); *BPH*, 60–62.

11   *Against Henry* has been identified, edited and translated into French by Monique Zerner: *Guillaume monachi contre Henri schismatique et hérétique* (Sources Chrétiennes 241, Paris, 2011 – too late to be taken fully into account here). Zerner has identified William of Arles as the author. Her work supersedes my translation in *BPH*, 46–60, of a later, elaborated version of the debate, also edited and translated by Zerner in this volume, on which my account of Henry's views in *The Origins of European Dissent*, 91–101, was based. I am more than grateful to Monique Zerner for her great generosity in sharing this extremely important discovery, and her principal conclusions about it, in advance of its publication.

8: Sheep in the midst of wolves

1   *MGH SS,* XII, 673.

2   For what follows, Uwe Brunn, *Des contestaires aux 'Cathares'* (Études augustiniennes, Paris, 2006), 80 ff. My treatment in this chapter and the remainder of the book of everything that happened in the Rhineland region, and hence of a crucial part of my argument, is heavily indebted to this work.

3   *PL*, 182, col. 76–80; *BPH*, 76–8.

4 Walter Map, *De nugis curialium: Courtiers' Trifles*, i. 20; ed. M. R. James, C.N. L. Brooke and R. A. B. Mynors (Oxford, 1983), 118–21; see below, 173–5.

5 *MGH SS*, XVI, 711. This burning is also noted, with no other information, in the slightly earlier Annals of Aachen.

6 Annales Brunwilarensis, *MGH SS*, XVI, 727.

9: Making enemies

1 *The Chronicle of Morigny*, quoted by Colin Morris, *The Papal Monarchy* (Oxford, 1989), 187.

2 Quoted in Morris, 339.

3 J. Rubinstein, *Guibert of Nogent: Portrait of a Medieval Mind* (New York and London, 2002), 30.

4 *Introductio ad theologiam*, PL, 178, col. 1056.

5 Dominique Iogna Prat, *Order and Exclusion: Cluny and Christendom Face Heresy, Judaism and Islam (1000–1150)* (Ithaca, NY, 1998).

6 John of Salisbury, *Historia Pontificalis*, iii, ed. and trans. Marjorie Chibnall (London, 1956), 8–9.

7 Gary Macy, *The Hidden History of Women's Ordination: Female Clergy in the Medieval West* (Oxford, 2008), Chapter 1.

8 *MGH SS*, VI, 389–90; William of Newburgh, ed. Howlett, 60–64; *BPH*, 62–5.

9 John of Salisbury, ed. Chibnall, 59–66; see also Bernard of Clairvaux, *Letters*, trans. Bruno Scott James (London, 1953), 329–32, and *BPH*, 66–71.

10 Bonizo of Sutri, trans. Robinson, *Papal Reform* 205.

11 Arsenio Frugoni, *Arnaud de Brescia* (Paris, 1993), 10–11.

12 Otto of Morena, *Historia (1153–61)*; *MGH SRG*, VII, 73.

13 Walter Map, i. 24, ed. James, Brooke and Mynors, 80–83; the Lombard anonymous, trans. T. Carson as *Barbarossa in Italy* (New York, 1994), p. 30.

14 Otto of Freising, *The Deeds of Frederick Barbarossa*, trans. C. C. Mierow (New York, 1966), 143–4; Peter Abelard's *'Ethics'*, ed. D. E. Luscombe (Oxford, 1971), 127.

10: Exposed to contumely and persecution

1 E. Martène and U. Durand, *Amplissima collectio* (Paris, 1724–33), 1252–70.

2 *MGH SS*, XIII, 286–7.

3 *PL* 195, col. 11–102; *BPH*, 88–94.

4 Hilbert Chiu, 'The Intellectual Origins of Medieval Dualism', M.Phil. diss., University of Sydney, 2009.

5 Mansi, XXI, col. 843.

6 Ralph of Coggeshall, *Chronicon Anglicanum*, 121–5; *BPH*, 86–8.

7 *Ann. Coloniensis maximi*, *MGH SS*, XVII, 778, 784–5; Mansi, XXI, col. 689–90.

8   Bouquet, XV, 790, 792, 799; *BPH*, 80–82.

9   Bouquet, XII, 343–4; *BPH*, 85–6. Hugh of Poitiers, *The Vézelay Chronicle*, trans. John Scott and John O. Ward (Binghamton, NY, 1992).

10   Frédéricq, *Corpus* II; *BPH*, 101–11. Cf. Simons, *Cities of Ladies*, 24–34.

11   *The Letters and Charters of Gilbert Foliot*, ed. A. Morey and C. N. L. Brooke (Cambridge, 1967), 207–10.

12   *The Life of Ailred of Rievaulx by Walter Daniel*, ed. F. M. Powicke (London, 1950), ci–cii.

13   William of Newburgh, ed. Howlett, 131–4; William Stubbs, *Select Charters*, 9th edn (Oxford, 1913), 173; *BPH*, 88–94.

14   Walter Map, ed. James, Brooke and Mynors, 118–21.

11: Sounding the alarm

1   William of Newburgh, II, 15, ed. Howlett, 136.

2   Mansi, XXII, 157–68; *BPH*, 94–8.

3   Gervase of Canterbury, *Opera historica*, ed. W. Stubbs, RS (London, 1879), 270–71.

4   Frederick L. Cheyette, *Ermengard of Narbonne and the World of the Troubadours* (Ithaca, NY, 2001), 288.

5   *PL*, 199, col. 1119–24; *PL*, 204, col. 235–40; *BPH*, 113–22.

6   Assize of Clarendon 21, David C. Douglas and G. W. Greenaway, *English Historical Documents II, 1042–1189* (London, 1953), 410.

7   J. H. Mundy, *The Repression of Catharism at Toulouse: The Royal Diploma of 1279* (Toronto, 1985), 239.

12: Drawing the lines

1   *H&A*, 168–70.

2   *H&A*, 170–73.

3   Lester K. Little, *Liberty, Charity, Fraternity: Lay Religious Fraternities in the Age of the Commune* (Bergamo, 1988) 20, 33–4; Frugoni, *Arnaud de Brescia*, 10–11.

4   Hugh Eteriano, *Contra Patarenos*, ed. Bernard, Janet and Sarah Hamilton (Leiden, 2004).

5   *Chron. Universali anonymi Laudunensis, MGH SS*, XXVI, 449.

6   Frances Andrews, *The Early Humiliati* (Cambridge, 1999).

7   Maureen C. Miller, *The Formation of a Medieval Church: Ecclesiastical Change in Verona, 950–1150* (Ithaca, NY, 1993), especially 117–41; Maureen C. Miller, *The Bishop's Palace: Architecture and Authority in Medieval Italy* (Ithaca, NY, 2000), 157–69.

13: Speaking of principles

1   *H&A*, 168–70.

2 Letters 73, 75, *PL*, 211, 371–2, 375, quoted by Cheyette, *Ermengaud*, 279.

3 Bouquet, XII, 447f.; Jean Leclerq, 'La témoinage de Geoffroy d'Auxerre sur la vie cistercienne', *Studia Anselmiana* (1953), 196–7.

4 *De fide catholica contra haereticos, PL*, 210, 366A.

5 Walter Map, ed. James, Brooke and Mynors, 124–7.

6 For the thirteenth-century version, Jacobus de Voragine, *The Golden Legend*, trans. William Granger Ryan (Princeton, NJ, 1993), I, 371–4.

7 Stephen of Bourbon, W&E, 209.

8 Cheyette, *Ermengaud*, 319–20.

9 W&E, 278–89.

10 Euan Cameron, *Waldenses: Rejections of Holy Church in Medieval Europe* (Oxford, 2000), 36–48.

14: The enemy at the gate

1 *PL*, 215, col. 654–7.

2 Quoted in R. H. C. Davis, *Medieval Europe from Constantine to St. Louis,* 3rd edn (London, 2006), 379; and Morris, *Papal Monarchy*, 427.

3 *Acta Sanctorum May V*, 86–9; *BPH*, 127–32.

4 Quoted by David Foote, *Lordship, Reform and the Development of Civil Society in Medieval Italy: The Bishopric of Orvieto, 1100–1250* (Notre Dame, IN, 2004), 116–7.

5 *Registrum Inn. III*, I. 298, *PL*, 214, col. 256.

6 *PL*, 215, col. 1147; 214, col. 904.

7 George W. Dameron, *Episcopal Power and Florentine Society, 1000–1320* (Cambridge, MA, 1991) 118–20.

15: To war and arms

1 *Registrum Inn. III*, X.149 (27 November 1207), *PL*, 215, cols. 1246–1248.

2 *The Song of the Cathar Wars*, trans. Janet Shirley (Aldershot 1996), 18.

3 Mark Pegg, *A Most Holy War* (New York, 2008), 65.

4 A literal translation of the words attributed to him by Caesarius of Heisterbach, *Dialogue on Miracles*, V. xxi, often rendered as 'Kill them all': *cf.* Malcolm Barber, *The Cathars: Dualist Heretics in the Languedoc in the High Middle Ages* (London, 2000), 211–12, n.20.

5 *Song of the Cathar Wars*, 21–2; Peter of Les Vaux de Cernay, *The History of the Albigensian Crusade*, trans. W. A. and M. D. Sibley (Woodbridge, 1998), 117.

6 *Song of the Cathar Wars*, 41, 48; Peter of Les Vaux de Cernay, 119–20.

7 Peter of Les Vaux de Cernay, 83–5.

8 *Song of the Cathar Wars*, 33.

9 Peter of Les Vaux de Cernay, 106.

10 Peter of Les Vaux de Cernay, 10–14.

11 Mark Pegg, *The Corruption of Angels: The Great Inquisition of 1245–46* (Princeton, NJ, 2001), 83–91.

12 Pegg, *Holy War,* 34–40.

16: Politics by other means

1 *H&A*, 173–4. For a complete translation of the canons, *Decrees of The Ecumenical Councils*, ed. Norman P. Tanner, 1 (Washington, DC, 1990).

2 Jacques de Vitry, quoted in John C. Moore, *Innocent III* (Notre Dame, IN, 2009), 288.

3 *The Chronicle of William of Puylaurens*, trans. W. A. and M. D. Sibley (Woodbridge, 2003), 74.

4 *The 'Liber Augustalis'*, trans. James F. Powell (Syracuse, NY, 1971), 7–10.

5 Miller, *The Bishop's Palace*, 166–9, from which this discussion is almost wholly derived.

17: The sleep of reason

1 John of Salisbury, *Polycraticus*, ii. 17, ed. K. S. B. Keats-Rohan (Turnholt, 1993), 105–6.

2 *The Register of Pope Gregory VII, 1075–1083*, trans. H. E. J. Cowdrey (Oxford, 2002), vii.21, pp. 351–2.

3 Edward L. Peters, *The Magician, the Witch and the Law* (Philadelphia, PA, 1978), 156–7.

4 Cf. Hugh Trevor-Roper, *The European Witch-Craze of the 16th and 17th Centuries* (Harmondsworth, 1967), 81.

5 Deborah Lipton, *Images of Intolerance* (Berkeley, CA, 1999), 5–13. For what follows, Alessia Trivellone, *L'hérétique imaginé* (Turnhout, 2009).

6 *Golden Legend*, II, 309.

7 *Annals of Worms, MGH SS*, XVII, 839.

8 *Annals of Worms*, 843; *Trier Chronicle, MHG SS*, 24, 402.

9 W&E, 268.

10 Ann E. Lester, 'From the Margins to the Center: Religious Women, the Cistercian Order, and the Power of Reform in Thirteenth-Century Northern France', International Congress of Historical Studies, Amsterdam 2010. http://www.ichs2010.org/programme.asp?find=Lester.

11 Augustine Thompson, *Revival Preachers and Politics in Thirteenth Century Italy* (Oxford, 1992).

12 *L'histoire du Catharisme en discussion: Le 'concile' de St. Félix (1167)*, ed. Monique Zerner (Nice, 2001).

13 *H&A*, 194–5.

14 'The Chronicle of William Pelhisson', trans. Wakefield, 209.

NOTES

18: The vineyard of the lord

1 Jörg Feuchter, *Konsuln und Büßer: Die städtischen Eliten von Montauban vor dem Inquisitor Petrus Cellani (1236/1241)* (Tübingen, 2007).

2 Wakefield, 250–58; for the provisions of Raymond of Peñafort, *H&A*, 198–200.

3 Pegg, *The Corruption of Angels*.

4 Partial trans., Wakefield, 242–9.

5 Partial trans., W&E, 269–74.

6 For Armanno Punzilupo, Lansing, *Passion and Purity*, 92–5; Augustine Thompson, *Cities of God* (University Park, PA, 2005), 211–12, 430–33; for Bompietro di Bologna, Lansing, 152–56.

7 Pelhisson, trans. Wakefield, 220.

8 *Golden Legend*, I, 255; Gerald of Frachet, quoted in Karen Sullivan, *The Inner Lives of the Medieval Inquisitors* (Chicago, IL, 2011), 104–5.

9 W&E, 274–8.

10 *Le liber de dubus principiis*, ed. A. Dondaine (Rome, 1938), 64–78; *BPH*, 132–45.

11 'L'hiérarchie cathare en Italie, I, Le "*De heresi catharorum*"', ed. A. Dondaine, *Archivum Fratrum Praedicatorum*, XIX (1949); *BPH*, 122–7.

12 'L'hiérarchie cathare en Italie, II', ed. A. Dondaine, *Archivum Fratrum Praedicatorum*, XX (1950); *BPH*, 145–54.

13 Hugh Eteriano, *Contra Paterenos*, passim. Bernard Hamilton's introduction to this treatise (1–102) makes the most learned and persuasive modern case for close links between Byzantine and Western heresy – if one accepts, as I cannot, the equation of Lateran III between 'Paterene' and 'Cathar' and the assumption that both mean 'dualist' there and thereafter (cf. his pp. 8–9 and p. 209 above).

14 Meyer Schapiro, *The Sculpture of Moissac* (London, 1985, 4–5); Constance H. Berman, 'Medieval Agriculture, the Southern French Countryside and the Early Cistercians', *Transactions of the American Philosophical Society*, 76/5 (1986).

Afterword: The war among the scholars

1 Trevor-Roper, 81.

GLOSSARY

Arianism the heresy of Arius, condemned by the Council of Nicaea (AD 325), for
teaching that in the Trinity the Son was not equal to the Father and Holy Ghost,
but in our period more generally, the sin of dividing the church

canon (i) a rule; (ii) a person whose life was governed by a Rule; (iii) one of the
governing body of a cathedral, with a share of its revenues

canon law the law of the church

clerk a man in holy orders; a literate person

commune a sworn association; hence the collective identity and governing body of a
city. Many were formed, especially in Italy, from *c.* 1100, generally dominated by
noble clans

consul title often given to the officers of the commune, usually chosen to serve for a
year; also often called *boni homines* – good men

contado the area surrounding a (normally Italian) city and subject to its jurisdiction

deacon a member of the clergy ranking below priests

desert fathers the early Christian hermits who lived with extreme austerity in the
Egyptian desert, the most famous being St Anthony (dates traditionally given as
251–356)

Donatism the heresy that the efficacy of a sacrament depends on the worthiness of
the minister

eucharist the sacrament of the body and blood of Christ, celebrated in the Mass

fathers of the church the leading thinkers and writers of the early church, including
Jerome (c. 331–420), Ambrose of Milan (340–97), Augustine of Hippo (354–430)
and (Pope) Gregory the Great (540–604)

Flanders approx equals modern Belgium and north-eastern France

Francia here, roughly the northern part of modern France and the French-speaking Low Countries, which had been ruled by Charlemagne but was not always ruled in its entirety by those who succeeded him as King of the Franks

inquisition (*inquisitio*) the device, originally of Roman law, of securing information by putting designated individuals on oath

Italy in our period only a geographical expression, but one which does not now carry unacceptable connotations: cf. Languedoc

Languedoc the name by which the region between the Alps, the Pyrenees and the Dordogne became known after the greater part of it was conquered and absorbed by the French crown (see Chapters 15–18). There is no accepted name for it before those events that does not imply a prejudgement of them. 'Midi' ('de la France') and 'Occitania' are open to similar objections. For this reason I have wherever possible preferred topographical designations.

legate a representative of the pope, with delegated papal powers

Low countries region around the deltas of the Rhine, Scheldt and Meuse rivers, including modern Netherlands and Belgium, parts of Germany and northern France

Manichees, Manichaeans alleged followers of Mani (d. 271), often applied in our period to those particularly suspected of abstention from meat and sex

mark a unit of weight, in principle 8 ounces = 160 silver *denarii* (pennies); in practice it varied considerably

neoplatonism a philosophical tradition stressing the corruption of matter: see pp. 16–17

nicolaitism the heresy of defending clerical marriage

popolo collectively, the groups that emerged in opposition to the noble communes in Italian cities from *c.* 1200: see p. 236

reliquary container for the relics of a saint, often splendidly decorated

sacraments religious rites regarded as conveying divine grace. Today in the Catholic Church they are: baptism, confirmation, the eucharist, penance, extreme unction, ordination and matrimony; but in the twelfth century their number and status were still undefined and often controversial.

simony the sale of spiritual powers: see Chapter 5

synod a council or assembly of clergy

Templar member of the religious Order of the Temple, founded in 1119 to protect pilgrims to the Holy Land, which rapidly became extremely wealthy and powerful

tithe proportion of crops and other produce paid in principle to the priest, and in practice to his ecclesiastical superiors or the secular lord (see pp. 72–3)

BIOGRAPHICAL INDEX
OF NAMES

Rather than attempt an illusory consistency in the forms and spelling of personal names I have allowed variants to assist differentiation among a very long cast of characters. They are indexed as they appear in the text.

John of Vicenza (d. after 1259), Dominican preacher 284–7
Josfred, bishop of Paris 1061–95 91
Julieta of Florence, 'daughter of iniquity' 239
Justinian I, Roman emperor 527–65, codifier of Roman law 8

Kulin, Ban, of Bosnia 237

Lambert 'le Bègue,' (d. ?1177), parish priest, accused of heresy 173, 175–9
Lambert, Malcolm D, historian 351
Landolf Cotta, Patarene leader 78
Landolf Senior, Milanese chronicler 36, 39–40,
Lanfranc, abbot of Bec, archbishop of Canterbury 1070–89, lawyer 29
Léger, archbishop of Bourges, (d. 1120) 109, 127
Léger, pupil of Gerbert, archbishop of Sens 1000–1032 26
Leo III, pope 795–816 82,
Leo IX (Bruno of Toul), pope 1049–54 83–4
Leo de Valvasssori, Dominican preacher 286
Letaldus of Micy, hagiographer 63
Leutard, farm worker, of Vertus 52–4, 67, 69
Lisiard, bishop of Soissons 1108–26 93
Lisois, canon of Orléans, confessor to Constance of Arles, burned alive 1022 15–17,
    20–23, 32–5, 40–42, 43–4
Losinga, Herbert, bishop of Norwich 1091–1119 145
Lothar, s. of Louis the Pious 28
Louis VI, king of France 1108–37 45–6
Louis VII, king of the France 1137–80 146, 172, 175, 187–8, 192
Louis VIII, king of France 1220–26 265, 267–8, 277
Louis IX, (St Louis) king of France 1226–70 282, 288, 293–4
Lucius II, pope 1144–5 158
Lucius III, pope 1181–5 205
Ludwig, count of Thuringia, husband of Elizabeth of Hungary 279

Manfred, bishop of Brescia 157
Marbod, bishop of Rennes 1096–1123, poet 104, 110–11
Maria, daughter of William of Montpellier 243
Mark, Lombard cathar 320
Markward of Anweiler 235
Marsilius, heretic of Cologne, burned alive 1163 3, 170
Map, Walter, Welshman and courtier of Henry II, author of *de nugis curialium* 136,
    159, 197–8, 221, 223, 277
Matthew Paris, chronicler 284

INDEX